*The Roland Legend in
Nineteenth-Century French Literature*

The Roland Legend in Nineteenth-Century French Literature

HARRY REDMAN, Jr.

THE UNIVERSITY PRESS OF KENTUCKY

Copyright © 1991 by The University Press of Kentucky

Scholarly publisher for the Commonwealth,
serving Bellarmine College, Berea College, Centre
College of Kentucky, Eastern Kentucky University,
The Filson Club, Georgetown College, Kentucky
Historical Society, Kentucky State University,
Morehead State University, Murray State University,
Northern Kentucky University, Transylvania University,
University of Kentucky, University of Louisville,
and Western Kentucky University.

Editorial and Sales Offices: Lexington, Kentucky 40508-4008

Library of Congress Cataloging-in-Publication Data

Redman, Harry.
  The Roland legend in nineteenth-century French literature / Harry Redman, Jr.
    p. cm.
  Includes bibliographical references and index.
  ISBN: 978-0-8131-5451-0
  1. French literature—19th century—History and criticism.
  2. Roland (Legendary character)—Romances—Adaptations—History and criticism.   3. Medievalism in literature.   4. Chanson de Roland.
  I. Title.
PQ283.R43   1991
840.9′351′09034—dc20   90-26581

This book is printed on acid-free paper meeting
the requirements of the American National Standard
for Permanence of Paper for Printed Library Materials.

∞

To my father

As Arthur is to England,
As Roland is to France. . . .
Archibald Rutledge

Contents

Preface　ix

Toponomy　xi

1　Vague Recollections and New Beginnings　1

2　Patriot Warrior　29

3　The Romantics' Roland　75

4　Magnificent Braggart and Doomed Lover　119

5　Despair, Hope, and Triumph　162

6　A Hero for All Seasons　206

Notes　219

Selected Bibliography　239

Index　241

Preface

This study came about rather accidentally, growing out of an exercise I sometimes give in teaching French lyric poetry of the nineteenth century. I ask students to compare poems treating the same idea or theme for structure, viewpoint, and artistic achievement. Vigny's "Le Mont des Oliviers" and Nerval's "Le Christ aux Oliviers," Baudelaire's "Le Flacon" and Sully-Prudhomme's "Le Vase brisé," and Baudelaire's "L'Albatros" and Mallarmé's "Le Vierge, le vivace et le bel aujourd'hui" lend themselves to this kind of juxtaposition. Encountering Albert Glatigny's beautiful and poignant "La Mort de Roland" enabled me one year to call on students to examine Vigny's "Le Cor" in relation to it. Glatigny's poem also made me curious about how other nineteenth-century writers might have viewed the ill-starred knight killed in an ambush on 15 August 778, as implacable enemies hidden in the Pyrenees Mountains swooped down and annihilated Charlemagne's rear guard in Roncevaux Valley while the Frankish main army was making its way back to Chasseneuil and Aix-la-Chapelle. I found many versions of the legend, and their literary merit proved as variable as their authors' imagination and skill. At least one unknown masterpiece has surfaced, Napoléon Peyrat's "Roland." For those who, like me, did not already know the poem, Glatigny's interpretation will be another worthwhile discovery, as will, I hope, Charles Fournel's moving "Romance de Roncevaux."

My investigation deals only with the Roland legend as it occurs in French belles lettres of the nineteenth century, although I have construed "belles lettres" and "nineteenth century" rather freely. The works examined span the period from 1777 to World War I. Plays, operas, poems, and prose fiction constitute most of the material, along with essays and selections from longer works by such authors as Michelet, Quinet, and Taine. Omitted is the scholarly writing of professional philologists and historians of medieval literature, whose research is familiar to those specializing in the literature of the French Middle Ages. An exception has been made in the case of Francisque Michel's publication of the Oxford Manuscript of the *Chanson de Roland* in 1837. Some creative writers took an interest in this process. Mérimée, for example, was Michel's friend and adviser. The edition, providing writers with a new account of the Roncevaux disaster, also left its mark on the period's literature dealing with Roland. A few authors, however, preferred to maintain a literary tradition that, with all its known inaccuracies, had established itself long before—the one that sprang from the *Pseudo-Turpin Chronicle.*

The works discussed in this study have been placed in approximate chronological order except in a few instances where palpable thematic kinships have argued against such an arrangement. The book does not examine the matter of possible foreign influences aside from one or two cases. Cultivated Frenchmen knew their Ariosto, and several authors may have known the sixth book of Andrea da Barberino's *Reali di Francia,* just as Simonde de Sismondi and Alfred Assollant had some knowledge of the Spanish *romanceros,* however little they may have relied upon them.

Of course, I have incurred a number of debts of gratitude in preparing this volume. While acknowledging them is inadequate payment, still it is with sincere pleasure that I thank Professors Robert W. Artinian, Gerard J. Brault, Robert F. Cook, Beatrice Jasinski, Hans-Erich Keller, Lucienne Lafosse, Pierre Le Gentil, Thomas A. Montgomery, David Powell, and Barbara Sargent-Baur, as well as Mrs. Knud (Liselotte) Andersson of the Tulane University Music Library, who have put their learning at my disposal, commented and suggested, and made my labors all the more enjoyable. I would also like to thank *Res Publica Litterarum* and *Studies on Voltaire and the Eighteenth Century* for allowing me to reprint here, with a few changes, my articles on Roland, the French Revolution, and Michelet.

Toponymy

Before scrutinizing the myriad faces nineteenth-century French authors assigned to Roland, the hero of the battle of Roncevaux, a word needs to be said about place-names that the various authors employed. On the Franco-Spanish border in the Pyrenees Mountains near Roncevaux Valley are several places that are associated, in legend at least, with the disaster in which Roland lost his life. One of these is Gèdre, a hamlet one passes through on the way to the site where most nineteenth-century French authors believed the massacre took place, and Gavarnie is another. Between Gèdre and Gavarnie is a barren valley known as Le Chaos or La Peyrade. More than twelve hundred years ago an earthquake, formerly thought to have been a volcanic eruption, sent huge quantities of rocks and stones toppling into the valley, where they lie about in fantastic disarray. For Taine the place was "la solitude morte et peuplée de débris." Creuzé de Lesser viewed it as an eerie, ominous wasteland. The period's most famous travel book poetically conceded that "cette nature morte, ces masses inertes et mutilées remplissent l'âme d'idées effrayantes et sinistres."[1] More imaginatively, Napoléon Peyrat liked to think that in the jumble of stone nature had erected an immense equestrian statue of Roland.

Beyond Le Chaos, Gavarnie boasts the Cirque de Gavarnie, an enormous natural amphitheater that Peyrat thought of as an immense mausoleum sheltering Roland's remains. Towering 2807 meters about this amphitheater is the famous Brèche de Roland, which has dazzled many tourists. Wordsworth wrote that he would like to "seek the Pyrenean Breach / That Roland clove with huge two-fisted sway, / And to the enormous labour left his name, / Where unremitting frosts the rocky crescent bleach." Striking at the mountains with his sword, Roland is supposed to have created this vast jagged declivity in the wall of rock high over the Cirque de Gavarnie. Only a practiced mountain climber could scale it on foot. On horseback Roland and his companions would have been hard-pressed to reach it, much less to move about once they got there. But then, we are in the domain of the superhuman. Le Marboré, another massive segment of the Pyrenees Mountains, is nearby. When authors mention Le Marboré generally they have in mind the Pic du Marboré, which towers over the Cirque de Gavarnie to the southeast. Even higher than the Brèche de Roland, it is equally spectacular.

Finally something should be said about the site where the ambush occurred. Roncevaux is actually a mountain pass, not quite a valley. Among writers of his day, Peyrat, who grew up in the region, was virtually alone in calling it a plain. Baron Isidore Taylor and Auguste Mermet would later agree. Today many people believe that the disaster did not take place there anyway, but rather in another mountain pass, the Somport, near Saragossa.[2] Still, Frenchmen writing in the nineteenth century held that the site of the catastrophe was a valley at Roncevaux. Maurice Bouchor and Alfred de Vigny called it "une sombre vallée." Hence, despite the redundancy, I have referred consistently to Roncevaux Valley, not questioning whether Roland died there.

*The Roland Legend in
Nineteenth-Century French Literature*

1
Vague Recollections and New Beginnings

For our purposes, it will be worthwhile to keep in mind what educated Frenchmen knew prior to the nineteenth century about the illustrious Frankish knight who perished in the slaughter that took place in Roncevaux Valley on 15 August 778. Actually, Roland and his legend were by no means unknown. To be sure, much of what was known came from Spanish and Italian Renaissance literature. In the Middle Ages there had been moreover a fanciful and highly didactic Latin narrative, not quite romance and not quite history, that, translated into the vernacular, made for entertaining reading. In time several French historians, two in particular, treated the disaster in which the hero and his companions were killed. In addition, natives and visitors to the Pyrenees Mountains reported a lively indigenous oral tradition which had corollaries in southern and central France and even along the Rhine River. People knew that a *Chanson de Roland* had once existed, and they presumed it was lying about somewhere, waiting to be discovered. Several redactions turned up as the nineteenth century began, and then, in a foreign library, the authentic song unexpectedly came to light. The song turned out to be an epic. Specifically, though, what did cultivated Frenchmen know about the hero it celebrated before the published epic told them his story?

For one thing, they had read about him in *Don Quixote*, in which Roland, "uno de los doce pares de Francia," and his death in the forlorn mountain pass are mentioned a number of times. As Don Quixote and Sancho Panza set out for El Toboso on their third adventure, they hear a plowman singing a version of the "Romance del conde Guarinos, almirante de la mar," which declares: "Mala la hubistes, franceses, / en esa de Roncesvalles." When Don Quixote comments, Sancho's reply evokes another ballad, the "Romance del moro Calaínos," in which Roland figures prominently.[1] Sancho also recalls that Roland's sword can be seen in the Armería Real in Madrid. Indeed, it was thought for centuries that a sword on display there had belonged to the ill-fated Frankish paladin.

Educated Frenchmen also knew Dante's *Divina commedia*, in which the hero is alluded to several times. In the *Inferno* XXXI, the narrator-poet, walking with Virgil, hears a horn being blown, so shrilly that it would have drowned out thunder. "Ma io sentí sonare un alto corne, / tanto ch'avrebbe ogne tuon fatto fioco, / che, contra sé la sua via seguitando. / Dopo la dolorosa rotta, quando / Carlo Magno perdé la santa gesta, / non sonò sí terribilmente Orlando." In the following canto Dante describes a circular frozen lake into which famous traitors have been cast, their heads protruding above the ice. Rather than in Antenora, where traitors to their country are confined, it is in Caina, that part of the lake reserved for those who have betrayed their relatives, that one discovers Ganelon, who, in delivering his stepson Roland into Saracen hands, also betrayed Charlemagne, his wife's brother.

Similarly, Roland is encountered in the *Paradiso* XVIII. Ascending higher and higher, Dante reaches the radiant circle, where Beatrice points out

> In questa quinta soglia
> de l'albero che vive de la cima
> e frutta sempre e mai non perde foglia,
> spiriti son beati, che giù, prima
> che venissero al ciel, fuor di gran voce,
> sì ch'ogne musa ne sarebbe opima.
> ....
>
> Così per Carlo Magno e per Orlando
> due ne seguì lo mio attendo sguardo,
> com' occhio segue suo falcon volando.

For those who did not read Italian, any number of translations were available, including Lamennais's poetic prose rendering, which appeared in 1855.

Then there were the Italian Renaissance works. *Orlando innamorato* and *Orlando furioso* and others, all extraordinarily popular, spawned a Roland literature totally different from what readers familiar with the *Chanson de Roland* look upon as authentic. While these works did little to bolster the paladin's image as a stouthearted medieval warrior, pious and rugged, they helped keep his name alive and transmit it to generations of French readers. This alien Roland had his following in France and for a time would acclimatize himself there, cropping up often in indigenous literature.[2] Save for occasional appearances in the early nineteenth century, he will concern us little in the present study. Eventually, as the French became increasingly aware of their native Roland, the imported one faded away.[3]

During the Classical Age this Italian Roland showed up in Lully and Quinault's opera *Roland*, performed at Versailles on 8 January 1685 and at the Palais Royal two months later. Despite Boileau's fear that it would encourage wives to commit adultery, the opera was much admired,[4] particularly some advice given the hero in act 5, scene 3: "Roland, courez aux armes: / Que la gloire a de charmes! / L'amour de ses divins appas / Fait vivre au-delà du trépas." The stern summons to duty has the ring of various songs that will be encountered through the French Revolution and Napoleonic wars. In 1778 Piccini and Marmontel rewrote the opera, reducing its five acts to three. It was a hit.[5] Roland had been killed exactly a thousand years before.

But what about the native Roland? French readers were aware there had once been a *Chanson de Roland*. They knew little about it, however, aside from the fact that, though lost, it might not have disappeared forever. Writing in the *Décade* on 21 March 1804, Charles Nodier mentioned that Roland was an epic character of whom Frenchmen could be proud. Ten years later, in the *Journal des Débats*, 8 January 1814, he conjectured that epic fragments centering around this hero must be lying about somewhere. Chateaubriand, as we shall see, even thought he knew where the *Chanson de Roland* might be gathering dust. Assurance that there had been such a thing came from Wace's account of the battle of Hastings in the *Roman de Rou* (1160), in which one learns that, in the Norman camp, a minstrel sang it on the eve of the contest in order to kindle the invaders' enthusiasm:

> Taillefer, qui mult bien chantout,
> Sor un cheval qui tost alout,
> Devant le duc alout chantant
> De Karlemaigne e de Rollant
> E d'Oliver e des vassals
> Qui morurent en Rencevals.

The nature of the song was anything but clear, but it was known that, as late as the Hundred Years War, it was still being sung. French knights hearing it at the battle of Poitiers (19 September 1356) were not destined to be victorious. The kind but luckless King Jean II, it is claimed, wondered aloud why there were no more Rolands to come to France's defense. A heartbroken soldier is supposed to have replied that France would have Rolands when she had Charlemagnes. Clearly, the Roland legend had not been forgotten. It was still remembered in the waning Middle Ages; Jean Molinet, in his *Faictz et dictz* and *Chronique*, mentions the hero several times.

Still, the great medieval epics, including those that deal with Roland, were by and large unknown. The *Bibliothèque universelle des romans* began changing this in 1777, shortly before Piccini and Marmontel's opera. In that year, complete with commentaries, it published a series of résumés of various epics as well as certain chivalric romances. In all of this Roland came in for his share of attention. Largely based on Italian works, the *Bibliothèque universelle*'s discussion nevertheless devoted some attention to those epics known to the well read or learned. Discussed also was the *Pseudo-Turpin Chronicle*. Bringing its discussion to a close, the editors mentioned the lost *Chanson de Roland* and, incredibly, proposed to reconstruct it. The resulting song was a series of yarns about Roland's childhood and early exploits, all imaginary.

To no one did it occur, apparently, that the real "song" might have been an epic. The "reconstruction," though far from great poetry, was nonetheless a step in the right direction. With it the reading public was invited to take an interest in a native Roland literature. Although its author did not realize it, the song was a first effort at continuing such a literature. When the French Revolution broke out, the little song was remembered. It would influence many a new one during the Revolution and First Empire. Over the next hundred years, Roland would be presented to the French public in various guises, almost all of them heroic.

Although Hugo considered it a barren year from the literary standpoint, 1817 contributed to the Roland legend. Mme de Staël, so concerned with the literature of chivalry, died that year, but a noteworthy essay appeared by Louis de Musset, a man who was very much alive.

Louis de Musset, marquis de Cogners (1753-1839), was Alfred de Musset's adored granduncle. As a young man, the marquis had written an epistolary novel, *Correspondance d'un jeune militaire* (1778), that attracted some attention. In his later years he expanded his interests and wrote a remarkable essay on Roland, based mostly on a manuscript. He was the first French author to comment upon the legend in the light of an Old French text.

The essay had been preceded by another one, "De l'épée considérée comme signe de religion et en particulier de l'épée de Roland," published in the transactions of an antiquarian society in 1809. Here Musset theorized that a sword, among certain ancient peoples, was believed to have supernatural powers. Moreover, it and the person wielding it were seen as protectors, avengers. Musset posited that a nobleman designated to carry a sword might have been called, in the language of the old Germanic tribes, a *herr of land*. In French this may have evolved into *erovland*, then into *Rovland*, and finally into *Roland*. Whatever the merits of his shaky morphological speculation, the author goes on to hint that perhaps Roland was not the given name of Charlemagne's nephew at all but referred instead to his functions. As a result of his deeds while using the sword, the name in time came to be associated with him as an individual. "Dans le onzième ou douzième siècle, lorsqu'on composa sur Charlemagne et ses douze pairs les fables que le génie de l'Arioste a rendues si aimables, on remit dans la main d'un jeune seigneur, le plus brave entre les braves, l'épée par laquelle le magnanime empereur commandait à tant de peuples. On donna à ce jeune seigneur un nom qui rappelle celui de l'*épée seigneur* ou *maître du pays*. On composa au paladin une légende des plus singulières; il fut mis au rang des saints dans plusieurs églises de France, et sa propre épée, à laquelle on donna un nom particulier, fut conservée comme une relique."[6] Roland's possible place in the hierarchy of sainthood would continue to interest Musset, and we shall see Mérimée, Alexis de Valon, and Frédéric Mistral taking up the question of whether Roland's sword had been kept in a church where it could still be seen. In passing, one notes Musset's opinion that the epics dealing with Charlemagne and his peers were written in the eleventh and twelfth centuries.

The marquis's primary essay on Roland is entitled "Légende du bienheureux Roland, prince français." It appeared eight years after the earlier one in the annals of the same antiquarian society, which by then had changed its name. If the author considers Roland "bienheureux," then he calls his uncle, in the opening paragraph, "Saint" Charlemagne. Musset declares Roland to have been the son of Princess Berthe, Charlemagne's sister. Berthe's first husband was Milon, Comte d'Angers et du Mans, but Musset gives credence to the suspicion that Roland could have been the result of the emperor's penchant for his sister. Whatever the case, Milon loved Roland and reared him to be an educated, accomplished knight. Roland had three brothers, Thierry, Geoffroy, and Baudouin. Drawing upon the *Pseudo-Turpin Chronicle* and assorted historical works, Musset states that Roland warred against the Bretons and, with Thierry, against the Huns.

Urged by St. James, who three times appears to him in dreams, Charlemagne sets out to conquer Galicia. After taking Pamplona and Compostela, he returns to France. Before long King Aigoland, a Saracen ruler, seizes the towns and begins persecuting the Christian population. Against "ce mécréant illustre," Charlemagne sends Milon, with Roland at his side. At a decisive battle Milon conquers Spain but is killed, while Aigoland flees. When the French withdraw, Aigoland once more takes possession of the disputed territories and even advances into France. Charlemagne then marches against him, pushes him back into Spain, and kills him. During this third French invasion Roland fights and kills Ferragus. Then it occurs to the emperor that Marsile and Baligant, entrenched in Saragossa, are Moslems and, despite placating, submissive words, could make trouble for him in future. On Roland's advice, Ganelon is chosen to treat with them. The mission is a perilous one, and Ganelon is irritated that he was selected. According to one thread of the Roland legend that Musset appears to accept, the widowed Princess Berthe has taken Ganelon as her second husband, thus making Roland Ganelon's stepson.

"C'est ici que l'auteur du *Poème de Roncevals* commence sa narration," Musset states. Hereafter he uses *poème* and *roman* interchangeably to designate the manuscript he consulted, the redaction of the *Chanson de Roland* that was formerly known as the Manuscrit de Versailles and is now called the Manuscrit de Châteauroux, which Raoul Mortier published in 1943.[7] Musset adds in a note that a certain M. Guyot des Herbiers was preparing an edition of the poem.[8] Claude Antoine Guyot des Herbiers was Alfred de Musset's maternal grandfather, who had been a member of the Conseil des Cinq Cents during the Directory and the Consulate. Something of a wit, he had tried his hand at writing and, in addition to other works, had authored a lengthy poem entitled *Les Heures* and another, in several cantos, about cats. When he died in 1828 his edition of the *Chanson de Roland* had not appeared, but in 1818 he had made a copy of the manuscript. This copy, used in the Bibliothèque Nationale in Paris, would serve as one of the bases of Henri Monin's famous thesis in 1832.

Musset cites numerous sources, but much of his material comes from the manuscript epic, which he summarizes and quotes at length. His essay follows the *Chanson de Roland* closely, since he is using a redaction of the poem. According to Musset, Ganelon connives with the Moors, then returns to the emperor's camp, bringing their promise of submission. The traitor asks that Roland be put in command of the rear guard as the main army sets out for home. This done, the Moors await their moment and then attack. Curiously, Musset declares Roland and the twelve peers victorious, even though all are killed in the ambush. Presumably he is referring to the emperor's return and pursuit of the villains. Since Musset is relying upon a version of the *Chanson de Roland,* unsurprisingly not only Olivier but also Archbishop Turpin share their comrade's fate. Musset adds that Roland's and Olivier's bodies are embalmed and taken to the Abbaye de St. Romain in Blaye. Charlemagne endows the institution and orders Roland's sword and horn to be hung over his tomb. Early nineteenth-century authors often mention the emperor's taking Roland's body to Blaye. Musset appears to be alone, however, in specifying that St. Romain's was an abbey church and in stating that Olivier's remains were interred there also.

Musset is also one of the rare early authors to devote any attention to Roland's feelings for Aude, the fiancée he left behind. Musset describes her as "l'unique objet de sa tendresse." Had they married, Roland would have been "le modèle des époux et des pères," he believes. Roland's brother Thierry and also Aude, who Musset calls Aure, beseech the emperor to try Ganelon. Ganelon is tried, convicted, and quartered. Justice is done, but the emperor's sorrow over his nephew's death remains.[9]

It is surprising to see several brothers in the poem, and one wishes the author had commented on them. Having a version of the epic at his disposal, he is, however, one of the first writers of the nineteenth century to place Turpin in Roncevaux Valley at the time of the ambush and hence to make him one of its victims. Other writers of the period, relying upon the *Pseudo-Turpin Chronicle,* have him return to France with his imperial master. Michelet liked to think that, in Charlemagne's era, all citizens and all soldiers were equal. Musset did not go this far, but he did believe that barons during the period constituted a special echelon in which all had the same status and were in every sense "compagnons."[10]

Musset notes that most readers date the *Pseudo-Turpin Chronicle* at about 1095. He did not think that this work, originally in Latin prose, was the lost *Chanson de Roland*. Such a work "convenait peu pour enflammer le courage des croisés," he observes. He contends that, first, there was a "chant de guerre." This war song, directed at soldiers about to fight Moslems in Jerusalem, must have pointed out that Moslems had once dared set foot in the Frankish empire and that Charlemagne's best soldiers had died in an encounter with them at Roncevaux. This call for vengeance against the Moors provided the basic plot for the epic, which was composed, Musset believed, after Philippe Auguste's reign.[11] That epic had to be the *Roman de Roncevals*, Musset's manuscript. After the epic came the *Chronicle*, the author reasoned. Musset asserted that Dante's source was not the *Chronicle* but rather the *Roman de Roncevals*. Alone among his contemporaries, he did not believe that what was sung at the battle of Hastings was the "chant de guerre" that served as the nexus of the epic or that it was the epic itself.[12]

Musset's theories and ideas concerning Roland, Roncevaux, and the *Chanson de Roland* are curious and, in some cases, uncanny. The writer is unique among his contemporaries in referring to Charlemagne as a saint. Similarly, he is the only one to confer the title "blessed" upon Roland, pointing out that some medieval French churches had elevated him to sainthood. It is true that the *Rolandslied* calls the noblemen slaughtered at Roncevaux "holy" lords around whose remains miracles have occurred, but, when Musset was writing, the *Rolandslied* had not yet been published.[13] However correct or incorrect Musset's views may be, they are the first French discussion based on familiarity with an authentic Old French text of the *Chanson de Roland*. Unfortunately, issued in an obscure publication, Musset's essay had no effect on what was being written about the Roland legend at the time.[14]

While a history of *Chanson de Roland* scholarship lies beyond the scope of the present study, still, in view of the wealth of plot material it would make available to writers beginning in 1837, we might profitably examine the discovery and dissemination of the epic in its present form. The *Bibliothèque universelle* and Chateaubriand believed that a manuscript must be hidden away somewhere, waiting to be discovered, and they were right. What they did not know was that there were various manuscripts and that most of them were hiding in faraway places.

Probably the first Frenchman in modern times to see the Oxford Manuscript was Abbé Gervais de La Rue. Fleeing the French Revolution, La Rue decided to sit out the storm in Great Britain, pursuing erudite interests at a safe distance. During his exile, he discovered the *Chanson de Roland* at Oxford

University. Unfortunately he did not mention it for the next forty years. He broke his silence in his *Essais historiques sur les bardes, les jongleurs, et les trouvères normands,* published in 1834. For both author and book Chateaubriand had high regard.[15] His comments, some of them astute, include an opinion about the manuscript's age: it belonged, the author decided, to the first three decades of the twelfth century.

In 1831 Edgar Quinet's *Rapport . . . sur les épopées françaises* had pointed out that, tucked away in two Paris libraries, a number of manuscript epics were waiting for someone to wipe away the dust and give them the attention that, as national treasures, they deserved. While calling for their preservation, Quinet also urged publication. At about the same time, Henri Monin, a student at the Ecole Normale, was looking for a thesis topic. Avoiding the beaten path, he chose to work not on an aspect of modern literature but on two manuscripts in the Bibliothèque Nationale, texts, far from perfect, of the *Chanson de Roland.* Today these complementary texts are known as the Manuscrit de Paris and the Manuscrit de Châteauroux. The latter was not totally unheard-of, since both Louis de Musset and Claude Antoine Guyot des Herbiers, had known and used it. The original that Guyot des Herbiers copied had once been in Louis XVI's library at Versailles. During the French Revolution it came into the possession of Comte Germain Garnier, Préfet de Versailles during the First Empire. From Garnier's estate, Antoine Jean Louis Bourdillon, a Swiss bibliophile and collector, acquired it in 1822. Soon after, Bourdillon began copying all the *Chanson de Roland* manuscripts he could find. In 1840 he published a translation of the one he owned, and in 1841 he issued a deplorable text in which he eliminated words and lines that he did not like, replacing them with readings from other manuscripts that suited him better. He published supplements to his text in 1847, 1850, and 1851. When he died in 1856, he left the original manuscript to the town of Châteauroux, and it was placed in the Bibliothèque Municipale.[16]

Aware that he was dealing with two versions of the same poem, which he called the *Roman de Roncevaux,* Monin scrutinized and compared them. He also transcribed a few hundred lines, bridging the passages of quoted material with summaries of what was being omitted. Numerous footnotes explained or translated obscure words and phrases. Unaware that the Oxford Manuscript existed, Monin sometimes had to speculate, but he speculated well, raising questions about the epic's origin and nature that *Chanson de Roland* scholars have debated ever since. Was this "une oeuvre littéraire destinée à être lue," he wanted to know, "ou n'est-ce pas plutôt un poème populaire formé peu à peu sur des traditions nationales, destiné à être chanté et à subir toutes les additions, tous les retranchements, toutes les transformations que la transmission orale ne peut manquer de faire subir à des traditions, même quand elles sont soumises à la forme poétique?" In the latter case, he reasoned, "ce roman

serait la fameuse *Chanson de Roland* que les soldats français chantaient encore au temps du roi Jean." Monin did not believe this, however, and theorized that there must have been more than one *Chanson de Roland*. Here he came close to what we now realize, that the poem simply exists in several different redactions. He also concluded that the poem must have had more than one author. It had been "composé de chants populaires . . , mais remaniés, mis en ordre et complétés. . . . Les récits qu'il contient ne sont pas une invention individuelle, mais des traditions nationales et universellement répandues." Discussing the thesis twenty years later in the *Revue des Deux Mondes*, Ludovic Vitet echoed Monin's queries. Vitet wondered whether the *Chanson de Roland* was "un de ces chants populaires dont personne n'est l'auteur, qui se transmettent comme ils sont nés sans que jamais l'écriture ne les recueille," or whether it was, on the contrary, "une oeuvre composée, une oeuvre écrite, un poème."[17]

Presented at the Sorbonne, Monin's thesis was published in 1832 and generated a great deal of excitement. The following year Michelet's *Histoire de France* praised it. Meanwhile, Francisque Michel gave it a rather severe *Examen critique*. Already Michel had found out about the Oxford Manuscript and alluded to it in his pamphlet. Hurriedly Monin made some "corrections et additions" to his thesis and had them bound with it. In these he readily admitted, as his critic contended, that the Oxford Manuscript might be older than the two texts he had used, but he was not interested in pursuing the matter. He did not believe, as his reviewer was inclined to do, that Turoldus was the epic's sole author.[18]

François Guizot, minister of public instruction, sent Michel to Oxford. The scholar copied the manuscript and then returned to Paris, where he prepared it for publication. Anything but secretive, Michel in 1836, on the eve of the edition's publication, showed it to Antoine Le Roux de Lincy. Le Roux de Lincy, quoting in modern French, discussed it in his *Livre des légendes*, which appeared before Michel's edition.[19] Michel's work, the *Chanson de Roland ou de Roncevaux*, appeared during the first week of February 1837.

In his *Revue des Deux Mondes* article in 1852, Ludovic Vitet, Mérimée's friend and predecessor as Inspecteur Général des Monuments Historiques, remarked that at last a good text of the *Chanson de Roland* was available. A modern French translation had also been needed, and François Génin had provided it.[20] Génin's edition and translation came out in 1850. (Etienne Delécluze, however, had published a translation several years previously.) Génin's version was reissued in 1852. A professional scholar, Génin was also cantankerous. Barbey d'Aurevilly loathed him, probably because of his venomous anticlericalism. Early in his career Génin took on Quinet, one of whose statements in the *Rapport* met with his disapproval. The disagreement was soon patched up, although Quinet did not retract the statement and even reprinted it.[21] Nonetheless, it was almost inevitable that Génin and Quinet should become allies, since both, in addition to being *universitaires,* shared deep anticlerical and republican convictions. In 1843, along with Michelet, they joined forces in a pitched battle with the Jesuits over public versus private education. Génin in *Le National,* Quinet in *Le Siècle,* and Michelet in *Le Constitutionnel* all belabored their common foe.

With other opponents Génin was less inclined to make peace, however. With a penchant for ignoring or dismissing colleagues' work, he had no dearth of adversaries. He attacked Paulin Paris, who criticized his edition of the *Chanson de Roland.* He also irritated and managed to alienate Francisque Michel, who came to detest him and delighted in calling attention to his blunders. Rancorous exchanges between the two went on for years. Michel was a friend of Mérimée, who took an interest in the squabble. While advising his friend to ignore his opponent's thrusts, Mérimée was nonetheless elated when in 1851 the Académie Française declined to award a prize to Génin's *Chanson de Roland* translation.[22]

Although contentious, Génin had produced a translation that made the *Chanson de Roland* accessible to those unwilling to cope with its linguistic problems but eager to read it. For those who could not bring themselves even to skim a translation, Vitet provided a detailed summary of the epic in his article, which Théodore de Banville would remember. Though with less detail than Vitet, Le Roux de Lincy had also summarized the *Chanson de Roland.*

With Michel and Génin's publications, the best, probably the oldest, text of the *Chanson de Roland* was available. Several editions, not to mention translations, appeared during the decades that followed. From this point on, most of those writing about Roland, including Auguste Barbier and Albert Glatigny, had either read the poem or knew something about it. Victor Hugo was one of those who did not bother, at least not for a long time.

A medieval compilation now known as the *Pseudo-Turpin Chronicle* gave to later ages an important corpus of material about the battle of Roncevaux and its tragic hero. Also known as the *Historia Caroli Magni et Rothlandi,* the *Pseudo-Turpin Chronicle,* highly didactic in content, is the work of an unknown French *clerc* writing around 1130 or 1140. Written in Latin, it was translated into French several times and well into modern times was considered authoritative. Although by the nineteenth century the *Chronicle* was known not to have been the work of Charlemagne's archbishop of Rheims, a number of writers such as Joseph Autran continued to draw episodes from it.[23]

The *Pseudo-Turpin Chronicle* is presented as a letter from Archbishop Turpin to Leoprandus, dean of the cathedral at Aix-la-Chapelle, telling about Charlemagne's achievements in Spain and Galicia. Charlemagne, Turpin informs his correspondent, was summoned to the peninsula by St. James, who appeared to the monarch in visions, urging him to subdue the pagans. Charlemagne set out with an army, and occupied Pamplona and converted the heathen who wished it, enslaving or killing the rest. During three years in Spain, he conquered the entire country. Having enlarged the basilica of St. James, he returned to France, building numerous churches as he made his way to Paris.

Then Charlemagne learns that an African Saracen, King Aigoland, has retaken Spain and killed large numbers of Christians. At the head of an army that includes Roland's father, Duke Milon d'Anglant, or d'Anglets, he retraces his steps. On the eve of an important battle, many of his men stick their lances in the ground and in the morning find that the lances have grown roots, bark, and leaves. Their owners cut off these lances near the ground, but from the roots whole groves, which can still be seen, spring up. In the battle that ensues, Milon is killed, but soon reinforcements arrive, the French win, and Aigoland flees to León.

Once more Charlemagne departs for France. Before he gets home, however, Aigoland assembles an immense pagan host. Taking Agen, in Gascony, he calls upon Charlemagne to meet him there and declare himself his vassal. Charlemagne eludes his foe, raises a large army in France, and returns, along with Turpin, Roland, Olivier, and Ganelon, among others. At Pamplona there are several engagements, and Charlemagne invites the pagan king to be baptized. For this purpose Aigoland arrives at his adversary's camp and finds the emperor and his men eating. Noticing that the clerics have plenty to eat while a dozen paupers seated on the ground are given very little, he is dismayed and, changing his mind, returns to his own camp. The lesson is not lost on Charlemagne, who hastens to make amends and provide for the needy in his camp. In the battle that takes place the next day, the Christians triumph and Aigoland is killed, only to be replaced by another heathen prince.

The next important episode in the *Pseudo-Turpin Chronicle* is Roland's duel with a pagan giant named Ferragus, whom the French knight overcomes and kills. Then the Saracens are defeated once more, this time in Cordova. Having conquered Spain again, Charlemagne establishes an episcopal see at St. James of Compostela. From Pamplona he sends Ganelon with a message to the Saracen princes, giving them the choice of paying tribute or becoming Christians. The princes temporize, bribing and conniving with Ganelon and preparing to attack. On Ganelon's advice, Charlemagne puts Roland in command of a rear guard made up of twenty thousand men. The main army, with Turpin and Ganelon, sets out for home. When the army disappears, the heathen fall upon the rear guard in Roncevaux Valley.

Roland accomplishes amazing feats, but the numerical odds are too great. Curiously, as the end draws near, he is thirsty. Durandal, his sword, presents a more serious problem, however. To prevent its falling into pagan hands, Roland strikes a marble boulder with it three times, hoping to break it, but he merely succeeds in splitting the rock. An occasional later writer, including

Sismondi, although drawing his basic material from the *Chronicle*, would allow him to break it. Roland then blows his ivory horn to summon his uncle. Charlemagne hears it but is dissuaded by Ganelon from turning back, and Roland realizes that he is doomed. He prays at length and finally breathes his last, his soul carried to heaven by angels. Turpin learns in a vision what has happened and tells Charlemagne. Baudouin, Roland's brother and companion, somehow escapes the massacre. Catching up with the emperor, he confirms the terrible news. The French return to Roncevaux, where the dead Roland and Olivier are found. Charlemagne pursues the culprits to Saragossa and punishes them, then goes back to Roncevaux, where Ganelon is placed on trial, his innocence or guilt to be decided by combat. Pinabel represents Ganelon and Théodoric, the accusers. When Pinabel is killed, the traitor is sentenced. After he has been quartered, the saddened French army returns homeward once more. Most of the dead are buried in Arles and Bordeaux. Olivier, however, is buried at Belin, while Roland is taken to Blaye and laid to rest in the church of St. Romain, with his sword at his head and his horn at his feet. Charlemagne, after endowing the church, proceeds to Paris and then to Aix. Turpin learns that the emperor died on 28 January 814. A postscript mentions that the archbishop himself died not long after his imperial master.

The *Chronicle* is filled with moralistic details. Miracles occur frequently, and theological debates either precede or punctuate the duels and battles. Aside from the miracles and debates, one of the *Chronicle*'s most prominent plot elements is Charlemagne's three invasions of Spain. Throughout, Archbishop Turpin is with the emperor, not Roland. The *Chronicle* gives Roland a brother whom he does not have in the *Chanson de Roland*, and whereas in the *Chanson de Roland* Ganelon is taken back to Aix to be tried, in the *Chronicle* he is tried and executed at Roncevaux. The two traditions are also at odds on other points. In the *Chanson de Roland* Roland's horn is left at the church of St. Seurin in Bordeaux, but his body, with the bodies of Olivier and Turpin, is interred at St. Romain's at Blaye. In the *Chronicle*, however, Olivier is buried at Belin and Turpin is not killed. The *Chronicle* represents still another variant that arouses reader interest: Roland's fiancée is absent. No doubt because of his insistence upon Charlemagne's being in Spain on a religious mission, the *Chronicle*'s author includes no element of profane love in his narrative, and Aude is not even mentioned.

Several nineteenth-century French authors were inspired by the *Chronicle*, actually lifting details or even whole episodes from it in elaborating their own versions of the Roland legend. Joseph Autran especially would remember his rich repository of Roland material.

Prior to the French Revolution, the Roland story had been told by several historians. Scipion Dupleix, with his *Histoire générale de France, avec l'estat de l'église et de l'empire,* was one of the most important. Writing his three-volume *Histoire générale* during the 1620s, he was basically an official historian. His commentary about the battle of Roncevaux is useful for understanding nineteenth-century French presentations of the Roland legend. His sources include Einhard's *Vita Caroli Magni* and *Annales regum francorum,* and probably he relied upon oral tradition as well.

In Dupleix's account, Aquitaine was to play a vital role. The author points out that a Spanish Christian king, Froila, had married a daughter of Eudo, duke of Aquitaine. Dupleix outlines the problems confronting both the Christian and Saracen rulers of Spain before Charlemagne's invasion of the Iberian Peninsula. At odds among themselves, the Saracens were in a particularly unsettled situation. One faction, ousted from power, sought Charlemagne's help against the other. Meanwhile, the Spanish Christians implored him to rid them of the same enemy. Finally the king agreed to intervene and crossed the Pyrenees Mountains with a large army, taking Gascony, Navarre, Pamplona, and Saragossa. Working their way through Navarre, the Gascons, whom Dupleix presents as Arabs, escaped and descended into Aquitaine. Future French writers differ about who attacked Roland. The most common literary tradition blames the Saracens, of course, but the Gascons, the Navarrese, and the Basques, as well as the Duke of Aquitaine and his vassals, are all accused.

Having achieved his goal in Spain, seconded by the Moors who called him in, Charlemagne returns to Pamplona, razes it to avoid leaving it garrisoned, and starts homeward. By now, however, the Saracen Gascons are refreshed. Just as important, they are accustomed to the rugged peaks through which the French must ride. Charlemagne is at the head of the main army wending its way home, and the Gascons have slipped into the narrow passes and are waiting for the rear guard. What happens next in Dupleix's account reverberates through many nineteenth-century evocations of the battle of Roncevaux. The cascading trees and rocks, in particular, appear repeatedly.

> Ces montagnars . . , qui estoient aux aguets sur les coupeaux voisins, roulans sur les François des pièces des roches entamées, des caillous, des arbres, et tout ce que la fureur leur mettoit en main, les mirent premièrement en désarroy, en escrasèrent plusieurs en ce tumulte, et puis contraignirent les autres de se précipiter avec un effroy et désordre incroiable dans la vallée prochaine: là . . . il les taillèrent en pièces sans qu'il en eschapât un seul, ainsi que le rapporte expressément Eginhard, secrétaire d'estat ou chancelier de Charles.
>
> Là moururent plusieurs braues et illustres seigneurs françois et entr'autres Roland, admiral ou gouuerneur de Bretagne. . . . Par cette défaite tout le bagage demeura aux Gascons, lesquels l'enleuèrent et l'emportèrent à la faueur de la nuict dans des cachots inaccessibles.
>
> La nouuelle de cette triste auanture estant portée au Roy, il fit tourner teste à son armée pour aller chastier ces bandoliers. Mais n'en pouuant attendre qu'un

second malheur, il fut conseillé de différer sa vengeance à une autre occasion plus opportune et continuer son chemin vers la France: emportant un regret extreme de cette perte inopinée, non pas pour le bagage mais pour tant d'illustres seigneurs et vaillans hommes, la mort desquels esteignit tout le contentement de ses signalées victoires. . . .

Charles, honorant la mémoire de ceux qu'il auoit chéris pour leur vertu durant leur vie, fit rechercher les corps des seigneurs de marque occis par les Gascons: lesquels il fit porter à Bourdeaus où partie d'iceux furent inhumés, aucuns au bourg de Belin à huict lieues de la mesme ville, et Roland en l'Eglise Sainct Romain de Blaye: ce qui donne sujet aux romans de chanter qu'il estoit comte de Blaye. L'on tient par tradition sur les lieux que l'espeé de Roland fut mise au dessus de son chef et sa trompe d'yuoire à ses pieds: laquelle a esté depuis traduite en l'église collégiale Sainct Seuerin lez Bourdeaus et son espeée à Roquemadour en Querci.[24]

In Dupleix's account, Charlemagne made only one incursion into Spain, as in the *Chanson de Roland*. Unlike the *Chanson de Roland*, however, Dupleix's *Histoire générale* does not have him pursue and chastise the villains. There is no mention of Olivier, Turpin, or Roland's fiancée Aude, but the historian does conclude by warning readers against "l'auteur de l'histoire qui court par les mains des hommes sous le nom de Turpin ou Tulpin, archevesque de Reims, lequel accompagna Charles en ses plus grandes entreprises." This, of course, is a reference to the *Pseudo-Turpin Chronicle*, which Dupleix summarizes. We note his statement that Roland was buried at Blaye, as well as his remarks about the hero's horn and sword. Roland's burial place and the fate of the horn and sword would preoccupy many nineteenth-century writers, and the sword's being at Rocamadour would come up more than once.

Voltaire saw history from the standpoint of reason, and he looked upon religion as something that, instead of springing from deep personal resolve, in most cases was more likely to arise from circumstances, perhaps even convenience or opportunism. Charlemagne's foray onto the Iberian Peninsula was not, as he saw it, a conflict pitting Christian against Moslem necessarily but one in which unstable alliances created a situation in which Moslems happened to find themselves at loggerheads with Moslems, and Christians with Christians. He illustrated his view in the *Essai sur les moeurs* (1756). In 778, he pointed out, Charlemagne made common cause with Ibnal, emir of Saragossa, against the latter's overlord but took care not to convert his new ally. Voltaire's Charlemagne obviously was not the devout Christian warrior whose every deed was undertaken with a view to advancing his faith. "Le prince français . . . s'allie avec des Sarrasins contre des Sarrasins; mais, après quelques avantages sur les frontières d'Espagne, son arrière-garde est défaite à Roncevaux, vers les montagnes des Pyrénées, par les chrétiens mêmes de ces montagnes, mêlés aux musulmans. C'est là que périt Roland son neveu. Ce malheur est l'origine de ces fables qu'un moine écrivit au onzième siècle, sous le nom de l'archevêque Turpin, et qu'ensuite l'imagination de l'Arioste a embellies."

Frenchmen writing on Roland in the early years of the nineteenth century, while they probably had read Voltaire, found more detailed, usable information in the work of another historian, Gabriel Henri Gaillard (1726-1806). Gaillard was an inactive lawyer and an active, prominent historian whose toil won him a seat in the Académie Française. Probably his most important work is his four-volume *Histoire de Charlemagne,* published in 1782. With its detailed account of Charlemagne's Spanish adventure of 778, it shows what well-read Frenchmen could have been expected to know about the expedition's historical underpinnings as the nineteenth century began. Revolution was in the air, and Gaillard showed his readers a less-than-ideal monarch, who commanded admiration but had weaknesses that the historian did not hesitate to condemn.

The third volume of Gaillard's book contains a "Histoire romanesque de Charlemagne et ses rapports avec l'histoire véritable," in which the author mentions objects, people, and events, real or unreal, associated with the Charlemagne and Roland legends. He points out that Durandal, "cette merveilleuse et magique épée donnée par Charlemagne à Roland," has its place in the legends. "Roland, près de mourir, casse la lame de Durandal et en jette bien loin les tronçons, afin qu'elle ne puisse jamais servir aux infidèles contre les Chrétiens."[25] The standard version holds that Roland tried to break his sword but failed. Victor Hugo and others were to be quite interested in the sword, its properties, and its fate.

Inevitably, Gaillard examines the *Pseudo-Turpin Chronicle.*[26] "Le roman publié sous le nom de Turpin, archevêque de Reims, et qui, comme tout le monde le sait aujourd'hui, n'est point de ce prélat, est le premier et le père de tous les romans de chevalerie. . . . Cette fabuleuse chronique, moitié légende, moitié roman. . . , fut fabriquée pendant le Concile de Clermont, tenu en 1095 . . . , où la première croisade fut résolue." Obviously, its purpose was to "échauffer les esprits et de les animer à la guerre contre les infidèles par l'exemple de Charlemagne, qui avoit eu en Espagne des succès contre les mêmes infidèles." It would be more than fifty years before the *Chanson de Roland* as we know it would be published. Gaillard could not predict, of course, that some scholars would come to believe that the epic itself was written for the same purpose he gives to explain the genesis of the *Pseudo-Turpin Chronicle.* According to the *Chronicle,* Gaillard points out, St. James appeared to the emperor one night and revealed the location of his burial place in Spain. He then ordered the monarch to conquer Spain, erect a tomb for him, and build a church in his honor. Obeying the command, Charlemagne departed. Turpin accompanied his master to baptize the vanquished. A creature of his era,

Gaillard does not fail to condemn "cet esprit d'intolérance et de prosélytisme."[27]

Dismissing the *Pseudo-Turpin Chronicle,* Gaillard emphasizes that, since there were virtually no other histories, it was long considered authentic. "Avant les siècles de bonne critique, les fables de Turpin avoient usurpé l'autorité qui n'est due qu'à la vérité. Le faux Turpin étoit seul connu, seul cru, seul cité. Ses fables étoient dans toutes les bouches; les poètes les avoient illustrées."[28] Future writers appreciated Gaillard but did not necessarily share his dislikes. The *Pseudo-Turpin Chronicle* continued to provide authors with material throughout the nineteenth century.

Gaillard also recalls stories about Charlemagne's sister Berthe and her marriage to Milon d'Anglante, comte d'Angers. Because the emperor disapproved, the couple went to live in a cave near Siena. Milon's disappearance and return are also related, as are episodes from Roland's childhood, during which the boy, believing his father to be dead, is his mother's only resource. How Roland took food from the emperor's table and brought it to his mother and how the emperor had him followed and became reconciled with his sister are narrated. Charlemagne's daughter Emma and her love for Einhard are described as well.[29] We shall see that Alexandre Dumas père used and embellished these anecdotes.

In Gaillard's treatment of Charlemagne, his era, and his wars, Prince Lucien Bonaparte and others may have discovered useful information. Charlemagne's brother Carloman died leaving a widow and two young sons. What became of these sons, to whose inheritance Charlemagne helped himself, is not clear. Apparently their mother fled to Italy, taking them with her, and eventually they fell into their uncle's hands. One, according to Gaillard, disappeared, while the other took religious vows. For Prince Lucien, the two princes' fate would be a problem. Gaillard calls their mother Gerberge, but Prince Lucien gave her a more euphonious name. Also treated in Gaillard's *Histoire* are Didier, king of the Lombards, and his son Adalgis. Moreover, one encounters two Lombard princes whose names occur in Prince Lucien's *Charlemagne ou l'église délivrée* and Marchangy's *Gaule poétique,* the dukes of Friuli and Benevento. According to Gaillard, Charlemagne beheaded a hostile Duke of Friuli, then awarded his duchy to a Frenchman. This explains why, in Prince Lucien's and Marchangy's works, a Duc de Frioul can stand out as one of the emperor's most trusted lieutenants. Likewise, Gaillard has the emperor eventually bestow the duchy of Benevento upon one of his own partisans. Finally, Tassilo, duke of Bavaria, is also deposed and his duchy given to someone else. Unlike Tassilo, Duke Naimes of Bavaria, so often encountered in the Roland legend, would be devoted to his master. Gaillard also has a great deal to say abut Wittikind, the Saxon chieftain who led numerous revolts against Charlemagne. One Saxon uprising was the immediate reason for Charlemagne's leaving Spain in 778, Gaillard observes.[30]

For our purposes, Gaillard's importance lies primarily in the *Histoire*'s account of Charlemagne's Spanish expedition. For Gaillard, Charlemagne and his soldiers were Frenchmen, not Franks. Like Dupleix, Gaillard claimed that the invasion was the result of several discontented Mohammedan princes' having appealed to Charlemagne. Gaillard reasoned shrewdly: "L'Espagne étoit toujours sous la puissance des Sarrasins," he wrote. However, "il étoit arrivé à ce peuple conquérant ce qui arrivera toujours aux peuples conquérans, d'être obligé de se diviser par l'effet même de la conquête.... Tout grand empire tend à se dissoudre" because of its size. Governors, having declared themselves independent kings, were now quarreling. Several of the weaker ones begged Charlemagne to come to their aid. The Frankish king hesitated, not sure that his conscience would permit an alliance with Mohammedans, even against other Mohammedans. Finally, enticed by the prospects of gaining territory and helping the persecuted Spanish Christians, he armed, crossed the mountains, and took Pamplona. Simultaneously another army, entering the peninsula by way of Roussillon, seized Barcelona. Navarre, Catalonia, and Aragon capitulated. All of the Saracen kings who had asked for help were restored. Ibinalarabi, the most important, was restored to the throne of Saragossa. Christians were freed from their obligations to Mohammedan rulers.[31] Charlemagne was accused of committing "horrible outrages" while setting things right, but Gaillard still reproaches him for not finishing the task. Momentarily, the historian has forgotten about the Saxons and their ill-timed revolt.

In any event, "Charlemagne rentroit dans ses états couvert de gloire et chargé de butin; mais la haine veilloit sur lui et l'attendoit au passage." Gaillard had already pointed out that Charlemagne had inherited bad relations with the Gascons and their discontented leader Lupus II and had mentioned the Duke of Aquitaine, another enemy. He had no doubt that those who attacked Charlemagne's rear guard at Roncevaux were Gascons. "Un duc de Gascogne étoit alors pour les Pyrénées ce qu'un duc de Savoie est pour les Alpes: il avoit la clef de l'Espagne," he observed.[32] As the French rode across the mountains onto the Iberian Peninsula, the Duke of Gascony let them pass unmolested. Either they moved too quickly or he thought it would be easier to pick them off later when, on the homeward trip, they would be hemmed in between the Moors and the mountains. When they returned, he was ready, but he dared not attack the main army. He waited and then swooped down upon the rear guard. Gaillard describes rocks being rolled down the mountainsides and crushing the victims.

> Il fondit en traître sur l'arrière-garde, qui ne s'attendoit nullement à cette brusque attaque, mais qui étoit prête à tout, étant composée des plus braves gens de l'armée: le bagage fut pillé, le choc fut même assez violent pour que l'arrière-garde, n'ayant pu être mise en désordre, fût taillée en pièces et pour que les

François y perdissent plusieurs guerriers distingués tels qu'Eginard, grand-maître de la maison du roi, Anselme, comte du palais, et ce Roland, neveu de Charlemagne, si célèbre par les romanciers et par les poètes mais dont l'histoire dit simplement qu'il étoit gouverneur des côtes de l'Océan Britannique et fils de Milon, comte d'Angers, et de Berthe, soeur de Charlemagne. Les François ne pouvant ni développer leurs forces ni se mettre en bataille ni atteindre un ennemi presque invisible, effrayés par la vue des précipices et par le bruit des torrens, étoient écrasés par de grosses roches qu'on rouloit sur eux du haut des montagnes ou percés par des flèches lancées d'un lieu sûr. C'est là cette fameuse journée de Roncevaux dont l'Espagne est encore si fière et où elle se vante d'avoir vaincu Charlemagne et ses douze pairs. Les François disent qu'on ne doit point se vanter d'une si lâche trahison; que s'il étoit possible d'en tirer quelque gloire, cette gloire serait un peu étrangère à l'Espagne; qu'elle appartiendroit à des voleurs montagnards, demi-François, demi-Espagnols, ou qui plutôt n'étoient ni l'un ni l'autre; qui avoient moins combattu qu'ils n'avoient pillé . . . ; que si les François essuyèrent un échec dans cette occasion, bien loin qu'il ait pu nuire à leur gloire, il semble avoir augmenté leur considération en Europe par l'importance même que l'Espagne attache à ce petit fait de guerre.[33]

Gaillard mentions a manuscript, probably Père Gabriel Daniel's *Histoire de France*, containing "la description d'une chapelle bâtie à trois cens pas de l'église de l'Abbaye de Roncevaux: sous cette chapelle est une cave au fond de laquelle l'auteur de la relation vit, à la lueur d'un flambeau, quelques ossemens." Around the chapel were thirty plain tombs, bearing no inscriptions. On the walls was a fresco depicting the battle of Roncevaux. Local tradition had it that Charlemagne "a fait bâtir cette chapelle, où l'on prioit pour les François morts à la journée de Roncevaux; que la cave est l'endroit où il les fit enterrer; que les trente tombeaux sont ceux des seigneurs les plus considérables qui périrent dans cette journée." The manuscript claimed that the populace allowed only Frenchmen to be buried in the area. There was no consensus among nineteenth-century French writers about where the slain knights were interred, but the issue recurs, and the chapel is evoked several times. Gaillard reports the tradition but neither endorses nor rebuts it. Concluding his discussion of the Roncevaux disaster, he notes that Charlemagne caught and hanged the Duke of Gascony, a deed the historian considered reprehensible.[34]

Gaillard records that Charlemagne reestablished Ibinalarabi as king of Saragossa and that in the conquered territories he set up a kind of satellite state. "Les provinces espagnoles qu'il avoit soumises . . . formoient une espèce de souveraineté particulière sous le titre de *Marche d'Espagne.*"[35] Immermann's fanciful *Das Thal von Ronceval* (1819) has Charlemagne confer the region upon Roland, making him its king. When Roland gets killed, it devolves upon his fiancée, a converted Moslem princess. In Alfred Assollant's novel *La Mort de Roland: fantaisie épique* (1860), another Moorish princess is made queen of the new territories. If Gaillard was correct, then Immermann and Assollant were not altogether inventing things.

Gaillard's *Histoire de Charlemagne* would be the standard history for many years. One of its chief claims to our attention lies in its stating that Roland's death was brought about by the hero's being crushed beneath rocks hurled down the mountains. The rocks, as well as trees, we have already encountered in Dupleix's *Histoire générale*. Later a number of writers would seize upon this detail, even adding to it. Not all, however, would agree that the Gascons hurled the primitive missiles.

Poet, dramatist, and novelist, Louis Ramond de Carbonnières (1755-1827) is best known today for his enthusiastic and poetic description of mountains. Pierre de Gorsse, in the section of *Villégiatures romantiques* devoted to Ramond, even calls him the Pyrenees Mountains' "inventor."[36] Ramond was born in Strasbourg, where Rouget de Lisle first sang the "Marseillaise." When the French Revolution broke out, the moderate Ramond greeted it with enthusiasm. Elected to the Assemblée Législative, he sat as a constitutional monarchist. When the political climate changed radically, Ramond returned to private life and managed to ride out the storm, but not without several narrow escapes. Meanwhile, his interest in nature, particularly in mountains, characterized his writing.

Ramond was both a disciple of Bernardin de St-Pierre and a precursor of Lamartine. Chateaubriand, Nodier, and Michelet admired him wholeheartedly. Sainte-Beuve, writing three *causeries* about him, saw him as an artist. Professor Cuthbert Girdlestone devoted an entire book to him.[37]

Ramond first visited the Pyrenees in 1787. For six years he had been secretary, confidant, and factotum to Cardinal de Rohan. When the cardinal got into difficulties over the Necklace Affair, Ramond retired with his exiled protector to retreats and then eventually to the Pyrenees Mountains. In time Ramond and the cardinal separated. Ramond entered politics but, with his moderate views, came under suspicion. Just days before the monarchy fell in 1792, he left Paris and returned to the mountains, believing that he could escape, if necessary, into Spain. With his sister, he stayed in his retreat at Gèdre for several years, spending most of his time collecting botanical specimens. Denounced in 1794, he was arrested near Gavarnie and imprisoned for a year at Tarbes.[38] He would return to politics, but only briefly, under Napoleon and the Restoration.

As the French Revolution was beginning, Ramond sought to popularize the mountains with his literate contemporaries, and he described them in great detail in the *Observations faites dans les Pyrénées* (1789). Only rarely, however, did Ramond allude to the legendary events that took place there in 778. The Brèche de Roland is discussed, but with little reference to the disaster it

witnessed. At one point the author calls it the "famous" Brèche de Roland. Later there is a bit more detail. "Au midi, c'étoit la base même des tours de Marboré, le gradin le plus élevé de l'amphithéâtre qui les porte, le rocher dans lequel est coupée la Brèche de Roland, rocher qui se prolonge en un long mur, si régulier qu'à cette distance on ne sait si c'est l'ouvrage de la nature ou de l'art et qui sépare distinctement l'Espagne de la France."[39]

Elsewhere the author invites his readers to use their imaginations. "Qu'on se figure une muraille de rochers, de trois cens à six cens pieds de hauteur, élevée entre la France et l'Espagne, et qui les sépare physiquement. Que l'on se figure cette muraille courbée en forme de croissant, en sorte que la convexité en soit tournée vers la France. Que l'on s'imagine enfin qu'au milieu même Roland, monté sur son cheval de bataille, a voulu s'ouvrir un passage et que d'un coup de sa fameuse épée il y a fait une brèche de trois cens pieds d'ouverture et l'on aura une idée de ce que les montagnards appellent la *Brèche de Roland*. Le mur a peu d'épaisseur; mais il en acquiert davantage du côté des tours de Marboré, qui s'élèvent majestueusement au-dessus de la porte et de toutes ses avenues, comme une citadelle que Roland auroit placée là, pour en défendre le passage. . . . Ici, tout est symmétrique, et Roland a travaillé sur un plan qui fait autant d'honneur à son esprit d'ordre qu'à la force de son bras."[40] Ramond goes on to call the area "un affreux désert."

Ramond intended to convey the region's picturesque though savage beauty, and the Roland legend was only incidental to his work. Clearly, however, the tradition had been kept alive in the mountains: the natives still referred to the Brèche de Roland and knew the legend of its creation. Moreover, Ramond alludes to the hero's "famous" sword. Another traveler, Jean-Florimond Boudon de St-Amans, a botanist, visited the region in 1788, and he provided additional evidence of the legend's vitality. Commenting on the Pic du Midi, "Telle est encore cette montagne sur les frontières de l'Espagne," he stated, "où l'on aperçoit une anfractuosité singulière qui représente une porte et que les gens du pays disent voir été formée par un coup de pied du cheval de Roland."[41]

While living in the mountains during the Terror, Ramond kept a diary, published in 1931 as *Carnets pyrénéens*, but it adds little to the author's work of 1789. It does record, though, visits to spots close to Gèdre, such as Le Marboré and the Brèche de Roland, which Ramond sketched. While at Gèdre, he spent time at La Peyrade, which Napoléon Peyrat would describe years later in his *Les Pyrénées, romancéro*.[42] Despite the fact that Ramond was not a native, he felt at home amid these barren, forbidding, but spectacular surroundings and would later sign one of his works "le solitaire des Pyrénées." Similarly, Napoléon Peyrat would call himself Napol le Pyrénéen.

As the Ancien Régime was coming to an end, another writer, a doctor, found time to publish his account of a trip through the Pyrenees Mountains.

The traveler was J.P. Picquet, and he called his book *Voyage dans les Pyrénées françaises*. Unlike Ramond de Carbonnières, Picquet was visiting terrain that he knew intimately, since he was born there in 1748. Later he would represent the Hautes Pyrénées in the Convention Nationale. Early in his work he notes that the mountains appear sterile and remarks that almost no famous individuals have ever lived in the region. "Ce tribut que l'on paie à la célébrité," he observes, "les Pyrénées ne le revendiquent qu'en faveur du héros d'Arioste et dans les paladins de Charlemagne." There is a chapter on Gavarnie, and the Brèche de Roland is mentioned as well.[43]

Residents of Bigorre, Picquet asserts, have shown special interest in Roland and his legend. "La valeur, la force, l'intrépidité de Roland s'étoient conservées par une tradition suivie. Les Bigorrais alloient tous les ans en pèlerinage à Roncevaux et à Blaye voir l'armure de ce héros. On voyoit dans cette dernière ville son tombeau, avec une épitaphe qu'on croyoit composée par Charlemagne lui-même, avant qu'on n'eût appris que ce grand homme ne savoit ni lire ni écrire. 'Tu patriam repetis, tristi nos orbe relinquis / Te tenet aula nitens, nos lacrymosa dies; / Sed qui lustra geris octo & binos super annos / Ereptus terris, justus ad astra redis.'"[44] Throughout the nineteenth century French writers disagreed about Roland's burial place, as well as the fate of his horn and sword. Picquet's opinion, based no doubt on the mountaineers' stories, is worth noting.

Picquet knew that a song or songs had transmitted the Roland legend orally among mountain folk. More than one poet had been involved, and there seemed to have been accretions. "Après tant de siècles et de révolutions dans les moeurs et dans le gouvernement," he wrote, "on retrouve les hauts faits de Roland et des autres paladins. La chanson de ce héros, composée par les successeurs des bardes et le chef-d'oeuvre de ces versificateurs barbares, s'est transmise de bouche en bouche; elle fait l'amusement des soirées villageoises." The song dated from the tenth century. It seems that the author has in mind a corpus of spontaneous compositions by untutored local poets, passed on by word of mouth. Picquet, then, comes close to the *cantilène* theory that Gaston Paris's *Histoire poétique de Charlemagne* would propound and make famous in the mid-1800s. Remarkably, Roland material was still being *sung* in 1789, long after the Middle Ages, and to my knowledge, Picquet is the only writer to mention this startling fact.

Picquet proceeds to quote in prose part of the song that he had apparently heard or at least heard about. "Roland affoibli par la perte de son sang, coupe un rocher en deux parts avec sa fameuse épée *Durandal*. On indique les vestiges des pieds de son cheval, et ceux de son passage en Espagne. Il sonne du cor en expirant; son dernier soupir est si terrible, que le cor en est brisé." Picquet adds that "L'Arioste n'a eu qu'à recueillir la féerie des peuples méridionaux et celle des romanciers gascons et espagnols du dixième siècle pour composer son

admirable poème."[45] Ariosto, of course, was dealing essentially with other adventures that he attributed to Roland.

Picquet's evidence that in the mountains Roland lore was transmitted orally is extraordinary. The existence of this material may explain aspects of nineteenth-century French treatments of the Roland legend that appear to have no written sources. Perhaps, for example, it accounts for the widespread contention, already encountered in the work of two historians, that Roland and his companions were crushed beneath a hail of trees and rocks. In 1817 another visitor, Etienne de Jouy, a minor Empire and Restoration poet, librettist, and playwright, learned about the local oral tradition. His *L'Ermite en province* narrates a chat with an elderly inhabitant, an uneducated shepherd, who was able to point out "l'endroit où se livra la terrible bataille entre Roland et Ferragus" and knew other pertinent details associated with the noble knight as well. This repository of information "savait dans ses moindres détails l'histoire de Roland."[46] We shall see that several other writers were aware of a local, oral tradition.

Much less attracted to the Middle Ages than most of his literary contemporaries, Stendhal, who never treated the Roland legend, noted that medieval poetry contains more events than psychological analysis. As a result, readers tend to attribute to the heroes sensitivities or even passions that they could never have had. "Nous *supposons* ce qui a dû être senti par les héros; nous leur prêtons généreusement une sensibilité aussi impossible chez eux que naturelle chez nous."[47] Probably most medievalists would not agree with Stendhal's complaint, but French authors writing on Roland in the nineteenth century saw their hero from their own particular perspectives. Thus the various Rolands do not resemble each other, and some, perhaps, have emotions that most medieval knights would not have been likely to experience. This merely intensifies the modern reader's enjoyment.

Stendhal had a friend whose comments, while they do not seek to probe the hero's character, should nevertheless be considered. Jacques Joseph Faget de Baure (1755-1817) was born in Orthez (Basses Pyrénées) in the Pyrenees Mountains. A precocious lad, at nineteen he was an *avocat général* at the Parlement de Navarre. He married Sophie Daru, Pierre Daru's sister and Stendhal's cousin, in 1802. With Daru's influential name behind him, he entered Napoleon's service, as Stendhal did, where his protector was an important administrative official. By 1811 he held the title Président de la Cour Impériale de Paris. He rallied to the Bourbons in 1814 and served on the commission that drew up the charter Louis XVIII granted his subjects that year. When Stendhal indicated a willingness to serve the new regime, his request fell on deaf ears. Faget de Baure, on the other hand, was elected to the Chambre des Députés, where he represented his native district and proved to be a decided conservative. Stendhal considered him a stimulating conversationalist, even though the two men held opposing views. In their discussions, Stendhal exalted Shakespeare, while Faget de Baure, a conservative in literature as well as politics, held out for Racine. Like Daru, Faget de Baure was interested in literature from a creative as well as a critical standpoint and wrote both poetry and prose.[48]

In 1818 Pierre Daru published Faget de Baure's posthumous *Essais historiques sur le Béarn*, which Chateaubriand praised, alluding to its "charme" and calling it a "petit modèle de goût et de clarté."[49] Faget de Baure's introduction contains an account of the French defeat at Roncevaux, which the author knew well. He held that the culprits were Gascons, pointing out that, after first alienating Lupus II, duke of Gascony, Charlemagne had then crossed the disaffected prince's territories en route to subdue the Moors. It was a costly mistake, as he discovered on the return trip. "Charlemagne traversa ses états, à la tête d'une armée, lorsqu'il entreprit la conquête de l'Espagne. Il y entra par les vallées du Béarn et de la Bigorre et se retira par celles de Navarre. Son arrière-garde fut coupée à Roncevaux par les Vascons-Navarrais, que Loup commandait; Charles y perdit l'élite de son armée," wrote Faget de Baure. The disaster lived on in the popular memory. "La défaite de Charlemagne est un de ces événements dont une tradition constante a perpétué la mémoire parmi les habitants des Pyrénées. Ils connaissent tous le nom de Roland. L'un vous montre cette montagne que le paladin entrouvrit d'un coup de cimeterre: on l'appelle encore la Brèche de Roland. . . . Près de Bayonne, on rencontre le château du Sarrasin Ferragus, et l'on voit à Roncevaux le tombeau des douze pairs. Enfin, on retrouve dans nos montagnes ces vieilles fables si chères à nos romanciers et qui, sous la main de l'Arioste, ont acquis un charme égal à celui de la mythologie."[50]

Faget de Baure was familiar with several sources of Roland lore. He had read and enjoyed *Orlando furioso*, and, since he mentioned Ferragus, he no doubt knew the *Pseudo-Turpin Chronicle* as well. His comments suggest that local legend endorses the idea that there had been a duel between the paladin and the giant, an episode found in the *Chronicle* but not in the *Chanson de Roland*. Faget de Baure loved the native mountain oral traditions that J.P. Picquet had described. Those traditions were to remain vital. Years later, Emile Vignancourt, introducing the second edition of his anthology of *Poésies béarnaises*, declared that the Roland legend was common among mountain folk. In their cradles, local people learned the "souvenirs historiques" as well as the "fabuleuses traditions" in which the region abounded, including the stories about the Brèche de Roland and the "empreinte du pied ferré de l'hippogriffe." They were likewise well aware of what had happened in "la fameuse vallée de Roncevaux."[51] Using these traditions, Faget de Baure believed that Roland and his companions were buried at Roncevaux, not in churches on the other side of the mountains, as both the *Pseudo-Turpin Chronicle* and the *Chanson de Roland* contend.

Founded in 1775, the *Bibliothèque universelle des romans* was the brainchild of Antoine René de Voyer d'Argenson, marquis de Paulmy (1722-87), who was its chief editor until December 1778. Another guiding spirit of the *Bibliothèque universelle* was Louis de La Vergne, comte de Tressan (1705-83), whose name remains associated with the *genre troubadour*. Tressan also translated *Orlando furioso* and part of *Orlando innamorato*, taking numerous liberties with his texts. Eventually Paulmy and Tressan came to a parting of the ways, and Paulmy withdrew from the enterprise. First with Tressan's help and then alone, J.F. de Bastide published the *Bibliothèque universelle*, which enjoyed great popularity, until the French Revolution.[52]

The *Bibliothèque universelle* gave summaries, often quite detailed, of various *romans*, interpreting the word as loosely as most of its readership did. Chivalric topics abounded, and in 1777 works about the Roland legend were summarized. The first of the July issues carried a résumé of the *Pseudo-Turpin Chronicle*. On two major points the author diverged radically from the original. He asserted that, before dying, Roland managed to break his sword, throwing the guard "bien loin." Still, he was buried with the pieces of both sword and horn. Likewise, when Ganelon was put on trial, someone named Sinabeat, rather than Pinabel, was his champion. The *Bibliothèque universelle*'s November and December issues focused on Esclava's *Noches de invierno*, Boiardo, Ariosto, Pulci, and Berni. *Garin de Monglane, Les Quatre Fils Aymon*, and the *Reali di Francia* supplied additional material. The articles appear to have been mostly written by Paulmy, and they constituted a readily available compendium of information about Roland for writers in the following years.

Paulmy concludes his discussion by mentioning the legend that there once existed a "famous" *Chanson de Roland*. Paulmy believed that for several centuries after Charlemagne, French troops had intoned the song as they went into battle to inspire enthusiasm. He asserts that it was sung for this purpose at the battle of Poitiers. Gathering dust in some library, he theorized, there could be a manuscript "dans lequel cette chanson se trouveroit transcrite dans son langage original." There might at least be "quelques fragments imparfaits et barbares." Much later, Charles Nodier thought so too, as did Chateaubriand, who held that somewhere the poem must be waiting to be discovered. As it turned out, Paulmy, Nodier, and Chateaubriand were right.

Paulmy was not interested in looking for the *Chanson de Roland*, but he speculated about its substance. Here he was not correct. "Il est probable," he wrote, "qu'elle ne contenoit point une relation de tous les hauts faits de Roland." To later soldiers, unlikely to find themselves in analogous situations, songs about such deeds would not have been particularly exhilarating. "Il est plus naturel de croire qu'on présentoit aux soldats le caractère de Roland comme un modèle à imiter et qu'on leur montroit le paladin comme un chevalier brave, intrépide, ardent et zélé pour le service de son roi et la gloire de sa patrie; qu'on leur ajoutoit qu'il étoit humain après la victoire, ami sincère de ses camarades, doux avec les bourgeois et les paysans; qu'il n'étoit point querelleur, évitoit l'excès du vin, et n'étoit point esclave des femmes." Paulmy did not stop there. Improbable as it seems, he set out to reconstruct the *Chanson de Roland* in keeping with his ideas. "Voici ce que nous croyons que chantoient nos soldats, il y a sept ou huit cens ans, en allant au combat," he declared.[53] He proposed that soldiers going into battle sang only the first seven stanzas, saving the others for their leisure in camp.

> Soldats françois, chantons Roland;
> De son pays il fut la gloire:
> Le nom d'un guerrier si vaillant
> Est le signal de la victoire.
>
> Roland étant petit garçon
> Faisoit souvent pleurer sa mère;
> Il étoit vif et polisson;
> Tant mieux, disait monsieur son père:
> A la force il joint la valeur;
> Nous en ferons un militaire;
> Mauvaise tête, avec bon coeur,
> C'est pour réussir à la guerre.
>
> Soldats françois. . . .
>
> Le père pensoit justemente;
> Car dès que Roland fut en âge,
> On vit avec étonnement
> Briller sa force et son courage;
> Perçant escadrons, bataillons,
> Renversant tout dans la mêlée,
> Il faisoit tourner les talons,
> Lui tout seul, à toute une armée.
>
> Soldats françois. . . .
>
> Dans le combat particulier
> Il n'étoit pas moins redoutable:
> Qu'on fût géant, qu'on fût sorcier,
> Que l'on fût monstre, ou qu'on fût diable,
> Rien jamais n'arrêtoit son bras;
> Il se battoit toujours sans crainte;
> Et s'il ne donnoit le trépas,
> Il portoit quelque rude atteinte.

Soldats françois. . . .

Quand il falloit donner l'assaut,
Lui-même il appliquoit l'échelle;
Il étoit le premier en haut;
Amis, prenez-le pour modèle:
Il passoit la nuit au bivac,
L'esprit gaillard, l'âme contente,
Ou dormoit sur un avresac
Mieux qu'un général sous sa tente.

Soldats françois. . . .

Pour l'ennemi qui résistoit
Réservant toute son audace,
Il accordoit toujours sa grâce;
L'humanité, dans son grand coeur,
Renaissoit après la victoire;
Et le soir même, le vainqueur
Au vaincu proposoit à boire.

Soldats françois. . . .

Quand on lui demandoit pourquoi
Les François étoient en campagne,
Il répondoit, de bonne foi,
C'est par l'ordre de Charlemagne;
Ses ministres, ses favoris
Ont raisonné sur cette affaire;
Pour nous, battons ses ennemis,
C'est ce que nous avons à faire.

Soldats françois. . . .

Roland vivoit en bon chrétien,
Il entendoit souvent la messe,
Donnoit aux pauvres de son bien,
Et même il alloit à confesse;
Mais de son confesseur Turpin,
Il tenoit que c'est oeuvre pie
De battre et de mener grand train
Les ennemis de la patrie.

Soldats françois. . . .

Il corrigeoit avec rigueur
Tous ceux qui lui cherchoient querelle,
Mais il n'étoit point querelleur;
Bon camarade, ami fidèle.

L'ennemi seul, dans les combats,
Trembloit, voyant briller sa lame;
Et pour le dernier des soldats,
Il se seroit mis dans la flamme.

Soldats françois. . . .

Au paysan comme au bourgeois
Ne faisant jamais violence,
De la guerre exerçant les droits
Avec douceur et bienséance,
De son hôte amicalement
Il partageoit la fricassée,
S'il ne faisoit point l'insolent,
Ni sa fille la mijaurée.

Soldats françois. . . .

Roland à table étoit charmant,
Buvoit du vin avec délice;
Mais il en usoit sobrement
Les jours de garde et d'exercisce:
Pour le service il observoit
De conserver sa tête entière,
Ne buvant que quand il n'avoit
Ce jour-là rien de mieux à faire.

Soldats françois. . . .

Roland aimoit le cotillon
(On ne peut guères s'en défendre),
Et pour une reine, dit-on,
Il eut le coeur un peu trop tendre;
Elle l'abandonne un beau jour
Et lui fait tourner la cervelle;
Aux combats, mais non en amour,
Que Roland soit notre modèle.

Soldats françois. . . .

Roland fut d'abord officier,
Car il étoit bon gentilhomme;
Il eut un régiment entier
De son oncle, Empereur de Rome:
Il fut comte, il fut général;
Mais vivant comme à la chambrée,
Il traitoit de frère et d'égal
Chaque brave homme de l'armée.

Soldats françois. . . .

Paulmy's song it not great poetry, but it influenced many subsequent writers. We note that Roland's childhood is evoked, but not as it was in the *Reali di Francia*. Roland's initiative and military exploits are emphasized, as one would expect. One is told that Roland never questioned the king's commands and that he was a good Christian, but not a zealot. Other stanzas in the song describe his temperament, conduct, and taste in women. On the latter point, Paulmy could not forget his Ariosto, although he intended to reconstruct a song that existed long before the Italian Renaissance went to work on his hero. His song has other unexpected moments as well. For today's readers familiar with the *Chanson de Roland*, Roland's moderation comes as a surprise. One notes, too, that his companions are seen as friends, never subordinates. Years later, just as unexpectedly, Michelet would stress what he wished to believe were the egalitarian principles governing the relationships of soldiers in that era. Paulmy's Roland is presented as a splendid soldier, worthy of emulation, but, curiously, not a word is said about the battle of Roncevaux. No enemies ever vanquish this mighty warrior, who survives each combat and goes on to greater achievements.

Paulmy's song would be remembered for its structure as well as its content. For the next several decades eight-syllable lines became standard for Roland songs, of which there were many. Paulmy's stanza form would also be roughly retained. In addition, writers would take care to introduce a refrain. Actual words, such as "soldats français," would even appear in the song's progeny now and then. Although he gave it a pronounced lilt, Paulmy provided no music for his song, but most of his successors were to do otherwise. Paulmy's song would be recalled as late as 1864, when Auguste Mermet drew upon it for a chorus in his opera *Roland à Roncevaux*.

2
Patriot Warrior

Before 1789 history and legend had generally presented Roland as Charlemagne's nephew, the sovereign's tried and trusty lieutenant, a stalwart, even superhuman, paladin fighting bravely and ultimately dying for God and king. During the French Revolution, while remaining a national hero and a champion held up for others to emulate, he came to be viewed as a militant patriot battling to preserve or extend France's boundaries and rid her soil of enemies, but his religious aura vanished and would not reappear for some time. Meanwhile, the domestic upheaval spent itself and order, little by little, returned. After several governments came and went, General Bonaparte gradually emerged as Napoleon I. If peace and tranquillity reigned at home, however, there was nothing but turmoil abroad. With wars of conquest the order of the day, Roland continued to be his country's aggressive champion, whatever changing circumstances demanded. But as the Napoleonic epic drew to a close and invaders poured across the borders, the reading public began to see a Roland who could be overwhelmed.

With the coming of the Revolution, interest in Roland quickened. The Assemblée Législative declared war on Austria on 20 April 1792, and France embarked upon a struggle with the rest of Europe that would last, almost uninterrupted, until 1815. As a staunch Gallic hero flaying his country's enemies, Roland became a symbol. The historical Roland's dedication to his faith and his king did not seem to diminish his appropriateness, even though his latter-day admirers were getting ready to dethrone and behead their king and then abolish Christianity.

Hardly had war been declared when Claude Joseph Rouget de Lisle wrote his stirring "Marseillaise" on 25 April. Two weeks later the young army officer wrote another patriotic song, "Roland à Roncevaux." The soldiers of the new order needed to be reminded that France could still produce heroes, although in winning distinction they might be killed. Except for the refrain, the lines are octosyllabic. Probably the author remembered that this was the meter used in the "Chanson de Roland" from the *Bibliothèque universelle des romans*. Roland is presumed to be addressing his comrades in the thick of the fray, and the refrain was timely in 1792.[1]

> Où courent ces peuples épars?
> Quel bruit a fait trembler la terre
> Et retentit de toutes parts?
> Amis, c'est le cri du dieu Mars,
> Le cri précurseur de la guerre,
> De la gloire, de ses hasards.
>
>> Mourons pour la patrie,
>> Mourons pour la patrie!
>> Mourons pour la patrie!
>> Mourons pour la patrie!
> C'est le sort le plus beau, le plus digne d'envie.
>
> Courage, enfants! Ils sont vaincus.
> Leurs coups déjà se ralentissent;
> Leurs bras demeurent suspendus.
> Courage, ils ne résistent plus:
> Leurs bataillons se désunissent;
> Chefs et soldats sont éperdus.
>
>> Mourons pour la patrie. . . .
>
> Je suis vainqueur, je suis vainqueur!
> En voyant ma large blessure,
> Amis, pourquoi cette douleur?
> Le sang qui coule au champ d'honneur,
> Du vrai guerrier c'est la parure,
> C'est le garant de sa valeur.
>
>> Mourons pour la patrie. . . .

Rouget de Lisle dispensed with history completely, but fidelity to history, of course, had nothing to do with his purpose. Roland was a national hero, and that is what counted. We all know that Roland was killed in his most important military engagement, but Rouget de Lisle has him come through it all, bleeding but triumphant, flaunting his wound as though it were a trophy and shouting victory. It was not the last time Roland would utter revolutionary propaganda. Rouget de Lisle does not identify Roland's adversaries, but contemporaries certainly realized that they were Austrians, not Moors.

"Roland à Roncevaux" achieved the distinction of being plagiarized. For the 1847 dramatic version of his novel *Le Chevalier de Maison-Rouge*, which takes place during the Terror, Alexandre Dumas père wrote a song called "Chant des Girondins." Alphonse Varney, music director at Dumas's short-lived Théâtre Historique, composed the melody. Dumas shamelessly lifted Rouget de Lisle's refrain, altering it slightly, for his own song: "Mourir pour la patrie! / Mourir pour la patrie! / C'est le sort le plus beau, le plus digne d'envie. / C'est le sort le plus beau, le plue digne d'envie."[2] Perhaps Dumas

had stumbled upon "Roland à Roncevaux" while writing his version of Roland's childhood, which he inserted in his *Chronique de Charlemagne* in 1842. With the Revolution of 1848, although the political changing of the guard caused a minimum of bloodshed and dying for "la patrie" was not very likely, Dumas's "Chant des Girondins" became enormously popular.

Rouget de Lisle found that his brief moment of glory would not win him permanent laurels. The Terror imprisoned him. After his release, prosperity continued to elude him. During the First Empire several official missions were entrusted to him, but he managed to "indisposer contre lui tout le clan des Bonaparte, l'Empereur en tête, par ses rapports d'une franchise intempestive." When the Bourbons returned, the erstwhile patriot pathetically tried to change his colors. Poems such as "Dieu conserve le roi," "Henri IV, chant héroïque," and the "Chant du Jura" with its lines "Vive le roi! / Noble cri de la vieille France" failed to ingratiate him with the new rulers. To survive, he relied upon his *romances*, for which he wrote both words and music. Because Béranger intervened, the Legion of Honor was awarded to Rouget de Lisle on 8 December 1830, after the July Revolution. The July Monarchy granted him a small pension.[3] He died in 1836, the same year as the last Bourbon king, Charles X. The title of his Roland song, if not the contents, would be used during the Second Empire, when Auguste Mermet titled his best-known opera *Roland à Roncevaux*.

After Rouget de Lisle's "Roland à Roncevaux," another Roland came along to stir up patriotic fervor. In a 1791 operetta that he called a *drame*, Michel Sedaine included a "Chanson de Roland." When he published the work two years later, he more than likely made it less representative of 1791 opinion and more responsive to events of 1793. When the operetta appeared, France was no longer a monarchy—not even the constitutional one under which Rouget de Lisle wrote his "Roland à Roncevaux." The Roland in Sedaine's song is a hero accustomed to victories as much as ever, but, like so many French soldiers in 1793, he is prepared to die in his country's wars. "Le plus bel instant de la vie, / C'est quand on meurt pour sa Patrie," he affirms.

On 9 April 1791 Sedaine and André Grétry, the composer, triumphantly produced their operetta *Guillaume Tell* at the Paris Théâtre Italien. Sedaine had worked on it in the Swiss mountains the previous summer.[4] In the operetta, set in the early fourteenth century, the Swiss are busy ridding themselves of their Austrian oppressors, represented by the evil Gessler. Perhaps France's unpopular Austrian queen inspired Sedaine's theme, but there is no way to know. By the time Sedaine's work was printed, she was a prisoner, and those who hated her exulted.

Publishing his operetta in 1793, with the Terror running its lethal course, Sedaine asserted that he had wanted to make his play even more "patriotic" than it was, though he named no obstacles. He had wanted, he said, to work the "Marseillaise" into a final scene. To the strains of this anthem he would have shown a band of *sansculottes* congratulating the Swiss for liberating their country from its cruel overlords and thus setting an example for others desiring freedom. Sedaine's remarks in all likelihood were a prudent lie; the author no doubt hoped that no one would remember that when *Guillaume Tell* was produced the "Marseillaise" was still unwritten. For that matter, *sansculottes* did not exist yet either. Nor does Sedaine tell his readers how he would have coped with having a mob of 1790s French revolutionaries rush off to Switzerland to compliment a band of early fourteenth-century mountaineers.

Sedaine's assurances concerning his libretto's patriotic intent smack of well-timed discretion. When the author penned his text, the French Revolution was still in a fairly moderate stage, but when it appeared in print, this was no longer true. For publication purposes, the writer's revolutionary zeal may well have been exaggerated. Sedaine's motives become even more suspect when we recall that Marie Antoinette had been a patroness. Moreover, his *Richard coeur de lion,* performed at court on 25 October 1785, contains a song with these words: "O Richard! ô mon roi! / L'univers t'abandonne. / Sur la terre, il n'est que moi / Qui s'intéresse à ta personne: / Moi seul dans l'univers / Voudrois briser tes fers." When the play was revived shortly before the Revolution, the song was remembered. At Versailles during a banquet on 1 October 1789, a military band struck it up and it became a kind of theme song for the royalists. In 1793, with the king beheaded, Sedaine would have been anxious to have such things forgotten. He seems to have taken no chances in revising his text. The year he died, his collaborator noted apologetically that when the operetta came out "l'énergie révolutionnaire devait se faire sentir" and then dismissed the matter. Sedaine's prudence paid off. The Convention Nationale voted on 2 August 1793 that, for a period of time thereafter, "republican" plays such as *Guillaume Tell* would be performed three times a week in state theaters.[5] Sedaine's published libretto is a revolutionary document containing several of the period's catchwords—*liberté, tyran,* and *patrie.*

As the Swiss villagers prepare to march away to fight their villainous masters' troops, an elderly protagonist, Melktal, turns to a young insurgent and reminds him, "Je t'ai entendu autrefois dire la chanson de Roland qui va au combat." The Swiss peasant around 1307 knows the *Chanson de Roland*? Not likely. Sedaine seems to have thought it was a song the legendary hero sang as he went into battle. Melktal invites his friend to recite it, but the young man insists that Melktal recite it himself. Melktal agrees, calling on the others to "faire chorus," and he narrates, or probably sings, the author's "Chanson de Roland." Its two stanzas do not have the same number of lines, nor do they correspond metrically. Both have different rhyme schemes, but both have a sort of refrain in the lines beginning "Mourons, mourons pour la Patrie," similar to Rouget de Lisle's refrain.

> A Roncevaux,
> Dans les clairs-vaux
> Roland courant à la victoire,
> Chantait tout haut
> Dans les clairs-vaux,
> Aux camarades de sa gloire,
> Aux compagnons de ses traveaux;
> "Mourons, mourons pour la Patrie;
> Un jour de gloire vaut cent ans de vie.
> Le plus bel instant de la vie,
> C'est quand on meurt pour sa Patrie.
>
> "Combien sont-ils?
> Combien sont-ils?
> Lorsque l'on vole à la victoire,
> Lorsque nous commande la gloire,
> On demande où sont les périls?
> Eh, qu'importe combien sont-ils?
> Mourons, mourons pour la Patrie;
> Un jour de gloire vaut cent ans de vie."[6]

The "Chanson de Roland" declaimed or sung, the battle is fought, Gessler's soldiers are crushed and exiled, and virtue triumphs. The *Chanson de Roland*, having helped win the day for William the Conqueror and his barons, has now done the same thing for a group of Swiss peasants and their William. Roland had been the right-hand man of an autocratic, if benevolent, monarch. Now his name and valor are being invoked to help commoners throw off a despot's yoke. The *patrie* is mentioned in the song, but there is no king. Roland, his *gloire* intact, is as much a hero as ever, yet his name is being used to bring about political upheaval. But if he has been democratized, he has also been secularized. No longer promoting a religious cause, he is heartily belaboring political and military foes. In short, we see here a Roland who has been put to work in the interests of a cause neither monarchical nor Christian. Sagaciously eying kings and prelates with suspicion, neither Rouget de Lisle nor Sedaine included their hero's uncle or Archbishop Turpin.

Finally, we note that Sedaine's Roland is less confident of victory than Rouget de Lisle's optimistic hero had been. While willing to die, Rouget de Lisle's Roland is wounded but victorious. By the time *Guillaume Tell* was published, Revolutionary France had had some wartime experience under its new leadership, and things were not going well. Sedaine's Roland half expects to be killed. We observe, however, that he makes no demands upon God to help him or to grant him salvation. If he is to be a martyr, then it will be to the *patrie*.

One of the earliest nineteenth-century works to show an interest in Roland was a play called *Guillaume le conquérant,* written by Alexandre Duval (1767-1842) and first staged at the Comédie Française in late 1803 or early 1804.[7] The First Consul was giving serious thought to invading the British Isles and was encouraging writers to prepare the French public. Duval resolved to "remplir le devoir d'un patriote." He may have been paid to do so. As minister of the interior, Lucien Bonaparte once asked another dramatist, Antoine Arnault, to produce a pamphlet that would appeal to honor and ignite conscripts' courage in order to "obtenir la paix par la victoire."[8] Later, as Prince de Canino, Lucien Bonaparte would write about honor and victories himself; his topic would be Roland.

Duval recalled that the *Chanson de Roland* was supposed to have been sung in the Norman camp on the eve of the battle of Hastings. In the play, then, the night before the battle, when William the Conqueror calls for a "chanson de guerre," it is decided that he and his men will hear "celle du brave Roland" (act 3, scene 7). There is no Taillefer in the play. Rather, Guillaume de Poitiers, a soldier whom his leader calls a "noble trouvère," sings, with a chorus' help, Duval's "Chanson de Roland." Each of its five eight-line stanzas is followed by a four-line refrain. For each of the first four stanzas the refrain is the same, but after the final one this refrain is altered to fit new circumstances. Familiar with the *Bibliothèque universelle*'s version of the Roland legend, Duval remembered Paulmy's octosyllabic "Chanson de Roland." He adopted the *Bibliothèque universelle*'s eight-line stanza form as well as its a b a b c d c d rhyme scheme, and, as Paulmy had done, he began each stanza with a masculine line. Finally, from the refrain of the older "Chanson de Roland" he took the first line of his own. Clearly, the *Bibliothèque universelle*'s song furnished Duval a model, but there are important differences. Duval did not forget that the purpose of his play was to incite the French to invade England, and the tone of the poem is patriotic. Roland is a serious, martial hero, and nothing is said about drinking or amorous dalliance.

> Où vont tous ces preux chevaliers,
> L'orgueil et l'espoir de la France? . . .
> C'est pour défendre nos foyers
> Que leur main a repris la lance.
> Mais le plus brave, le plus fort,
> C'est Roland, ce foudre de guerre;
> S'il combat, la faux de la mort
> Suit les coups de son cimeterre.
>
> Soldats français, chantons Roland,
> L'honneur de la chevalerie,

Et répétons en combattant
Ces mots sacrés, Gloire et Patrie!

Déjà mille escadrons épars
Couvrent le pied de ces montagnes;
Je vois leurs nombreux étendards
Briller sur les vertes campagnes.
Français, là sont vos ennemis;
Que pour eux seuls soient les alarmes;
Qu'ils tremblent! tous seront punis! . . .
Roland a demandé ses armes!

Soldats français. . . .

L'honneur est d'imiter Roland,
L'honneur est près de sa bannière;
Suivez son panache éclatant;
Qu'il vos guide dans la carrière.
Marchez, partagez son destin:
Des ennemis que fait le nombre?
Roland combat: ce mur d'airain
Va disparaître comme une ombre.

Soldats français. . . .

Combien sont-ils? combien sont-ils?
C'est le cri du soldat sans gloire;
Le héros cherche les périls,
Sans les périls, qu'est la victoire?
Ayons tous, ô braves amis,
De Roland l'âme noble et fière;
Il ne comptait les ennemis
Qu'étendus morts sur la poussière!

Soldats français. . . .

Mais j'entends le bruit de son cor
Qui résonne au loin dans la plaine. . . .
Eh quoi! Roland combat encor?
Il combat! . . . O terreur soudaine!
J'ai vu tomber ce fier vainqueur;
Le sang a baigné son armure:
Mais, toujours fidèle à l'honneur,
Il dit, en montrant sa blessure:

Soldats français! . . . chantez Roland,
Son destin est digne d'envie:
Heureux qui peut, en combattant,
Vaincre et mourir pour la patrie!

Duval took his cue from the *Bibliothèque universelle*, but he also recalled Rouget de Lisle and Sedaine. In the final refrain, "Son destin est digne d'envie" was inspired by "Roland à Roncevaux," while the line "Combien sont-ils? combien sont-ils" comes straight from the second stanza of Sedaine's "Chanson de Roland." Like his two predecessors, Duval took care not to identify his hero's enemies. There is some ambivalence too about whether Duval's Roland is killed. He is struck down, he bleeds, but one does not see him die. Perhaps he will live on, continuing to conquer for his country.

Napoleon temporized, and the invasion of Great Britain never occurred. Nevertheless, Duval's patriotic anthem, set to music by two different composers, Etienne Méhul and Alexandre Choron, was an instant success. Under the title "Chanson de Roland," it was destined to become one of the era's better known patriotic songs.[9] Much later, in what may have been a bid to ingratiate himself with the restored Bourbons, Duval would claim that some of the First Consul's creatures had pointed out that the stanza recounting Roland's supposed death had been a veiled warning that a French expedition against England was doomed. At its second performance the censors are supposed to have closed the play. Alas, the Bourbons banned it also.[10]

Duval's story about running afoul of the First Consul is highly improbable. The dramatist had written a song that caught on, and Napoleon seems to have made no move to stifle it. His soldiers sang it, set to Méhul's music, throughout their campaigns. Philothée O'Neddy dismissed Méhul's "sombres chants de guerre" as oppressive, but the public disagreed. In the 1840s Duval's "Chanson de Roland" would be included in the collection *Chants et chansons populaires de la France*, for which Antoine Le Roux de Lincy, a medievalist and Bibliothèque de l'Arsenal librarian, wrote an introduction. The Oxford Manuscript had been published, and Le Roux de Lincy summarized it for his readers. Observing that modern treatments paled in comparison with the original epic, he nevertheless had kind words for Duval's song, which, he said, "ne manque pas d'élévation, et sous ce rapport mérite de succéder au chant séculaire tombé dans le domaine de la science et que le peuple ne comprend plus aujourd'hui."[11] Duval's "Chanson de Roland" remained popular for years and from time to time was reissued.

At about the same time, another French writer took an interest in the Roland legend. Claude Auguste Nicolas Dorion (1768-1829) was a staunch monarchist during the Revolution and the Restoration. In 1817 and 1824 he vied for a chair at the Académie Française but succeeded neither time. He published an epic, *La Bataille d'Hastings ou l'Angleterre conquise*, in 1806. At the battles of Ulm and Austerlitz in 1805, Napoleon had crushed his Continental enemies. His power was near its zenith. Possibly Dorion decided that the French emperor was now secure and that he should seek his favor and protection. The time seemed perfect for an epic inviting Napoleon to invade Great Britain, as a French duke had done in 1066.

Dorion did not hesitate to alter names and events. England was France's traditional enemy. Thus King Harold's men are Englishmen rather than Saxons, and Duke William leads not a band of Norman adventurers but an army of Frenchmen. Harold, incidentally, is called Eralde in the poem, making it possible for the poet to avoid an aspirate *h* that might have given him an unwanted extra syllable at times.

La Bataille d'Hastings came out in 1806 in ten cantos. Fifteen years later Dorion would rearrange the cantos into a dozen. In Dorion's new ordering, the battle of Hastings starts in the ninth canto. The contending armies are lined up, ready for battle. God is invoked and naturally declares for the French. Then, "Taillefer entonnait d'une terrible voix / L'hymne que de Roland consacre les exploits. / Répété dans les rangs, redit dans les murailles, / L'hymne antique allumait le désir des batailles." The words are not given. Unlike the rest of the poem, Dorion's account of the singing of the *Chanson de Roland* is spirited. The poet realized that it must have been a martial air that bolstered soldiers' courage, but he did not speculate further.

Dorion knew Wace's account but took liberties in order to add interest. According to the *Roman de Rou,* after intoning the *Chanson de Roland,* Taillefer asked Duke William to let him deal the initial blow in the battle about to take place. Soon the carnage was under way. Claiming the honor promised him, the soldier-bard struck the first blow, but an Englishman's lance pierced him below the chest an instant later. Dorion elaborates, adding details of his own. King Harold, not an anonymous soldier, punishes the warrior-minstrel for his valor.

> Des sommets du rempart, Eralde à Taillefer
> Lance deux javelots armés d'un triple fer:
> Un trait perce le col en traversant la bouche;
> Le guerrier mord le bois avec un ris farouche;
> Son front frappe la terre; il vomit tout son sang;
> De pénibles sanglots font haleter son flanc:
> Il meurt. "Va," dit le roi, "par des sons plus funèbres
> Réjouir maintenant le prince des ténèbres,
> Chantre insensé. . . ."[12]

Dorion made certain he had blood and pathos in abundance. Two lances were aimed at the noble minstrel, although only one reached its mark. Instead of a single wound below the chest, we see the fatal spear enter its brave victim's neck and go through his mouth, making him bite the wood and die with a horrible grin on his face. None of this is in Wace, but it does enliven Dorion's account. Most of *La Bataille d'Hastings* remains a pedestrian effort, though, and on the whole the poem richly deserves the oblivion into which it quickly fell. If Dorion was inviting Napoleon to follow Duke William's example and invade Great Britain, then the invitation fell on ears that needed no encouragement.

The emperor simply never felt the moment right for such a bold undertaking. The invitation does not appear to have advanced Dorion's fortunes in the least. When the Bourbons returned, he rallied to them, but to no avail.

Through the nineteenth century, Taillefer, unlike Roland, lost ground as a literary subject. One of those remembering him in mid century was Gustave Le Vavasseur (1819-96), a minor poet and prose writer. He was a Norman, dedicated to the memory of heroes who had added luster to his province, like Taillefer and William the Conqueror. Le Vavasseur had read the *Chanson de Roland*, and he believed that the Norman conquest, like the battle of Roncevaux, also deserved its epic. Presumably Dorion's work did not meet his specifications.

Le Vavasseur did not produce that epic, but he did write a double sonnet called "La Chanson de Roland." As an epigraph he quoted four lines from the original epic, part of Roland's farewell to Durandal. Roland recalls that with the sword he has conquered England.[13] Le Vavasseur compares Taillefer to Roland, whose ghost he imagines riding with the heroic minstrel, urging him on: "Et l'ombre de Roland, le brave sans pareil, / Galopait avec lui sur la terre frappée." Later Roland's soul takes possession of the modern champion: "L'âme de son héros passe dans le jongleur." Taillefer pretends at one point that his own sword is Durandal, and he addresses it in words reminiscent of the *Chanson de Roland*: "'Durandal,' disait-il, 'hé! claire et blanche épée, / Miroir d'acier poli flamboyant au soleil, / Tu vas reprendre encor un bain chaud et vermeil, / Dans le sang des Anglais où Roland t'a trempée.'" Le Vavasseur appears to consider Roland a saint and invokes him, asking that he pray for the invaders.

Taillefer fought bravely but was killed, and his courage set an example. Emulating him, the Norman soldiers swept everything before them and won the day. Although a casualty himself, Taillefer had made Duke William a king. The poet remarks in his last two lines, "Et les Normands disaient: Pourquoi pleurer nos morts? / On peut perdre Roland quand on a Charlemagne."[14]

Charles Hubert Millevoye, the best of the later French Preromantic poets, concerned himself with Roland in three poems, none of which was his best work. In the first poem, "Ancienne Chanson de Roland," the young poet, following the lead of Rouget de Lisle, Sedaine, and Duval, showed Roland as a patriot. The poem was set to music, as its predecessors had been. Putting *ancienne* in his title permitted the fledgling author to acknowledge the other songs and suggest that his own was more authentic. When it came out in the *Chansonnier des grâces* in 1805, the introduction declared that "le refrain et le premier couplet de cette chanson guerrière sont, à fort peu de mots près, les mêmes qui se chantaient à la tête des armées de Charlemagne; le reste n'est point parvenu jusqu'à nous. M. Millevoye a essayé d'en rajeunir quelques expressions et l'a augmentée de deux couplets."[15] Just where M. Millevoye might have unearthed the *Chanson de Roland* fragment he was supposed to have been modernizing was not disclosed. Millevoye had located no part of the lost song, of course. He had simply taken the *Bibliothèque universelle*'s "Chanson de Roland" and lifted the first stanza and the refrain, retouching them and adding two stanzas of his own. Strangely, however much the *Bibliothèque universelle*'s "Chanson de Roland" had been drawn upon over the previous thirteen years, no one appears to have detected the poet's real source.

With the alterations in italics, Millevoye's first stanza and the refrain appear below. The poet's changes had nothing to do with rejuvenating the song. Some were merely stylistic, and others sought to put Roland's childhood disposition in a better light. Thus the *Bibliothèque universelle*'s "mauvaise tête" became "grand caractére." Similarly, in the new version, the little boy "sometimes" made his mother weep, not "often."

> Roland, *dit-on, encor enfant,*
> Faisait *parfois* pleurer sa mère;
> Il était vif et *pétulant;*
> Tant mieux, *tant mieux,* disait son père;
> A la force il joint la valeur,
> Nous en ferons un militaire;
> *Grand caractère* avec bon coeur,
> C'est pour réussir à la guerre.
>
> Soldats français, chantons Roland!
> *De la patrie* il *est* la gloire:
> Le nom d'un guerrier si vaillant
> Est le signal de la victoire.

Updating the refrain, Millevoye declares that Roland *is*, not *was*, the man his country points to with pride; he still serves it with his sword and his fame. In addition, the *Bibliothèque universelle* had said of the hero that "De son pays il fut la gloire." From 1792 onward, however, the watchword in French war songs was *patrie*, not *pays*, and Millevoye made the adjustment. Pierre Ladoué in his 1912 thesis erroneously stated that the poet had found the materials for the "Ancienne Chanson de Roland" "dans nos vieilles chroniques."[16] The remainder of the *Bibliothèque universelle*'s song had far from disappeared. Millevoye just decided not to use it.

The rest of Millevoye's poem is original, although it remains in the tradition and mood of the Revolutionary and Napoleonic Roland songs. Throughout, the poet retains the usual meter and rhyme scheme. He shows his hero growing up, learning to be a soldier, excelling in his profession, and saving his country. The patriotic warrior is conspired against, but, not succumbing to his enemies' evil plots, he survives undaunted and triumphant. He does not die. Like the work's recent predecessors, the "Ancienne Chanson de Roland" names no specific foes. Millevoye's two original stanzas are as follows:

> Roland grandit sous les lauriers;
> Avec lui grandit son courage.
> Auprès des plus braves guerriers,
> De vaincre il fit l'apprentissage.
> De gloire sentant l'aiguillon,
> Pour son pays il prit la lance,
> Et sut mériter grand renom,
> En déployant grande vaillance.
>
> [Refrain]
>
> Roland devint preux chevalier;
> Et, l'âme de gloire occupée,
> Des Français fut le bouclier
> Aussi bien qu'il en fut l'épée.
> On voulut flétrir son grand coeur,
> On voulut abréger sa vie. . . .
> Mais des complots il fut vainqueur,
> Et le fut encor de l'envie.

The *Bibliothèque universelle*'s "Chanson de Roland" seems to have had no musical accompaniment. Millevoye's words, however, were set to music by Jacques Marie Beauvarlet-Charpentier (1766-1834), who composed romances and patriotic songs.

After the "Ancienne Chanson de Roland" Millevoye next presented Roland in the short epic *Charlemagne à Pavie* (1808). The emperor, fearing Roland dead, calls upon Morgan le Fay to tell him what has become of "le fier Roland, mon neveu, mon ami." With her supernatural powers, "la docte fée" sees Roland victimized by unrequited love. Suddenly she breaks off, announcing that the story will be told one day by someone wiser than she. Before concluding, however, she predicts the battle of Roncevaux: "C'est un mortel: Arioste est son nom. / N'entends-tu pas la voix aérienne / De ton Roland signaler les travaux? / Avec sa gloire elle chante la tienne: / Dans l'univers tu n'as plus de rivaux; / Console-toi, même de Roncevaux!"[17] Obviously, the poet was thinking here about *Orlando furioso*.

Millevoye later wrote a shorter narrative poem called *Emma et Eginhard* (1812), and this time his presentation of Roland was more in keeping with the *Chanson de Roland*. Roland has been killed, and the Germans are in revolt. As Charlemagne and his soldiers are about to leave to quell the distant insurrection, a minstrel, accompanying himself on an anachronistic guitar, sings a *romance* designed to kindle the warriors' enthusiasm. One of its three stanzas assures the men that Roland's ghost will be watching over them as each tries to outdo the other in valor: "Lance en arrêt, marchez, vaillants rivaux! / Le fier Roland préside à vos travaux, / Le fier Roland qui rendit sa grande âme / En défendant, aux champs de Roncevaux, / Son Dieu, son roi, son pays, et sa dame."[18]

The Middle Ages were one of Millevoye's characteristic themes. Ladoué believed that the poet's patriotism led him to interest himself in that period.[19] Regardless of motivation, the poet came close to the *genre troubadour* when he presented Roland as a soldier who fought not only to serve God, king, and country but also to defend his lady. Millevoye was evidently unaware that courtly love did not exist in Roland's day, but he could see clearly that there was a place for traditional values in Napoleon's France. In dying, Roland had been his country's champion. Now, once more, poets could admit that he had also been the champion of his monarch and creator.

In the nineteenth century Théophile Dumersan and Noël Ségur brought out several collections of popular French songs, the best known of which is *Chansons nationales et populaires de France*. Included in it is a piece with the simple title "Roland," which, like Duval's "Chanson de Roland," was a call to arms. The author listed was a certain Houdart.[20] The words were set to music by Martin Pierre D'Alvimare or Dalvimare (1772-1839), whose political convictions supported the Ancien Régime. As a young military officer, he was on duty at the Tuileries Palace on 10 August 1792, the day the monarchy fell. Escaping the massacre, he went into hiding for a time, then emerged and learned to support himself as a harpist and composer. Interested in *romances* with a medieval flavor, he would later compose a *Renaud de Montauban*.

What seems to be the first edition of "Roland" lists the author as Léon de La Mothe H.[21] The poet was almost certainly Baron Etienne Léon de La Mothe-Langon (1786-1864), who used the name La Mothe-Houdancourt during the First Empire.[22] He appears to have transformed Houdancourt into yet another pseudonym, Houdart. A royalist, he would one day write a poem called "Louis XVI dans sa prison." Monarchism, however, did not prevent a certain amount of enlightened opportunism. Dalvimare became Empress Josephine and Queen Hortense's harp instructor and one of the emperor's court musicians. Similarly, using the name La Mothe-Houdancourt, La Mothe-Langon wrote odes commemorating episodes in Napoleon's career, including "Ode sur le mariage de leurs majestés impériales et royales" (1810) and "Ode sur le baptême de S. M. le roi de Rome" (1811), written when the new heir was born. With Napoleon's fall, La Mothe-Langon calmly reverted to his family's orthodox monarchist principles. In 1824 he wrote a novel, *Monsieur le préfet*, that may have inspired certain pages in Stendhal's *Lucien Leuwen*.

During the First Empire, La Mothe-Langon collaborated with Dalvimare several times. In 1810 he provided the words for *Renaud de Montauban* and the romance "Le Marquis Olivier." At about the same time the two associates wrote their "Roland," which became immensely popular.[23] According to the *Dictionnaire de biographie française*, it was almost a national anthem. The poem, in lilting, octosyllabic verse, has three stanzas. La Mothe-Langon borrowed his form, including the rhyme scheme, from the *Bibliothèque universelle* and Alexandre Duval. There is no formal refrain, although the first and last stanzas have a common final line.

> Le roi des preux, le fier Roland,
> Français, au danger vous appelle;
> Auprès de son glaive sanglant
> Marche la Victoire fidèle.
> Le paladin et les soldats,
> Nobles enfants de la vaillance,
> Chantaient en allant au combat:
> "Vive le roi! vive la France!"
>
> En vain les Maures valeureux
> Opposaient leur triple barrière,
> Roland s'est élancé sur eux,
> Ils ont tous mordu la poussière.
> "Sont-ils nombreux, leurs escadrons?"
> S'écriait un jeune trompette.
> Roland dit: "Nous les compterons
> Le lendemain de leur défaite."
>
> Et nous qui marchons sur ses pas,
> Nous que la même ardeur anime,
> Français, dans les jours de combats
> Suivons cet exemple sublime!
> Que son feu brûle dans nos coeurs;
> Que la victoire nous devance;
> Et répétons ces mots vainqueurs:
> "Vive le roi! vive la France!"

In La Mothe-Langon's time, the national origin of Roland's adversaries was not usually named. Here, however, his opponents are Moors, and they are "valiant," an unusual touch given the times. The song implies that Roland crushed them at Roncevaux. Obviously, the purpose of battle cries is not historical accuracy. The poem has a brisk, martial tone, heightened by Dalvimare's music, and its strident cadences are almost as compelling as those of the "Marseillaise." When the song appeared, Napoleon had created a new aristocracy, and once more Roland's nobility could be implied. He was the "roi des preux," and he and his comrades were "nobles enfants de la vaillance." In most respects the poem, characteristic of the period that produced it, is altogether worthy to take its place among the other Roland songs spawned by the Revolutionary and Napoleonic eras.

Friendly to Napoleon or not, many writers were convinced that his era had witnessed events deserving poetic, even epic, treatment. Tacitly or otherwise, some, such as J.B. Barjaud (1785-1813), compared the new age with that of Charlemagne. Admiring Napoleon, Barjaud sought his favor with two odes on the birth of the King of Rome. Soon a few literary prizes came his way, and then, on 24 January 1813, he solicited an army commission, which was granted two months later. He quickly earned distinction, but he was fatally wounded at the battle of Leipzig. In two different collections, however, he had published fragments of an epic, *Charlemagne*. Lest his readers miss the parallels between France's modern emperor and her medieval one, the poet showed the earlier monarch carrying a shield emblazoned with Napoleon's insignia. Barjaud's Charlemagne went into battle protected by a "bouclier d'abeilles parsemé."

In the first canto of *Charlemagne*, the old emperor is at the gates of Rome. Outstanding among the knights with him is Roland, with his superhuman might.

> Roland des paladins que la France a vu naître,
> Le plus impétueux et le plus fort peut-être;
> Roland qui seul détache et soulève un rocher
> Que dix guerriers en vain tenteraient d'arracher
> Et qui, déracinant le tronc noueux d'un chêne,
> Dans sa robuste main le balance sans peine.
> Sous deux sourcils d'ébène étincellent ses yeux,
> Le soleil qui souvent le brûla de ses feux
> A dévoré les lis de son mâle visage,
> Son front hâlé respire une fierté sauvage.
> Une armure d'airain couvre ses bras nerveux;
> ....
> Tout prêt pour les combats, le guerrier d'une main
> Tient l'orbe ensanglanté d'un bouclier d'airain,
> Et l'autre devant lui fait marcher une lance,
> Dont l'oeil épouvanté suit la grandeur immense.[24]

In addition to unusual strength, Barjaud insists upon his hero's manliness. Barjaud is also one of the few authors to assign him specific physical traits: his Roland is deeply tanned and has black hair.

Aimé Martin (1786-1847) was a minor though prolific literary figure who had married Bernardin de St-Pierre's widow. When it became prudent to do so, he tardily decided that Napoleon had been a tyrant. Still, he conceded that the reign furnished poets an almost inexhaustible source of material.[25] Martin was a Roland enthusiast. In 1814 he gave a course at the Athénée de Paris on literature of the twelfth, thirteenth, and fourteenth centuries. Except for some discussion in the *Mercure de France*, little is known about the course, and Martin's lectures seem not to have been published. Martin had deficiencies in the field, and he drew heavily upon the *Bibliothèque universelle*. The *Mercure* reviewer, L.A.M. Bourgeat, thought him *aimable* as a lecturer but voiced reservations. In the March issue he suggested that "M. Aimé Martin, séduit par le charme des idées chevaleresques, a peint trop en beau les siècles de la chevalerie. . . . Au reste, tous les faits qu'il a cités sont vrais; mais il les a vus avec l'oeil de la prévention et n'a pas cru s'écarter de la vérité en embellissant leurs details."[26] With the Allied armies getting closer to Paris and French resistance becoming more spectacular, Martin succeeded in making his audience curse Ganelon as he narrated Roland's heroic death at Roncevaux.[27] With Napoleon exiled to Elba, Martin would champion the new order, but in his course he still raged at the enemy at the gates.

In 1815, when the real *Chanson de Roland* was still unknown, Bonaventure de Roquefort (1777-1834) published *De l'état de la poésie françoise dans les douzième et treizième siècles*, which had won a contest sponsored by the Institut de France five years earlier. The prizewinner doubted whether Charlemagne really had the peers and courtiers literature had ascribed to him. Roland, however, he considered authentic. Among the peers, he wrote, "celui qu'on doit le moins oublier est le fameux Roland, qui périt à Roncevaux par la trahison du perfide Ganelon de Mayence." He had not heard of the *Chanson de Roland*, but he did have notions, not always exact, concerning the *Pseudo-Turpin Chronicle*, which he considered a tasteless compilation of "traditions," "récits," and tall tales.[28]

Then Creuzé de Lesser's epic appeared. During the French Revolution, the First Empire, and the Restoration, Auguste François Creuzé de Lesser (1771-1839) served in diplomatic and administrative posts, while producing comedies and operetta librettos as well as several translations. Around 1812 and 1813 he had become interested in the Middle Ages and chivalric romances. Stendhal had a low opinion of his ability. The Bourbons made him a baron on 28 March 1818, and after the July Revolution he resigned as Préfet de l'Hérault and retired to private life.

In 1815, on the eve of Napoleon's return from Elba and the Hundred Days, Creuzé de Lesser published *Roland*, a long decasyllabic verse epic. Somewhat altered but still interminable, its forty cantos reappeared in the author's posthumous *La Chevalerie* in 1839. Creuzé de Lesser knew the *Pseudo-Turpin Chronicle* but attached little importance to it. His Roland owes much more to Boiardo, Pulci, Berni, and especially Ariosto. Still, he viewed his own creation as a more admirable figure, "toujours noble dans sa simplicité et souvent sublime sur les champs de bataille." Moreover, he was a Frenchman, "chanté enfin par un homme de sa nation."[29] The poet was too complacent, but he knew that a *Chanson de Roland* was sung in medieval French armies to inspire valor. He speculated that the lost work must have shown the paladin as "un vrai et redoutable héros." He made up a "Chanson de Roland" of his own and inserted it in his narrative. Like others we have seen, it resembles its ancestor, the *Bibliothèque universelle*'s "reconstruction." Creuzé de Lesser imagined that it was sung during the hero's lifetime, even by Roland himself.

> Chantons le chef le plus vaillant
> Qu'ait jamais chéri la victoire.
> Soldats français, chantons Roland:
> Il fera chanter notre gloire.
>
> Honneur à ses faits glorieux,
> Et malheur à ses adversaires!
> La voix de son cor belliqueux
> Sonne la mort des téméraires.
>
> Chantons. . . .
>
> L'ennemi, bientôt éperdu,
> Devant Roland fuit comme une ombre.
> Ce n'est qu'après l'avoir vaincu
> Qu'il veut bien en savoir le nombre.
>
> Chantons. . . .
>
> Quand la victoire a prononcé,
> Ce fier lion change de rôle;
> Le rival qu'il a terrassé
> Devient un ami qu'il console.
>
> Chantons. . . .
>
> A plus d'un officier brutal
> Il offre un exemple admirable:
> Bien qu'il soit un grand général,
> Pour le soldat il est affable.
>
> Chantons. . . .
>
> Seulement on reste surpris
> Que ce paladin héroïque
> Ait pendant si longtemps, gratis,
> Escorté la belle Angélique.
>
> Chantons. . . .
>
> Imitons ses coups inouis:
> Evitons ses délicatesses.

> Poussons autant nos ennemis;
> Mais respectons moins nos maîtresses.
>
> Chantons. . . .
>
> Il cherchait, esclave imprudent,
> Une maîtresse trop chérie:
> Mais son amour le plus ardent
> Est désormais pour sa patrie.
>
> Chantons. . . .

The seventh stanza is added when some soldiers chant the song to the hero as he comes out of the long delirium caused by his amorous misadventures. Recovered, Roland goes on to worthier deeds, taking along his sword and his famous horn that can be heard six miles away. Obviously, nothing in this suggests that Creuzé de Lesser took note of the Oxford *Chanson de Roland* that Francisque Michel published when, late in life, he reworked his own epic.

Once Angelica departs for her own kingdom, Roland is put to his most demanding tests. In Spain, King Marsile is still a threat, and Charlemagne puts Roland in command of an expedition to deal with him. Arriving in the Pyrenees Mountains, Roland beholds Le Chaos, the Cirque de Gavarnie, and Le Marboré, but he experiences less pleasure than horror at the spectacle. He sees "le sublime du laid."

Before long Roland encounters Ferragus, the giant, and wins a terrible duel with him. In extremis, the giant asks to be received into the victor's faith and is baptized. Then Roland pushes on, leaving nothing but victories in his wake. Marsile sues for peace. Notified, Charlemagne sends Ganelon to treat with him, and then assumes personal command of the army. Marsile accepts harsh terms but then conspires with the ambassador, who hates the emperor's nephew. The main army starts home, leaving Roland to protect its rear. Intruders in a rocky wilderness inhabited by mountaineers who side with their adversaries, Roland and his twelve thousand soldiers must make their way through Roncevaux Valley. With its "hideuses beautés," it is a dismal spot indeed.

> Autour de vous le torrent solitaire
> Avec l'autan dispute de fureurs:
> L'oiseau de proie, accouru de son aire,
> Semble accuser vos pas usurpateurs.
> Sur le tapis de la neige incertaine
> Le pied tremblant ne se pose qu'à peine
> Où le sentier, au regard attristé,
> Offre l'ennui de son éternité.

In this forbidding landscape two hundred thousand pagans fall upon the Frenchmen. From high in the mountains, a hail of rocks begin to pelt the victims trapped in the gorge below. No Olivier has to plead with the commander to blow his horn: he does it immediately. Charlemagne hears the call but is dissuaded from turning back. Meanwhile, Roland urges those who can to escape, but no one is willing to leave him. Olivier is killed, and then, brandishing Durandal, Roland rids the world of Marsile. He sounds the horn again, and this time the French turn back, arriving in time to see Roland expire. Several drive Ganelon and his clan into a corral and hack them to death. The Saracens, awed and contrite, are not punished. On the spot where Roland and his men made their last stand, the emperor founds "un pieux édifice." Henceforth, travelers will find rest where a hero met death. Nothing is said about burial plans.

Alluding to the famous slash in the Pyrenees Mountains, Creuzé de Lesser writes: "De ce haut fait d'un héros si vaillant / Sur ces rochers vit la trace hardie; / Et l'on y voit la Brèche de Roland / Qui comme lui s'est beaucoup aggrandie." To keep his sword from falling into pagan hands, Roland, thoroughly spent, tried to destroy it by striking it against hard mountain rock, at first unsuccessfully. Then,

> Sur d'autres rocs, dans sa douleur extrême,
> Il porte en vain d'autres terribles coups.
> Plus Durandal paraît indestructible,
> Et plus Roland en ce moment terrible
> A la briser montre un noble courroux.
> Dans un espace où la roche est disjointe,
> De son épée il enfonce la pointe,
> Et, destructeur de ce qui lui fut cher,
> Par un effort tristement mémorable,
> En deux éclats le preux incomparable
> A fait voler l'incomparable fer.
> Près du torrent le tronçon lancé roule.

Before dying, he takes the two pieces and arranges them in the shape of a cross: "cette épée, instrument de sa gloire, / Forme une croix qui prie encor pour lui." In neither the *Pseudo-Turpin Chronicle* nor the *Chanson de Roland* does the hero succeed in breaking his sword. Creuzé de Lesser permits him not only to break it but also to make a cross with it. While he thinks this unusual cruifix is still praying for its owner, however, he expresses no opinion about its fate.

Creuzé de Lesser intended to graft an indigenous legend onto an imported plot. Insofar as this happened, it came about in the last canto. A thrilling poet Creuzé de Lesser is not, but his narrative has an odd originality. For one thing, inserting a "Chanson de Roland" reminded readers that the protagonist was their own national hero, not a foreigner. Then the poet added his own touches. More than most writers, he evoked the grim setting for the massacre. He also made Bernardo del Carpio one of Roland's adversaries. Del Carpio, in this version, sneaked away during the fight. Charlemagne's sending Roland to cope with problems on the Iberian Peninsula, then changing his mind and arriving to take charge himself is an unexpected plot feature. Just as unique is the punishment meted out to Ganelon and the other enemies of Roland. One is surprised to learn that, aside from the pagan emir, he had cohorts. We note also that Charlemagne founded a hospice on the site where his nephew and the men with him were slaughtered. The hospice will crop up again, though sometimes it will be a commemorative chapel.

Creuzé de Lesser concluded his epic with a song addressed to France's modern heroes. The first of its five stanzas follows:

> Héros couverts des plus justes honneurs,
> Nobles guerriers, gardiens de nos murailles,
> Vous que toujours, généreux défenseurs,
> On vit briller et survivre aux batailles,
> Assez de chants, illustrant vos vertus,
> Célèbreront vos faits, votre génie:
> Je me consacre aux preux qui ne sont plus,
> Honneur aux preux tombés pour la patrie!

The last line, repeated at the end of each of the other stanzas, serves as a refrain. Enthusiastic though it was, the song was not destined to save Napoleon's France. Four months after it appeared, the French were routed at Waterloo and Allied armies once again occupied Paris.

These were sad times for patriots, and some thought of revenge. Not long after Creuzé de Lesser's epic, Népomucène Lemercier's five-act tragedy *Charlemagne,* first performed 27 June 1816 at the Comédie Française, showed a moment in the emperor's life when Roncevaux was still a bitter memory. Lemercier's Charlemagne had not pursued the attackers after the battle. Somewhat later, the emperor sends his son Louis to punish the culprits. As Alcuin tells his imperial master, "J'arrive d'Aquitaine, / Sire, heureux d'apporter la nouvelle certaine / Des exploits des Français contre les Sarrasins." He adds that "de l'illustre Roland punir les assassins" is a task that the emperor's son has carried out successfully.[30] Here Lemercier may have been remembering Dupleix, who held that Charlemagne, on learning about the disaster, had turned around to go punish the villains. When he was told that this action would probably lead to another disaster, he decided to wait for a more opportune moment. Voltaire thought the moment never came.

After Lemercier, another dramatist showed the Franks from their enemies' viewpoint. First produced at the Odéon on 16 March 1843, Ferdinand Dugué's *Gaïffer* presented Duke Waifar as a hero with a cause, struggling to keep Pepin and Charlemagne from consuming his little country. In a decisive battle against the invaders, Waifar is wounded, and his army loses. Then someone wonders aloud if what has happened might not be for the best. Under Charlemagne, a great new age could be dawning: "Du sein de l'ombre épaisse on le verra paraître, / Ce point encor perdu dans l'horizon brumeux / Nous éblouira tous de ses rayons fameux." To the duke such a thought is revolting, and he dies a bitter man. Neither Charlemagne nor Roland is ever seen on stage.[31]

Lucien Bonaparte, prince de Canino (1775-1840), was one of Napoleon's younger brothers. At a critical moment his quick thinking and oratorical skill made 18 Brumaire and the First Empire possible. As an author he is best known for a novel, *La Tribu indienne*. When the Académie Française was reorganized in 1803, he became a member, but a year later, after a dispute with his brother, he settled close to Rome and gave his Académie Française stipend to Pierre Jean Béranger, then a new poet. Lucien Bonaparte made peace with Napoleon and returned to France during the Hundred Days, and thus the Restoration not only proscribed him but also excluded him from the Académie.

Lucien Bonaparte had an independent spirit. When the First Consul ordered him to dissolve his second marriage, he refused and withdrew to the Papal States. There he acquired the estate of Canino, and Pope Pius VII bestowed on him the title of Prince de Canino. On 17 May 1809 France annexed the Papal States. Fearing his brother's wrath, Prince Lucien decided to move to the United States. En route a British frigate took him prisoner. A short stint in Malta preceded internment in England, where he purchased another estate, Thorngrove. At Thorngrove he lived until 1814, when he was authorized to leave. While at Thorngrove he completed his epic, *Charlemagne ou l'église délivrée*, which he claimed to have begun in 1804 in the Papal States. He published the epic in 1814 in Rome and London. He returned to Paris, and in 1815 *Charlemagne* was issued there. Prince Lucien, owing his title to his brother's adversary Pius VII, with whom he was on excellent terms, gave his Charlemagne close ties to his own pope.

The most unattractive feature of *Charlemagne* is the singsong quality of its alexandrines. Prince Lucien was aware that rhyming alexandrine couplets produce a droning effect but considered this inherent in French versification.[32] Trying to minimize the monotony, he contrived to introduce variety into his verse. His intentions were laudable, but the results were not. Hoping to achieve musicality, he decided to use ten-line stanzas. Each line is an alexandrine except for the sixth, which has six syllables. The rhyme scheme, *a b b a c c d e d e,* is novel but soon becomes as monotonous as the traditional couplets. Add to this the author's tired vocabulary, his circumlocutions, and his overworked inversions, and the net result is dull reading indeed.

In writing his epic, Prince Lucien faced a dilemma. To be sure, he looked upon Charlemagne as an authentic hero. Yet Charlemagne had serious flaws, and Prince Lucien felt ambivalent about him. Perhaps at times he equated him with his own brother. Certainly he had good reason to be aware of Napoleon's negative qualities. Regarding Charlemagne, he remarked in a note, "Clovis lui-même s'abreuva du sang de beaucoup de ses parents. Les historiens semblent oublier que des misérables couverts de crimes ne peuvent jamais être de grands hommes; et qu'au lieu d'une admiration insensée, l'horreur et l'exécration sont les seuls sentiments que doivent inspirer de tels princes."[33]

Prince Lucien's Charlemagne has two serious marks against him. First, he usurped the crown that his brother Carloman had left to his own sons. Charlemagne's second flaw has a direct bearing upon the epic's plot. Didier, king of the Lombards, wished to seize Rome. To prevent France from coming to the pope's aid, he made an alliance with Charlemagne, sealing it with the hand of his daughter Armélie. Charlemagne already had a wife but nevertheless accepted Armélie, partly because Ganelon had urged him to do so. He then repudiated her predecessor Adelinde, who retired to a convent. As heroes are wont to do, Prince Lucien's Charlemagne saw his error in time. Remembering his sacred vows to Adelinde, he dismissed her rival and rushed off to save the Holy See. Redeemed, he pledges to uphold the Church and advance the faith.

Persisting in his lofty resolution, Charlemagne meets Didier and the Lombards beneath the walls of Rome. In the fierce battle, Charlemagne reminds God that he has been promised victory and asks that the promise be kept. A heavenly voice reassures him, the battle is won, and he is proclaimed emperor. Eventually he experiences a belated urge to return their kingdom to the nephews he has robbed. Carloman, who has gone to heaven, appears to his widow Laurence and tells her that he believes all of France should be united under a single ruler, adding that his two sons should enter the Church. Charlemagne keeps his stolen crown.

Prince Lucien's epic has little in common with Millevoye's *Charlemagne à Pavie,* although there are occasional reminders that the two authors were familiar with the same Roland tradition in Italian literature. Both deal with aspects of Charlemagne's adventures in Italy, and both include Didier, king of the Lombards, as well as Didier's son Adalgis and other characters. Aside from this, there are few similarities.

In the introduction to his epic, Prince Lucien admits that he has taken liberties with history but implies that he has done so in order to condense his material and thus unify the action.[34] No doubt he also hoped to add interest. If historical fact was an encumbrance, then he was prepared to dispense with this kind of authority. Like Chateaubriand in the *Génie du christianisme*, his introduction rejects Boileau's dictum that Christianity and the epic do not mix. Prince Lucien's Charlemagne is God's agent, and he can call out to the Lord and expect a quick answer, not to mention help.

Charlemagne's readers first encounter Roland about where Italian Renaissance literature left him. The son of Milon and described as Comte d'Angers, he is killed early in the narrative. Prince Lucien proves innovative in making him more rash than he is elsewhere in French literature before 1837. His impetuous nature breaks out in connection with Queen Adelinde's repudiation and banishment. He is devoted to Adelinde and when he embarked on the adventures related in *Orlando innamorato* and *Orlando furioso*, she was queen. On his return he discovers that she has been supplanted and dismissed. Standing alone and brooding, he is almost a Romantic hero: "Un paladin fameux / Reste seul éloigné de la foule importune / Son front triste et pensif, son regard dédaigneux / Semblent désapprouver l'allégresse commune."

Disapproving looks soon gave way to heated words as Roland chides the other knights for rallying to their new sovereign. Charlemagne, knowing his nephew's worth, has overlooked some previous outbursts. But now when, somber and quick-tempered, Roland denounces the new queen and castigates his uncle's "égarements" and even "honte," Charlemagne is incensed, although, at least to himself, he concedes that his nephew's accusations are justified. Here the Prince de Canino, who had refused to divorce his own wife to please his brother, might have been reproving Napoleon for getting rid of Josephine and marrying Marie Louise. Judiciously, Olivier urges moderation and leads Roland away. When Armélie clamors for the young man's death, her new husband refuses, but several courtiers, including Gaiffre (Waifar) and the "perfide" Ganelon, promise her that their swords will punish "le superbe Roland." Some of the courtiers are no doubt envious, but all consider that, at some time or other, the brash young peer has humiliated them. Most dislike the king also. Thus it seems that Ganelon has personal reasons for wanting Roland dead, but the ambition and wrath of an insecure queen consort provide motivation.

Roland, "le preux mélancolique," decides to leave Paris, and when enemies, intending to put him to death, arrive at his house, he is not there. An altercation then breaks out between Ganelon and Einhard, who champions the absent peer, and Ganelon receives a mortal wound. Dying, he admits his misdeeds and warns the king, who is summoned, of the plot against Roland's life. Implicating himself, he names the other conspirators. By allowing Ganelon to die at this point and in repentance, Prince Lucien has introduced a drastic change in the familiar narrative.

Prince Lucien reminds his readers in the introduction that Pepin had put down several revolts engineered by dukes of Aquitaine and Gascony. Waifar and Lupus, their descendants, are just as unruly and hate Charlemagne, Pepin's son. Mischief, then, can be expected. "Maîtres du passage des Pyrénées, souvent alliés aux sarrasins, ils s'entendaient avec tous les ennemis de la France.... Le fameux Roland, neveu de Charlemagne, périt à Roncevaux par leur trahison."[35]

If Roland is headstrong, he is also naive. He left Paris with Olivier and Roger, a character from *Orlando innamorato* and *Orlando furioso* and now one of Roland's closest friends. Hardly have the three comrades crossed the Loire River when a young knight accosts them and tells them that the Duke of Gascony needs Charlemagne's help in driving the Mohammedan Almansor from his states. Bidding Lupus's messenger to tell Charlemagne that he will handle the matter himself, Roland and his companions ride into Tarbes, Lupus's capital. As his men rush to Roland's banner, Lupus, envious and piqued, has second thoughts. Itier, his evil counselor, reminds him that Pepin had put his father to death and that bad blood exists between him and the French monarch, Roland's uncle. The devious counselor takes it upon himself to mend relations with Almansor. He advises Lupus to feign cooperation with Roland and then, with the Moors, to kill the young paladin. The unsuspecting Roland, meanwhile, has put the Moors to flight. He pursues them and soon is in the "gorges profondes" of Roncevaux. The next day shepherds are supposed to lead him as he continues to chase the fleeing Moors, but thanks to Itier, no guides will arrive. Roland has fallen into a trap.

At this point in his epic Prince Lucien contends in a note that Charlemagne's incursion into Spain is hearsay. "La vallée de Roncevaux, si fameuse dans les chroniques de ce siècle, est sur la frontière d'Espagne et de Gascogne.... Tous les romanciers en vers et en prose ont dit qu'à Roncevaux Charles et les douze pairs furent battus par les Espagnols et que Roland et la plus grande partie des pairs y perdirent la vie. Charles n'alla jamais en Espagne."[36] Charlemagne, in any case, is not supposed to have been at Roncevaux. But Roland, Olivier, Roger, and the soldiers with them will not have to face their enemies alone. Still in their midst are some Christian Gascons who admire Roland and, at his side, are bent on pursuing the Moors.

Urged on by Itier, Lupus joins Almansor during the night. Many of the Gascons follow their duke. Almansor has already prepared his attack: trees have been cut down, boulders are in place. "Des arbres abattus ont comblé les sentiers; / Sur tous les mamelons, les roches suspendues / Peuvent du sein des nues / Rouler à chaque instant dans le creux des ravins." Morning breaks, and the paladin quickly discovers problems in his camp. No guides appear, and there have been many desertions, leaving him with scarcely a hundred men. Nevertheless, he hurls himself at the foe, and the wicked Itier is the first to be killed. Others follow, struck down by Roland's "glaive terrible." Soon the treacherous Gascons are in headlong flight.

Roland and his comrades do not yet realize that they are trapped. From high in the mountains, Lupus, with some of his allies and men, observes what Roland has done to the bulk of his army. Exasperated, he topples the first huge rock, setting off an avalanche that crushes the French soldiers below. "Mille rocs, aussitôt détachés à la fois, / Roulent de toutes parts sur le dos des montagnes, / Et d'un nouveau tonnerre ébranlent les campagnes." As for

> Les chrétiens abattus, écrasés sous leur poids,
> ....
> Ils meurent sans défense;
> Les uns, précipités sur le bord du torrent,
> Au milieu de ses flots terminent leur carrière;
> D'autres sont entraînés par un roc bondissant
> Qui s'enfonce avec eux dans le sein de la terre.

Accompanying the rocks and trees is a hail of arrows.

Soon a gigantic stone pulverizes Roger, and only Roland and Olivier are left. Joining arms, the two attempt to scale the mountains where their adversaries are entrenched. Pushing his friend aside, Roland tries alone to fight his way upward, but to no avail. "Il voit son bouclier, sa lance en mille éclats," and his sword is useless. The end comes, "et du sein de la nue / Tombe le roc fatal, ministre de la mort." "Déchiré," Roland soon feels life ebbing away. He asks God to forgive his sins and grant him salvation. He also acknowledges that he has been impulsive and admits that the deaths of so many French soldiers are his fault. In Olivier's arms, he calls upon his friend, should he survive, to dedicate himself to Charlemagne and to France. Charlemagne must be asked, moreover, to pardon his rash nephew, who died fighting for him. Finally, Roland enjoins Olivier to assure "celle qui m'est chère" that he was thinking of her at the moment he died.[37] Roland's death scene here probably inspired Achille Michallon's *La Mort de Roland,* shown at the 1819 Salon.

Olivier does not live to carry out Roland's last wishes. So great is his emotion that, when Roland dies, he falls dead near his friend. Soon a new avalanche of stones hurtles into the "vallée affreuse." "Mille rocs meurtriers sont lancés de nouveau: / Ils roulent en grondant . . . et sous la même pierre / Les deux nobles amis ont trouvé leur tombeau!" Much later, Satan exults as he contemplates the site: "Il aperçoit au fond de l'étroite vallée, / Sous les vastes débris d'une roche écroulée, / Les squelettes épars et le fer des héros." The bodies have not been buried. Even later, Waifar visits the scene and sees the oaks and pines, the rocks. Carloman's widow arranges for a funeral service in a rustic local chapel. In the eulogy Roland is hailed as "l'honneur des chevaliers" and "la terreur des plus fameux guerriers," The priest concedes that Roland was hotheaded, even a bit mad, but he would be forgiven. His banner, armor, and sword are buried at the battle site.[38] Probably the chapel Prince

Lucien is referring to is the Chapelle de Charlemagne. Mostly destroyed by fire in 1884, it was still standing at the time he was writing, and ruins are visible in present-day Ibañeta. In some form the chapel existed at least as early as the ninth century.[39]

Prince Lucien's *Charlemagne* may contain some contemporary allusions other than the harsh words possibly aimed at Napoleon. As in Roland's day, the French were having serious reverses in Spain when he was finishing his epic, a coincidence that contemporaries would have noted at once. Also, among those "Qui du trône français soutenaient la puissance, / L'honneur de leur patrie, et les pairs de leur roi," it is asserted that "Henri, duc de Frioul, vieux soldat de Pépin, / Sert noblement le fils comme il servit le père." After overrunning the northern part of the peninsula, Napoleon declared himself King of Italy. Friuli was part of the conquered territory and thus a French dependency. Prince Lucien may be alluding discreetly to G.C. Du Roc or Duroc, one of Napoleon's most competent and beloved aides, who was rewarded with the title Duc de Frioul in 1808. In 1813 he died of wounds in Silesia, which Charlemagne had annexed in 775, taking Friuli a year later. Likewise, one of Armélie's sisters is married to a cruel, authoritarian Duke of Benevento, who may represent Talleyrand, Napoleon's minister of foreign affairs. Upon his treacherous minister Napoleon had bestowed the titles Duc and Prince de Bénévent in 1806. At about the time Prince Lucien was completing his epic, Talleyrand deserted his imperial master and helped restore the Bourbons. After the Congress of Vienna returned Benevento to the Holy See, he would be known as Prince de Talleyrand.

Prince Lucien did not know the *Chanson de Roland*, of course, and he chose not to draw upon the *Pseudo-Turpin Chronicle* for any vital episodes or even details. Most of the sections of *Charlemagne* dealing with Roland sprang from the poet's imagination, resulting in a highly original version of events. Prince Lucien, for example, had his own ideas about the disaster at Roncevaux. He rejected the notion that Charlemagne had ever set foot in Spain and constructed his plot accordingly. Roland's presence in the Pyrenees Mountains is not related to a crusade against the Spanish Moors but is merely the result of his leaving his uncle's court. Marsile, the Mohammedan prince, described as "généreux," "vaillant," and "ennemi de la fraude et du crime," is not involved in the evil deeds. On the other hand, in Prince Lucien's version, Ganelon is awarded a more active role than one might expect. Presumably conniving with the king's border enemies, he appears to have foreseen which direction the young peer would take on leaving Paris and schemes to place an armed guard in the mountains, with orders to descend upon and kill the knight and his companions. Roland, however, never reaches this point.

Prince Lucien's Roland, like the hero of the yet unpublished *Chanson de Roland,* is rash and headstrong, as he is in Ariosto and Boiardo. As in the medieval epic, these characteristics bring about his and his companions' destruction. Prince Lucien also picks up on two rather widespread components in Roland literature, although he deviates somewhat from the mainstream tradition. He identifies the hero's assailants as Gascons, but he does not, as Scipion Dupleix had done, make these "Gascons" Mohammedans who had hidden out in the mountains of Gascony. Instead, Prince Lucien's Gascons are Frenchmen who occasionally find themselves allied with Mohammedans. Prince Lucien also supported the tradition, still somewhat unusual at the time, that, already dying, Roland was finally crushed beneath an avalanche of trees and rocks.

Other elements in *Charlemagne*'s Roland account are original. For example, the horn is not mentioned. As the author presented him, of course, Roland did not need one, since the French king was nowhere near when disaster struck. In most other versions of the story, Olivier dies before Roland, but here the deaths are reversed. Moreover, the ambushed French soldiers are buried in a mass grave, not by Charlemagne but by mountaineers. A coffin is provided for the hero eventually, but presumably his remains, along with those of Olivier, were interred in the common grave. His sword and armor are buried on the site rather than in churches in southern France, as the *Pseudo-Turpin Chronicle* contends. Finally, Prince Lucien's Ganelon, never tried or punished, dies in Paris full of remorse. This is a surprising development indeed. But he was by no means the only conspirator. Armélie and her supporters, who go free, are at least as guilty as he is. Creuzé de Lesser's Ganelon had French allies too, we recall. Disappointingly, in Prince Lucien's poem Charlemagne never grieves over the hero's death. Perhaps he was too busy slaughtering Lombards to have much time for lamentation. Although Ganelon had warned him of the plot to kill Roland, he did nothing to abort it or even arrest the conspirators.

Whatever his reservations about his brother, Prince Lucien was a Frenchman who admired his compatriot's bravery. At a critical moment in France's history, circumstances forced him to live in a nation at war with his own country. From a distance, *Charlemagne* may have had touches of veiled literary applause for French gallantry. Prince Lucien's story, the product of historical ignorance, poetic license, and bold imagination, is very different from the usual one.[40]

Probably *La Gaule poétique* of Louis Antoine François de Marchangy (1782-1826) was not intended as a *roman à clef*, but at points it can be read as such.[41] Regarding himself as Charlemagne's successor, Napoleon was not one to discourage people who chose to compare him with his illustrious predecessor. When the earliest volumes of Marchangy's work appeared, Napoleon was locked in a death struggle with most of the rest of Europe, as Charlemagne had been centuries before. What the author said about the medieval emperor had a sinister appropriateness for his modern successor. "Tandis que l'Orient et l'Occident enfantent de nombreuses armées pour attaquer la France, son héros, calme à la vue de tant de périls, assemble ses milices intrépides."[42] In the third volume, published in 1815, the author deals with Roland. He visualizes Theudo, king of the Huns, assembling an army and preparing to attack Charlemagne. One of Charlemagne's trustiest lieutenants is Henri, duc de Frioul, and in the enemy ranks is a malevolent Duc de Bénévent. Gaillard's work and Prince Lucien Bonaparte's *Charlemagne* mention them. Like Prince Lucien, Marchangy could have been introducing two names immediately recognizable to contemporaries. Napoleon's Duc de Frioul, killed at a critical moment, was one of the First Empire's best generals. In the sinister Duc de Bénévent many readers would have seen an allusion to Talleyrand, who betrayed Napoleon in 1814. At about the time the third volume of *La Gaule poétique* was being printed, the author underwent a metamorphosis himself. He had ardently admired Napoleon, but with the Restoration, he switched allegiances. A learned barrister, he served the Bourbons well, crippling adversaries with an oratorical skill that commanded even liberal enemies' respect.

While Marchangy's background was modest, he added the noble particle to his family name. Among his contemporaries, he made the name famous, though it has not remained so. Marchangy was a conservative, which no doubt hurt him in some quarters. Stendhal was to create a Julien Sorel who was only too willing to compromise his liberal principles in order to succeed in Restoration society. Nevertheless, disliking Marchangy, Stendhal dismissed *La Gaule poétique* as tiresome. Mérimée shared his opinion but advised handling so important a political figure and so popular an author with caution. Hugo's *Les Misérables* called the poet a "faux Chateaubriand," and Flaubert, in *Par les champs et par les grèves*, derided his "sempiternelle poésie des tourelles, des demoiselles, du palefroi, des fleurs de lis de l'oriflamme de saint Loius, du panache blanc, du droit divin et d'un tas d'autres sottises." But some contemporaries were of a different mind, including George Sand. Charles Durozoir, writing in Michaud's *Biographie universelle,* praised the author for his "coloris frais et brillant" and for his inventiveness as well.[43] To modern tastes *La Gaule poétique* may seem ponderous and dated, but when it came out most readers devoured it. By 1834 it had run into five editions.

Compared with other historical novels and dramas of the period, *La Gaule poétique* is well researched. Not surprisingly, in his notes the author mentions the *Bibliothèque universelle* as well as Ramond de Carbonnières. Part history, part romance, *La Gaule poétique* is reminiscent of both the *Recherches de la France* and *L'Astrée*. As Chateaubriand had done in the *Génie du christianisme* with *Atala* and *René,* Marchangy intended to provide French authors with a demonstration of a thesis. His thesis was Mme de Staël's. In *De l'Allemagne*, she had proposed medievalism as a field that literary artists should cultivate. In his long prose poem, Marchangy treated his readers to an idealized overview of great episodes in Gallic civilization from the Franks' invasion to the end of the seventeenth century.[44] His particular interest was the Middle Ages. He believed that Charlemagne had ushered in an intellectual golden age. Like the Marquis de Paulmy before him, he theorized about the lost *Chanson de Roland* but wisely made no effort to reconstruct it. He did, however, produce a version of the Roland legend that is intuitive and, at times, poetic.

La Gaule poétique's first two volumes appeared in 1813. Volume 3, published two years later, contains a "Chant funèbre en l'honneur de Roland," the author's treatment of the legend. Charlemagne, preparing to move against the Huns, reviews his troops while the author apostrophizes the absent Roland, "le plus vaillant de tous les Français, invincible Roland." Roland's death is still recent, and black crepe is hanging on the helmets and shields of his comrades. Marching off to war, these soldiers sing a lament in the fallen hero's honor that is an imaginative recapitulation of events at Roncevaux. Notwithstanding his extensive documentation, Marchangy did not hesitate in composing his dirge to embroider, to discard, to invent. The "Chant funèbre en l'honneur de Roland" is the result.

In Spain and Navarre, at Pamplona and Saragossa, Roland has taken the lead in France's war with the infidels, killing Aigoland and Ferragus.[45] Because of him, "sur les bords de l'Ebre l'altier Sarrasin voit l'arbre de son orgueil abattu." Now the war is over, and Roland tells the assembled French legions to return to their "patrie impatiente." Their absence "a trop longtemps désolé vos amours et refroidi la cendre de vos foyers hospitaliers," he adds. He informs the men that he and some companions will bring up the rear, protecting them lest the defeated Moors seek revenge. In Marchangy's version, this is Roland's idea. No Ganelon proposes it, no emperor consults the peers and makes the ultimate decision. Roland's comrades salute their leader and acquiesce. If they consent to precede him, they answer, it is merely to announce his exploits and prepare the hero's welcome. Fate had decreed otherwise. "Le sort les dément et secoue son front inflexible et sévère," the author observes.[46]

The main army rides away and soon disappears in the distance. Roland is now alone with a few select companions, including Olivier. Watching him are the awestruck Moors. Roland and the others, suspecting nothing, chat about hunting and love while riding toward the French border. "Leur âme loyale et généreuse ne soupçonnait point d'embûche ni de traîtres." Yet there were villains close at hand, and soon they would attack. In the passage that follows, the author's images well convey the momentary stillness, the danger, and Roland's confidence: "L'amant de la belle Angélique suit le long défilé qui menait à nos frontières. Les sommets des hautes Pyrénées répandaient une nuit éternelle sur cet étroit sentier que resserrent les escarpements des rochers sourcilleux, et que dominent des masses pendantes et des forêts redoutées. A travers ces horreurs et ces ombres sinistres, Roland passe avec sécurité. Tout à coup un bruit sourd fait retentir la triple chaîne des échos sonores. Le preux, sans s'effrayer, lève les yeux et voit la cime des monts hérissée de soldats nombreux."[47]

Was it the Moors who attacked? With Einhard and others, Marchangy believes that the culprits were Gascons. The hidden enemies call out to Roland that he must die. Then an avalanche of arrows, trees, and stones pour down upon the hapless French soldiers like a summer hailstorm crushing a harvest. The scene is devastating. The attackers "font rouler des rochers énormes, qui, dans leur chute, détournent le cours des torrents, entraînent les neiges amoncelées. L'onde égarée écume et mugit, l'avalanche tonne et foudroie, des gouffres nouveaux ouvrent leurs flancs ténébreux d'où s'exhalent des feux souterrains." It would seem that the whole universe would have to perish in order to guarantee Roland's death. His comrades all dead, Roland is alone in the tumult. "Il plane sur le chaos; il lutte avec la nature; il triomphe de la mort qui l'assiège sous mille aspects divers." Beneath the rain of debris, this "paladin immortel" falls into the depths of a ravine. Like a man possessed, he springs back, striking out vigorously but with despair. He seizes his sword and thrashes about with it, pulverizing trees and splitting rocks. The author reminds us in a note that mountain people still point to what they call the Brèche de Roland, believing that "ce paladin la fit d'un coup d'épée." Roland at last blows his horn, "et le son qu'il en tire roule comme un tonnerre dans les gorges de Roncevaux; les monts ont tremblé, l'air a frémi, les bêtes féroces regagnent leurs tanières, le géant se cache entre les pins de la colline, et la sentinelle des châteaux lointains s'inquiète à ce bruit surnaturel qui se fait entendre jusqu'à l'armée française."[48]

The army hears Roland's horn and arrives in time to witness the hero's death. "Elle a soudain connu le danger de Roland, car lui seul pouvait faire résonner avec tant de force le belliqueux instrument des forêts et des champs. Mais à mesure qu'elle s'avance à son secours, le bruit s'affaiblit, et le cor n'était plus animé que par les derniers soupirs de Roland; il expirait.... Les veines de son col robuste avaient éclaté, ses poumons déchirés vomissaient à longs flots son sang qui bouillonnait; il expirait, et nos bataillons, entourant les bords de l'abîme, gémissent pendant trois jours sur le plus magnanime et le plus courageux des guerriers."[49] When Charlemagne's men have sung the dirge, they ride away to fight the Huns.

Perhaps there may be indirect allusions to specific individuals in Marchangy's prose poem, but there was a broader comparison to be made. Certainly, the "Chant funèbre" evokes the battle of France, and one recalls how in 1813 and 1814 the French, overwhelmed by sheer numbers, were evacuating occupied territories and were being driven back, steadily, toward Paris. Hounded in the north and east by inexorable Austrian, German, and Russian advances, they were simultaneously pushed out of Spain through the

Pyrenees Mountains by the determined, relentless Wellington. On 25 July 1813 there was even another battle of Roncevaux. The French, who up to this point had been the victors in almost all their engagements, had to contend with resuscitated armies they had once devastated.

The "Chant funèbre en l'honneur de Roland" handles the Roland legend freely. With Creuzé de Lesser and others, Marchangy insists upon the ominous appearance of the massacre site. Roland decides on his own to protect the army's rear, and Charlemagne is not even mentioned in the "Chant funèbre" itself. Olivier is named only once. There is no Turpin, no Ganelon, no Aude. Durandal is never named, although Roland's feats with his "redoutable épée" are crucial to the poem. When in desperation Roland finally blows his horn, the veins in his neck rather than those in his head burst. Now and then the author adds details of his own, such as Roland's lungs shredding during the bootless effort. Moreover, to make Roland correspond to contemporary ideas of a medieval knight, Marchangy allows for a love interest, reminding us that Roland has been Angelica's lover. Interestingly, Roland is a marvelous soldier, valiant and even superhuman, but he remains modest to the end. He is also patriotic, referring to "nos illustres bannières."

One of Marchangy's chief surprises is that, while the French Revolution is past, there is still no religious element in the poem. Roland is a soldier who does his duty and does it admirably, but whether crushing Saracens or fending off Gascons, that duty is secular. There is no *merveilleux chrétien*. As he dies, Roland does not pray. There is no chaplain on hand in this poem, and in his absence, Roland does not remember to commend his soul to God.

Marchangy's narrative moves at a much more rapid pace than Prince Lucien's does, and the author sustains reader interest much better than the author of *Charlemagne ou l'église délivrée*. Marchangy was not a great poet, but neither does he deserve scornful dismissal. Using his imagination freely, he tells us, for instance, that the main army mourned the hero for three days before embarking on a new military expedition. The poet's imagery is evocative: "rochers sourcilleux," for example, describes picturesquely the high, curving mountaintops. Likewise, the author evokes the rain of missiles hurtling down the mountainsides more energetically and skillfully than Prince Lucien did. Details of the falling stones picking up snow as they tumbled down the cliffs and altering the course of creeks and rivers are colorful and gripping. Well-chosen verbs help also: the avalanche "tonne," the water "mugit." The author's depiction of nature trembling when Roland blew his horn contributes to the pathos of the situation and creates suspense. The "Chant funèbre" is not a durable prose poem, but it is a highly imaginative retelling of the Roland story.

During the Restoration, the novels of Vicomte Charles Victor d'Arlincourt (1788-1856) had a following.[50] The best known is the Gothic novel *Le Solitaire*

(1821), which went through numerous editions. Arlincourt's drama and poetry did not have as much success. A contorted style earned him the nickname "l'inversif vicomte." His father had been a *fermier général* under Louis XVI and was guillotined during the Revolution. Under Napoleon the son held several government posts, the principal one as a Conseil d'Etat auditor. He was with the French army in Spain as a civilian. At Napoleon's fall, he quickly discovered a passionate love for the Bourbons and was rewarded with an appointment as Maître des Requêtes. After the July Revolution, Arlincourt remained loyal to the Bourbon cause, retired to his estate, and wrote novels hostile to Louis Philippe. He revered the Middle Ages and decorated his château in "Gothic" style. Like Horace Walpole at Strawberry Hill, he lived in what to him and his contemporaries was medieval splendor.

In *De l'Allemagne* Mme de Staël had advised modern French poets to treat episodes from their country's medieval past. "La littérature des anciens," she wrote, "est chez les modernes une littérature transplantée: la littérature romantique ou chevaleresque est chez nous indigène, et c'est notre religion et nos institutions qui l'ont fait éclore."[51] Arlincourt considered the suggestion a good one and put it into practice. Of those treating the Roland legend, he was the only French writer of his era to hint that he was acting on Mme de Staël's advice. He was also alone in presenting Charlemagne as a young man.

Arlincourt held Marchangy's *La Gaul poétique* in high regard, mentioning it several times in his preface and notes. He began his own epic, *Charlemagne ou la Caroléide*, during the First Empire years, and part of it was written in Spain. The poet no doubt hoped to please Napoleon, who liked to be compared with his great predecessor. Fragments of the work appeared in 1810, but Napoleon had been exiled before it was finished. Altering his manuscript as new circumstances dictated, the poet published it in 1818. He said in his preface that he had chosen a native protagonist whom all Frenchmen, whatever their political biases, could acclaim. "Honneur à tout Français qui sut illustrer sa patrie et combattre noblement pour elle, n'importe à quelle époque et sous quel étendard," he declared.[52]

The action begins as the Saxons are staging their third rebellion. Arlincourt's knowledge of history was far from irreproachable, but he shared the deficiency with many of his fellow writers. Arlincourt was equally ignorant of even rudimentary architectural evolution: his hero wakes up one morning as the epic begins in his Gothic palace. No Romantic, that hero still, in the radiance of a brilliant dawn, admires nature: "Au fond d'un vieux château, de gothique structure, / Où l'art s'étoit flatté d'embellir la nature, / Charle, à l'aube du jour, s'arrachant au sommeil, / Déjà de la nature admire le réveil." Dressed in his armor, Charlemagne strides to his council chamber and addresses his captains. Past victories are enumerated, and the decision is made to end the Saxon revolt. In Arlincourt's time, some of the German nations were prominent in the coalition that had just defeated and occupied France. Seeing Charlemagne warring with his German contemporaries and bringing them to heel would please many French readers, and the poet knew it.

Arlincourt's epic, like that of Prince Lucien Bonaparte, has a preface, notes, and twenty-four cantos, but it is not divided into patterned stanzas of equal length. Except for occasional lyrical outbursts, the meter is alexandrine, with masculine and feminine rhymed couplets alternating. While the verse is not quite pedestrian, it is not exceptionally good. It is hard to comprehend that the *Premières Méditations poétiques* would be published only two years later.

Early in *La Caroléide*, Arlincourt lists the noble barons present for Charlemagne's council of war. Roland, having been killed in Spain, is of course not there. "Noble Roland! jadis, parmi tous ces héros, / Tu t'élevois superbe . . . O fatal Roncevaux! / Que maudit soit ton sol où la gloire succombe! / Ton immortalité s'assied sur une tombe," the poet exclaims.[53]

In a brisk encounter with Saxon enemies, two of Charlemagne's most valued men are killed. Comrades carry their bodies into a wooded area for burial, their shields, as in Marchangy's "Chant funèbre en l'honneur de Roland," covered with crepe. As the bodies are being carried away "soudain, selon la loi des preux, / En l'honneur des guerriers dont la mort fut célèbre / Tous en choeur de Roland chantent l'hymne funèbre." Arlincourt was aware that a "hymne de Roland" had once existed. In his notes he states that he has set out to give his readers an idea of what it must have been. "Je n'ai prétendu en donner qu'une imitation," he modestly asserts.[54] His own song presents his version of events at Roncevaux. Detail and wording reveal that he remembered the versions of Prince Lucien and Marchangy, and possibly those of Creuzé de Lesser and others as well. Undoubtedly the idea of inserting a dirge in his work came from *La Gaule poétique*. Marchangy wrote in poetic prose, however, and Arlincourt stuck to rhyming couplets.

Arlincourt's "Hymne funèbre de Roland" generally follows the tradition of the Roland songs produced during the Revolution and First Empire. There are significant differences, however: no music was written for it, and the stanzas are unequal in length. Moreover, each line has ten syllables instead of the usual eight, and the four lines serving as a refrain occur only at the beginning and end of the song, with a curious inversion the second time. The first refrain reads: "Il est tombé le vainqueur d'Agramand! / Mais Dieu lui seul a pu vaincre Roland: / Il est tombé l'orgueil de la patrie! / Mais nul mortel ne lui trancha la vie." At the end of the dirge the order of the two couplets is reversed.

Following the introduction is a stanza declaring the dead hero to have been not only a mighty warrior but also a charitable friend and a faithful lover, although no sweetheart is identified. Next, the poet narrates the disaster at Roncevaux. In the song there is no mention of Olivier, who, one presumes, was with the emperor, riding on ahead. He survives and, much later, participates in the war against the Saxons. When Roland blows his horn finally, he does it on his own initiative. Ganelon and Turpin do not figure in Arlincourt's hymn. As the song opens, Charlemagne's Spanish campaign is over, and the French are returning home. Nothing is said about a rear guard, but clearly Roland and his unnamed companions are at a considerable distance from the main army.

> Déjà Roland, du fond de l'Ibérie,
> Revient vainqueur au sein de sa patrie:
> Entre deux monts dont le front touche aux cieux,
> Il passe . . . Hélas! leur sommet sourcilleux
> De Sarrasins tout à coup se hérisse . . .
> Route funeste! au bord du précipice,
> Rocs et sapins qu'arrachent les brigands,
> Sur le guerrier s'écroulent foudroyants.
> L'abîme attend l'avalanche tonnante;
> L'onde égarée écume mugissante;
> Sous le torrent, des gouffres ténébreux
> Ouvrent leurs flancs, d'où jaillissent des feux
> Que suit la mort: un Dieu tonne invisible:
> Il sembleroit en ce désordre horrible
> Que l'univers doit périr écroulé,
> Pour qu'il soit dit:—Roland fut ébranlé.
>
> Ses compagnons ont roulé dans l'abîme:
> Roland lui seul, Roland, l'effroi du crime!
> Quand rocs et monts croulent sur ses héros,
> Debout encor plane sur le chaos:
> Seul, menaçant une horde parjure,
> Le paladin lutte avec la nature.
> L'éboulement des arbres renversés,
> Les pics tombants, les rochers fracassés,
> Sont les degrés, montée inaccessible,
> Que le héros escalade invincible.

In what ensues, Arlincourt borrows heavily from Prince Lucien Bonaparte, although here Roland is alone. Roland's scaling a mountain where the Saracens are entrenched and falling into a ravine comes from Prince Lucien's work and from Marchangy's "Chant funèbre en l'honneur de Roland." His violent thrashing about with his sword is a Marchangy touch.

> Déjà Roland touche au sommet gravi:
> Epouvantés, les Sarrasins ont fui:
> O jour fatal! les ruines mouvantes
> Qui l'élevoient s'éboulent mugissantes.

> La force en vain roidit ses bras nerveux;
> Le désespoir hérisse ses cheveux . . .
> Si près de vaincre! . . . effroyable supplice!
> Roland retombe au fond du précipice.

Enraged, Roland draws his sword: "Il fond les rocs, et le sol qu'il divise / A retenti sous les arbres qu'il brise. / La cataracte, au milieu du torrent, / Tombe à grand bruit . . . L'impétueux Roland / S'y jette, il veut s'opposer à sa course, / Et repousser les ondes vers leur source." Roland thinks of his horn and blows it.

> Sur sa poitrine un cor est suspendu . . .
> Il le saisit, il en tire, éperdu,
> Des sons roulants, semblables au tonnerre:
> L'air en frémit, au loin tremble la terre.
> De ces déserts les monstres rugissants
> Rentrent troublés dans leurs antres sanglants;
> Et le pasteur du vallon solitaire
> Croit avoir ouï la trompette dernière.

The howling monsters that go back into their dens are no doubt the same vicious beasts that, in Marchangy's "Chant funèbre," return to their lairs when the hero sounds his horn, making a noise like thunder. A great distance away, Charlemagne hears the "son fatal" and rushes back. He is, of course, too late. "Hélas! alors qu'il arrive au torrent, / Le dernier son expire avec Roland. / Il est tombé l'orgueil de la patrie! / Mais nul mortel ne lui trancha la vie: / Il est tombé le vainqueur d'Agramand! / Mais Dieu lui seul a pu vaincre Roland."

Arlincourt's poem is not a great one, but it does show that during the years preceding the publication of the Oxford Manuscript, there was a ready market for retellings of the legend of Roncevaux. Arlincourt's popularity is suggested by the fact that Horace Vernet illustrated *La Caroléide*. Busy putting the finishing touches on his *Méditations poétiques,* Larmartine noted in 1819 that the epic was being highly praised. Six years later, Sainte-Beuve claimed in one of the *Premiers lundis* that Arlincourt was "un attentat perpétuel aux lois éternelles et sacrées de la raison."[55] A large segment of the reading public did not go along with the judgment. The year before the critic's solemn pronouncement, *La Caroléide* had a second edition.

To her Romantic contemporaries, Amable Tastu was an important poet. Encouraged by Empress Josephine, she began writing in her teens. She treated themes such as the past and death in poems that make her, in the evolution of French verse, a sort of midpoint between Millevoye and Lamartine. One of her earliest collections deals with the Middle Ages. Entitled *La Chevalerie française*, it appeared in 1821 and was accompanied by an introduction, a vocabulary, and explanatory material.[56] In her *notices historiques* the author declares that in 1370, returning from a military mission in Castile, Bertrand Du Guesclin crossed Roncevaux Valley. There he paused and prayed "devant le tombeau de Roland, à l'endroit même où il périt." Tastu quotes the prayer and uses a sentence from it in a poem called "Duguesclin au tombeau de Roland." She describes the poem's setting: "De ce vallon, où gît l'honneur de France, / Le sol fatal a vu tomber Roland." According to the poet, on the site, a tomb actually existed and Roland literally reposed "sous cette pierre." Du Guesclin beseeches God to grant him the "Coeur généreux, valeur et prud'hommie / De celui-là qui repose en ce lieu." He wishes to obtain the "Heur de mourir en beaux jours de batailles, / Comme autrefois mourut ce fier Roland!" When that happens, he hopes that his name, like that of Roland, will be remembered by future generations of soldiers.

La Chevalerie française also contains a poem the author called "Olivier et Roland." In the historical introduction for this poem, Tastu narrates Charlemagne's expedition into Spain, his return, and the attack on the rear guard. According to the poet, the villain was Lupus, duke of Gascony. Alluding to the battle of Roncevaux, she mentions that "ce fait est consacré par un monument." Then she summarizes the account given in the *Pseudo-Turpin Chronicle*, adding some touches of her own. She says that, on hearing his nephew's horn, Charlemagne at first did not respond but sent Baudouin, Turpin, and a certain Thiodoric to investigate. Before dying, Roland succeeded in breaking his sword, and the pieces were buried with him. Tastu also summarizes Gabriel Daniel's *Histoire de France*, which Gaillard had mentioned in 1782. In writing his work, the author points out, Fr. Daniel used a manuscript, dated 15 December 1707, that discussed the presumed battle area, its traditions, and its curiosities. The manuscript described a chapel three hundred paces from the monastery at Roncevaux and mentioned a cellar beneath the chapel where thirty tombs and some bones could be seen. There were no inscriptions on the tombs, but on the chapel walls, along with a fresco depicting the battle of Roncevaux, were several names, including those of Olivier and Roland. Tastu adds, "La tradition du pays est que Charlemagne a fait bâtir cette chapelle, où l'on priait pour les Français morts à Roncevaux; que la cave est l'endroit où il les fit enterrer; qu'enfin les trente tombeaux sont ceux des principaux chevaliers qui périrent dans cette journée." One may guess that the tombs are the monument the author had referred to earlier. The chapel, of course, is the one that could still be seen in the early 1880s, which Ramón Menéndez Pidal discusses in *La "Chanson de Roland" et la tradition épique des Francs*.[57]

"Olivier et Roland" consists of five eight-line stanzas of octosyllabic verse. The poem deals with Roland's last stand, but in the two initial stanzas, the first addressed to the Pyrenees Mountains and the second to a body of French soldiers, the poet may also have been thinking of the imperial army as it crossed back into France in 1813, hounded by Spanish guerrillas and British soldiers. The poem follows in its entirety.

> Eternels remparts de la France,
> Recevez nos soldats vainqueurs.
> Du retour la douce espérance
> Fait déjà palpiter leurs coeurs.
> L'écho surpris de la montagne
> Répète cet hymne guerrier,
> Qui joint au nom de Charlemagne
> Ceux de Roland et d'Olivier.
>
> Arrêtez, Français intrépides,
> Redoutez un funeste sort;
> Arrêtez, de ces monts perfides
> Sur vous s'élancera la mort.
> De toutes parts, sur votre tête,
> Je vois les rochers s'ébranler;
> L'arc est tendu, la lance est prête,
> Et le sang français va couler.
>
> Jamais, au moment de combattre,
> Roland compta-t-il l'ennemi?
> Il lui reste encor pour l'abattre
> L'honneur, son bras, et son ami.
> Ces héros, soutiens de la France,
> Méritaient un destin plus beau;
> Mais tant d'exploits et de vaillance
> N'obtinrent, hélas! qu'un tombeau.
>
> Deux fois les échos de la plaine
> Ont répété le son du cor;
> Malgré cette alarme soudaine,
> Charlemagne balance encor.
> Cours; s'il réclame ta présence,
> Ce n'est point pour sauver ses jours:
> Roland doit trembler pour la France,
> Quand il appelle du secours!
>
> C'en est fait, l'amitié fidèle
> En vain court aux champs des combats;
> En vain une terreur nouvelle
> A chaque instant hâte ses pas,
> Ses regards, errans dans la plaine,
> Lui redemandent le guerrier. . . .

> Roland expirait sur l'arène,
> Près du corps sanglant d'Olivier.

Like the Revolutionary Rolands, this one is a patriot, trembling not for himself but for France. Romantic touches, however, appear as well: fate, for example, overtook the hero, who deserved "un destin plus beau." Charlemagne reaches the scene in time to see his nephew die. From the second stanza it is clear that the poet credits the tradition in which Roland was killed not by arrows and swords alone but also by rocks hurled from the mountains.

Today Amable Tastu is no longer considered a major poet, and it is easy to dismiss her unlikely medievalism, her *faux ancien*. Nevertheless, it harmonized with her era's concept of the Middle Ages. Contemporaries such as Chateaubriand and Lamartine applauded it, and Sainte-Beuve complimented her "sensibilité toute réelle."[58] "Olivier et Roland" probably will not find its way into anthologies of nineteenth-century French poetry, but it gives us additional proof of a vigorous Roland literature in France prior to the publication of the Oxford Manuscript.

Early in *Les Misérables* Victor Hugo included a chapter on the year 1817. From every standpoint, the author thought, it was a bad year. After Waterloo and Napoleon's being hustled off to St. Helena, Allied troops were still on French soil. And the literary atmosphere was dreary as well.[59] That year a play about Roland appeared that the author must have missed, for, had he seen it, he would have criticized it.

Jean Guillaume Antoine (or Auguste) Cuvelier de Trie (1766-1824) studied law, then became a soldier. Having been wounded, he was discharged. Next, he tried his hand at drama. Endowed with a talent as facile as it was modest, he left no masterpieces but is credited with inventing the *mélodrame*, a genre that in the early nineteenth century enjoyed a tenacious success one would be hard put to explain on rational grounds. Cuvelier was known as "le Corneille du boulevard," a title he shared with Guilbert de Pixérécourt. Often military heroes dominated his productions, as in *La Mort de Turenne* and *La Mort de Kléber*. Frequently he collaborated with Léopold Chandezon, and in 1817 the two men offered the theatergoing public *Roland furieux*, described as a "pantomime chevaleresque et féerie en quatre actes avec des prologues." Not melodrama or true pantomime, it was an example of *pantomime dialoguée*, a bastard genre with which Cuvelier de Trie's name has become associated. The play featured music, ballets, and also the "machines" that the public loved, so that supernatural beings, good and bad, could materialize from nowhere, disappear into thin air, and perform all kinds of unlikely feats. There is some dialogue, though not much. The scene changes with incredible swiftness, and sounds such as thunder and music constantly emphasize the action. Perhaps suspecting that their "pantomime" was less than a momentous artistic achievement, the two authors merely signed themselves "MM. Cuvelier et Léopold" when their play was published. The Cirque Olympique, where it was performed, became famous, and Cuvelier de Trie helped it do so.

Cuvelier de Trie and Chandezon relied upon a basically Italian Roland plot, but they felt free to change it at will. They tell their readers in an introduction that Alcina, the enchantress, has been made into a male sorcerer. Angelica descends upon Charlemagne's court not in Paris, but in the mountain passes that divide France from Spain. No brother accompanies her. More important, the authors have rearranged familiar episodes and even created new ones.[60] As remarks at the beginning and end would seem to bear out, their aim in writing the play was probably patriotic. Foreign soldiers were strutting about everywhere, and public morale needed a boost.

Roland furieux begins in hell, where groups of devils are making instruments of war. Alcimar, the sorcerer, is presiding over a council of evil magicians. People and events in France have him worried. "Cette France glorieuse," "cet immortel royaume," he calls it. Charlemagne has vowed to destroy the sorcerers, and he just might succeed. The country owes its happiness to "la richesse de son sol et surtout au courage de ses guerriers," chief among whom is Charlemagne's nephew, the invincible Roland. Protected both by heaven and the powerful, benign fairy Logistille, he is invulnerable. Soon he will marry the beautiful warrior Marphise, and should this happen, the couple will no doubt produce a race of bellicose offspring capable of annihilating the wicked magicians. Alcimar reveals his strategy for coping with the threat: the sorcerer intends to instill love, jealousy, and hatred into Roland so that he will lose his reason. "Une fois sa raison aliénée, le charme qui le protège sera détruit, et . . . sa force surnaturelle sera nulle ou tournera contre lui-même," he tells his cohorts. He adds that Angélique, queen of Cathay, will arrive that day to enlist Charlemagne's help in wresting her country from a usurper. In the Ardennes Forest, which crops up occasionally in fictional accounts of Roland's childhood, there is a magic fountain. For convenience, Alcimar has moved it to another forest close at hand. Drinking its water changes love to hate. Alcimar plans to have Marphise give Roland a drink from it, making the paladin lose interest in her. A look from Angélique will do the rest. The assembled wizards cheer their leader and swear to support his schemes.[61]

The action occurs in the Pyrenees Mountains. In the course of a vigorous hunt, Roland kills a monster. Later he is exhausted and thirsty. Marphise goes to the magic fountain and gets water for him. After drinking it, he repels her attentions. Then, looking into the fountain, he sees a beautiful woman's image in the water. Soon she comes into view, and Roland falls in love immediately. Angélique asks to be introduced to Charlemagne, expressing the hope that Roland will help win back her country for her. Roland, only too eager to be of service, goes with her to meet the emperor. Stunned, Marphise looks on, while Astolphe, her brother, tries to console her. He is Roland's best friend and does not understand.

In act 2 the French are in their tents between battles with Saracen enemies. King Agramant, at the head of his pagan hordes, is hiding in the woods. At a signal from Alcimar he will attack. The sorcerer is convinced that "les chrétiens surpris fuiront . . . devant le croissant victorieux." This done, the magicians could breathe more freely, but if Roland's new love turns to hatred and the hero loses his mind, the rewards for the conspirators would be even greater.

Meanwhile Roland presents the Queen of Cathay to Charlemagne. She implores the emperor's aid, and help is promised. She sits down beside the throne, and a celebration is about to begin when a stranger appears. Disguised as a pagan ambassador, Alcimar announces that the queen must be turned over to Agramant. If not, a combat between Christian and Saracen knights will decide the issue. Naturally, Charlemagne refuses to surrender his guest, and a combat ensues. Roland heads the French contingent, and, with Astolphe at his side, he soon wipes out the Moors. Angélique is saved, but this has only been a diversion. Alcimar's signal is given, and suddenly pagan troops sweep through the French camp. French arms are victorious, however, and the Moors quickly flee. Médor, a Saracen knight's young squire, is seriously wounded by Roland. Wandering away from the fighting, Angélique comes upon him, takes pity on the "jeune et beau sarrasin," and tends him. As he revives, she falls in love with him and he with her. Roland discovers them and flies into a jealous rage, falling to the ground and lying motionless in the darkness. At this point, incredible as it may seem, the audience is treated to a look at Roland's senses. "Une flamme bleuâtre s'élève de la tête de Roland et se perd doucement dans les airs." The bluish substance, one is told, is Roland's reason. Alcimar is on hand, needless to say, orchestrating events. He tells the other magicians that things are going well. Roland's reason is being dispersed "au sein des airs, vers un endroit inaccessible, où elle restera sous la garde des génies du mal." The sorcerers vanish and Roland awakens. Hearing nuptial music and seeing Angélique and Médor heading for a temple, he brandishes Durandal and loses control. As he tries to prevent the engagement ceremony, pagan knights surround and arrest him.[62] The pagans no longer harbor ill will toward Angélique, especially when she agrees to become Agramant's vassal.

Act 3 shows Roland in prison, mad and chained. Remembering the one he loves and his rival, he throws off his chains and breaks through the prison wall. He reaches Agramant's palace when the couple has just been united, and as bride and groom disappear, he goes on another rampage. Again he falls exhausted, and again he is imprisoned, this time in a cave. Finding his armor and sword, his friends assume him to be dead. His battle gear is given to

Marphise, who erects a memorial to him. Through trickery Agramant gets possession of Durandal and drives it into Marphise's bosom. Astolphe arrives in time to witness his sister's death. At that moment Logistille, the demented knight's protectress, appears and reassures the heartbroken brother. Astolphe must travel to the moon, "l'astre des nuits," and collect Roland's reason. Suitable transportation is provided. Astride the hippogriff and armed with a golden lance, he springs, dauntless, into the firmament. As he does so, Angélique and Médor, to the spectators' immense relief, can be seen departing for Cathay. The authors neglect to mention whether the usurper who made it necessary for Angélique to come to France in the first place has been ousted.

Act 4 opens with Alcimar, riding a winged dragon, arriving on the moon to warn the evil spirits guarding Roland's senses, which are being kept in a crystal globe that gives off a bluish light. Astolphe reaches his destination, overpowers the evil spirits, seizes the crystal globe, and hurries back to earth, his mission accomplished. Alcimar and Agramant then decide to put Roland to death. Before they can do this, however, a voice orders Astolphe to open the jar and release the contents, which drift toward the captive knight. "La flamme . . . vient se placer doucement sur la tête du paladin, bientôt elle n'est plus visible." Roland is once more in possession of his wits. "Je me reconnais," he cries, "ma raison a repris son empire." In addition, the spell that had made him love Angélique is broken. He emerges from the cave. The evildoers, their power gone, are soon dispersed, and Logistille appears. At her command, Roland touches Marphise's tomb with Durandal, and his fiancée comes back to life. The Moors are in chains. Charlemagne is seated on his throne, surrounded by his military leaders. Before the curtain falls, Logistille gives Roland a stirring celestial commission: "Toi, Roland, je te rends à l'honneur, à la gloire," she tells him. "Ta patrie t'attend, ton roi t'appelle. Conduis à la victoire nos immortelles phalanges, achève de délivrer la France des ennemis qui l'oppriment, et va prouver au monde que nos fertiles campagnes peuvent produire à la fois le laurier de Bellone et l'olivier de Minerve."[63]

This piece of rhetoric no doubt brought cheers as the audience remembered France's recent heroic achievements and compared them, necessarily, with her present humiliation at the hands of the Allied occupation forces. Logistille's ringing words are reminiscent of the Revolutionary and Napoleonic Roland songs. Cuvelier de Trie and Chandezon did not create a dramatic masterpiece, but they did use Roland, as their recent predecessors had done, as a symbol of French military glory, suggesting that the enemy should be driven out. Diplomatic, not military, efforts would bring this about a year later. By coincidence or otherwise, the treaty was signed in Charlemagne's capital of Aix-la-Chapelle in 1818.

Before Cuvelier de Trie and Chandezon, Millevoye had touched upon the Italian Roland tradition in his *Charlemagne à Pavie*. Later, although Balzac would allude to it, that tradition would have little place in French creative writing as native literature exploiting the legend began to achieve greater importance.[64]

The Swiss historian, critic, and political economist Jean Charles Léonard Simonde de Sismondi (1773-1842) was a friend of Mme de Staël. He published his *Histoire des Français* over a period of more than two decades; the second volume, which treats Charlemagne and his immediate predecessors, appeared in 1821. Like Chateaubriand and other authors of his day, he knew Ariosto and the *Pseudo-Turpin Chronicle*. He also knew the Spanish *romanceros*.

Prone to belittle Charlemagne and his motives, Sismondi discusses the Frankish ruler's foray into Spain in 778. A Protestant, Sismondi may have been somewhat biased. "Charles saisit avec empressement l'occasion . . . d'étendre sa domination sur l'Espagne," he wrote, noting that Moorish princes seeking his help had invited him to come. Convoking and reviewing his armies at Chasseneuil Palace, he divided them into two main bodies, which entered Spain by way of Pamplona and Roussillon and then joined ranks beneath the walls of Saragossa. After razing Pamplona's walls, Charlemagne placed his own men in the important positions, thus irritating Saracens who otherwise would have been his allies. The kings of Navarre and Asturias, along with Lupus, duke of Gascony, made common cause with the Mohammedan governor of Saragossa, "que les romanciers ont nommé Marsilio." Hearing that Wittikind, the Saxon leader, had incited a rebellion in Germany, Charlemagne left Spain, and hurried home to put down the revolt, unaware that he had irritated so many people.[65]

"Les Gascons et les Navarrais, dont l'origine était commune, parcourant leurs montagnes avec une rapidité qui les distingue encore aujourd'hui. . . , dressaient des embûches à Charles. . . , comme il traversait la vallée de Roncevaux, si fameuse dans les romans." While the Frankish hosts made their way through the valley, their enemies struck. Sismondi quotes Einhard's *Vita Caroli Magni* account of events, mentioning Roland, along with the other heroes. "C'est là tout ce que l'histoire nous a appris sur le paladin Roland et sur cette bataille de Roncevaux, si célébrée par les romanciers et par les historiens espagnols des temps postérieurs," Sismondi concludes.[66]

Sismondi believed that Roland had to exist, but he also believed that people's view of their hero's exploits with time took on unwarranted proportions. Folklore, to which the Spanish *romanceros* contributed and which *Orlando furioso* expanded, established the Roland legend.[67] "Un génie tel que celui de l'Arioste aurait pu créer la célébrité de Roland," he declared, but he pointed out that a legend existed before Ariosto. Sismondi was not too far from the *cantilène* theory of the *Chanson de Roland*'s origin when he held, in connection with episodes in the *Pseudo-Turpin Chronicle*, that "on doit les regarder moins comme l'invention d'un romancier que comme le dépot des fables et des légendes qui circulaient alors parmi le peuple."[68] To Sismondi, the *Pseudo-Turpin Chronicle* had little historical value, but as a repository of tales, it was something he did not care to dismiss.

Speculating about Roland, Sismondi reached a hypothesis that later writers have not pursued. He doubted that the paladin was Charlemagne's nephew. Indeed, he suspected that Roland was much older than the emperor and that his real service to France had occurred in Charles Martel's time. Sismondi based his ideas partly on the fact that Einhard is the only historian who alludes to Roland and that even then he is mentioned as just one of several Frankish casualties at Roncevaux. "C'est contre les Sarrasins que tous les romanciers supposent que Roland signala sa vaillance," Sismondi points out. Implicit in his argument is that the Franks' major clashes with the Moors were on Frankish soil earlier in the eighth century and that Gascons, perhaps along with Asturians and Navarrese but not Saracens, waylaid them at Roncevaux when Roland was an old man. Thus, if Roland covered himself with glory at the Moors' expense, his feats would have to have been accomplished at an earlier date than is generally assumed, because it was much earlier that the Franks found themselves pitted against Saracens. Here Sismondi is referring to Charles Martel's defeating the Moors at the battle of Autun in 725 and the battle of Tours or Poitiers in 732. Though convinced that a Roland took part in the fighting at this time, he adds that "le héros des romanciers n'était plus jeune lors de la bataille de Roncevaux." As a lad Roland could have been present at the Franks' defeat at Narbonne in 720, and, five years later, he could have distinguished himself in the defense of Nîmes, Carcassonne, and Autun. He could have won laurels in 729 during the war in Aquitaine and in 732 at the battle of Poitiers. He may even have continued to measure swords with the Saracens after Charles Martel died. Hence, Sismondi believes that Einhard's Roland was someone else or that he was much older than later accounts surmised. Unable to demonstrate his thesis, Sismondi speculates: "Roland n'est . . . nommé par aucun historien, mais aucun capitaine de Charles Martel ne l'est mieux que lui. La ressemblance de nom de ce Charles et de Carloman avec Charlemagne aura plus tard causé l'erreur du peuple et des romanciers."[69] Sismondi's deductions are novel, to say the least. Whereas a number of nineteenth-century creative writers and essayists took liberties with Roland's career, none ventured to pursue this particular line of thought.

Sismondi's historical depiction of Roland is unusual in several other respects. Charlemagne's setting out on his Spanish expedition from Chasseneuil Palace is a rare detail. Coupling Navarre with Gascony in the attack on the rear guard is unusual also. In Prince Lucien Bonaparte's work, Navarrese shepherds, sorrowful and tender, mourned and buried the slain victims. Finally, Sismondi's contention that in the popular mind the *Pseudo-Turpin*

Chronicle could have had little importance in propagating the Roland legend is noteworthy. For Sismondi, popular lore made its way into the *Chronicle* instead of vice versa.

When Sismondi published *De la littérature du midi de l'Europe* in Paris in 1813, he was more inclined to admire Charlemagne than he would later be in the *Histoire des Français*. In 1813 he held that Charlemagne and his peers' deeds constituted "l'histoire . . . la plus éclatante du moyen âge," a story that had imprinted upon the centuries "un sentiment d'étonnement et d'admiration." The emperor himself was "un héros propre à la chevalerie, un point brillant au milieu des ténèbres."[70]

Even by the standards of his own day, Sismondi was hardly a student of Old French. Essentially he was a gifted dilettante. Little concerned with epic scholarship and as yet unaware of the substantial body of Roland material in other idioms, except for Ariosto, he declared that the emperor and his peers had inspired a collection of chivalric romances, all French. He viewed the Roland legend as basically a moment in the evolution of French literature. Like most of his French contemporaries, including Abel Villemain, he made little or no distinction between *épopée* and *roman de chevalerie* and generally preferred the latter term. The *Chanson de Roland* as we know it was unknown at the time, and since Sismondi did not know Louis de Musset's article, he naturally believed that the oldest *histoire merveilleuse* dealing with the ambush in Roncevaux Valley was the *Pseudo-Turpin Chronicle*, which he dated from about 1085. Turpin's name he believed to be an invention and insisted upon calling him a *romancier*.[71]

Sismondi was wrong in thinking that the *Chronicle* was written before the First Crusade, but his deductive process was sound. He believed that the *Chronicle*, imbued with the spirit of the age that produced it, displayed a kind of religious zeal markedly different from the one the First Crusade set in motion at the end of the eleventh century. "Ce qui frappe avant toute chose et dans cette chronique et dans tous les romans qui en sont nés, c'est l'enthousiasme des guerres saintes contre les infidèles. . . . Mais ce qui n'est guère moins remarquable, c'est une occupation des guerres d'Espagne, des Maures d'Espagne, de tout ce qui est espagnol, qui n'est point d'accord avec l'esprit de la première croisade. . . . La chronique de l'archevêque Turpin contient seulement l'histoire de la dernière expédition de Charlemagne en Espagne, à laquelle il est invité miraculeusement par l'évêque Saint-Jacques de Galice, ses victoires sur le roi maure Argoland, les combats singuliers du paladin Roland et de Ferragus, la mort de Roland à Roncevaux, et la vengeance de Charlemagne." Such a preoccupation, Sismondi held, is not in keeping with the spirit that launched the First Crusade in 1096. Gaillard, we recall, disagreed. Sismondi believed that the *Chronicle* dated rather from "l'époque où Alphonse VI, roi de Castille et de Léon, fit en 1085 la conquête de Tolède et de la Castille Nouvelle. Il fut suivi dans cette expédition glorieuse par un grand nombre de chevaliers français qui passèrent les Pyrénées pour combattre les infidèles auprès d'un grand roi." These people's motivation was not the same as that which animated the Crusaders a decade or so later. For Alfonso and his soldiers, "Il s'agissait de porter des secours à des frères, à des voisins, qui adoraient le même Dieu et qui vengeaient des injures communes, dont le romancier semblait renouveler le souvenir," whereas the First Crusade's purpose was to aid not men but God. While it is "toute pleine de miracles" and "animée par un ardent fanatisme," the *Chronicle* shows no interest in the East, no zeal for the Holy Sepulchre.[72] Thus Sismondi dated the *Chronicle* around 1085, before the First Crusade.

According to Sismondi, the *Pseudo-Turpin Chronicle* was not intended as art or entertainment but rather as history. Amazing as it may seem, the miraculous deeds it recounted conditioned the French public to accept them as truth. Later these deeds would be recorded in *Les Chroniques de St-Denis*. The events in Roland's life would later inspire epics that by then the public was prepared to accept as fact.[73]

The *Pseudo-Turpin Chronicle* is not such an epic, yet it contains the seeds of a direction French literatue would take during the next several centuries. Moreover, the *Chronicle* is not without interest in itself.

> Ce sont alternativement des faits incroyables de guerre et des miracles, de la superstition monacale pour le ciel, de la crédulité monacale pour les événements de la terre. On y voit déjà quelques enchantements; la redoutable épée de Roland, Durandal, ne peut porter de coups sans ouvrir de blessures; Ferragus est partout le corps enchanté et invulnérable; le terrible cor de Roland, avec lequel il sonne à Roncevaux pour demander des secours, est entendu jusqu'à Saint-Jean-Pied-de-Port, où Charlemagne était avec son armée; mais le traître Ganelon empêche le monarque de porter du secours à son neveu. Roland, perdant toute espérance, veut briser lui-même son épée, pour qu'elle ne tombe pas entre les mains des infidèles et ne se teigne jamais dans le sang des chrétiens; il frappe contre des arbres élevés, contre des rochers; mais rien ne résiste à la lame enchantée, conduite par un bras si puissant: les chênes sont renversés, les rochers volent en éclats, et Durandal est encore entière. Roland enfin l'enfonce presque jusqu'à la garde dans une pierre dure et, la tournant avec violence, il la brise entre ses mains. Alors il sonne encore du cor, non plus pour demander des secours, mais pour annoncer aux chrétiens sa dernière heure; et il le fait avec tant de force que ses veines éclatent et qu'il meurt inondé de son propre sang.[74]

The legend is "assez poétique," Sismondi concedes, "et indique une imagination brillante." But something is lacking that keeps the chronicle from being an epic or a novel of chivalry. "Pour que ce fût un roman de chevalerie, il y faudrait des femmes et de l'amour, et jamais il n'y est question ni des unes ni de l'autre." Again Sismondi is at odds with Gaillard, who regarded the *Pseudo-Turpin Chronicle* as the first of the French chivalric romances.

Sismondi had reservations about the *Pseudo-Turpin Chronicle* as epic or chivalric literature. Some of these can be ascribed to his religious background, but not all.[75] By the time he wrote the *Histoire des Français*, he was even doubtful about Roland's having been Charlemagne's nephew. Nevertheless, despite his doubts and prejudices, his discussion, with its nervous, rapid prose, is compelling. His look at Roland as a historical and literary figure is one of the more intelligent examinations of the paladin during the period that preceded the publication of the Oxford Manuscript of the *Chanson de Roland*.

3
The Romantics' Roland

Under the regimes that followed the French Revolution, a new generation of writers came upon the scene, bringing with it new outlooks and interests. Some called attention to localities, monuments, even weaponry popularly associated with Roland and his exploits. Others, spurred on by recent speculation and discoveries, urged locating, preserving, and publishing old manuscript epics, including those that involved the mighty champion. Proving that the *Chanson de Roland* was a legitimate epic, Homeric in structure and details, was a vital matter to at least one author. While during this period there was some interest in what Roland could have been like as a little boy, especially his attitude toward his parents and his precocious military gifts, once the hero reached manhood, the new literary generation saw him as the invulnerable bulwark of his faith and his monarch and the virtually incomparable exemplar of knighthood. Although nearly invincible in human terms, to this generation he was an eminently tragic personality, the victim of an inexorable fate that ultimately struck him down. Whether, betrayed and perhaps abandoned, he died on a battlefield defending lofty concepts or whether he managed to survive only to have his heart broken by a catastrophe awaiting him when he returned from the wars, destiny had willed that he was not to know enduring happiness in this life.

As Chateaubriand crossed Spain in 1807, returning to France from the Middle East, he thought about Roland. He remembered him notably in an ode begun at the time. Obviously Chateaubriand had been to see the Brèche de Roland: "Dans les monts que Roland brisa de sa vaillance, / Je contais à sa lance / L'orgueil de mes dangers, tentés pour des plaisirs."[1] The pleasures and exaggerated dangers are a personal detail. Just back from a daring adventure in Jerusalem, Chateaubriand had had a romantic rendezvous with Natalie de Noailles in Spain. In his wake would come a professional soldier. A year later Napoleon overran Spain, just as Charlemagne had in 778. Neither emperor had much lasting success.

In publishing the *Génie du christianisme* in 1802, Chateaubriand did not know the *Chanson de Roland*. Had the poem been available, it would have enhanced the book's general thesis urging the merits of Christianity as a source of artistic inspiration, especially in those chapters about the committed warrior of the Middle Ages. Even so, Chateaubriand mentions Roland several times in his work. Once Roland is invoked in connection with what the author, although he had never seen it, believes to have been his burial place. "Dans cette gorge des Pyrénées," he writes, "voilà l'hôpital de Roncevaux, que Charlemagne bâtit à l'endroit même où la fleur des chevaliers, Roland, termina ses hauts faits: un asile de paix et de secours marque dignement le tombeau du preux qui défendit l'orphelin et mourut pour sa patrie." Chateaubriand is referring, of course, to the chapel or hospice that eighteenth- and nineteenth-century visitors were shown and which the emperor was thought to have established. Subsequent excavations do not support the notion that the structure could have dated from such a remote era.[2]

That Chateaubriand knew the Roland tradition becomes even clearer when the author observes much later in the *Analyse raisonnée de l'histoire de France* that Charlemagne "avait dans ses armées des héros à la manière de Roland" and that "les romanciers du douzième siècle . . . ont pris Charlemagne [et] Roland . . . pour leurs héros." He was aware that even in the Middle Ages Roland had been an important literary figure. He alludes several times to the *Pseudo-Turpin Chronicle*, which he calls a *roman*. Surprisingly, he does not discuss Roland in the *Analyse raisonnée*, even though he mentions the disaster at Roncevaux, remarking that Charlemagne "refoule les Sarrasins en Espagne. La défaite de son arrière-garde à Roncevaux engendre pour lui une gloire romanesque qui marche de pair avec sa gloire historique."[3]

The July Revolution ended Chateaubriand's political career, but from this period dates some of his most introspective historical writing. The *Etudes historiques*, published in 1831, studies France from Julius Caesar to the barbarian invasions. In the sixth of these studies the author points out that "les nations entières, dans leur âge héroïque, sont poètes," thereby suggesting his concept of the origin of epic literature. The study treats the Huns, the Goths, the Gauls, the Franks, and the Normans. The author cites Augustin Thierry's *Histoire de la conquête de l'Angleterre* and quotes the famous lines from Wace's *Roman de Rou*: "Taillefer, qui mult bien chantout, / Sor un cheval qui tost alout, / Devant le duc alout chantant / De Karlemaigne e de Rollant / E d'Oliver e des vassals / Qui morurent en Rencevals." Chateaubriand comments that the Normans' war songs culminated eventually in the *Chanson de Roland*, which may imply his belief that the song already existed in some inchoate form. "Ces rhythmes militaires," he observes, "se viennent terminer à la *Chanson de Roland*, qui fut comme le dernier chant de l'Europe barbare." Chateaubriand was not sure of the *Chanson de Roland*'s length or its nature, alluding to it as "cette ballade héroïque."[4] If he knew the *Bibliothèque universelle*'s reconstruction, he did not deem it worth serious consideration.

Suspecting that the original song must exist somewhere, Chateaubriand wondered whether researchers might not be able to locate it in the library of Kings Charles V, VI, and VII. A royal library used to be housed in the Abbaye de St-Denis, and this is probably what Chateaubriand had in mind. As it happens, *Les Grandes Chroniques de France*, also known as *Les Chroniques de St-Denis*, do indeed contain an Old French Roland narrative.[5] Chateaubriand's readers were naturally aware that the *Chanson de Roland* is said to have been sung at the battle of Hastings. Chateaubriand reminds them that it was also sung at the battle of Poitiers in 1356. Since Michelet would later claim the same thing, it is worth noting that Chateaubriand insists that Charlemagne was surprisingly meticulous, both at his court and in his army, about observing democratic procedures.

To accompany his translation of Milton's *Paradise Lost*, Chateaubriand published an *Essai sur la littérature anglaise* in 1836. He necessarily had to discuss William the Conqueror's invasion, and with almost no changes, he lifted his material from the *Etudes historiques*. Again he quoted Wace's *Roman de Rou*. This time, but without explanation, he added that Geoffroy Gaimar knew more about Taillefer than the *Roman de Rou*'s author had known. The hazy allusion is to the *Estoire des Engleis*, an Anglo-Norman chronicle written around 1140. Less than a year after the *Essai sur la littérature anglaise*, Francisque Michel published the Oxford Manuscript of the *Chanson de Roland*. For later editions of his works, however, Chateaubriand did not retouch his previous utterances in the light of the new material.

When France invaded Spain in 1823, Victor Hugo assured French soldiers that as they crossed the mountains Roland was looking down approvingly from heaven. Chateaubriand was the French minister of foreign affairs at the time of the invasion, and he liked to take credit for it. His two nephews participated. Chateaubriand's memoirs mention "ces ducs et ces comtes de la cour de Charlemagne, qui, après avoir combattu contre les Sarrasins, fondaient des couvents."[6] Perhaps the author knew that Roland is said to have endowed religious establishments.

Sainte-Beuve, a contemporary who disliked Chateaubriand, compared him to Roland. In his *Chateaubriand et son groupe littéraire* the critic complained that Chateaubriand's prose, unlike Rousseau's, was devoid of sustained developments and that it was characterized instead by spasmodic, convulsive progressions. This did not mean that the author's style was any less spectacular. On the contrary, "sa plume est comme l'épée de Roland: il sait qu'à chaque coup il en fera jaillir des éclairs." Sainte-Beuve had a certain grudging admiration for Chateaubriand the political journalist and statesman. In his *Notes diverses sur Chateaubriand*, published with *Chateaubriand et son groupe littéraire*, he again compared Chateaubriand to Roland. Chateaubriand, he conceded, was a formidable opponent. "C'était un magnifique duelliste de plume, un paladin que tentaient les hasards de la lice; il croyait, comme Roland à Roncevaux, qu'il suffirait seul, au besoin, à pourfendre toute l'armée des infidèles et qu'il n'en serait jamais réduit à sonner du cor d'ivoire pour appeler le vieux Charlemagne à son secours." This is how, for example, Chateaubriand championed the freedom of the press.[7] Although he never wrote about it directly, Sainte-Beuve seems to have been familiar with the *Chanson de Roland*.

Sainte-Beuve mentioned Roland before the Oxford Manuscript's publication, however, in the *Revue des Deux Mondes* on 1 June 1832, when reviewing Paulin Paris's edition of the *Roman de Berte aux grans piés*. Berthe aux Grands Pieds married Pepin and thus became Charlemagne's mother as well as the mother of Charlemagne's sister, also named Berthe in most accounts. "D'elle naquit la femme de Milon d'Ayglant, mère du brave Roland," notes the critic toward the end of his review, which later appeared as one of the first *Lundis*.[8]

Sainte-Beuve probably suspected that he was not at his best when talking about medieval literature. Still, at the University of Liège in 1848 and 1849 he gave a course that he called the Cours d'Ancienne Littérature. Twenty-four lessons were devoted to the Middle Ages, but there were strange gaps. In general, epic literature was neglected, and the *Chanson de Roland*, published more than a decade earlier, was not discussed. From 1858 to 1861 the critic was once more a literature professor, this time at the Ecole Normale. In one of his classes there, he suggested that a comparison might be made between Roland and Olivier's duel in *Girart de Vienne* and Victor Hugo's "Le Mariage de Roland." Thus, while he was unaware of some of its intricacies, Sainte-Beuve proved that he at least had not forgotten the Roland legend.[9]

Alfred de Vigny's poem "Le Cor," which appeared in *Poèmes antiques et modernes* in 1826, was written in December 1824 at Orthez or Pau. The poet, then an army captain, had been stationed on the Spanish border in and near the Pyrenees Mountains since 1823. He had expected to be sent into Spain with the French army that delivered King Ferdinand VII from his constitutionalist captors. To French conservatives the invasion had become a sacramental venture, a crusade in which devout French monarchists would crush the infidel Spanish parliament—Roland and the Moors, in short. The invading French, led by a French prince, were known as the Hundred Thousand Sons of St. Louis. It was in this context and from this viewpoint that Vigny composed his poem. On 1 September 1824 he wrote a friend that he was going to visit the Cirque de Gavarnie and the Brèche de Roland. Next day he examined the sites.[10]

The poet's interest in Roland was not new. In Rouen in 1821 he had written a drama called *Roland*, based on Ariosto. Ill one day eleven years later, he reread and burned it. By this time, the only thing its author still liked about it was a line referring to Jesus, "Fils exilé du ciel, tu souffris au désert." Quoted in the *Journal d'un poète*, this line is almost all that remains of *Roland*. Late in 1823 Vigny considered rewriting it. This time his hero would not have been Ariosto's madman but the actual legendary or historical character. "C'est le Roland de l'histoire qu'il veut mettre en scène," a friend recorded. The new play would have had three acts, but only some notes and a few lines of verse have survived.[11]

The play did not materialize, but a poem, "Le Cor," did. However, *Roland* and "Le Cor" were not the only manifestations of the poet's interest in the Roland theme. On 12 July 1851 he took notes for a poem he planned to call "Le Miroir de Roland." One of the lines the poet may have intended to use was "Souvent le front est doux et le coeur est sauvage," perhaps a résumé of how the poet envisaged his hero.[12] A few years before "Le Cor," Vigny had written "La Neige." Like "Le Cor," it was a *conte en vers*. It narrated the story of Charlemagne's daughter Emma and her lover Einhard. As he would do with the Roland legend, the poet took liberties here with the traditional plot elements. Emma is the "blanche Emma, princesse de la Gaule," but her suitor is not her father's councilor or historian but a mere page, which no doubt makes him a more romantic character.

Vigny's sources are not clear. Perhaps he consulted Jean Dusaulx's *Voyage à Barèges*, dating from 1796.[13] Gaillard's *Histoire de Charlemagne* has also been proposed. There may be no connection, but an Abbé Gaillard was once the poet's tutor. Moreover, Vigny could have used the *Bibliothèque universelle*. Undoubtedly he knew Marchangy's *La Gaule poétique*, and probably he was familiar with the Roland songs of the Revolutionary and Napoleonic eras as well. Since Archbishop Turpin in the poem is with Charlemagne when the battle of Roncevaux takes place and hence does not get killed, the poet may have looked at the *Pseudo-Turpin Chronicle* also. Another likely source is a folk song called "Le Cor des bois," for which the German composer Friedrich Silcher (1789-1860) wrote a modern setting in 1816. The song begins with the lines, "Au fond du bois / J'aime la voix / Du cor qui retentit, / Du cor qui retentit." The last stanzas, more serious and sadder than the others, also seem to have overtones in "Le Cor."

> Le son du cor
> Exprime encor
> La plainte et les regrets,
> La plainte et les regrets,
>
> Quand son soupir
> Fait retentir
> L'écho de nos forêts,
> L'écho de nos forêts.[14]

Vigny had personally viewed the supposed site where the Franks' rear guard was wiped out. Possibly an additional visual source was Achille Michallon's watercolor, *La Mort de Roland*, in which the paladin is shown dying in Olivier's arms, the victim of a rock that was cast down a mountain slope. Vigny could have seen the painting at the Paris Salon of 1819, where it attracted a great deal of attention. Whatever his written, visual, and oral sources, the poet's own imagination, his own sensitivity, contributed as much as anything else to the poem's elaboration.

Vigny's version of the Roncevaux disaster is written in verse that is as sad as it is exquisite and lofty. Of the barren wasteland where the ambush occurred, Jules Vodoz declared that "en présence de ce spectacle imposant. . . , le souvenir de Roland inspire au poète des vers incomparablement beaux: beaux par la pureté de son, beaux aussi par l'accent de mélancolie qui s'en dégage. . . . La grandeur épique de Roland y est rendu d'une façon remarquable."[15] Vodoz, writing nearly a century after the poem's composition, was correct. "Le Cor" remains one of the best and most touching works Vigny ever created. It is written in *rime suivie* alexandrines, and words like *preux* and the archaic verb *ouïr* give it, linguistically at least, a certain medieval character.

In the first of the poem's four divisions, the writer evokes the dismal sound of a horn reverberating in the stark mountain passes and wonders whether the ghosts of the knights slain at Roncevaux ever return: "Roncevaux! Roncevaux! dans ta sombre vallée / L'ombre du grand Roland n'est donc pas consolée!"

When the poem's second movement begins, the battle of Roncevaux has already taken place, and almost all of the French participants have been slaughtered: "Tous les preux étaient morts, mais aucun n'avait fui." Olivier is dead, but though his end is near, Roland is still alive. One of the Moors taunts him and calls on him to surrender, seeing that he is going to die anyway. Disdainfully, Roland refuses, and someone detaches a huge rock and rolls it down a mountain slope toward him. With this, the hero succumbs at last.

The third and longest segment of the poem depicts Charlemagne riding back into France with Turpin beside him, followed by the main corps of the French army. The men are confident. After all, Roland is in command of the rear guard: "Roland gardait les monts; tous passaient sans effroi." Then suddenly the horn is heard. For a time the emperor rides on, pensive and disturbed. The horn, insistent, is heard again. Like his master, Turpin hears it but does not know what it is. Vigny at this juncture could not be relying upon the *Pseudo-Turpin Chronicle*, in which the archbishop hears no horn and only learns about the disaster in a vision. Vigny's Charlemagne senses trouble: "Il craint la trahison, et, tandis qu'il y songe, / Le Cor éclate et meurt, renaît et se prolonge." Now he is certain that there has been a catastrophe, and he exclaims: "Malheur! c'est mon neveu! malheur! car, si Roland / Appelle à son secours, ce doit être en mourant. / Arrière! chevaliers, repassons la montagne! / Tremble encor sous nos pieds, sol trompeur de l'Espagne!"

In the poem's final and shortest section, Charlemagne and his men reach the battlefield and inspect the carnage. On the horizon can be seen the fleeing Moors' banner. The emperor and Turpin see Olivier and Roland's bodies lying at the bottom of a stream, crushed by a rock. "Le plus fort dans sa main élève un Cor d'ivoire, / Son âme en s'exhalant nous appela deux fois," remarks Turpin. The poet concludes, eerily, with the melancholy exclamation: "Dieu! que le son du Cor est triste au fond des bois!"

In "Le Cor" Vigny is at his best. As so often happens in nineteenth-century treatments of the Roland legend, Roland is not struck down, ultimately, by a sword thrust, nor does he die of weariness when the battle is over. He is crushed, rather, by stone. In Vigny's retelling of the story, however, the hero is not pulverized beneath an indiscriminate torrent of rocks aimed at the entire rear guard. Instead, he is killed when a rock is hurled at him specifically for having scorned the idea of surrendering to a Moor. "Si je me rends, / Africain, ce sera lorsque les Pyrénées / Sur l'onde avec leurs corps rouleront entraînées," he tells his tormentor. Indeed, a rock is dislodged and comes careening down the mountainside, taking his life. Even so, he dies without surrendering.

When Charlemagne becomes disturbed at the horn's insistence, it is Archbishop Turpin who tries to persuade him that Roland's dying call must be something else. In other versions, usually Ganelon does this. "Ce sont des pasteurs / Rappelant les troupeaux épars sur les hauteurs," Turpin suggests, but he has other explanations as well. For a churchman, spirits are unusually important in his thinking, and he is even a little superstitious. Pointing out that "on voit dans le ciel des nuages de feu," he notes that "deux éclairs ont relui, puis deux autres encor." He attributes the phenomenon to "des âmes / Qui passent dans les airs sur ces vapeurs de flamme." It could also be "la voix étouffée / Du nain vert Obéron qui parle avec sa fée." Finally Charlemagne decides for himself that something is amiss and gives the command to turn back. When the French return to the ambush site, Olivier and Roland have breathed their last. Turpin's credulous but poetic hunch may have been right. Perhaps the sparks he saw in the sky earlier were the dead men's souls taking flight.

"Le Cor" is a powerful poem. Eventually Ange Flégier, a noted composer of the late nineteenth century, set it to music. Arranged for a bass voice, it is intense and dramatic and has become the composer's best-known song. In time Emanuel Geibel translated the poem into German, putting it with his *Übersetzungen französischer Lyrik*.

Decades after Vigny wrote "Le Cor," Jules Laforgue seemed to have recalled it in two poems that came out posthumously in *Derniers vers* (1890). Though neither is a Roland poem, both "L'Hiver qui vient" and "Le Mystère des trois cors" show an interest in horns reminiscent of the earlier work. "L'Hiver qui vient" is an evocative piece suggesting the modifications in an individual's life brought on by the change of seasons. The dreary approach of winter is paralleled by the distant sound of horns in a forest inundated with

dead leaves. "Les cors, les cors, les cors mélancoliques, mélancoliques." In "Le Mystère des trois cors" each horn is given human attributes. Laforgue remembers that in his predecessor's poem the instrument was "reborn," that eventually it "burst" and "died." In Laforgue's work, "Un cor dans la plaine / Souffle à perdre haleine" One horn seems to be Roland's. So vigorously had the *Chanson de Roland*'s hero blown his horn that his temples had ripped open. Similarly, Laforgue's personified horn seems as though it has veins in its forehead that are on the point of splitting as the instrument is blown. "Celui de la plaine / Sent gonfler ses veines, / Ses veines du front," and a few stanzas later Roncevaux is mentioned. At the end of the poem, all three horns are found "dead." If "Le Mystère des trois cors" echoes "Le Cor," Laforgue has also read and recalled the *Chanson de Roland*, which contains the detail about blood vessels in the paladin's head bursting.

Laforgue wrote his poems at the German imperial court, where he held an appointment in the dowager empress's household. Charles Fournel, who had held a similar position at the Prussian court in the 1840s and 1850s, wrote his "Romance de Roncevaux" in Berlin also.

When he was fifteen, Jules Barbey d'Aurevilly wrote an elegy called "Aux héros de Thermopyles" (1825), encouraging the Greeks in their struggle for independence from Turkey. He urged the Christian Greeks to strike down the Mohammedan Turks: "que ta vaillance / Abatte les fiers Musulmans," he wrote, addressing himself to the Greek nation collectively. Such a stand prepared him to view the Roland legend, in which Christian is pitted against Saracen, with particular feeling.

Two Barbey d'Aurevilly works contain probable allusions to "Le Cor." One is *Un Prêtre marié* (1864). Like many an Aurevillian hero, Néel de Néhou belongs to the old aristocracy, which has noble traditions. At one point Sombreval and his daughter, whom Néel loves, are in a cemetery and a mob is threatening to kill them when they emerge. Néel, "chevaleresque et généreux comme il était," comes to their rescue. The idea that harm could come to the girl stirs his blood. "Cette idée . . . éleva en lui comme le cri de l'amour frappé, qui l'appelait, qui lui sonnait la fanfare suprême du cor de Roland à Roncevaux!" As heroic as Roland but more successful, Néel manages to rescue the embattled father and daughter.[16]

Even earlier Barbey had referred to the Roland legend in his diary. On 21 September 1836 he described having asked his brother Léon, who in a few days was leaving for a seminary, to postpone his departure long enough for the two of them to visit. Perhaps letters never reached their destination, but, receiving no answer, Barbey concluded that none had been sent. He compared the pleas he had addressed to his brother with Roland's desperate call for help at Roncevaux. Not only our brothers but most of those whom we love sooner or

later turn a deaf ear when we want or need them, he complained. "Je l'ai prié à plusieurs reprises et il ne m'a pas même répondu. Je suis resté seul et *inentendu* comme Roland à Roncevaux. . . . Nous avons tous un Roncevaux dans notre vie, tôt ou tard. Nous appelons les absents, nous sonnons de notre cor d'ivoire et en vain! Ce cor qu'ils connaissaient si bien et qui avait pour eux . . . de si poignants appels, cette voix amie qu'ils proclamaient irrésistible et qui les eût ramenés du bout du monde, ils l'entendent qui demande, qui crie, qui meurt d'appeler, et ils ne viennent pas! Nous teignons l'ivoire de notre cor inutile de la pourpre du sang de notre coeur déchiré. Ce sang dont nous comptons les gouttes, ils ignorent que ce sont eux qui le font couler. Comme Roland, nous ne sonnons plus bientôt à ces vides échos qui nous raillent, nous nous préparons à mourir seuls; comme Roland, la rage d'être abandonnés ne nous fait pas fendre les rocs de nos épées, mais nous devenons rocs nous-mêmes en attendant que la mort nous ait broyés, sans nous rendre plus insensibles ni plus froids!"[17] Like Vigny, Barbey suggests that Roland died pulvérized. With Barbey it is no more than a suggestion, however.

Given the circumstances, Barbey's comparing himself with Roland is an exaggeration, of course. In any event, the author had misinterpreted Roland's horn blast getting no response, although Michelet much later would take the same position. The people Roland was trying to summon were by no means indifferent to his plight. Because of his pride, he simply waited too late to blow his horn. Once Charlemagne realized that Roland must be in trouble, he and his men reacted quickly enough.

Barbey's view of Roland provides an original explanation for the hero's slashing at the rocks with his sword. Exasperated that no one answered his call, he slammed his sword against the mountainside. Accounting for the Brèche de Roland's creation in this manner is as unique as Heine's suggestion that the doomed knight had been trying to open up an escape route for him and his men. Regarding Barbey and his brother, relations were never the same. Referring to Léon twenty years later, Jules told a friend that "pour lui depuis longtemps mon cor de Roland ne sonne plus."[18]

Barbey retained his interest in Roland. One of his best tales in *Les Diaboliques* (1874), "Le Bonheur dans le crime," alludes to the *Chanson de Roland*. On leaving the army, a certain M. Stassin has opened a *salle d'armes*. Without sons, this skilled fencing master transmits his art to his only daughter, who was given the unlikely name Hauteclaire. Stassin was told by the baby's godfather that any child of his "ne doit se nommer que comme l'épée d'un preux." Thus Olivier's sword provides the little girl a name.[19] Because it contained the name Claire, it must have seemed a better choice than Durandal.

One of the nineteenth century's best poems based on the Roland legend was written by a poet who today is virtually unknown. He was born and reared in the Pyrenees Mountains near the Arise River. Nurtured in the region's lore and traditions, he naturally referred to a local hero as a Roland.[20] A private tutor, Protestant minister, and poet, Napoléon Peyrat (1809-81), or Napol le Pyrénéen, as he liked to call himself, was involved in the movement to revive Provençal as a literary idiom. Now, if he is remembered at all, it is for his *Histoire des pasteurs du désert* (1842), a study of French Protestantism from the revocation of the Edict of Nantes to the Revolution of 1789.

Peyrat arrived in Paris in 1831. There, through Béranger, he met various literary celebrities, including Lamartine, Hugo, Lamennais, and Sainte-Beuve. Politically active, he worked with Lamennais to help liberal candidates in the 1837 Chambre des Députés elections. Much later, Sainte-Beuve, who liked Peyrat's *vers naturels*, half promised to write an article "embrassant la totalité de votre oeuvre" but seems never to have done it. Napoléon Peyrat died unnoticed in 1881. To Anatole France, he was "le plus ignoré des poétes de 1830," and that is still true.[21] A fine poet, he deserves attention.

His "Roland" had a complex publication history. In 1833, under the author's pen name, the poem came out in Stéphane Ajasson de Grandsagne's collective volume, *Anthologie des poètes français vivants*. In 1862 it appeared in another collection, Eugène Crépet's *Les Poètes français*, with an introduction by Charles Asselineau. Peyrat printed a considerably revised version the following year in a work of his own, *L'Arise, romancéro religieux, héroïque, et pastoral*. Although "Roland" underwent several revisions, the *Chanson de Roland* left no mark on any of its various states. In all versions, for instance, Archbishop Turpin accompanied Charlemagne and did not die with Roland, as he did in the epic.

The reworked "Roland" in *L'Arise*'s Deuxième Livre (1863) is a good basic text. Here the author describes his work as a *ballade* and also as a *hymne*. Some years later Anatole France would call it "une ode dans une épître." It was dedicated to Prosper Timbal, a prominent Toulouse attorney. The poem is composed of twenty-three regular alexandrine and octosyllabic stanzas, each having six lines with an *a a b c c b* rhyme scheme. In the first stanza the poet bids his verse to wing its way to Toulouse and there greet Timbal as he awakens. Except for the last four stanzas, the remainder of the poem is a narrative in which the author speaks to his friend directly. The poem is filled with allusions to towns, creeks, rivers, and mountains that give the poem regional coloration. Timbal is invited to gaze at the mountains, which resemble a colossal wall from the era of the giants. Alluding to the Brèche de Roland, the poet declares that Roland, with his sword, gave the mountains their serrated outline: "Roland le paladin / Qui dentela ces monts, et de ce vaste Eden / Ebrécha les grandes murailles, / Qui sculpta Canigou, Marboré, Moradal, / Faisant, en longs éclairs, tournoyer Durandal / Dans ses gigantesques batailles!"

Establishing the antecedents of his plot, the poet tells his correspondent that, having killed Roderick, the last king of the Visigoths, the Spanish Moors have extended their control to the Pyrenees Mountains. One day, with his leopards, one of the emirs is tracking an old bear and climbs a mountain from which he can see Toulouse. Dazzled, he decides to wrest the wondrous land from its emperor, Charlemagne. With his hordes he crosses into France and is at first victorious. Highly cultivated, Peyrat's Moors are musical, cosmopolitan, and wealthy. "Ces brillants Sarrasins," the poet calls them. In France they set about wooing the local damsels, whom they serenade: "Ils chantaient sur des luths d'ébène aux socles d'or, / Célébraient nos beautés qui de leur minador / Berçaient leur coeur aux sérénades." Love, these songs assure them, will make the French women renounce their faith. Nevertheless, the women decline to take the risk, knowing that a Moslem woman must share her man with a hundred others. Resisting, they are finally abducted and spirited away.

Charlemagne learns what has been happening and explodes in anger. Turpin goads him to action, assuring him that God will give him victory over the philandering miscreants. Peyrat has provided him with a most unusual reason for venturing into Spain. With Roland and Renaud de Montauban, a holdover from Ariosto, Charlemagne sets out with a huge army to pursue the amorous Moors and their fair booty. The truculent archbishop goes along too, blessing "l'ost franc devant Rocamadour." Conspicuously missing is Olivier. Deciding to give battle, the emir chooses his terrain with care, entrenching his armies in the mountains and leaving the plains to the French. Turpin, looking at the mountains, is not disconcerted, nor are his companions. The battle lasts three days. Roland's feats are heroic, and so are the author's images: "C'est alors que Roland / Fit bondir son cheval, tel qu'un griffon volant, / De Gèdre aux cimes remuées, / Jusqu'au Marboré sombre, et de sa Durandal / Sculpta son haut cylindre aigu, pyramidal." Thrashing about with his sword as he mauls his adversaries, Roland has created the famous mountain breach. His making his horse leap upward, "tel qu'un griffon volant," into the tortuous crags recalls, in addition to Ariosto, an allusion in Faget de Baure's description of the Brèche de Roland in the *Essais historiques*. Faget de Baure had asserted that the mountain residents all knew Roland's name and enjoyed pointing out to the visitor the sites associated with the hero and his exploits. One mountaineer would show a visitor the Brèche de Roland, "l'autre vous indique l'endroit où l'hypogriffe s'arrêta après avoir franchi d'un saut un espace de quatorze lieues, et vous reconnaissez l'empreinte de de ses pieds ferrés."[22] Like Faget de Baure, Peyrat was a native and was writing from firsthand knowledge. Clearly, though, a smattering of Italian literary detail had crept into local legend or vice versa.

Charlemagne wins the three-day battle, but the emir believes that he himself will ultimately be the victor. After all, the French emperor is still encircled in the valleys beneath the mountains. "Il est mon prisonnier! Le cirque colossal / Sera sa colossale tombe!" the emir exults. Seated high on the lofty mountain peaks as though on a throne, he is protected by his guards and soldiers—the storms, glaciers, avalanches, and rushing streams. Moreover, he is protected by the winter. Peyrat's is the only version of the Roland legend suggesting that the Roncevaux disaster took place in the wintertime. But the emir will not need nature's warriors.

Roland's tragedy is narrated in a single stanza. The poet tells his readers that "Loup, fils de Gaïfer, marche au fils de Pépin." Lupus, the disgruntled duke of Gascony, is marching against Charlemagne, avenging his father's grievances against an old opponent's successor. He is also avenging the emir. What occurs next can be disorienting to readers familiar with the *Chanson de Roland:* "Charles, ses douze pairs, l'archevêque Turpin, / Roulent sur leur camp qui s'effare. / Roland meurt, et le Franc fugitif frissonna / Lorsque entre les deux mers, de mont en mont, sonna / Le tonnerre de la fanfare." Peyrat may mean here that, as the emir watches, Lupus wipes out the rear guard while tracking the emperor and the main army, his real goal. Charlemagne, hearing his nephew's call, turns back and rushes into the wrongdoers' camp, exterminating them. Terrified, the duke escapes into the mountains but knows that he will be hunted down and punished. Probably, though, Charlemagne has not left yet; probably no detachment is lingering behind to cover a main army's withdrawal. If such is the case, then Charlemagne, Roland, Turpin, and all the others were in Roncevaux Valley, facing the enemy together. Roland, however, is the only main character who gets killed. Whatever the author's intent, there is no doubt that in one place the emperor descends upon Lupus's forces and routs them. The "Franc fugitif," then, is the disobedient vassal who, in his flight, shudders when he hears the victorious emperor's exultant musical celebration, perhaps a Te Deum, reverberating in the mountains. Faget de Baure tells us that Charlemagne had him kidnapped and hanged.[23] Curiously, the moment Lupus enters the picture the emir vanishes. Nor are we sure that Roland ever blows his horn. Of course, if he is fighting at his uncle's side, there is no reason for him to do so. This highly ambiguous stanza suggests a most unusual version of the events in Roncevaux Valley.

The next two stanzas are a lament on Roland's death. More capably than his predecessors, the poet is doing what Marchangy and Arlincourt did. Although other treatments insist that Roland's remains, along with his horn and sword, were taken elsewhere, this one assures us that Roland, his horn, and his sword are still where the hero was struck down. Supernatural, Romantic touches abound: centuries later, Roland's horse can still be seen and heard, searching for his dead master. The forlorn Aude haunts the spot also, mourning beside her lover's grave every night, only to vanish at dawn. Whether as a mortal or a ghost, Aude does not appear at Roncevaux in any other nineteenth-century French version of the legend except for Mermet's opera *Roland à Roncevaux*. In Peyrat's words,

> Gloire à Roland vaincu! Gavarni garde encor
> Tes os, ô paladin, ton épée et ton cor,
> Tes brèches, tes tours triomphales!
> La nuit, le pâtre entend ton cheval éploré,
> Qui boit à la cascade et paît au Marboré,
> Et t'appelle dans les rafales!
>
> Dans tes songes de guerre, et de gloire et d'amour,
> Dors, paladin fidèle! Au dernier rai du jour
> Chaque soir, doux fantôme pâle,
> Ta jeune amante, Auda, vers ta tombe descend
> Et gémit jusqu'à l'heure où le matin naissant
> Teint les monts d'un reflet d'opale!

While Aude plays no essential role in this poem and is not mentioned until near the end, her spectral appearances on the battlefield long after her fiancé's death contribute to the poem's emotional impact, deepening its pathos.

The poem's last two stanzas proclaim the author's patriotism and state his political views, which not all historians would endorse. In "La Guerre d'Espagne" Victor Hugo had hailed the French armies sent into Spain to deliver Ferdinand VII from his unruly Cortes. Like Hugo, Peyrat was certain that Roland was watching as modern French soldiers rode into Spain. Unlike Hugo, he recalls in "Roland" not those Frenchmen who in 1823 invaded Spain to rescue a highhanded king but rather those who in 1808 overran it to place Napoleon's brother Joseph on the throne and, as the poet saw it, to sow freedom in their wake. Such a cavalier view of history must be attributed to the poet's enthusiasm, not to his common sense. It had never been the habit of French soldiers marching or riding into Spain to bestow freedom. Apart from the material gains involved, Charlemagne had gone there to impose his religion upon the inhabitants just as, centuries later, Napoleon stormed in to make one of his brothers king, regardless of the Spainards' wishes. Still, Peyrat's idea was tenacious. Years later, Jean Richepin, who also wrote about Roland, would make the same curious remark, asserting that Napoleon "Sur le monde ébloui semait les *Droits de l'homme*."[24] In deploying such a personal concept of history, Peyrat and Richepin were in good company. Using much the same line of reasoning, Stendhal liked to think that the invading French armies aroused nationalism and spawned a desire for independence when they descended upon Italy in 1796.

Concluding his poem, Peyrat compares Napoleon with Charlemagne. Addressing Roland's memory, he asks:

> Nos pères, du soleil et du canon bronzés,
> Sont morts aussi, mordant leurs vieux sabres brisés
>   Sur toutes ces cimes d'Espagne!
> O Roland, tu les vis lorsqu'ils tombaient ainsi!
> Réponds, était-il grand notre empereur aussi
>   Comme ton oncle Charlemagne?
>
> Ah! si vers l'Ebre un jour passaient vers Roncevaux
> Nos soldats, nos canons, nos tambours, nos chevaux
>   Et nos chants tonnant dans l'espace,
> Dresse-toi dans ta tombe et regarde, ô Lion!
> C'est plus que Charlemagne et que Napoléon,
>   Car c'est la Liberté qui passe!

Of the other two versions of "Roland," the more important is the "Roland" that appeared in *Les Pyrénées, romancéro,* in 1877. The other appeared in a poetry collection published by Alphonse Lemerre in 1883, two years after the author's death. With only minor changes, this version is a reprint of the earliest known one, the "Roland" published in the anthology of living poets in 1833. Fundamentally the 1833, 1863, and 1883 versions are the same: all use the six-line stanza form, the same metrical plan, and the same rhyme scheme. Variants, however, are numerous. The 1877 version, a bit more enthusiastic and vivacious than the one just examined, seems the oldest of the three, but this is a mere guess. With its thirty-three stanzas, it is the longest as well. Both the 1863 and the 1883 version appear to be condensations of the poem as published in 1877.

Several differences between the three texts might be noted. The 1863 and 1877 versions are dedicated to Prosper Timbal. The 1883 poem has no dedication, though the poet is addressing a close friend. In the 1863 and 1877 poems, the Moors have killed King Roderick at Jerez, while in the 1883 poem one is simply told that the Goths, or Visigoths, have been defeated there. Nor is it certain that the emir who decides to take Toulouse in the 1863 and 1883 poems is the one pitted against the Franks in the 1877 poem, in which he is called Emir El-Mouménim, not mentioned in the other two poems. In the 1863 "Roland" the contest between Franks and Moors lasts three days. In the 1883 version it goes on for a month, and in the 1877 version it stretches out over a hundred days. Another feature of the 1883 version is that the Moors are less patient when courting their French sweethearts, brutalizing them when rejected. By 1883 Aude has disappeared from the poem.

On learning about the Moors' incursion into France, Turpin, concerned about the invaders' drunkenness and their conduct with women, exhorts his imperial master to drive the wanton interlopers out. He does so in measured tones in the 1863 and 1877 poems but chooses a somewhat comic phrase in the 1883 one: "Sire, disait Turpin, ne souffrez pas ainsi / Qu'un Africain maudit vienne croquer ici / A votre barbe vos pucelles." By 1883 Turpin has ceased to be disturbed by the Moors' drinking. A more significant variant occurs in the 1877 poem: Charlemagne not only observes what is going on but actively directs operations against the intruders. The stanza in which this variant occurs is a particularly good one, especially the lines stressing the exotic Moors' contrast with the French knights: "Charles, du Mont Nora, Moussa, du Salao, / Commandaient la bataille immense, et de là-haut / Voyaient d'Elna à Fontarabie / S'entre-choquer leurs camps, auriflors, olifants, / Emirs contre barons, chevaux contre éléphants, / La France contre l'Arabie."

Roland battled furiously. In almost identical stanzas, the 1877 and 1883 poems tell the reader how certain he was that he would win out: "Et Roland rugissait, et des vautours géants, / Des troupeaux d'aigles bruns volaient en rond béants, / Faisant claquer leurs becs sonores, / Et Roland leur disait: 'Mes petits oiselets, / Un moment, vous allez avoir bons osselets / Et belles carcasses de Maures.'" While despatching Moors, Roland paid due attention to his cleanliness. In the 1877 poem, "On combattit cent jours: Roland, de mont en mont, / Jetait leurs corps à l'aigle et leur âme au démon, / Qui hurle et glapit par saccades. / Les âmes chargeaient l'air comme un nuage noir, / Et Roland et Renaud, tout sanglants, chaque soir / S'allaient laver dans les cascades." By 1883 Roland was bathing alone: "Et notre bon Roland, en riant, chaque soir, / S'allait laver dans les cascades."

Despite his confidence, Roland is finally killed. Peyrat's heartiest tribute to his hero in the 1877 version of the poem occurs in stanzas 30 and 31, in which, perhaps remembering Marchangy and Arlincourt, the poet introduces an abbreviated dirge. Referring to landmarks at the site where Roland fell, the poet exclaims:

> Gloire à Roland vaincu! Ton nom est immortel!
> Le cirque est ton cercueil! Le Cône est ton autel!
>   L'isthme immense ton mausolée!
> Deux golfes orageux, Narbonne et Cordouan,
> Et l'épopée, au bord de ton double océan,
>   Lyre, olifant, strophe étoilée,
>
> Célèbrent ton trépas, glorieux paladin!

The final stanza of the 1883 poem differs from the concluding lines of the 1863 and 1877 poems. Roland is presumed to have died young, but the passing of time, coupled with the adulation that has accumulated over the centuries, warrant the poet's describing his veteran hero as an *old* lion. Then, as in the previous versions, the poet invites him to rise up and watch if French troops should ever file through Roncevaux Valley again: "Lève-toi pour les voir, lève-toi, vieux lion: / Plus grande que ton oncle et que Napoléon, / Viens voir la liberté qui passe!" Once more the poet returns to his messianic concept of advancing French armies trailing freedom in their wake. Possibly the poet is alluding to the Moors' eventually being driven out of Spain. He might also be proposing that, once again, the French go in and put an end to the political disorder that characterized Spain's affairs during so much of the nineteenth century, perhaps imposing a republic.

Several contemporaries were struck by the poem. Charles Asselineau's notice in *Les Poètes français* (1862) praised poem and poet. With "Roland," wrote the critic, Peyrat in 1833 "se plaçait du premier coup entre les *Odes et ballades* et les *Orientales* et . . . manifestait . . . les qualités, tant recherchées alors, du pittoresque, de la couleur, de l'image vivante et voyante" The poet had not set his poem in a contrived location but rather in one he knew intimately. "Les images riches et correctes sont frappantes de vérité. Ce n'est plus un pays deviné, rêvé, recréé pour ainsi dire par l'imagination puissante d'un poéte grand magicien, mais un pays vu, compris et admirablement rendu en quelques coups d'un savant pinceau." The poem had been written, in short, with "une exécution magistrale." Asselineau's friend Baudelaire, who presumably read "Roland" in the 1862 anthology, also liked the poem and planned to quote it in *Mon coeur mis à nu*.[25]

Peyrat's bold images were not lost on one highly cultivated reader. For Anatole France, who was to write on the legend himself, "Roland" was "une belle oeuvre d'art." In an article on the 1883 anthology, the critic extolled the poem, calling attention to its "splendeur" and, referring to the era of the 1830s, describing it as "un des plus beaux poèmes de cette période." Not all critics would endorse his remark that the poet had left "la pièce de maîtrise la plus belle et la plus complète de l'art de son temps."[26] Had the critic known the poem's other, longer versions, perhaps he would have felt this even more keenly.

Fernand Gregh in his *Portrait de la poésie française au XIXe siècle* (1936) described "Roland" as "un admirable morceau de poésie," marvelous and magnificent. Peyrat, "un jour d'inspiration, avait écrit d'un trait cet admirable poème encore un peu 'troubadour' ça et là, mais par ailleurs d'une forme si moderne, et plein de détails réalistes qui anticipaient même sur les audaces de Hugo." Compared to Hugo, the poet "est moins grand, mais plus vrai." He is a literary phenomenon, "le Rimbaud du romantisme."[27] The praise is deserved, but with one reservation. Even though Peyrat devoted his energies mainly to his pastoral duties after publishing "Roland," he did not turn his back on poetry, as Rimbaud did after *Une Saison en enfer*.

While certainly his best, "Roland" is not Peyrat's only reminiscence of his hero. The second book of *Les Pyrénées, romancéro,* contains a poem called "La Peyrada," which tells readers that a traveler going from Gèdre to Gavarnie will see an immense pile of natural debris where the elements have carved a likeness of Roland and his horse, "un concassement colossal, dont l'Arni / Ronge les roches ruinées. / Salut, ô Peyrada! La bataille et l'effroi / Sculptent sur ton chaos Roland, son palefroi." The poem takes its title from La Peyrade, also known as Le Chaos or Le Chaos de Coumély, a tiny community midway between Gèdre and Gavarnie in the Hautes Pyrénées. It is believed that in the eighth century, before the battle of Roncevaux, a severe earthquake distributed the pile of rocky debris in such a way that local people have detected in it a stone image of Roland and his horse.

Another poem, "Bertran de Born," evokes Roland's call for help as he blew his horn to summon the emperor. The author forgets, of course, that in "Roland" his protagonist never blew his horn. The horn, described here as "La trompe merveilleuse, faite / D'un tonnerre incrusté d'une dent d'éléphant," is kept at Blaye, where, according to the poet, it was deposited miraculously after its owner's death: "Blaye a de plus le cor d'ivoire / De Roland, d'où s'exhale une vapeur de gloire. / Un ange avait sauvé le superbe oliphant." The poet also mentions the death of Roland, the "paladin au prodigieux fer," at the hands of "le basque / Loup, chef de nos tribus, Loup, fils de Gaïfer." Again it is Lupus who does the dirty work. He is presented here as a Basque tribal chief, however, not as a proud noble or a virtually independent vassal.

Napoléon Peyrat, after writing one of his century's most remarkable poems, slipped into oblivion. Beyond a doubt, his work as a minister brought certain compensations. Yet his constantly retouching the best of his poems and occasionally writing others demonstrates that the artist was not entirely stifled by the clergyman. Peyrat had trouble distinguishing Charles Martel's and Charlemagne's periods. Still, "Roland" stands out because of its startling imagery, at once deft and vigorous. The poem is also an intensely personal, highly original rendition by an extraordinary poet who spent his formative years in the Pyrenees. Barren and dismal, the region inspired little but horror in Creuzé de Lesser. To Peyrat, who knew the secret of making it come alive, it was an Eden in which catastrophe occurred.

In 1841 Edgar Quinet was appointed to the Collège de France, where he was expected to lecture on the literature of southern Europe. Essentially a philosopher and historian, he was, like his friend Michelet, an anticlerical activist, and he contrived to spend much of his class time on current religious controversies. Other interests made him the first to recognize the cultural significance of Old French epics, many of which were in Paris libraries. To urge their identification and preservation, Quinet turned to a new minister of public works, Comte Apollinaire d'Argout. To him in 1831 Quinet addressed his *Rapport à M. le Ministre des Travaux Publics sur les épopées françaises du douzième siècle restées jusqu'à ce jour en manuscrit dans les Bibliothèques du Roi et de l'Arsenal.* Quinet pointed out that, like France's architectural monuments, these epics constituted a national treasure. Not only should the epics be preserved, but they also ought to be published. "Je ne sache pas qu'aucune entreprise plus nationale puisse être présentée à votre intérêt," he wrote, "que de ressusciter ces merveilleux poèmes en qui nous trouvons tous les types les plus purs du génie et qui rejettent en arrière de près de cinq siècles sa grande ère littéraire et poétique." He concluded by pointing out that "ces monuments sont de ceux qui semblent avoir été tenus en réserve pour le temps où l'art national, après avoir épuisé toutes les voies et cherché toutes les solutions, ne peut plus retrouver de vie et de naturel qu'en se renouvelant dans les sources indigènes qui lui étaient restées inconnues."[28] The appeal was both articulate and opportune, but the government took no action. The medieval aura that surrounded so much of the current literature stimulated no official move to preserve and publish that literature's antecedents, the authentic primitive treasures for which Quinet was pleading.

In *Rapport . . . sur les épopées françaises,* Quinet contended that France's medieval epics had grown out of national traditions. He added that "les poèmes franks qui se groupent autour de Charlemagne ont adopté le grand vers héroïque de dix ou de douze syllabes." At the time, the statement, repeated in the *Histoire de la poésie,*[29] produced a minor disagreement with François Génin. *Poèmes franks* might suggest that to Quinet the epics were originally Frankish poetic narratives that were finally set down in the twelfth century. This view is not wholly consistent with remarks he would later make about epic poets.

In 1837 Quinet thought of himself as a cultivated reader, not as someone "ébloui par le fanatisme commun aux érudits." A fanatic he was not, at least in academic matters, but he may have been too modest. Virtually alone among his contemporaries, he distinguished between romance and epic. Between 1831 and 1840 he published several articles in the *Revue des Deux Mondes* on epic poetry that he would later work into the *Histoire de la poésie,* which deals with only two kinds of verse, both medieval, the romance and the epic. The article that concerns us is "L'Epopée française," published in the *Revue des deux Mondes* on 1 January 1837.[30]

Quinet believed that the European social structure collapsed when Rome did. The Middle Ages dawned, but there was no society. During the medieval period several poetic genres developed more or less simultaneously. "L'hymne, la légende, le chant guerrier, le lai des bardes, voilà les premiers rudiments de l'art en France," he declared. As these sprang up, "il y avait une poésie et point de poèmes, comme il y avait des débris de peuples et point de peuple, des hommes et point de société." Then in the twelfth century society was miraculously born, resulting from a mating between Christianity and feudalism. An inspired new architecture came into existence, and "des compositions épiques de trente, de quarante, de soixante mille vers éclatent presque à la fois, dans des dialectes naissants." Then, "pendant que la société se formait de l'alliance de l'église et de la force barbare, l'épopée qui devait la représenter se formait de l'alliance de la légende et du chant de guerre." Two genres had combined to create the epic. The epic poets were composing their poems in the Homeric tradition, Quinet insisted. "Le même intérêt qui, chez les anciens, s'était attaché à la guerre de Troie, devait s'attacher, pendant le moyen âge, au souvenir des guerres contre les Sarrasins."[31] If Quinet had in mind here the intentions of individual poets composing epics, then his remarks do not agree with the idea that each epic was an agglomeration of earlier, shorter poems.

To Quinet, the most startling feature of French epic literature is that events taking place at the time the epics were being constituted are almost absent from the works themselves, a view Sismondi had already touched upon. Amid events such as the crusades, epic poets were glamorizing a past era. Nearly three decades later Gaston Paris, in the *Histoire poétique de Charlemagne*, agreed. Charlemagne's epoch, he wrote, became "pour des siècles, l'âge d'or vers lequel on tournait sans cesse les yeux."[32] Marchangy's *La Gaule poétique* showed that long after the Middle Ages the idealization process had gone on unabated. Quinet failed to see that, despite their preoccupation with past events and dead heroes, epic writers in the twelfth century were by no means avoiding current issues. Traits admired in their contemporaries were being exaggerated and ascribed to the epic heroes. When these poets despatched Charlemagne and his men to exterminate miscreants in distant, exotic places, the ventures were much like the contemporary Crusades.

Quinet also pointed out that religion and love are subordinated to political concerns. "L'intérêt politique y passe toujours avant l'intérêt romanesque," he added. Whereas epics are but little concerned with lovers, they contain a wealth of fathers, wives, sons, sisters. Moreover, according to Quinet, epics present a complete picture of the whole feudal structure. Charlemagne's principal vassals "sont d'origine franke et barbare. Leurs exploits se rattachent à l'établissement de la féodalité. Ils en sont les champions et les héros." Astride his horse Veillantif, which Quinet mistakenly calls Valentin, and brandishing his sword Durandal, Roland is such a champion.[33]

Without mentioning the epic's title, Quinet summarizes one of the main episodes of *Girart de Vienne*. Learning that Charlemagne's empress has boasted that she once humiliated him by contriving to have him kiss her foot in the dark, Girart with his whole clan rebels against the emperor. When the revolt reaches a stalemate, a champion is selected from each side: Roland represents his imperial uncle, and Olivier, the rebels. Facing Vienne on an island in the

Rhone River, the two heroes, both brave and accomplished, have at one another. If Quinet's admiration is obvious, so is his conviction that the epic is in spirit Homeric.

> Dans une bruyère, deux paladins de Charlemagne, Olivier et Roland, sont aux prises l'un avec l'autre. Le combat dure depuis un jour entier; les deux chevaux des chevaliers gisent coupés en morceaux à leurs pieds; le feu jaillit des cuirasses bosselées; le combat dure encore; l'épée d'Olivier se brise sur le casque de Roland.—Sire Olivier, dit Roland, allez en chercher une autre, et une coupe de vin, car j'ai grand' soif. Un batelier apporte de la ville trois épées et un bocal de vin. Les chevaliers boivent à la même coupe; après cela, le combat recommence. Vers la fin du second jour, Roland s'écrie:—Je suis malade, à ne vous le point cacher. Je voudrais me coucher pour me reposer. Mais Olivier lui répond avec ironie:— Couchez-vous, s'il vous plaît, sur l'herbe verte. Je vous éventerai pour vous rafraîchir. Alors Roland, à la fière pensée, reprend à haute voix:—Vassal, je le disais pour vous éprouver. Je combattrais encore volontiers quatre jours sans boire et sans manger. En effet, le combat continue. Plusieurs événements du poème se passe, et l'on revient toujours à cet interminable duel. Les cottes démaillées, les écus brisés, rien ne le ralentit. Le soir arrive, la nuit arrive; le combat dure toujours. A la fin, une nue s'abaisse du ciel entre les deux champions. De cette nue sort un ange. Il salue avec douceur les deux francs chevaliers; au nom du Dieu qui fit ciel et rosée, il leur commande de faire la paix, et les ajourne contre les mécréans à Roncevaux. Les chevaliers tout tremblans lui obéissent; ils se délacent l'un à l'autre leurs casques; après s'être entrebaisés, ils s'asseient sur le pré en devisant comme vieux amis.[34]

From this battle scene Quinet draws conclusions. "Voilà le seigneur féodal dans ses rapports avec Dieu," he affirms, and he adds, "Tout cela n'est-il pas singulièrement grand, fier, énergique? Le tremblement de ces deux hommes invincibles devant le séraphin désarmé, n'est-ce pas là une invention dans le vrai goût de l'antiquité, non romaine, mais grecque, non byzantine, mais homérique?" There ought to be a painting commemorating the scene, Quinet felt.

Quinet's source of information about *Girart de Vienne* is not clear. The entire epic had not been published at the time he was writing, and in October 1777 the *Bibliothèque universelle* had printed a condensed version giving few of the details he mentions.[35] In 1782 Gaillard's *Histoire de Charlemagne* had mentioned the poem but had not delved into the plot. At the Bibliothèque Nationale, Uhland had transcribed it in 1810 and 1811, and when his friend Immanuel Bekker prepared a critical text of the *Roman de Fierabras* somewhat later, the poet made his transcription available to him. Bekker's edition, published in 1829 and including 4060 lines of *Girart de Vienne*, may have been Quinet's principal source.[36] There is always the possibility that at some point he pored over the original epic itself, perhaps when he was writing his *Rapport . . . sur les épopées françaises.*

In January 1837, when Quinet's article appeared, the Oxford Manuscript of the *Chanson de Roland* had not been published. Nothing in the *Rapport* or "L'Epopée française" indicates that the author had seen or studied any of the other manuscript versions. He did know Monin's thesis, however, and his remarks about the Roland legend, except for the duel with Olivier, are based upon it. Monin referred to the epic as the *Roman de Roncevaux*, but Quinet preferred to think of it as the *Poème de Roncevaux*.[37] The poetry, in spite of its "idiome embarrassé," he considered sublime. In addition, while events are perhaps not reported quite the way they happened, there is in these compositions "une vérité plus vraie que l'histoire." Quinet's final words return to the matter of conception and structure:

> Roland, à Roncevaux, est resté seul vivant de toute l'arrière-garde avec l'archevêque Turpin. Les Sarrasins vont l'atteindre. L'archevêque est descendu dans la vallée pour lui chercher à boire. Roland évanoui se relève sur son séant; il sonne de son cor d'ivoire pour appeler Charlemagne à son secours. Dans ce dernier moment, il adresse ses adieux à son épée, sa fameuse Durandal. De peur qu'elle ne tombe entre les mains des mécréans, il veut la rompre contre le rocher; mais c'est le rocher qui se brise. A la fin il l'enfonce jusqu'à la garde dans le granit; il la met en pièces en la tournant dans ses mains. Après cela il souffle de nouveau dans son cor jusqu'à ce que sa poitrine se brise. Et ce grand cri, plus fort que celui d'Achille, retentit dans toute la chevalerie et la noblesse de France jusqu'à la fin du moyen âge. Voilà l'individualité du grand vassal, seul avec lui-même et son épée.[38]

In his insistence upon Homer's Achilles, Quinet is recalling his article on the *Iliad* and the *Odyssey* that appeared in the *Revue des Deux Mondes* on 15 May 1836. Cuvelier de Trie and Chandezon had likewise seen Roland as an Achilles, despite their reliance upon Ariosto. Without developing the point, Victor Hugo would compare the two heroes as well. His *L'Ane*, calling attention to the speed with which time eludes humankind, observed that "l'avenir s'envole" with "l'emportement d'Achille et de Roland."[39]

In summarizing Roland's death, Quinet does not draw upon the *Poème de Roncevaux* exclusively. For several details he is probably relying upon his own imagination. Durandal crumbles as, determined that it not fall into heathen hands, Roland tries to smash it against a rock. Finally, Quinet writes, "il la met en pièces en la tournant dans ses mains." The *Poème de Roncevaux*, the *Chanson de Roland*, and the *Pseudo-Turpin Chronicle* all insist that the sword neither shatters nor breaks. The July 1777 *Bibliothèque universelle*, however, allows the paladin at least to damage his sword, asserting that, "animé d'une fureur héroïque" and having tried in vain to destroy the weapon, Roland "plonge la pointe de son glaive dans le plus dur des rochers; et quand elle y est bien enfoncée, il casse lui-même la lame et en jette bien loin le tronçon qui lui restoit dans les mains."[40] Quinet again relies upon his own inventiveness when narrating what takes place as Roland blows his horn for the last time. In the *Poème de Roncevaux* and the *Chanson de Roland*, his temple bursts. In the *Pseudo-Turpin Chronicle* it is the nerves and veins of his neck. In Quinet's account, Roland's chest explodes, a personal touch indeed.

The *Poème de Roncevaux* is only one of the epics Quinet mentioned in his article. He sparkled with enthusiasm for authentic medieval epic literature, which in 1837 was just beginning to capture readers' attention. At times he displayed remarkable insight. One could quarrel with his assertion that the love element is largely missing in medieval epics. After all, in *Girart de Vienne* Aude and Roland meet and fall in love. But the most surprising aspect of Quinet's Roland discussion is that it underwent no serious modification in light of subsequent discoveries. "L'Epopée française" appeared in January 1837. One month later Francisque Michel published the Oxford Manuscript of the *Chanson de Roland*. Yet in republishing his article, Quinet never emended it with the new text in mind.

Because of his anticlerical remarks in class, Quinet's course at the Collège de France was suspended in October 1843. The writer traveled for a time in Spain and had occasion to think about Roland again. As his coach crossed the border into Spain one night, he was struck by the quietness of the moonlit expanse surrounding him. "Le soir arrive, la lune se lève; au loin les cascades réveillent l'écho du cor de Roland," he wrote. But gone are the frenetic passions that once covered the area in blood. Later at the Armería Real he saw the sword that was supposed to have been Roland's.[41] Did he recall claiming that Roland had managed to destroy it? Returning to France through the Pyrenees Mountains, he heard a chance sound that reminded him of Roland's horn. To the liberal Quinet, the sound of Roland's horn blowing was the sound of freedom, emanating from France and inspiring other nations. Napoléon Peyrat in his "Roland" had proclaimed a similar idea. "Voilà les Pyrénées aux flancs verdoyants," Quinet wrote. "J'entends, de l'autre côté de Roncevaux, à travers la vallée, un souffle lointain; il vibre comme s'il sortait de la poitrine d'un blessé. Les passants me disent: Ce n'est rien; c'est le bruit d'un torrent qui s'épuise. Et moi, je vous dis: Espagnols, Portugais, Italiens, Polonais, vous tous qui attendez ou espérez quelque chose, c'est le cor de Roland; c'est la respiration de la France; c'est le souffle d'un grand peuple, livré, navré, qui se réveille de sa léthargie pour appeler à soi tout ce qui souffre et pâtit et veut vivre sur la terre."[42] Like the Revolutionary and Napoleonic Rolands, this one is made to serve the author's political convictions.

Late in life Quinet published his strange novel, *Merlin l'enchanteur*. In it such characters as Mohammed, Robin Hood, and Mirabeau mill about. Roland and Durandal are mentioned. At one point Merlin is said to be "plus amoureux que Roland," an allusion not to the epic Roland but to the Italian Renaissance one. While his role is small, Turpin also appears. He is seen completing his chronicle and then planning to live in solitude on a mountain.[43] Little in Quinet's previous discussion of Roland suggests that the author attached any value to the *Pseudo-Turpin Chronicle*. In any event, he calls attention to the postscript with which the *Chronicle* ends and points out that the archbishop did not retire to a mountaintop. Still exercising his episcopal functions, he is supposed to have died not long after writing the *Chronicle*.

Jules Michelet was a Romantic historian, with the Romantic love for history as perpetual movement and panoramic spectacle. And while he did not invent it, he no doubt contributed to the contemporary fixation on the Middle Ages. His contemporaries would lose interest in the period when Romanticism had run its course, and he eventually decided that the Middle Ages, or at least the high Middle Ages, had not been the *aetas aurea* he had once thought. Throughout Michelet's evolution, however, Roland incurred no blemishes.

The *Tableau de la France* is an extensive introduction to the second volume of the *Histoire de France*, a volume that came out in 1833. Thus it dates from the period when the author still looked enthusiastically upon the Middle Ages as one of civilization's great moments. Furthermore, it is written in a harmonious and exciting prose that thrilled the French public. In the book, as Lucien Refort remarked in 1949, Michelet enunciated the concept, long before Taine and the Naturalists, that people are the product of their ancestral and environmental circumstances.[44] The various groups, including the Celts, Romans, and Germans, that settled in or crossed what is now France, have all left traces on the land and its people, according to Michelet. He was at enormous pains to call attention to the traits that, to him, distinguish Normans, Bretons, Provençals, and others. At the Pyrenees Mountains, Michelet contends, an immense natural wall defines the French border, and the inhospitable people who live there open and close the passes to let travelers through, at least if they wish to do so. "Portiers irritables et capricieux, las de l'éternel passage des nations, ils ouvrent à Abdérame, ils ferment à Roland; il y a bien des tombeaux entre Roncevaux et la Seu d'Urgel."[45] Often Michelet did not bother with details—another Romantic quirk—and hence he is likely to confuse the Cirque de Gavarnie and the Brèche de Roland. In any case, he believed that Gavarnie, at the southwestern limit of France, was the scene of a momentous historical event.

Relying upon a manuscript tradition of Einhard, Michelet wrote in the *Histoire de France* that at Roncevaux "les Francs . . . perdirent beaucoup de monde, entre autres . . . le fameux Roland." He noted also that "La brèche immense qui ouvre les Pyrénées sous les tours de Marboré . . . n'est autre chose, comme on sait, qu'un coup d'épée de Roland." The "comme on sait" suggests how well known the author believed this aspect of the Roland legend to be. Michelet added that Roland's horn was kept for a long time at Blaye and thus accepted a tradition reported by Scipion Dupleix. But the southwestern extent of France had been the theater of an event not only historical but also, to the author, poetic. "Une immense poésie historique plane sur cette limite des deux mondes, où vous pourriez voir . . . Toulouse ou Saragosse. Cette embrasure de trois cents pieds dans les montagnes, Roland l'ouvrit en deux coups de sa Durandal. C'est le symbole du combat éternel de la France et de l'Espagne, qui n'est autre que celui de l'Europe et de l'Afrique. Roland périt, mais la France a vaincu."[46] France's winning out over Africa presumably alludes to the French presence in North Africa that had begun in 1830, shortly before Michelet's pronouncement, and that the author apparently felt would continue.

Treating the Frankish empire and its events in chronological order, Michelet had occasion, even earlier in the *Histoire de France* and prior to the *Tableau*, to mention Roland. Encouraged by contending parties and interests, wrote the historian, the Franks advanced into Spain, led by a king described not as venerable and wise but rather as insouciant. Michelet's Charlemagne is at least as anxious to acquire new territory as he is to spread religious doctrine. In Michelet's account,

> C'était . . . l'année 778, où les armées de Charlemagne recevaient un échec si mémorable à Roncevaux. L'affaiblissement des Sarrasins, l'amitié des petits rois chrétiens, les prières des émirs révoltés du nord de l'Espagne, avaient favorisé les progrès des Francs; ils avaient poussé jusqu'à l'Ebre, et appelaient leurs campements en Espagne une nouvelle province, sous les noms de marche de Gascogne et marche de Gothie. Du côté oriental, tout allait bien, les Francs étaient soutenus par les Goths; mais à l'Occident, les Basques, vieux soldats d'Hunold et de Guaifer, les rois de Navarre et des Asturies, qui voyaient Charlemagne prendre possession du pays et mettre tous les forts entre les mains des Francs, s'étaient armés sous Lope, fils de Guaifer. Au retour, les Francs, attaqués par ces montagnards, perdirent beaucoup de monde dans ces ports difficiles, dans ces gigantesques escaliers que l'on monte à la file, homme à homme, soit à pied, soit à dos de mulet; les roches vous dominent et semblent prêtes à écraser d'elles-mêmes ceux qui violent cette limite solennelle des deux mondes.[47]

Michelet feels sure of his facts up to this point, but in the passage that follows he is less certain. He does not say whether the Roncevaux massacre was an attack on Charlemagne's principal army or an ambush of a contingent in the rear. Nor does he commit himself concerning the Saracens' involvement in the slaughter, and he only speculates about the role of the Basques. Clearly Michelet has seen a Roland poem, since he refers to a poet's account of the hero's death. In a note he alludes to Monin's thesis, which had caused a great stir not long before:

> La défaite de Roncevaux ne fut, assure-t-on, qu'une affaire d'arrière-garde. Cependant Eginhard avoue que les Francs y perdirent beaucoup de monde, entre

autres plusieurs de leurs chefs les plus distingués et le fameux Roland. Peut-être les Sarrasins aidèrent-ils; peut-être la défaite commencée par eux sur l'Ebre fut-elle achevée par les Basques aux montagnes. Le nom du fameux Roland se trouve dans Eginhard sans autre explication: *Rotlandus proefectus britannici limitis*. La brèche immense qui ouvre les Pyrénées sous les tours de Marboré, et d'où un oeil perçant pourrait voir à son choix Toulouse ou Saragosse, n'est autre chose, comme on sait, qu'un coup d'épée de Roland. Son cor fut pendant longtemps gardé à Blaye sur la Garonne, ce cor dans lequel il soufflait si furieusement, dit le poète, lorsque, ayant brisé sa Durandal, il appela, jusqu'à ce que les veines de son col en rompissent, l'insouciant Charlemagne et le traître Ganelon de Mayence. Le traître, dans ce poème éminemment national, est un Allemand.[48]

Like Faget de Baure and Sismondi, Michelet held that Charlemagne had been inviting trouble when he invaded Spain, alienating those who should have been his natural allies. Michelet had told the story in essentially the same way in the *Précis de l'histoire de France*, published in 1833. Curiously, in the detailed narrative of the battle of Hastings in the *Histoire de France*, there is no mention of Taillefer or of a *Chanson de Roland*.[49] Years later, however, Michelet would refer to the matter in the introduction to *La Renaissance*.

After his early treatments, Michelet next considered the Roland legend in 1855, in the introduction to the seventh volume of the *Histoire de France*, the first of the volumes dealing with the Renaissance. By this time the Oxford Manuscript of the *Chanson de Roland* had been published. Michelet, a typical Romantic, opened his remarks with a resounding paradox. "La tyrannie du Moyen Age commença par la liberté," he wrote. At the dawn of the French Middle Ages individuals were equal, as contractual relationships demonstrate, the historian theorized. When people joined together to fight, it was not because one individual had the power to compel the others to do so but because all understood that their combined strength gave them a better chance of achieving their common ends. The association was one into which all parties entered freely and from which each could withdraw at will. During the twelfth century social relationships evolved dramatically, so that by the end of Louis IX's reign, a hierarchical matrix of masters and subordinates—lords, vassals, and serfs—had been established. The people were no longer their own masters, no longer their comrades' equals. Writing reflected the changing social phenomena. The primitive, robust literature shows a people united against common enemies. "Rien entre l'empereur et le peuple. Les Roland, les Olivier n'en sont nullement séparés; ils ne sont que le peuple armé. C'est ce qui fait la grandeur étonnante de ce poème," the *Chanson de Roland*. By Louis IX's time, writers had become "des gens de lettres modernes qui pouvaient vivre aussi bien au siècle de Louis XV."[50]

But in the "sublime" *Chanson de Roland*, the oldest of the epics (which the writer dated at around 1100), the warriors still take part in battles on an equal footing with one another. Here, Michelet contended, "j'entends la forte voix du peuple et le grave accent des héros."[51] One has trouble imagining Charlemagne, Roland, and their subordinates as democratic in their relationships. Presumably Michelet missed in the *Chanson de Roland* such lines as those in which Gautier de l'Hum declares that he is Roland's vassal: " 'E jo od vos,' ço dist li quens Gualters, / *'Hom sui Rollant,* jo ne li dei faillir.' " Michelet's view has the merit, at least, of being almost original. We recall that Marchangy's Roland did not order the main army to ride ahead. He simply invited it to do so.

Michelet, the plebeian's champion, came to believe that the Middle Ages had been much less marvelous than he had once supposed. As he grew older and more liberal in his social attitudes, the *peuple* became even more important in his thinking. In the *Chanson de Roland* he detected the people's clarion voice. Long before he began republishing the *Histoire de France* in 1871, emperors and kings had lost their appeal and, indeed, a considerable amount of their historical significance for him. Charlemagne had become not unconcerned but heartless, and the people had made great strides. Roland, too, had become more sympathetic. Though "brutal," he was natural and direct. The people, with their imperfections, Michelet had come to look upon as a kind of God principle, but they were a god capable of turning a deaf ear. In the *Chanson de Roland,* Roland is the people's representative. The *éclaircissements* that the anticlerical Michelet wrote for the new edition of the *Histoire* reveal that Roland died for the people, just as Jesus did. He even had his Judas, Ganelon. "Le héros qui meurt pour la chrétienté est un héros chrétien, un Christ guerrier, barbare; comme Christ, il se voit abandonné, délaissé. De son calvaire pyrénéen, il crie, il sonne de ce cor qu'on entend de Toulouse à Saragosse. Il sonne, et le traître Ganelon de Mayence et l'insouciant Charlemagne ne veulent point entendre. Il sonne, et la chréticnté pour laquelle il meurt s'obstine à ne pas répondre. Alors il brise son épée, il veut mourir. Mais il ne mourra ni du fer du Sarrasin, ni de ses propres armes. Il enfle le son accusateur, les veines de son col se gonflent, elles crèvent, son noble sang s'écoule: il meurt de son indignation, de l'injuste abandon du monde."[52] Roland is abandoned by everyone, including his uncle. Barbey d'Aurevilly had also seen the emperor as an unnatural uncle, ignoring his nephew's despairing call for help.

Michelet's new conclusions are certainly arresting. The parallels between Roland and the Messiah are ingenious but overstated. Historically, Roland died in an encounter that was essentially a military operation, although its religious overtones cannot be discounted. The *Chanson de Roland's* Ganelon, unlike Judas, betrayed not only one individual but also that individual's companions. Moreover, Roland dies because the Moors, the Basques, or the Gascons have wounded him, not because, abandoned, he no longer has the will to live. One is almost startled that Michelet does not try to relate Jesus' pierced side to Roland's bursting veins. Yet Michelet's analogy cannot be dismissed. As Michelet saw it, Roland had been abandoned by those in whose interests he was dying, including an indifferent uncle, who, according to the author, allowed him to die. One is immediately reminded of Jesus' words on the cross, asking why his Father had forsaken him. Michelet also appears to assume that Roland's body remained at Roncevaux, buried beneath the rocks. Michelet points out that, like Christ, Roland was interred in stone. "Grande comme la lutte, haute comme l'héroïsme, est la tombe du héros, son gigantesque *tumulus;* ce sont les Pyrénées elles-mêmes." Michelet's ultimate interpretation of Roland as a Christ figure, unexpected but eloquent and personal, commands readers' attention with its originality.[58]

Michelet continued to use Roland as a reference point. Toward the end of his life, he discussed the Pyrenees Mountains, along with the Alps and other mountain ranges, in *La Montagne* (1868). The writer mentions how hard it is to cross the Pyrenees at certain times of the year, adding, "La fameuse Brèche de Roland qu'il ouvrit de sa Durandal était naguère encore à grand'peine franchie par le contrebandier, le bandit poursuivi."[54]

One of the nineteenth-century authors subscribing to the view that Charlemagne's rear guard was annihilated at Roncevaux by stones rolled down the mountainsides was Jacques Albin Simon Collin de Plancy (1794-1881). At the beginning of his long career Collin de Plancy claimed to be Danton's nephew, but his claim is doubtful. Nonetheless, under his own name and a variety of others, he turned out an incalculable number of books, most of which are forgotten today. Probably his best-known work is his *Dictionnaire infernal*. Collin de Plancy was liberal and anticlerical in his earlier years, writing virulent diatribes mostly against the Jesuits, whom he hated as much as Génin, Quinet, and Michelet did. In the 1830s he was converted, and his point of view changed.

Interested in the Middle Ages and in legends as well as religion, Collin de Plancy turned naturally to Charlemagne. His historical novel *La Reine Berthe au grand pied et quelque légendes de Charlemagne* seems to have been first published in 1842. The portion dealing with Charlemagne is called an appendix and mostly consists of anecdotes about the King of the Franks. In one, related in the chapter "Roncevaux," the author explains the circumstances leading to the monarch's incursion into Spain.

Charlemagne, according to this account, was spending the winter at Herstal, one of his palaces. To a military council and pageant he held at Paderborn came an emir proposing an alliance and expedition against another Moslem ruler. Charlemagne decided that going along with the emir's plan might forestall Moorish intrusions into his own territory. Leaving an army to watch the Saxons, he hurried to Aquitaine, raised troops, and rode into Spain, accompanied by some of the peers. The *Dictionnaire infernal* had given a different reason for the invasion, one more in keeping with literary tradition. There the author had written that Charlemagne "ne porta la guerre en Espagne que parce que saint Jacques lui apparut, pour l'avertir qu'il retirât son corps des mains des Sarrasins."[55] In spite of his new religious fervor, by 1842 Collin de Plancy apparently no longer saw this as the real reason.

With the Moors fleeing as he advanced, Charlemagne took Pamplona, Saragossa, and Barcelona, conquering all the territory between the Pyrenees Mountains and the Ebro River. Then he crossed back into Aquitaine, victorious, bringing with him an imposing amount of booty and a number of hostages. Guarding the main army's rear was Roland, "son neveu, commandant militaire de la Bretagne." Unable to defeat the Franks in open battle, the king's enemies fell upon the rear guard in Roncevaux Valley. "Là un revers cruel vint troubler le triomphe de Charlemagne. Ses ennemis n'avaient pu le vaincre; des traîtres lui firent subir plus qu'une défaite."[56] For the moment, the author does not identify the villains.

The account of events is told in fast-moving prose.

> Comme la nombreuse arrière-garde traversait les Pyrénées, lorsqu'elle entra dans la vallée de Roncevaux, elle s'aperçut tout à coup que les gorges des défilés étaient gardées de toutes parts et toutes les montagnes couvertes de soldats qui faisaient rouler sur les nôtres des quartiers de rochers. Ce fut bientôt un horrible champ de mort. Les soldats que commandait l'intrépide Roland gravissaient les rochers pour atteindre l'ennemi. L'ennemi fit la moitié du chemin. Un bataille sanglante se livra tout le jour; car aucun des guerriers de Charlemagne ne voulut se rendre. En vain, disent les vieilles traditions, le neveu du roi, le brave Roland, fit retentir les sons puissants de son cor pour demander secours; Charlemagne ne l'entendit point. Roland, dont la force surnaturelle et le courage merveilleux ont été chantés par toute la terre, le brave Roland, de qui la chanson guerrière a si longtemps guidé nos soldats, combattit et mourut dans la vallée de Roncevaux; aucun de ceux qui le suivaient ne survécut pour apporter la nouvelle de ce carnage.[57]

Their work done, the villains absconded. "Les traîtres se dispersèrent après cette action," wote Collin de Plancy. "Mais Charles, qui se réjouissait de s'être fait des vassaux en Espagne (ils restèrent fidèles) et d'avoir affranchi les chrétiens de ce pays de tout tribut envers les Musulmans, apprit bientôt la perte qu'il venait de faire. Il découvrit le chef de cette trahison, c'était Loup, duc des Gascons. L'infâme fut arrêté, jugé, et pendu, et les Bretons, qui s'étaient révoltés en l'absence de Roland, battus et soumis."[58]

Collin de Plancy does not mention the location of the Moorish hostages at the time of the ambush. Readers are left to suppose that they must have been with Charlemagne. Historically, however, the main purpose for the attack on Roland may have been to rescue the hostages, which implies that they were with him. Regardless, Collin de Plancy's villains were the Duke of Gascony and his men, who were bent on their own mischief and not on rescuing Moorish hostages, whose fate is not explained. The author also contends that part of Spain remained loyal to the Franks.

Other details are of greater interest. Turpin is never mentioned, for example. The battle, readers are told, lasts one day. Stones are rolled down the mountain slopes upon the rear guard, but, as in Gaillard's *Histoire de Charlemagne*, nothing is said about trees. As in Prince Lucien Bonaparte's *Charlemagne*, despite the falling rocks pelting him at every step, Roland starts up the mountainside in an effort to reach his attackers. The assailants come halfway down the mountain to meet him, so much of the battle actually takes place on the slopes. Probably without knowing it, Collin de Plancy thus comes close to historical accuracy in placing the combat scene not in Roncevaux Valley but in the mountains themselves. Collin de Plancy's Roland is no proud hero disdaining to call for help. His Roland is ready to blow his horn when the need arises, but unfortunately Charlemagne does not hear the sound. The most unexpected plot feature in this anecdote, however, is that Ganelon plays no role in the action. Presumably this is due to the author's assumption that Gascons rather than Saracens perpetrated the wrongdoing. Readers do not find out how Charlemagne learned about the disaster, nor is anything said about the victims' burial. It is not clear how much the author knew about the *Chanson de Roland*.

Writing in his *Dictionnaire critique des reliques et des images miraculeuses* (1822), Collin de Plancy called Roland Charlemagne's "neveu prétendu." Here he provided details that he did not incorporate into the later *Berthe au grand pied*. In the *Dictionnaire critique* he told readers that Roland died at Roncevaux in 778, adding that he had been beatified. "On l'a béatifié," he wrote. "Du moins les légendaires le mettent au nombre des bienheureux." Louis de Musset had also referred to Roland as "blessed."

Collin de Plancy mentions in the *Dictionnaire critique* that Roland's sword had been deposited at Notre Dame de Rocamadour, presumably because Roland visited the church once. "On raconte que Roland, visitant un jour cette chapelle, fit présent à la Vierge d'autant d'argent que pesait son braquemar." At some point the sword vanished and was replaced. A later writer would claim that this was at the time of the French Revolution, but Collin de Plancy disagrees. "Il s'égara dans les guerres de la Ligue, et les prêtres le remplacèrent par une lourde masse de fer que l'on continue d'appeler l'épée de Roland. Les femmes du pays allaient en pèlerinage toucher ce braquemar afin de devenir fécondes." Sterile women likewise venerated something else at the church in Rocamadour, the author added in a comic twist. This was "une vieille statue du preux chevalier." "Celles qui avaient le désir d'être mères allaient gratter un peu le mollet du bienheureux, qui avait une jambe si usée qu'elle ne tenait plus à rien. Elles buvaient cette poudre dans de l'eau et ne tardaient pas de se trouver grosses, après toutefois qu'un homme avait aidé au miracle."[59]

Collin de Plancy's "Roncevaux," more serious than the writer's earlier handling of the Roland theme, is a spirited piece of prose writing. Regrettably the author made no effort to make his characters lifelike and did little to provide them with motivations. They act because it is expedient, as in the case of Charlemagne's deciding to invade Spain, or because they can settle some vague grudge, as when the Gascons suddenly fall upon the unsuspecting rear guard. No delicate shading colors their thinking as they reach their decisions and translate these into action.

Alexis de Valon (1818-51) was a talented young writer who in 1847 married Cécile Delessert, daughter of Mérimée's mistress. Valon may have known Francisque Michel's edition of the *Chanson de Roland,* but certainly he was familiar with François Génin's edition and translation. On 1 February 1851, in the midst of a controversy raging between Génin and Michel, he published an essay in the *Revue des Deux Mondes* in which he mentioned that "Roland, tué à Roncevaux, offrit, en 778, à Notre-Dame de Rocamadour un don en argent du poids de 'son bracmar ou épée,'" adding that, following Roland's death shortly afterward, the sword itself was carried to Rocamadour. Valon went on to point out that, during the Revolution, "cette fameuse Durandal que Roland, près de mourir, craignait tant de voir tomber en des mains peu vaillantes," is supposed to have been removed, "remplacée par un coutelas de fer informe . . . qui ne doit ressembler en rien à cette arme incomparable qui taillait, sans s'émousser, des brèches dans les montagnes." Then Valon quoted from the *Chanson de Roland,* including part of Roland's address to his sword as he is about to die: "E, Durandal, cum es et clere et blanche! / Cuntre soleill si luises et reflambes!" Valon added that, in Rocamadour and its environs, local people revered Durandal, believing that both it and its modern substitute could make childless women conceive.

Valon's comments are notable for several reasons. First, in spite of his using the plural, the author was not implying that there was more than one Brèche de Roland. Rather, he was referring to the *Chanson de Roland*'s laisse 205, in which, on arriving at Roncevaux, Charlemagne finds scars on three different rocks, suggesting that Roland had hacked at all of them. Second, like Scipion Dupleix, Valon asserted that Durandal had indeed been taken to Rocamadour after its owner's death. Collin de Plancy had already associated Roland with Rocamadour. Similarly, Napoléon Peyrat had informed his readers that the French army, chasing the Moors, had paused in Rocamadour, where Archbishop Turpin had blessed the troops. In addition, Valon's detail concerning the sword's disappearance at the time of the French Revolution is a curious one, as is the local conviction in and around Rocamadour that touching the sword, or even the one that may have taken its place, could make barren women conceive.[60]

Francisque Michel and Prosper Mérimée were close friends, and Mérimée's correspondence reveals that the short story writer was aware of the controversies between Michel and Génin. Curiously, the Middle Ages had not always interested Mérimée. Once he told a friend that "tant de gens qui m'ennuient se sont jetés à corps perdu sur le moyen âge qu'ils m'en ont dégoûté."[61] Whether or not the remark was serious, the attitude it expressed would not last. In 1834 Mérimée was appointed Inspecteur Général des Monuments Historiques, succeeding his friend Ludovic Vitet. Three years later he was named secretary to the new Commission des Monuments Historiques. Mérimée was responsible for identifying, preserving, and restoring a number of medieval art works and buildings. He traveled a great deal and was in the Pyrenees Mountains at various times. There was little about France's medieval churches, including the one at Rocamadour, that he did not know. Stories about Durandal and the sword that is said to have replaced it would no doubt have reached his ears. Young Valon had been a friend of his, and he may have been thinking of the *Revue des Deux Mondes* article when in a letter to Francisque Michel on 15 January 1853 he mentioned "l'épée de Roland conservée à Rocamadour."[62] Nothing suggests that Mérimée believed that the hero's sword had vanished and had been replaced.

Mérimée had little to say about the *Chanson de Roland*, but he had read it with care. To a correspondent who had just translated *El Cid* he declared that, patriotism aside, the Spanish epic was a greater masterpiece than the French one. As transmitted to modern readers, the *Chanson de Roland* did not sound as though its author or authors had witnessed the events it narrates. He observed that Napoleon, comparing Homer and Virgil, insisted that Homer had been a soldier, a sailor, and a traveler writing about familiar things. Virgil, on the other hand, had been a man of letters describing farm life and warfare without ever having put his hand to the plow or the sword. "N'en pourrait-on pas dire autant des auteurs du *Cid* et de *Roland?*" Mérimée wondered. "Le Français est déjà un poète de salons, tandis que l'Espagnol a vécu de la vie sauvage qu'il décrit."[63] Michelet had looked upon the *Chanson de Roland* as a robust poem, holding that literature did not lose its virility until about the time of Louis IX. Mérimée thought that when the *Chanson de Roland* took shape, this had already come about.

In 1851 Mérimée told Francisque Michel that the Académie Française had decided not to award a prize to Génin's translation of the *Chanson de Roland*.[64] According to Mérimée, one member of the prize committee considered the language of the translation so obscure that a reader would have to consult the original to understand it.

With Peyrat and Mistral, Mérimée and Valon are almost the only authors to mention Rocamadour, which means "amateur de la roche." There is indeed a chapel there, and it is evoked by one of Mérimée's contemporaries, Eugène Rosary. Rosary's book *Les Pèlerinages de France* (1865) tells of miraculous cures that took place in the chapel, which existed during Roland's lifetime. Rosary adds that "un grand nombre d'illustres personnages vinrent y rendre leurs hommages à la vierge Marie. La tradition place au premier rang Charlemagne et le fameux Roland, son neveu; elle ajoute que Roland voua son épée à la madone et laissa en argent à la chapelle le poids de cette épée. Après sa mort, la terrible Durandal fut apportée à Rocamadour, suivant l'ordre qu'il en avait donné; et ce glaive ayant été perdu dans les siècles suivants, on le remplaça par une lourde masse de fer, qu'on nomme encore l'épée de Roland et qu'on montre aux visiteurs, dans la chapelle de Saint-Michel."[65] Rosary does not associate Durandal's disappearance with the French Revolution. Nothing is said either about the local belief in the power of the sword to encourage conception. Rosary's remarks do, however, confirm Valon's and Mérimée's suggestions that the sword or a substitute was believed to be in Rocamadour. But one must not discount Collin de Plancy's statement that the real Durandal disappeared at the time of the Ligue. Perhaps it was a new one placed in Notre Dame de Rocamadour during the late Renaissance that vanished at the time of the Revolution. Thus, the sword on display in Valon's day and in Frédéric Mistral's may have been the third to hang there.

Like Napoléon Peyrat, Frédéric Mistral was dedicated to furthering Provençal as a modern literary idiom. A devout Christian and a staunch conservative versed in local and national traditions, he was an ideal poet to write about Roland. He counted among his close friends the medievalists Paul Meyer and Gaston Paris. A Roland tradition, both oral and literary, flourished in Provence, and Mistral may have known the Old Provençal *Cansó d'Antiocha*, which Meyer published in 1883 and which contains a digression on the ambush at Roncevaux. Similarly, he could have known the Provençal *Rollan a Saragossa* and *Ronsavals*. But the oral tradition would have offered sufficient material. On 24 December 1871 Mistral informed Meyer that Roland had left "diverses traces dans la tradition orale de notre pays." Listing examples, he mentioned a hill in Arles "sur laquelle monta Roland pour examiner l'armée sarrasine." He added, "Je ne vous parle pas du *sabre de Rouland* suspendu autrefois dans l'église de Rocamadour," alluding to a church that would reappear in a sonnet he wrote more than three decades later. He also called his correspondent's attention to the presumed Pas de Roland in Roussillon, the Brèche de Roland near Luz, the Vau de Roland at Roncevaux, and the Tombeau de Roland near Bédaille, not far from the Spanish border. Meyer, with a scholar's caution, was dubious. "Vous vous donnez une peine inutile pour chercher des traces de Roland dans le Midi," he warned on 1 February

1872. For example, the weapons on display near the battle site were not authentic. "Les armes de Roland conservées à Roncevaux sont du XIIe siècle," much too late to have belonged to Charlemagne's nephew.[66]

Years later Mistral was still convinced that Arles bore traces of Roland's presence. To Gaston Paris in 1888 he noted, "Vous attribuez avec raison aux tombeaux antiques des Aliscamps d'Arles la source des légendes et poèmes relatifs à une bataille perdue par les chrétiens contre les sarrasins. On montre encore par là le tombeau de Roland."[67] Mistral was not the only nineteenth-century French writer to hold that Roland's body had been placed in a tomb. Peyrat and Victor Hugo had thought the same thing. The tomb's location, however, was a matter for disagreement.

Mistral eventually composed a sonnet about the paladin he persisted in claiming as a local hero. Entitled "Lou Duran-Dai" ("Durandal") and dated 27 August 1905, the sonnet appeared in the initial number of the short-lived *Revue du Sud-Est* in 1906.[68] Six years later it was reprinted in the collection *Lis Óulivado (Les Olivades)*. The Provençal poem follows:

> N'avès ausi parla, segur, dóu Duran-Dai,
> L'espaso que Rouland traisé dins le fendudo
> E qu'à Roco-Amadou se vèi enca pendudo:
> Daiavo, acò se dis, sèt lègo avans lou tai.
>
> Rouland, en se vesènt à soun darrié badai,
> Aplempougnè la lindo e, la sachènt vendudo
> Au Mouro Sarrasin, de-bado à la perdudo
> N'en piquè lou roucas pèr la roumpre. Un dardai,
>
> Lou dardai de l'arcié, bandiguè tal eslùci
> Que touto la rapino, astour, gerfau e rùssi,
> S'envoulèron d'amount en radant, esfraia.
>
> Ansin, bèl estrambord qu'as empura ma vido,
> Pousquèsses, quand sara ma lengo enregouïdo,
> Sus le nible faurèu longo-mai dardaia!

The French translation reads:

> Vous avez ouï sans doute parler de Durandal,
> L'épée que brandissait Roland dans les trouées
> Et qu'à Rocamadour on voit encore pendue:
> Elle fauchait, dit-on, sept lieues avant le tranchant.
>
> Roland, lorsqu'il se vit à son dernier soupir,
> Prit à deux mains l'épée, et, la sachant vendue
> Au Maure Sarrasin, en vain éperdument
> Il en frappa le roc pour la rompre. Un éclat,

> Le fulgurant éclat de l'acier, jeta un tel éclair
> Que les oiseaux de proie, vautours, gerfauts et buses,
> S'envolèrent, planant dans le ciel, effrayés.
>
> Ainsi, bel enthousiasme qui m'as enflammé ma vie,
> Puisses-tu, quand sera roidie ma langue,
> Sur les rapaces fauves longuement rayonner!

Parnassian in concept, Mistral's poem depends largely upon visual effects, although there is an important personal statement at the end. The pathetic, dying hero realizes at last that he and his sword have been "sold" to the Moors. Desperately, he tries to break the sword by striking it against rock, but only a chip is detached.

The poet reminds his Provençal readers that they can view the miraculous sword at close range. In a letter to Meyer, Mistral claimed that it had been hung in a Rocamadour church. Much earlier Scipion Dupleix had seemed to agree. Mistral's sonnet leads one to assume that the poet believes that it is still there for all to behold. Thus he appears not to concur with Alexis de Valon's contention, which Meyer was to echo, that the sword was removed, perhaps at the time of the French Revolution, and replaced by a more modern weapon. Mistral, unlike Collin de Plancy and Valon, does not mention barren women wanting to touch the sword.

Concluding his poem, Mistral hopes that his "bèl estrambord," like Roland's sword, will continue to encourage others long after his death. Presumably this enthusiasm reflects the ardor with which the poet had stressed Christian commitment and the zeal with which he had advocated writing in Provençal.[69] To Mistral both causes involved heroic battles, even crusades.

Alexandre Dumas père's *Chronique de Charlemagne* appeared in 1842 as one part of a volume of three loosely connected stories about the early Middle Ages.[70] In 1867, somewhat reordered, the "chronicle" was incorporated into the author's *Les Hommes de fer*. The material about Roland in the *Chronique de Charlemagne* consists of two anecdotes treating the hero's childhood, both of which would have been suitable for children. Dumas's work anticipated Adolphe d'Avril's *Les Enfances Roland*, published half a century later.

Entitled "Comment le bon empereur Charlemagne, après avoir retrouvé sa fille Emma et son secrétaire Eginhard, retrouve sa soeur Berthe et son neveu Roland," the first of Dumas's Roland anecdotes recapitulates the emperor's sister Berthe's falling in love with a handsome, valiant knight named Milon, whose fortune consisted of his spear and his sword. Convinced that her brother would never permit a union, Berthe had married her lover in secret and run away with him. The two wandered for a long time, "sans que leur fortune s'accrût d'autre chose que d'un fils, qui avait reçu au baptême le nom de Roland."

In Spain Milon took part in the king of Aragon's war with the Saracens. When the Aragonese fled, Milon was captured and taken to Tunis. With her son, Berthe left Spain, crossed France, and went to Germany, intending to plead with her brother to use his influence to obtain her husband's release.

Reaching Aix-la-Chapelle, however, she lacks the courage to approach her brother. When she admits to her young son that she is hungry, he promises to bring her something to eat. A few days before he had seen a number of kitchen helpers carrying food into the palace for the emperor's dinner. He heads for the palace, boldly enters the dining hall, and, without saying a word to anyone, selects the most succulent dish and leaves with it. Charlemagne signals a servant to follow the lad. Roland gives the food to his mother, who devours it, only to realize that her thirst is as great as her hunger had been. Roland returns to the palace. When he enters the dining hall, the emperor's cupbearer has just filled his master's gem-studded goblet with wine. Roland takes the cup and starts to leave. This time the emperor stops and questions him, but the boy tells him that "rien n'est trop beau ni trop bon pour une fille de roi et pour une soeur d'empereur." There is no reason to believe that Roland knows Charlemagne is his uncle. The emperor allows him to leave but tells him to return with his mother after she has drunk the wine. Taking this as divine intervention, Berthe returns with her son. Charlemagne forgives all and sends a deputation to the king of Tunis with twenty Mohammedan prisoners to be exchanged for Milon. The mission succeeds, and three months after Roland's visits to the palace, Berthe is reunited with her husband and Roland with his father.[71]

Dumas's other anecdote about Roland is called "Comment six des plus braves chevaliers de la cour de Charlemagne se mirent en quête du géant à l'émeraude, et comment ce fut le petit Roland qui le combattit et le mit à mort." During a council, Charlemagne and his peers decide to march against the infidels, who have invaded Germany. Later Archbishop Turpin tells the emperor that he cannot fail to win if he possesses a particular piece of the true cross containing a rare emerald. Once the emerald belonged to King Pepin, but it is now embedded in the shield of a giant miscreant who lives in the Ardennes forest. Charlemagne announces to the peers that he will award a duchy to the person who retrieves the precious stone. Six of the most illustrious set out immediately, including Milon and Turpin. The archbishop is no novice soldier: "Le vaillant prélat avait passé plus d'une fois son étole et son rochet par-dessus une cuirasse, et il ne maniait pas moins gracieusement la lance du chevalier que la crosse de l'éveque."

Roland knows that he is still too young to fight giants but believes that he is strong enough to go along as a squire, holding his father's sword and spear. Milon, hoping that his son will indeed grow up to be an accomplished knight, agrees to this apprenticeship. On reaching the Ardennes Forest, the six knights separate, increasing the likelihood that one of them will encounter the redoubtable giant. Milon decides to explore an isolated path, and his son tags along. Hot and tired, Milon lies down beneath a pine tree at noon to take a nap. After an hour Roland sees deer rushing down a nearby mountain, pursued by a ten-foot-tall horseman carrying a shield encrusted with the lost emerald. Roland's first impulse is to awaken his father, who somehow has managed to sleep through the commotion, but he decides against it. Milon needs his sleep, and Roland is already holding his father's weapons, although they are too big for him, as is Milon's horse. Unruffled, Roland takes them and slips quietly away.

Roland confronts the giant, who ridicules so diminutive a would-be opponent. Nonetheless, Roland mortally wounds his adversary on the first charge. Circling the fallen giant, he ascertains that his enemy is dead and, with his father's sword, removes the emerald from the giant's shield. Then, after washing his face and his father's spear in a stream, he returns to the place where Milon is still sleeping and goes to sleep himself. At seven o'clock in the evening Milon wakes up and, followed by Roland, sets out to look for the giant. He finds the dead giant and sees that his horse, armor, shield, sword, and spear are gone. Milon laments the nap he has taken and, accompanied by his son, makes his way back to Aix. As the two ride along, Roland deftly substitutes the emerald for the ornament in his father's shield.

Each of the six peers presents the emperor with a trophy belonging to the dead giant but denies having killed him. When Charlemagne sees the emerald in Milon's shield, his delight knows no bounds. Soon Roland confesses that he killed the monster himself. Since Roland is too young to be given the duchy promised as a reward, it is handed over to his father to be kept in trust. Next day, wearing the emerald at his neck, Charlemagne rides off to battle the infidels and, as Turpin had predicted, sweeps everything before him.[72]

Dumas did not invent either of these anecdotes. Ultimately both go back to Andrea da Barberino's *Reali di Francia*. More probably Dumas found his material in the *Bibliothèque universelle* or Gaillard's *Histoire de Charlemagne*.[73] He was not one to reproduce material slavishly, of course. He took what he wanted, embellished upon it, and let his exuberant imagination do the rest. Aside from their entertainment value, Dumas's stories are interesting for several reasons. Relating lesser-known incidents in Roland's career, they expanded and popularized the legend. Dumas increased the importance of Milon, and he made Roland more believable, showing the future paladin coming from a happy home and having warm relationships with his parents. Young Roland is presented as a daring little warrior, but nothing in the stories foreshadows the battle of Roncevaux. Dumas's Roland is a modest lad, not the proud hero that he will become by the time he appears in the *Chanson de Roland*. Moreover, readers see Archbishop Turpin as a military man, quite apart from his duties as archbishop of Rheims. Those who know the *Chanson de Roland* realize that, arriving at Roncevaux, he has had experience on the battlefield.

In writing these stories, Dumas merely put the finishing touches to his focus on Roland. A year earlier he related an unusual tale that he had heard on his travels. With Ida Ferrier, he had descended the Rhine River in August and September 1838. Dumas visited Aix-la-Chapelle and Charlemagne's tomb and along the way collected stories. Near Coblenz his boat sailed between Rolandswerth and Nonnenwerth. Here he heard the Roland anecdote that he repeated in his *Excursions sur les bords du Rhin* (1841).[74]

Rolandswerth is a hamlet on the river's edge, and rising high above it on a basalt rock is Rolandseck, the ruins of a medieval castle. According to Dumas, Charlemagne had called his vassals to join him at Ingelheim and go fight the Saracens in Spain. Going up the river to answer the call, Roland stopped at a castle. Its owner, an elderly nobleman named Raymond, was delighted to receive Roland and ordered his daughter, the beautiful Hildegonde, to serve him. "Peu importait à Roland par qui il serait servi pourvu que le dîner fût copieux et que le vin fût bon," remarks Dumas. When Roland's eyes met those of the châtelaine, the inevitable happened. Agitated, Hildegonde spilled wine on the floor. Comte Raymond pressed Roland, planning to leave the next day, to postpone his departure for a week. Duty called, but so did love. Roland tarried. "Au bout de ces huit jours, les deux amans ne s'étaient point parlé de leur amour, et cependant, le soir du huitième jour, Roland prit la main d'Hildegonde et la conduisit dans la chapelle. Arrivée devant l'autel, ils s'agenouillèrent tous deux d'un même mouvement." Roland then took a solemn oath. "Je n'aurai jamais d'autre femme qu'Hildegonde," he declared. The damsel swore that should anything prevent her from becoming Roland's wife, she would dedicate herself to God. The count was told about the engagement, and Roland took his leave.

A year went by. "Roland fit des merveilles, et le bruit de ses prouesses retentit des Pyrénées aux bords du Rhin." This good news was soon followed by bad. "Tout d'un coup on entendit vaguement parler d'une grande défaite, et le nom de Roncevaux fut prononcé." Nothing more was known. Then one evening a stranger appeared at the castle, a knight who had been one of Roland's comrades. Hildegonde hesitated a moment, then mentioned Roland's name. "Alors le chevalier raconta comment, dans la gorge de Roncevaux, entouré de Sarrasins et se voyant seul contre cent, il avait sonné de son cor pour appeler l'empereur à son secours, et cela avec une telle force que, quoiqu'il fût à plus d'une lieue et demie, l'empereur avait voulu retourner; mais Ganelon l'en avait empêché, et le bruit du cor s'en était allé mourant, car c'était le dernier effort du héros. Alors il l'avait vu, pour que sa bonne épée Durandal ne tombât point entre les mains des infidèles, essayer de la briser sur les roches; mais, habituée à fendre l'acier, Durandal avait fendu le granit, et il avait fallu que Roland enfonçat la lame dans la gerçure et la brisât en appuyant dessus. Puis, couvert de blessures, il était tombé à côté des tronçons de son épée, en murmurant le nom d'une femme qui s'appelait Hildegonde." Aside

from the fiancée's name and the disputed question of whether the hero had been able to shatter his sword, Dumas's digressive narrative closely follows, up to this point, the usual account of Roland's death. Still, there is no mention of Olivier, Turpin, or the emperor's reaction to the disaster. After this recital of Roland's last stand, the author returns to his story, which is a radical break with literary tradition.

On hearing the stranger's words, Hildegonde quietly turns to her father and reminds him of her oath. "Demain, avec votre permission, j'entrerai au couvent de Nonnenwerth," she announces. As Dumas explains it, "Il lui semblait que plus elle serait séparée de la terre, plus elle serait rapprochée de Roland." Comte Raymond respects Hildegonde's commitment and sadly gives his consent to her plans. From her uncle, a bishop, she obtains permission to shorten her noviciate, and at the end of three months, she is a nun, irrevocably.

Less than a week later Roland appears at Comte Raymond's door to claim his bride. His friend had been wrong. Obviously he is very much alive, but his wounds were serious and his convalescence took time. Thunderstruck, the old count leads his guest to the chapel and there explains his daughter's terrible step. Next morning, on foot and unarmed, Roland makes his way to a mountaintop overlooking the convent. As he reaches the spot, the nuns are at compline. "Au milieu de toutes ces saintes voix qui montaient au ciel, il y eut une voix qui vint droit à son coeur." The voice belongs to his fiancée. Stretching out on a rock, he spends the night there. At dawn, when the nuns sing matins, he hears the voice again. At eleven o'clock the nuns come outside. One sits alone under a willow beside the water. She is dressed like the others and wears a veil, but the sorrowful paladin knows intuitively that she is Hildegonde. He resolves to build a hut on top of the mountain and live in it as a hermit, as close as possible to his beloved.

Every day for the next two years, Roland listened and watched, silently. A special voice would be heard whenever the nuns sang. Each day at the same hour a nun would come and sit alone in the same spot. As time passed she walked more and more slowly. Finally one evening Roland did not hear her voice, nor did he hear it the next morning. Eleven o'clock came and went, but she did visit her tree at the water's edge. Starting at four o'clock, several nuns dug a grave beneath the tree. Then the entire community escorted a coffin to the freshly dug grave. In the coffin lay Hildegonde, wearing a crown of flowers. For the first time in two years, no veil covered her pale face. To Roland Hildegonde's death was a final blow. "Trois jours après, un pâtre qui avait perdu sa chèvre grimpa jusqu'au sommet de la montagne et trouva Roland assis, le dos appuyé contre la muraille de son hermitage et la tête inclinée sur la poitrine. Il était mort."

Dumas's treatment of Roland's adult life, or at least its romantic side, is almost a singular phenomenon in French literature. We see no Aude. There is no emphasis on the paladin's religious motives in fighting the infidels. Indeed, the military expedition is rather marginal, serving as a means to separate the lovers. Roland's surviving Roncevaux is the story's most remarkable feature, of course. Part of Dumas's originality lies in the skill with which he combined a local German legend with the usual narrative of the battle of Roncevaux. Years later Adolphe d'Avril would have a survivor live to recount the massacre, but the story of a surviving Roland who returns to marry his fiancée would turn up only two more times in nineteenth-century French literature.

Though rare in France, the account of a Roland who returned to marry his fiancée only to learn that she had taken final vows used to be common along the banks of the Rhine River.[75] In 1840 the German poet Ferdinand Freiligrath published *Rolands-Album*, an anthology of poems based on this curious variant. Dumas, who heard the alternate legend while traveling in Germany in 1838, is one of the few French authors to use it. He was not the only one to hear it, though. In *Le Rhin* Victor Hugo pointed out that in a localized legend Roland dies "non à Roncevaux des coups de toute une armée, mais d'amour sur le Rhin, dans le couvent de Nonnenwerth."[76] Xavier Marmier mentions Roland and the castle tower and its ruins but says nothing about the tragic love story said to have unfolded there.[77] Before long, however, another French author would look into the matter more carefully.

In 1841 Franz Liszt discovered Nonnenwerth and decided that the picturesque island, with its romantic associations, would be an ideal place for him to spend summers with his mistress, Marie d'Agoult, and their three children. Mme d'Agoult and her lover arrived toward the beginning of August. Not long before, an arch, all that remained of the tower in a castle Roland was thought to have built overlooking the convent to which his fiancée had retired, had collapsed during a winter storm. Thanks to Ferdinand Freiligrath, who had organized a subscription for the purpose, the arch had just been restored. The convent itself was now a hotel. Mme d'Agoult took what had once been the abbess's quarters and at least once appeared dressed as a nun.[78]

Two years later, François Ponsard, on the threshold of a brilliant career as a dramatist, joined Mme d'Agoult's circle of intimate friends in Paris. In the summer of 1850, traveling in Switzerland and Germany, he visited the island where she had spent several summers. Apparently she had recommended her hotel. On 10 August Ponsard recorded his impressions in a letter to her. "Ma première station," he wrote, "a été à Rolandseck. Je n'a pas voulu passer devant Nonnenwerth sans saluer votre île. Je voulais loger dans l'île mais votre hôtel, qui avait été un monastère, est devenu un pensionnat de demoiselles. Je me suis établi à Rolandseck, qui est en face de l'île, et j'y ai passé deux jours."[79] The site inspired a poem, which the author included in his letter.

A month earlier Ponsard had enclosed twelve lines of the poem in a letter to Egédie Decazes, to whom he wrote that he had seen "les vieux châteaux ruinés qui couronnent les coteaux du Rhin." Roland's castle, or rather its ruins, impressed him the most. "Rolandseck est un château bâti par Roland; c'est là et non pas à Roncevaux qu'est mort le neveu de Charlemagne," he wrote. "Sa fiancée, le croyant mort à la guerre, avait pris le voile dans un couvent. Roland, désespéré, construisit une tour sur la roche, d'où il apercevait le monastère. Là, il passait ses journées à regarder les murs qui renfermaient son amante. Un jour, il vit creuser une fosse: c'était celle de sa fiancée. Le lendemain, il mourut lui-même."[80]

Called "Galésinde au couvent" and subtitled "légende," the poem was published in the author's *OEuvres complètes*, in which, instead of 1850, it was dated 1859. As sent to Mme d'Agoult, the poem contains nine stanzas, each with four decasyllabic lines. The caesuras, curiously, come after the fifth syllable in each line, not the fourth. Concluding the poem is a seven-line strophe. Six lines are regular alexandrines with a *rime suivie* pattern, while the last, four-syllable line rhymes with none of the preceding couplets. In reworking his poem for publication, Ponsard omitted the last strophe. It was a mistake, for the lines provided his poem with a touching conclusion and commentary. Ponsard also inserted two stanzas narrating Roland's adventures after his encounter with the Moors. Another stanza was revised, bridging the gap between the inserted material and the rest of the poem.

Charlemagne, who is both king and emperor in Ponsard's account, issues a call to his vassals to join him in an expedition against the Moors, whom he hopes to convert.[81] Roland answers the call. Taking leave of his fiancée, he reminds her that on his return they will marry. Ponsard must not have considered the damsel's name euphonious, since he changed it to Galésinde. In her castle tower, Galésinde watches and waits, but her lover does not come back. At last his page appears: "Votre sire est mort," he announces, adding that "L'empereur des Francs, le roi Charlemagne, / A perdu là-bas ses meilleurs barons." Galésinde receives the news in silence. Her reaction, however, is swift: "Galésinde pâle autant qu'une morte / Ne dit rien, nul pleur ne mouilla son oeil. / Mais le lendemain se ferma la porte / Du couvent prochain sur l'amante en deuil."

In the published version, Ponsard inserted two stanzas relating what happened on the other side of the Pyrenees Mountains and explaining how Roland escaped death.

> Or, dans Roncevaux, la gorge maudite,
> Où par trahison sont morts tant de preux,
> Après la bataille, un pieux hermite
> Aperçut Roland qui rouvrit les yeux.

> Il avait au poing un tronçon d'épée;
> On voyait fendue au-dessus de lui
> La roche en granit qu'il avait coupée
> Et par où les boeufs passent aujourd'hui.

Thus in passing the poet explains the Brèche de Roland.

Regaining consciousness and "bien pansé," Roland set out for home, but he was too late: "Mais, à son retour, il sut que sa mie / Avait pris le voile au prochain couvent." Heartbroken he resolves to live as close to her as he can: "Lors, sur le sommet d'un roc solitaire, / Le comte Roland bâtit une tour / D'où son oeil plongeait dans le monastère, / Qu'il regardait tant que durait le jour." Not even this consolation would last. Months or years rolled by. "Une fois, il vit dans le cimetière / Une tombe neuve, un nouveau cyprès. / Il comprit pourquoi. La nuit tout entière, / Il pleura sa mie et mourut après." Ponsard's concluding remarks, discarded in the *OEuvres complètes*, add a Romantic touch.

> Ainsi mourut Roland. Sur le rocher assise,
> La vieille tour regarde encor la vieille église.
> Le château de Roland par le lierre couvert
> S'appelle Rolandseck, le couvent Nonnenwerth.
> Dormez, amants, dormez sous l'herbe et les décombres!
> Sans doute vers minuit se visitent vos ombres.
>   Dormez en paix!

In Ponsard's poem Dumas's plentiful details have vanished, and the plot has changed a little. The heroine has no distraught father. There is no engagement scene in a chapel, and no compassionate bishop shortens the postulant's novitiate. Roland builds a castle with a tower, not a hut. Ponsard adds details lacking in the earlier version, most of which link the traditional story to the local legend that once flourished on the banks of the Rhine. For Ponsard, Charlemagne invades Spain not to protect the Christians there, but to convert the Moors, thus eliminating the need for protection. The reader does not know how successful his mission has been. In any event, the invasion over, the emperor disappears. Presumably he has ridden ahead with his army's main contingent, as is usually the case. As in Dumas's version, neither Olivier nor Turpin is mentioned as having been at the battle of Roncevaux. Roland is attacked and the rear guard is annihilated, but nothing is said about Charlemagne's returning to punish the culprits. Roland has his horn, but whether he uses it or not is never stated. The battle over and his enemies gone, the paladin is lying where he fell, presumed dead, still clutching what remains of the sword with which he had hacked an opening in the mountains. Regaining consciousness, he is discovered by a kindly hermit who nurses him back to health.

We know the rest. The poet, while he mentions that the nun's cloister and part of the knight's tower can still be seen, does not add that the melancholy heroine's retreat has become in modern times first a hotel and then a boarding school.

Despite Dumas's and Ponsard's treatments, the story of Rolandseck never caught on in France. Ponsard told Mme Decazes that it was just a legend and no one was interested in legends.[82] Perhaps a better explanation would be that French authors and readers were little inclined to see their hero as a German soldier dying on the banks of the Rhine River. Whatever the case, the scenario would not reappear in French literature for several decades, and even then it would be significantly modified.

Gustave Kahn spent the years 1890 to 1895 in Belgium, close enough to the Rhine River to collect some of the region's lore for use in his *Livre d'images*. One of the "images" tells the tale of Roland's ill-fated love for a girl who, thinking her fiancé dead, enters a religious order. It is essentially the story that appealed to the vigorous imaginations of Dumas and Ponsard, but this version contains significant variants.

Kahn's "L'Image Roland" appeared first in the *Revue blanche* during the summer of 1897 and was soon reprinted in the author's *Livre d'images*, published on 6 October. The poem has been rightly described as a *conte en vers*. Less accurately, it has been said that, unwilling to treat "une légende . . . ou un sujet tout fait," the poet approached it with his characteristic desire to be different.[83] Kahn had predecessors, so this is not altogether true.

Kahn appears to suggest that the battle of Roncevaux took place in the evening. Roland survived it, owing his life to divine intervention.

> Car Roland n'est pas mort au soir de Roncevaux!
> Mais sauvé du péril par l'aide des saints anges,
> il suivit sa piété, comme les flèches d'argent
> du courant se dirigent vers la mer sans limite.
> Il fut le pèlerin que la forêt abrite
> de son manteau charitable et des réseaux
>   touffus de ses sentiers d'asile.

In literary accounts of Charlemagne's retaliation, angels have been known to put an end to a duel between Olivier and Roland and also to bear Roland's soul to heaven. Kahn is the only French writer, however, to have them actually save the hero, permitting him to survive the disaster.

Eventually this unique Roland will face another catastrophe. Driven now not by warlike aspirations but by a need to provide for his soul's well-being, "il s'en allait priant sous l'azur et les branches." His conscience is troubling him, maybe due to the deaths he caused by allowing his pride to keep him from blowing his horn soon enough at Roncevaux. The problem is never spelled out. "Et les pas de Roland visitèrent maintes landes / et gravirent les glaciers dans l'aurore des cimes / et redescendirent, glissant aux abîmes / où le torrent se joue des brindilles des chênes, / et s'arrêtèrent au seuil candide des hermites / pour demander la route au vieillard en prière." Roland's travels have taken him to unusual places, and he has even scaled glaciers. Finally he reaches the Eternal City. There, lost in a crowd,

> il reçut de l'Evêque de Rome le signe
> et la parole qui lavent le pécheur, et qui délient
> sa conscience enchaînée près des crocs des remords;
> alors il s'en revint beau comme un grand cygne
> et tranquille et blanc, le pas ferme et l'oeil doux
> vers la contrée natale et vers l'amour jaloux
> qu'il retrouvait en lui, pour Hilberte la belle
> aux yeux berceurs, au corps de pêche et mirabelle.

His conscience finally at rest, Roland can now return to his birthplace and his sweetheart, who in Kahn's version is named Hilberte.

Unfortunately for the lovers, Charlemagne's soldiers returning from Spain had said that Roland had been killed at Roncevaux. Unlike Aude, Hilberte does not die on hearing the news but retires to a convent to mourn the fallen hero.

> La tendre Hilberte
> s'en alla parmi les voiles d'étamine et de pierre
> du cloître, pour prier en pensant à la perte
> éternelle de sa meilleure âme, au val creux
> d'Espagne: et sa vie esseulée
> elle la voulut parmi l'amour divin enlinceulée
> comme une opale tendre en un coffret d'ivoire
> et ses yeux se détournèrent du passé noir.

Roland, on his way home to reclaim his fiancée, walks past the convent. "Encore portant la sombre bure," he hears his fiancée's lament. Realizing that she has taken vows and can never be his wife, he falls dead. Her voice

> toujours plus haut s'élançait sur les débris
> d'un grand coeur de couleur et d'un corps de héros
> car Roland, ayant reconnu et compris
> le son de la voix unique,
> la vie le délaça de sa dure tunique
> aux pointes intérieures d'acier d'adversité
> et Roland gisait ici, le coeur brisé.

Thus Roland dies, not at Roncevaux, but near his home in the Rhine Valley. Whether that home was on the French or the German side is never stated. Possibly it was near Aix, but more likely it was in or near Cologne, since in this area the legend of a Roland who survived military disaster and returned home to get married has been popular.

Departing from the traditional Roland story, Kahn took liberties with the tale Dumas and Ponsard had related as well. Like Dumas, Kahn mentioned the heroine's singing. On the other hand, Dumas's scene in a chapel is missing. So is Ponsard's charitable hermit who nursed Roland back to health. Kahn sends his hero on a pilgrimage, which is absent in Dumas and Ponsard. The three authors give their heroines different names. Like the others, Kahn's version clearly bears its author's personal stamp. Unlike Dumas and Ponsard, Kahn stresses Roland's piety. While Charlemagne's nephew is generally presented as devout, we do not expect details such as the haircloth shirt with studs or nails inside. Kahn also comments upon his hero's good looks and mentions his "oeil doux," whereas the others do not. All three make Roland more of a lover than usual. The *Chanson de Roland* does not imply that its protagonist would have been likely to die for human love, but this is precisely what kills him in Dumas, Ponsard, and Kahn. In all three authors' versions we see events more from the hero's tragic standpoint than from the heroine's. Apparently the disconsolate nun never learns that her fiancé is hovering only a few feet away from her. We note, in Kahn's version, that he dies before she does.

Kahn's verse is extraordinarily musical and linguistically daring. Hilberte's "vie esseulée" and "enlinceulée" arrests readers' attention, as do other striking images. The saddened heroine's putting her life away as though it were "une opale tendre en un coffret d'ivoire" is an imaginative description of her withdrawal from the world.

At the Odéon on 4 December 1897, the poem was recited at the fifth Samedi Populaire de Poésie Ancienne et Moderne.[84]

4
Magnificent Braggart and Doomed Lover

During the middle years of the nineteenth century, oral tradition, guidebooks, and tourists continued to perpetuate the Roland legend. Creative writers, sometimes adhering rather closely to the basic story but often extremely imaginative, added their own touches. Using an archaic word or expression here and there, several endeavored to suggest an appropriate medieval atmosphere. Writers also wondered what became of Roland's horn and sword after their owner's death. Continuing to view their protagonist as impetuous but essentially pathetic and noble, they tended to think of him, more than in the past, not only as a soldier but as a lover, and some took an interest in Aude and her grief when he died in the line of duty. A few highly fanciful authors allowed their imaginations free rein and invented adventures and exploits found in none of the traditional accounts.

For an edition of Duval's "Chanson de Roland," Antoine Le Roux de Lincy wrote an introduction in which he observed that modern treatments of the Roland legend had attained neither the *Chanson de Roland*'s "noble sentiment" nor its power. Perhaps he was too hasty. A short poem appeared about the time he was writing that deserves a careful reading. In 1843 Auguste Barbier concisely stated his view of the legend. Neglected today, Barbier had a solid reputation among his contemporaries. Rimbaud called him an imbecile, but he was not speaking for all his fellow poets.[1] Leconte de Lisle and Baudelaire, for example, admired Barbier. Best known for his mordant political satire, in calmer moments he wrote his *Rimes héroïques*, which contains a sonnet with the simple title "Roland." Barbier starts in medias res.

Olivier

> Vaillant préfet des Marches de Bretagne,
> Ne vois-tu pas sur les monts accroupis
> Plus de guerriers qu'une vaste campagne
> N'étale aux cieux de verdoyans épis?

> Roland
>
> Cher Olivier, je vois sur la montagne
> Un grand amas de païens insoumis,
> Prêts à broyer les vainquers de l'Espagne
> Sous l'épaisseur de cent rocs ennemis.
>
> Olivier
>
> Roland, Roland, souffle en ton cor d'ivoire,
> Et que son bruit perçant la gorge noire
> Jusques au roi par les vents soit porté.
>
> Roland
>
> Crier à l'aide, ah! c'est bon pour des femmes,
> Cher Olivier, tirons plutôt nos lames:
> Mieux vaut la mort que telle lâcheté.

Like Le Roux de Lincy, Barbier had read the *Chanson de Roland* carefully. He had been swept away by the epic's "caractère poétique," and he was convinced that the medieval poem had a foundation in historical fact.[2] In writing his own poem he kept the older one in mind and appears to have expected his readers to do the same. Readers are presumed to know that Charlemagne has invaded Spain and that he has struck out for home, leaving a smaller unit to cover the main army's withdrawal. Readers also need to remember that "Roland est preux, mais Olivier est sage." Perhaps too late, Olivier suspects trouble and consults Roland. He eventually calls upon his friend to blow his horn and summon help, but Roland, as brash as he is brave, considers such an act cowardly and declines. He and his companions will face the enemy alone and hope for the best. Readers know that his foolhardiness causes the rear guard to be wiped out.

Casting the poem in dialogue form helped Barbier use the poem's fourteen lines to maximum effect. Regarding Roland as "poetic" despite his brashness, the author made him basically sympathetic. Barbier recalled the *Chanson de Roland*'s ten-syllable lines and adopted the meter himself. The verse is smooth, and the "vaste campagne" with its "cieux de verdoyans épis" shows a good feeling for nature. The paladin and his companions are killed by adversaries "Prêts à broyer les vainquers de l'Espagne / Sous l'épaisseur de cent rocs ennemis." Like Collin de Plancy, Barbier does not mention trees, and he reminds his readers of Roland's position as military commandant of Brittany. Unlike Collin de Plancy, however, he relies upon the *Chanson de Roland* and makes his villains Moors rather than Gascons.

Not all of his contemporaries appreciated Etienne Jean Delécluze. Sainte-Beuve remarked that he was sometimes "un béotien émoustillé." Stendhal and

Mérimée, on the other hand, liked and admired him. His interests, like theirs, were varied. Art critic for the *Journal des Débats*, Delécluze was a painter and novelist who also wrote historical works. Romanticism was on the wane when he was writing, and while he had the Romantics' interest in the Middle Ages, he looked at the period with the sober eye of a Realist.

Delécluze published his *Roland ou la chevalerie* in 1845, dedicating the two-volume work to his nephew Viollet-le-Duc, the architect who, spurred on by Mérimée, carried out the restoration of so many medieval castles and churches. Whereas the initial volume is a treatise on chivalry in literature, the second contains a complete translation, one of the first, of the *Chanson de Roland*. The book bears witness to how much Monin and Francisque Michel's earlier labors had attracted cultivated readers' attention.[3] It also prepares modern readers, as it did the author's contemporaries, to examine some of the later treatments of the Roland legend with more insight.

Delécluze assumes without question that Turoldus, whoever he might have been, authored the *Chanson de Roland*. He calls attention to the poem's "esprit monacal" and concludes that the author had been handling material from an earlier era. He refers to the epic as the *Chanson de Roland* but considers it acceptable to call it the *Poème de Roncevaux*. Not convinced that Roland was Charlemagne's nephew, he calls him "un personnage à peu près imaginaire, dont les poètes et les romanciers ont fait le héros, le chevalier que tout le monde connaît aujourd'hui par le poème d'Arioste." Real or imaginary, Roland is no less a model of what the Christian hero ought to be. He and the other knights are dedicated to personal achievement but seldom forget that their basic allegiance is to Charlemagne. "C'est à peine si les guerriers qui y figurent oublient, une ou deux fois, la soumission due à leur chef pour faire des exploits au profit de leur gloire personelle." In the *Chanson de Roland* "la chevalerie est encore purement héroïque. Dans ce récit, il ne se trouve ni événement fantastique, ni aventure amoureuse."[4]

Delécluze attaches a great deal of importance to the manner in which love is presented in the *Chanson de Roland*. Pointing out that, chronologically, medieval literature was first "héroïque," then "galante," then "romanesque," he labels the *Chanson de Roland* heroic, since the love element is almost absent, at least in the men. Roland, "en mourant sur le champ de bataille, ne prononce pas même le nom de celle à qui il devait être uni, et qui devait bientôt mourir de douleur en apprenant sa fin." As for Aude, whom Delécluze calls Alde, "on retrouve l'amour fort, mais simple, chez la femme, comme quand elle n'est pas encore devenue une idole pour l'homme et que les grands déchirements du coeur sont presque exclusivement son partage." Again, "ces secrets du coeur féminin étaient tellement cachés avant que la galanterie eût fait une science de l'amour que les hommes ne les soupçonnaient même pas; et en effet le Roland de la *Chanson*, lorsqu'il est mourant à Roncevaux, non seulement ne témoigne point de regret en reportant son souvenir sur sa fiancée qui mourra à cause de lui, mais le nom d'Alde ne vient même pas sur ses lèvres, et tout ce qui reste de force de corps et d'énergie d'âme est employé à chercher les moyens de briser son épée pour qu'elle ne tombe pas entre les mains de ses ennemis." Delécluze makes a good point when he declares that the *Chanson de Roland*'s concept of love demonstrates that the traditions and materials utilized in the poem's elaboration were venerable. "Tel était l'amour en réalité, avant l'introduction de la *gaie science* des troubadours," he writes.[5] The *Chanson de Roland* antedates courtly love. The idea is commonplace enough to modern readers, but it was new when Delécluze wrote.

Delécluze contrasts the *Chanson de Roland*, or at least its basic contents, with the *Pseudo-Turpin Chronicle* and reasons that the latter is practically a chivalric romance and hence was written much later. "Si ce dernier livre est presque déjà un roman de chevalerie, l'oeuvre de Turold est encore une sévère et fort belle épopée." Beyond this Delécluze does not speculate about the period in which the *Chanson de Roland* was written or when its components were assembled into one poem. He makes no attempt to introduce linguistic evidence of age, but he was not interested in the *Chanson de Roland* from a philological standpoint. This is not to say that he was blind to the poem's linguistic features. For example, in his translation he retains the *aoi* at the end of the *laisses* in which it occurs but admits that he does not know what the word meant. "Est-ce un cri de guerre, une exclamation admirative ou un avertissement donné au ménétrier qui accompagnait le chant du jongleur? C'est ce que les savants n'ont pu décider; et j'avoue que je n'ai pas été plus heureux qu'eux dans mes recherches."[6] Specialists still do not agree.

Charles Magnin, an eminent critic in his day, assessed Delécluze's book in the *Revue des Deux Mondes* on 15 June 1846. Magnin did not agree with the author on various points but nevertheless called the *Chanson de Roland* an "oeuvre patriotique et sévère, sagement contenue dans les bornes de la vraisemblance." At least it had no other "invraisemblance que les prodigieux coups d'épée de Roland, d'Olivier et de l'archevêque Turpin." The critic admired the poem, describing it as "la première et la plus belle de nos anciennes épopées françaises" and delighting in its "mâle et noble poésie." With its natural, childlike, unadorned directness and its almost Homeric structure, it was devoid of the excessive complications that would characterize later French chivalric literature. The poem, he declared, "n'admet d'autre merveilleux que le merveilleux biblique et chrétien." He pointed out that it had already become famous.[7] Although there were exceptions, from this point on most French writers treating the Roland legend knew the poem.

Charles Théodore Fournel, born in Metz on 24 March 1817, studied at the Collège de Metz and became a teacher. From 1844 to 1854 he was in Berlin as tutor to the Prussian royal children, including the future Frederick III. While in Berlin he was an intimate of two writer compatriots, Paul and Louise Ackermann. In 1856, having returned to France, he was sent to Orléans as a German teacher. Later he held the same post at Tournon.[8] He died on 14 June 1869.

Fournel's poetry went almost unnoticed during the author's lifetime and has fared no better since. Gustave Vapereau, writing in the *Année littéraire* in 1863, derided its "pieuses fadeurs" and dismissed it.[9] Earlier Victor Hugo may have paid the poet an indirect tribute. Fournel's first collection of verse, *Ombres et rayons*, came out in 1840. In May of the same year Hugo's *Les Rayons et les ombres* appeared. Perhaps Hugo got his title from Fournel.[10] To Gabriel Fauré, Fournel's "vers archaïques ont le charme des vieilles enluminures et la douce coloriée des vitraux." Mallarmé, who considered the poet something of a Pre-Raphaelite, would have agreed. At Tournon he and Fournel were colleagues, and the two men proved compatible. Mallarmé admired and liked the older poet, whom he mentioned as early as 1864, preferring him to his other associates. In writing "Sainte," he may have chalked up a debt to Fournel.[11]

Fournel's *Poésies* (1848) appeared at an inopportune moment. The *Bibliographie de la France* announced it on 5 February, and the Revolution of 1848 broke out less than three weeks later. No one noticed the book. In any event, it contains Fournel's treatment of the Roland legend, a poem entitled "Romance de Roncevaux." *Romance* by this time had long since lost its strict meaning of a poem or song, divided into stanzas each followed by a refrain, telling a love story. For the Romantics it was often a ballad. When Fournel used it, the term referred merely to a narrative poem. Fournel's calling his poem a *romance* also reflects his familiarity with German poetry.

Fournel presented his readers with a personal view of Roland, keeping the traditional elements that suited his purposes, altering or discarding those that did not. Nothing in the poem tells us that Roland is the emperor's nephew, but he comes across, as usual, as very rash. Burdened or blessed with a "coeur trop altier," he readily admits that he is "superbe." He scorns advice or simply dismisses it, but on the other hand, he is both pious and brave. His two "conseillers en guerre" are Olivier and Turpin. Even the Moors honor "Turpin, le prêtre chrétien." Archbishop Turpin's noble character stands out in particular when he makes peace between the two principal warriors in his camp. When Turpin, Roland, and Olivier realize that they are doomed, they must prepare for death. Aware that Roland is sorry for his role in the disaster, the prelate exhorts Olivier to set aside his anger at Roland so that both, as Christian soldiers, can command the pagans' respect as they die. Despite events at Roncevaux, a heavenly victory awaits them, Turpin continues. As far as earthly matters are concerned, Charlemagne will make sure that his men are buried. Fournel assumes that his readers know the basic plot and consequently does not point out that the emperor arrives too late nor that the Moors are punished and Ganelon executed. Charlemagne's purpose for being in Spain is never mentioned, and finally, Turpin's assurances that the emperor will bury the dead is not followed up. The *Chanson de Roland* assures readers that the matter is resolved, but Fournel's poem does not show it being done.

Divided into five segments of unequal length, the "Romance de Roncevaux" is written in four-line stanzas, each line having seven syllables. Masculine and feminine lines alternate in an *a b a b* rhyme scheme. Although his poem lacks the gentle melancholy that pervades Vigny's "Le Cor," Fournel uses his own poetic devices with considerable skill. Many of his images, while simple, are appropriate and evocative. For example, when Charlemagne rides back into Spain at the head of his army at dusk, the poet observes that "Bientôt l'ombre vint s'asseoir / Sur les monts." Fournel also contrives to add interest to rather pedestrian statements. Instead of asserting that Marsile's army was made up of more than a hundred thousand men, for instance, he announces that the pagan king's men numbered "Cent fois mille et plus encore." On occasion an archaic construction or a word such as *ouïr, gésir,* or *félon* reminds the reader that the characters and their deeds belong to the medieval period. Despite his friendship with the Ackermanns, both atheists, Fournel was devout. Ever present in his poem is the theme of Christians versus infidels. Given the serious problems the French were having establishing their authority over Mohammedan North Africa, such a theme would have been natural at the time. Fierce devotion to their opposing creeds motivates the principal characters and heightens their credibility. Fournel even has Charlemagne accuse the Spanish Moors of rebelling against the true faith.

Like Barbier's "Roland," the "Romance de Roncevaux" begins in medias res. King Marsile has already been defeated, and he swears that he will get revenge that very day. Much later the reader learns that Ganelon has been sent to him on a peace mission and that he has told Marsile that the place to strike is Roncevaux Valley. High atop a mountain overlooking the valley, Marsile promises Mohammed, "prophète du vrai Dieu," that if he succeeds in his present venture he will burn and destroy Rome. With this, he rides down the mountain, followed by his hordes, toward Roncevaux.

Singing martial songs, Charlemagne and the main army are heading back to France. Roland, Archbishop Turpin, "les preux," and ten thousand men remain behind to oppose Marsile's one hundred thousand. Instead of being a routine rear guard contingent, they "Fermaient le passage au More," as though an attack on the main army were expected.

While Turpin conducts a prayer service before the attentive, reverent soldiers, Olivier, who has seen Marsile and his army, dashes forward, beseeching Roland to blow his horn and recall the emperor. Roland declines, pointing out that his horn has never summoned help in any combat. Olivier argues that this time the dust, the noise, the armor shining in the sun and blinding them could spell serious trouble. Convinced that God will come to their rescue, Roland continues to dismiss Olivier's appeal, whereupon Olivier brings up his fiancée: "Ne meurs point ainsi loin d'elle." This too Roland brushes aside, asserting rather sententiously that, when there is a battle to be fought, the man who trembles and slinks away to lie in a woman's arms is no soldier. Trying a different approach, Olivier tells his companion that all his men will die with him and weeping Christians will ask where they have gone. Roland remains obdurate. The Moors, he believes, would ridicule what would be construed as his terror were he to call for help. At last he realizes that his enemies are about to strike. Raising his hand toward heaven, he makes a vow. "Que Dieu seul soit mon secours, / Tant qu'au poing j'aurai mon glaive," he shouts, and, calling upon his sword to gleam with Moorish blood, he rushes off to battle.

The Franks, whom Fournel calls "les chrétiens," are surrounded in no time. All are aware that their situation is hopeless, but Roland is spared their reproaches. Outnumbered, they predict that "Les chrétiens, avant le soir, / Périront dans la mêlée" and vow to die in the holy cause. This revives Roland, who sees Turpin in pursuit of Marsile. He also sees Olivier, killing like a madman but roaring that there is no hope. Roland regrets that he declined to sound his horn earlier and wonders whether the emperor would hear it now, on the other side of the mountains. Olivier tells him not to bother the emperor at this point: "Pour si peu ton cor ne sonne." The emperor can already see "les tours de France." It is better for the men who have remained behind to die like heroes. Even so, the victorious Moors will be able to say that "l'âme vaine / De Roland, contre les siens, / A plus fait que notre haine!" Olivier concludes with a reproof, reminding Roland that the disaster must be laid at his door: "Retombent sur ton orgueil, / Les flots du sang de nos frères: / Et dans nos foyers en deuil, / Les flots des larmes amères!"

Olivier then goes off to prepare for death. Turpin has heard the exchange and admonishes Olivier, urging him to be calm and asking him to spare his friend, who deplores his bad judgment. Now everyone needs to think about God, Turpin declares. In the meantime Roland should sound his horn, so that perhaps the emperor will return and at least bury his men. The Moors will be impressed at seeing Christians living and dying like brothers. There can be no doubt, of course, that the Franks will die, but in heaven they will have their victory. Turpin's zeal inspires the men, and they rush back into the fray.

Meanwhile, the main army is happily cantering along, singing war songs. Privately Ganelon gloats, knowing what awaits the rear guard. His pleasure abates, though, when a sound is heard in the distance. Charlemagne realizes that Roland is calling him and turns pale. Ganelon tells him that the sound is merely the wind sighing in the mountain pines. When the emperor insists, Ganelon tries to dismiss the sound by wondering whether, thinking about his sweetheart, Roland "fait chanter en choeur / Les échos des monts pour elle." The moment is ominous, and the poet makes his reader sense the inauspicious hush: "Et le bruit s'élève encor, / S'élève et bientôt retombe . . . / Au couchant le soleil d'or / Descendait comme en sa tombe." Roland's insistent horn portends doom. Charlemagne at first suspects, then is convinced, that there has been treachery. He looks back and observes that "l'horizon / Gronde sombre sur l'Espagne."

Ganelon makes a last effort to explain the sound of the horn. Perhaps, he suggests, Roland, still excited about his recent battles, is chasing a rabbit, blowing his horn as he does so. Or maybe, he adds sarcastically, the hero has been bitten by a horsefly and, with his "courroux superbe," is bellowing like a bull. Charlemagne reasons that such a cavalier attitude could be hiding reprehensible motives or conduct. He recalls that Ganelon had been sent to King Marsile to dictate peace terms. Remembering the Moors' wealth, Charlemagne thinks that Ganelon may have struck a criminal bargain with his enemies. At that moment the horn is heard again, and the poetry is both suggestive and compelling: "Et le son du cor plus fort / Dans l'ombre au loin recommence, / Pareil au dernier effort / D'un mourant criant vengeance." Studying Ganelon's troubled face, Charlemagne loses his last doubts, curses "le vil Judas," and has him arrested and chained. The emperor and his men turn back toward Spain. He hopes to hear the horn once more, but instead there is "partout nuit et silence." The atmosphere is dramatic and grim, boding ill.

In the poem's final movement the somber atmosphere is maintained as the emperor and his men ride back across the mountains into Spain. The poet describes the scene in splendid images.

> Bientôt l'ombre vint s'asseoir
> Sur les monts; et la vallée
> Reposait paisible au soir,
> Sombre et de brume voilée.
>
> Où sont, où sont, Roncevaux,
> Roncevaux, triste vallée,
> Guerriers, armures, chevaux,
> Et les cris et la mêlée?

Actually it is over. The Moors, knowing the emperor will return as soon as he hears the horn, have rushed in, done their work, and sped away. They have killed Olivier, Turpin, and all the others save one. Roland, mortally wounded, is still alive. Carrying his horn and leaning on his sword, he makes his way through the carnage. Tired and broken, he sits down in the shade of a tree on a mountain road. He does not know that the emperor is rushing back, but he listens all the same.

He addresses first his horn and then his sword, recalling how in the past the horn has called men into battle and announced their victories. For once its voice has been lost, but it must not fall into the Moors' hands. Roland dashes it against some rocks and breaks it. To his noble sword he declares that he must soon die. He decides to destroy it, but more than six times he raises it in the air with both hands and, with a mighty thrust, strikes the rock to no avail. Only the rock crumbles. Exhausted and in extreme pain, Roland crawls toward a chasm and drops his sword into it. With that he murmurs a short prayer, asking to die. His wish is granted.

> "Donne enfin paix à mon coeur
> Sur mon noir chevet de pierre."
>
> Et les bras en croix, Roland,
> Les yeux tournés vers la France,
> Sur les hauts rochers s'étend,
> Pâlit, et reste en silence.

The next morning at daybreak, Charlemagne and the main army return to the battle site. The emperor and his men, "tous en pleurs, tous en prière," contemplate the aftermath. In death as in life Roland is the spectacle that arrests everyone's attention: "Roland gisait sur la pierre, / L'armée était alentour." Even though Roland is impetuous and does not listen to good advice, his prowess and his religious convictions and fervor make him heroic. With his deeds in battle and his exemplary death, he seems to atone for his shortcomings. Perhaps the poem ends too abruptly, but the conclusion is no less dramatic. The reader knows that sooner or later virtue will triumph. Yet Fournel does not moralize in his poem. His closest approach to didacticism occurs when, brushing aside Olivier's arguments and entreaties, Roland brashly refuses to summon help. God, Roland contends, will help him. While this might be true, Fournel believes, Roland should have taken some precautions of his own. But Fournel's poem implies that Roland's goodness and heroism more than compensate for his human flaw, his unwillingness to heed sound advice.[12]

The "Romance de Roncevaux" demonstrates Fournel's familiarity with an earlier German poem, Friedrich de La Motte Fouqué's *Romanzen vom Thale Ronceval* (1805).[13] Like his German predecessor, Fournel labeled his poem a *romance*, dividing it into sections, all unequal in length. As in the German poem, these are in turn divided into four-line stanzas. La Motte Fouqué had used trochaic tetrameter. Similarly, Fournel decided upon short lines of seven syllables each. Both La Motte Fouqué and Fournel called Marsile "Marsilias."

Roland's sword Durandal is Durandarte in La Motte Fouqué and Durandart in Fournel. More strikingly, Hauteclaire, Olivier's sword, was dubbed Anteclara by La Motte Fouqué and Anteclare by Fournel.

Neither the *Romanzen vom Thale Ronceval* nor the "Romance de Roncevaux" mentions that Roland is Charlemagne's nephew, but it is clear in both that the emperor has a special attachment to the young knight. When Fournel's Olivier pleads with Roland to blow his horn, his entreaties follow La Motte Fouqué rather closely. The German Olivier, as well as the French one, beseeches Roland to remember his fiancée and his men. When Roland refuses to blow the horn and the inevitable showdown with the pagans becomes a calamitous reality, Fournel again follows his predecessor's lead in having Olivier upbraid his friend, using nearly the same language. In both poems Archbishop Turpin intervenes and reconciles the two men. Charlemagne, too far away to save the day, can already see the "towers of France" when he finally hears the horn. In both poems Ganelon resorts to essentially the same arguments as he tries to convince the emperor not to turn back, and in both the emperor reacts in the same manner. In neither poem does the reader see Olivier and Turpin die. The dead Roland, in both poems, is found with his arms outstretched, as though on a cross. Finally, Marsile's oath that he will burn Rome figures in both works. These parallels indicate that Fournel knew the German poem quite well and that he borrowed a number of details from it.

When Fournel published his "Romance de Roncevaux," the *Chanson de Roland* had appeared, though Fournel did not necessarily know the poem. If not, how can we account for Archbishop Turpin's presence at the battle of Roncevaux? La Motte Fouqué had placed him there, but in 1805 La Motte Fouqué could not have known the *Chanson de Roland* or the *Rolandslied*, neither of which were published at that time. For this detail he relied upon Stricker's *Rhythmus de Caroli Magni Expeditione Hispanica*, a thirteenth-century narrative. Stricker in turn had had access to a manuscript version of the *Rolandslied*, in which Turpin fought and died with the others.[14]

Fournel was not merely adapting a German work, however moving he may have found it. Between his poem and the German one there are notable differences. Roland appears, in La Motte Fouqué's poem, to accept his inability to destroy his sword and dies clutching the weapon. Fournel's hero is made of stronger stuff. He drags himself to a crevice and drops his sword into it. Fournel's conclusion points to another basic difference between the two poems. In the "Romance de Roncevaux" Charlemagne and the main army return and find Roland and the other peers dead. The poem ends with this dismal but dramatic scene. La Motte Fouqué added an episode, showing the emperor after he crosses the mountains into Provence. There the disconsolate monarch calls upon St. Giles, a hermit whom an angel has informed about the disaster. The hermit presents a book about the ambush to his visitor and assures him that the disaster was God's will. All told, Fournel's simple denouement is probably more effective.

Some travelers to the Pyrenees Mountains were not reminded of Roland. Adolphe Thiers, the future politician and historian, visited the region in November and December 1822, but his book *Les Pyrénées et le midi de la France* does not mention Charlemagne's ill-fated rear guard. Thiers's silence is unusual. Most travelers and guidebooks have much to say about the battle of Roncevaux. The most popular of the guidebooks was probably A. Philibert Abadie's *Itinéraire des Hautes-Pyrénées*, first published in 1819. Abadie considered the Cirque de Gavarnie impressive and admired "la cime blanchie du Marboré, la Brèche de Roland, et les pompeuses tours qui dominent l'amphithéâtre. . . . Sur ces formidables remparts qu'on croirait bâtis par les anciens géans, au pied de ces sublimes tours, combattirent autrefois Agramant, Ferragus, Marsile, contre les preux de Charlemagne. Au-dessus, Roland, monté sur son cheval de bataille, transperça une montagne de sa terrible épée et s'ouvrit un chemin qui devait le conduire chez les Maures et à la victoire."[15] Abadie must have thought that the tourist trade would be hurt if the area he was praising was the scene of a tragic defeat. The references to Agramant and Ferragus suggest that the author's sketchy documentation came from folklore, the *Pseudo-Turpin Chronicle*, *Orlando innamorato*, and *Orlando furioso*. Although the *Chanson de Roland* was published at the beginning of 1837, Abadie did not bother to revise this passage in the edition of his guidebook for the tourist season that year.

A perceptive traveler interested in the written and unwritten lore about the battle of Roncevaux was Baron Isidore Taylor, enlightened administrator of the Comédie Française. A member of the French expeditionary force that invaded Spain in 1823, he served with distinction. After the campaign he resigned his commission and traveled. When the Duc de Montpensier announced his intention to vacation in the mountains in 1843, the baron sent him some notes. At the same time the baron published a book, *Les Pyrénées*. When describing what was presumed to be the battle site, Taylor was one of the few writers of his time to call it a plain rather than a valley. On leaving the Château d'Orthez, he records,

> nous nous rendîmes à l'abbaye de Roncesvalles, communément nommée abbaye de Roncevaux, cet autre grand souvenir des temps poétiques de la chevalerie. L'abbaye se compose de vastes et solides bâtiments. . . . Mais ici la pensée ne s'occupe ni du monastère ni des cénobites, elle est tout entière au nom fameux que ce lieu rappelle, à l'immense désastre dont il fut le théâtre, aux morts illustres dont il fut le tombeau. C'est en 778 que la fortune de Charlemagne vint échouer à Roncevaux par la trahison de Lupus, duc de Gascogne. C'est là que le paladin Roland a trouvé sa fin glorieuse. La bataille où il a succombé s'est livrée dans la

plaine, près du village de Barguette, à un quart de lieue au midi de l'abbaye. Les montagnards montrent encore à quelque distance une ruine nommée l'hôpital de Roland. C'est là que ce guerrier, blessé à mort, s'est réfugié au moment de mourir. Lorsque nous avons visité Roncevaux, l'abbaye étoit encore habitée par des moines. Ces bons pères montroient avec orgueil des armes qui, disoient-ils, avoient appartenu au héros chanté par l'Arioste. Ils faisoient surtout remarquer deux boules de trois pouces de diamètre, attachées par deux chaînons de fer à un manche de deux pieds de long, garni de fer aux deux extrémités, masse d'armes terrible dont un géant seul pouvoit se servir.[16]

Clearly Taylor believed that Lupus, duke of Gascony, not the Moors, set up the ambush that cost Roland his life. His tone suggests that he had reservations about the objects and ruins that mountaineers and monks were showing. Gaillard claimed that Archbishop Turpin's slippers used to be pointed out also. Taylor was dubious, but his mentioning such things demonstrates that a lively oral tradition had been preserved and was still being passed on.

Taylor was aware of historical writing about the Roncevaux disaster. He comments that "l'histoire n'a laissé sur ce grand fait de la bataille de Roncevaux que des détails aussi incomplets qu'incertains. Elle est restée dans ce vague qui se prête si bien aux fictions de la poésie. C'est à la poésie seule aujourd'hui qu'il faut demander des souvenirs qui ont plus de merveilleux que d'authenticité, mais auxquels l'imagination prête toujours un grand charme." Then the author embarks upon a lengthy discussion of the *Chanson de Roland*, ending with a quotation in modern French. Taylor must have made his own translation, since no printed one had yet appeared. For Taylor, one of the merits of this kind of poem is that it is "l'expression naïve et simple des moeurs du peuple qu'ils mettent en action sous nos yeux." Returning to the question of tradition, the author underscores his conviction that "les chants historiques . . . sont l'expression des sentiments nationaux, l'aliment principal des traditions, le premier anneau de cette chaîne qui nous rattache par l'intelligence aux souvenirs historiques les plus reculés. . . . Pour le peuple, le chant historique, c'est l'histoire."[17]

Taylor makes a curious observation concerning the Franks' withdrawal from Spain in 778: "Depuis cette célèbre retraite de Charlemagne, les Français, dans presque toutes les retraites qu'ils ont exécutées, ont toujours éprouvé des revers ou de grands désastres." He was no doubt thinking of Napoleon's reverses in Russia, the Peninsula War, and the battle of France, which had occurred during his lifetime. Even so, did he know the extent to which the retreating French had been able to hold their advancing enemies at bay? As the British were driving them out of Spain in 1813, there had been a short but momentous halt. At a modern battle of Roncevaux, Marshal Soult defeated his opponent, Sir G.L. Cole, on 25 July. Soult's victory, however, could not stave off the inevitable, at least not for long.[18]

In the mid–nineteenth century another visitor would comment upon

Roncevaux, again from the literary standpoint. Nevertheless, he was not as taken with the *Chanson de Roland* as Taylor had been. Commissioned by a publishing house, Hachette, to write a travel book, Hippolyte Taine traveled in the Pyrenees Mountains in 1854. The result was a *Voyage aux eaux des Pyrénées* (1855). Taine returned in 1855 and 1856 and reworked his book as *Voyage aux Pyrénées*, published in 1858.

As Jean Fourcassié pointed out, Taine was not yet "le doctrinaire du réalisme." Though not a Romantic, he had the Romantic feeling for nature and was awed by the spectacle of the mountains. He was reminded of the *Chanson de Roland*, which he quoted, and its author. Taine assumed that there was only one author, an individual with a predilection for the enormous and the miraculous. "Il aime le merveilleux et se plaît aux histoires gigantesques. Dans la bataille de Roncevaux, tout grandit, et à l'infini. Les preux tuent toute l'arrière-garde des Sarrasins, cent mille hommes, puis l'armée du roi Marsile, trente bataillons, chacun de dix mille hommes. Roland sonne le cor, et la clameur arrive à trente lieues jusqu'à Charlemagne, dont les soixante mille hautbois se mettent à retentir." The epic's characters are uncomplicated, "des esprits et des âmes d'enfants."[19] For the moment, Taine had nothing to say about the *Chanson de Roland*'s poetic qualities.

Less than a decade later, Taine would judge the *Chanson de Roland* more harshly. His prolonged contact with English literature may have altered his taste, and he seemed ready to endorse the remark Voltaire attributed to Nicolas de Malézieu, that the French do not have epic mentalities. In the first volume of the *Histoire de la littérature anglaise* (1863), Taine vented his spleen against his compatriot poets. "Nulle race n'est moins poétique," he complained. He noted that there was no dearth of French epics, but their artistic achievement leaves much to be desired. Homer took time to call attention to the wonders of nature, but the French epic poet only gives facts, "sans s'attarder aux rêves du coeur ou devant les richesses du paysage." Taine declared that the *Chanson de Roland* was the best of the Old French epics, but he expressed only qualified admiration. "Voulez-vous ouvrir le plus ancien, le plus original, le plus éloquent, à l'endroit le plus émouvant, la *Chanson de Roland*, au moment où Roland meurt?" he asked his readers. "Le conteur est ému, et pourtant son langage reste le même, uni, sans accent, tant ils sont pourvus du génie de la prose et dépourvus du génie de la poésie. Il donne un abrégé des motifs, le sommaire des événements, la suite des raisons affligeantes, la suite des raisons consolantes. Rien de plus. Ces hommes voient la chose ou l'action en elle-même, et s'en tiennent à cette vue. Leur idée demeure exacte, nette et simple, et n'éveille pas une image voisine pour se confondre avec elle, se colorer et se transformer. Elle reste sèche."[20] Using Génin's edition, Taine quotes in a note the *Chanson de Roland*'s account of its hero's death.

Taine reacted here against his earlier, more enthusiastic view of the poem,

with its enormous dimensions, its simple, uncomplicated characters, and its supernatural interventions. His disappointment is based, of course, on his personal aesthetic and the resultant meagre latitude he was willing to allow epic writers. An epic had to be Homeric. Obviously Taine did not share Quinet's view that the Old French narratives dealing with Roland were quite Homeric in both concept and execution.

At about the same time, Taine commented in the *Philosophie de l'art* (1865) that true heroes are to be found only in a people's primitive literary works. He was in agreement with Michelet in this. "Les créatures vraiment idéales," he wrote, "ne naissent abondamment que dans les époques primitives et naïves, et c'est toujours dans les âges reculés, à l'origine des peuples, parmi les songes de l'enfance humaine, qu'il faut remonter pour trouver les héros et les dieux. Chaque peuple a les siens; il les a tirés de son coeur; il les nourrit de ses légendes; à mesure qu'il s'avance dans la solitude inexplorée des âges nouveaux et de l'histoire future, leurs images immortelles luisent devant ses yeux, comme autant de génies bienfaisants chargés de le conduire et de le protéger. Tels sont les héros dans les vraies épopées . . , Roland dans nos vieilles chansons de geste."[21] In explaining the grandeur of legendary heroes and the need humanity experiences for them, Taine still does not retract his contention that French epics are devoid of real poetry. His remarks demonstrate how sensitive he was to what he considered the essence of poetry to be. The *Chanson de Roland*, he thought, simply did not have it.

Taine had a friend, Maxime Du Camp, who was quite interested in the Roland legend. According to Edmond de Goncourt, Taine played a role early in 1880 in getting him elected to the Académie Française.[22]

Today Maxime Du Camp (1822-94) is remembered for little except his friendship with Flaubert. An inveterate traveler, gifted photographer, editor of the *Revue de Paris,* and novelist, he also tried his hand at poetry. *Les Convictions* (1858) contains a poem about Roland. Called "Le Cor d'ivoire," it is dated August 1857. Symmetrical in design, it is divided into three sections. The first and third, each having four stanzas, are identical in structure and length. The middle section, like a scherzo, offers a harmonious change of pace, with its three stanzas and different meter. The verse is not memorable, but the poem expresses some worthwhile, original thoughts about Roland, his horn, and his death.[23]

When the action begins, Roland is in the mountains, facing the enemy alone. Presumably his companions have all been killed. While no Olivier is there to tell him to do so, the hero repeatedly blows his gem-studded horn. The countryside quivers from the blasts, and the effort costs the stalwart knight his little remaining strength.

> Le preux Roland, au pied de la montagne
> Environné du Maure triomphant
> A grand effort sonnait de l'oliphant
> Pour appeler son oncle Charlemagne;
> Pâle et sanglant il sonnait coup sur coup;
> Le dernier son fit trembler la campagne
> Et lui rompit les artères du cou.

No one answers his call, and no one ever comes, not even later. As in Michelet, Du Camp's Roland has been abandoned. He sinks down on the bloodsoaked earth that will be his deathbed and awaits the end. Beating his chest like any other penitent about to die, he kisses his sword's crosslike handle and murmurs his last prayers. He struggles to stand up. Seizing his horn, he hurls it into the distance before dying exhausted, "le lança loin de lui dans l'espace; / Le cor gémit montant vers le ciel bleu; / Après avoir suivi des yeux sa trace, / Roland tomba, rendant son âme à Dieu!"

In the poem's second movement the poet wonders what became of the horn. Is it hidden among the rocks, in the grass or brush? Is it hanging in a tree? Have clever sorcerers discovered it and spirited it away? Could the Moors have found it and hung it, as a trophy, in a mosque? Disdaining to be looked upon by pagan eyes, did the hero's horn fly away into the heavens, where it shines like a star?

The poet answers his queries in the final stanzas of the poem. Perhaps, indeed, the horn has supernatural properties. It fell back to earth, landing at the same spot from which it was thrown. Roland had hurled it so far, however, that he died before it returned.

> Le cor d'ivoire est enfoui sous terre
> A l'endroit même où Roland l'a jeté
> En ivoquant le Dieu de vérité;
> Nul enchanteur, nul sorcier solitaire,
> Nul Maghrebin, nul Maure valeureux
> N'a pu trouver dans sa retraite austère
> Cet oliphant que sonnait l'ancien preux.

The horn will remain hidden until it signals the arrival of humankind's deliverance. The poet does not clearly specify whether this will be Jesus' Second Coming or Judgment Day.

> Un jour viendra, par Dieu fixé d'avance,
> Où, scintillant enfin à tous les yeux,
> Le cor, brisant l'oubli silencieux
> Qui le retient sans écho ni puissance,
> Eveillera l'ombre de notre nuit

> Et sonnera la grande délivrance
> Dont nous cherchons l'écho dans chaque bruit.

One day, then, the horn will be unearthed and sounded by an extraordinary man, ardent, intrepid, and uncompromising.

> L'homme hardi dont la lèvre robuste
> S'approchera du cor mystérieux
> Sera choisi, vaillant et glorieux,
> Pour mettre à fin notre labeur auguste;
> Il sera fort, inflexible et fervent,
> Et, dans son coeur, il saura que le juste
> N'hésite pas quand Dieu dit: En avant!

Taking the instrument, he will stride over mountain and plain, through field, forest, and city, wherever sound can be heard: "Il s'en ira sonnant à perdre haleine, / Et cette fois Charlemagne viendra!" This man could be Gabriel, or even Christ. Perhaps a special soldier of the Lord, he has been chosen because of his virtues to place himself at the head of the elect, marching forward to establish God's kingdom on earth.

Du Camp at this time was about to sail away to help Giuseppi Garibaldi try to put an end to the popes' temporal power. Given Du Camp's anticlericalism, his still-liberal views on other matters, and his commitment to what he called social poetry, it is likely that he was converting a chivalrous medieval ideal into what he may have considered its modern expression, social justice. Before the French Revolution made him a patriot, Roland traditionally had been the servant of an earthly and a heavenly king. Now Du Camp seems to have stirred him with a social mission. This time, as the call is sounded, someone in a position to accomplish necessary reforms will respond, or so the poet believes.

The chief flaw in Du Camp's poem is its vagueness. The author drew little, if anything, from the *Chanson de Roland*. Relying upon the *Pseudo-Turpin Chronicle*, he had Roland burst blood vessels in his neck rather than his temples as he blew his horn, contrary to the *Chanson*. In other respects Du Camp is highly original. Roland, by the time he died, was alone at Roncevaux. No Olivier is mentioned, and the pious knight makes no attempt to destroy his sword. The horn, on the other hand, is of supreme importance. It waits until some later hero, worthy to be Roland's successor, leads mankind into a new, happier era.

Although he never treated the entire Roland story or even the battle of Roncevaux directly, Victor Hugo was interested in the legend and even invented an episode or two of his own. This interest began showing up as early as the *Nouvelles Odes* (1824). One manifestation was "La Grand'mère," a *ballade* that the author dated 1823. Two children hope that their grandmother will tell them a story, and they suggest Roland and his adventures. Among other things, they would like to know "si le noir démon craint plus, dans ses royaumes, / Les psaumes de Turpin que le fer de Roland."

"La Guerre d'Espagne," written the same year, celebrates the French Bourbons' invasion of Spain. Louis XVIII was rescuing his cousin Ferdinand VII from an unruly parliament bent on forcing the king to accept a liberal constitution. To the French and their Spanish supporters, this was a crusade. Among conservatives, the army sent to deliver the king and throttle his godless parliament was referred to as the Hundred Thousand Sons of St. Louis. Hugo voiced the dominant opinion when he wrote that these men were in pursuit of "de nouveaux infidèles." The invasion was a success. Eventually, having become a liberal and an anticlerical, the poet would decide that it had been wrong. But for now, he hailed it and in the process claimed that monarchy and war were inseparable, affirming that "On ne peut te briser, sceptre de Charlemagne, / Sans briser le fer de Roland!" Chateaubriand, the French minister of foreign affairs, noted in his memoirs that the invaders' second corps passed through Roncevaux Valley.[24] Hugo appears to have been aware of the itinerary.

As the French troops were sweeping into Spain, Hugo imagined that Roland's ghost, "assis sur sa tombe célèbre," was watching and approving, pleased with the reincarnations of the medieval knights who had rushed to the defense of God and king. "Roland! N'est-il pas vrai, noble élu de la guerre, / Que ton ombre, éveillée aux cris de nos guerriers, / Aux champs de Roncevaux lorsqu'ils passaient naguère / Les prit pour d'anciens chevaliers?"[25] With the First Empire's soldiers in mind, Napoléon Peyrat would recall these lines a decade later. "Assis sur sa tombe célèbre" indicates that Hugo, like Prince Lucien Bonaparte, believed the paladin had been buried in Roncevaux Valley. Subsequently he would not be sure that the body had been interred, but he stuck to his conviction that, on the Franks' withdrawal, it was left behind.

Twenty years later, during his annual vacation with Juliette Drouet, Hugo traveled in Spain. On 4 August 1843 he saw Roncevaux, with its endless stretches of mountains. He also took in the Cirque de Gavarnie, "le colosseum de la nature." In *Les Travailleurs de la mer* (1866), he would remember having seen the Brèche de Roland, which had been almost a disappointment. "La Brèche de Roland n'est pas si fabuleuse qu'elle en a l'air. . . . La balafre du travail humain est visible sur l'oeuvre divin," he wrote. His reaction was equivocal.[26]

In 1846 Hugo would again think of the Roland legend in "J'aime un groupe d'enfants," later included in *L'Art d'être grand-père*. For Hugo, as for Dumas père, Roland's childhood had a certain attraction. Unlike Dumas,

Hugo resorted to pure invention. Hugo's brief episode pictures the future knight as a blond, good-humored little boy playing in the fields with two friends after their fencing lesson. Precocious, he is on his way to becoming a redoubtable fighter. Already "rempli de projets et de voeux," he likes flags and banners.[27]

While Hugo undoubtedly knew Quinet's "L'Epopée française," it is certain that he looked at another article as well, though he may have read it superficially. Using this article, he would write several poems, including "Le Mariage de Roland" and "Aymerillot," which, on the basis of handwriting, can be dated around 1850.[28] Later the poet jotted down additions to these poems and to "Le Petit Roi de Galice." Some of the developments he eventually incorporated, others he discarded.

In addition to Quinet, the author who provided Hugo with his written source material was Achille Jubinal (1810-75). A member of the Faculté des Lettres of the University of Montpellier, Jubinal was a professor who, like Michelet, Quinet, and Taine, had his courses suspended because he held unpopular opinions.[29] Having flourished under the July monarchy, Jubinal's academic career came to a halt with the regime. Jubinal became a republican, then quickly rallied to the Second Empire. Although he was born in Paris and would die there, in the Corps Législatif he soon represented Bagnères de Bigorre, in the Pyrenees Mountains. His *Letters sur les Pyrénées*, published in 1848, he reworded and expanded. As *Les Hautes-Pyrénées*, it reappeared in 1858. Although the book mentions the Brèche de Roland, it could not have told Hugo anything about the famed paladin. Medieval literature was Jubinal's chief interest, and he wrote numerous articles and books on it. For Hugo, Jubinal's most important publication was an article entitled "Quelques romans chez nos aïeux." Appearing in the *Journal du dimanche* on 1 November 1846, it summarized *Girart de Vienne* and *Aymeri de Narbonne*, plus other epics.[30] Hugo handled his source material with extraordinary freedom, altering, adding, and inventing whenever he liked. Quinet and Jubinal offered a point of departure. Hugo's imagination did the rest.

"Le Mariage de Roland" first appeared in the *Revue des Deux Mondes* on 1 September 1859. No doubt its purpose was to whet the public's appetite, for the same issue announced the forthcoming publication of the first series of the *Légende des siècles*, which would include it. In the poem Roland and Olivier are adversaries in a duel to the finish. Since Hugo does not explain why they are fighting, the reader, remembering Quinet, must reconstruct the situation. Girart, lord of Vienne, thinks he has a grievance against his monarch. Charlemagne, on the other hand, is exasperated at what he views as the arrogant behavior of a turbulent vassal who, with his entire clan, has retired to his castle and is making war upon his sovereign. Eventually each side designates a champion to uphold its cause in single combat. Olivier and Roland are to duel for Girart and Charlemagne, respectively. They meet to settle their relatives' dispute on an island in the middle of the Rhone River. At this point the poem begins.

Already the two men are accomplished warriors, but they look like mere boys. The poet describes them as "deux pages blonds, roses comme des filles." Only the day before, these serious, determined antagonists had been "deux enfants riant à leurs familles." Now circumstances have made them grim opponents. They have been fighting since dawn: "Ils luttent, noirs, muets, furieux, acharnés." Long before we see them, each has killed the other's horse. Evenly matched, they belabor each other for five days, to no avail. When Olivier at one point disarms Roland by knocking Durandal into the river, he courteously discards his own sword, and the two men continue their battle using uprooted trees as clubs. Throughout, Hugo maintains an impartial stance. His protagonists, meanwhile, acquire a fervent admiration for each other. Finally, realizing that neither will ever subdue the other, they conclude that honor has been satisfied and that they can make peace. Abruptly, Olivier proposes an alliance.

> Roland, nous n'en finirons point.
> Tant qu'ils nous restera quelque tronçon au poing
> Nous lutterons ainsi que lions et panthères.
> Ne vaudrait-il pas mieux que nous devinssions frères?
> Ecoute, j'ai ma soeur, la belle Aude au bras blanc,
> Epouse-la.
>
> —Pardieu! je veux bien, dit Roland.
> Et maintenant buvons, car l'affaire était chaude.
>
> C'est ainsi que Roland épousa la belle Aude.

During the struggle, Olivier breaks his sword. A truce is called so that he can procure a new one. His father sends him Hauteclaire. Hugo decided to call it Closamont, as Jubinal had done.[31] Often, however, he departed radically from the Quinet and Jubinal summaries of *Girart de Vienne*. In the epic, for example, Roland and Olivier's duel lasts one or two days, not four or five.[32] At one point the antagonists consider resting, Olivier offering to fan his weary opponent while he catches his breath. Quinet felt that Olivier was being ironic. To Hugo, on the contrary, the offer was an exquisite knightly gesture.

Hugo deviated from his source material in more significant respects than this, however. For one thing, he makes Girart the father of Olivier and Aude, whereas in the epic he is their uncle. The reader is startled too at the enthusiasm with which Hugo's Roland jumps at the idea of marrying Aude, whom in this account he has never seen. In *Girart de Vienne* he has had a long conversation with her. More important, in *Girart de Vienne* Roland and Aude are engaged but do not marry. Although the ceremony is not shown, Hugo tells us that the wedding took place.

The poet's most noticeable deviation, and perhaps his most unaccountable one, involves the duel's termination. In "Le Mariage de Roland" Olivier brings about the denouement by suggesting the match between his sister and his adversary. In *Girart de Vienne* an angel comes down from heaven and orders the two champions to desist, telling them that their energies and prowess will soon be needed in a worthier cause. That Hugo gave his poem a conclusion from which the miraculous is eliminated is perplexing, since the poem appears in a section of the *Légende des siècles* devoted to Christian epic cycles.

Toward the end of the nineteenth century, several authors interested in the Roland legend took Hugo to task. One of them, Joseph Fabre, remarked that the poet had narrated the duel "avec grand éclat, mais aussi avec de regrettables outrances qui sentent la rhétorique at révoltent le sens commun." He did not elaborate.[33] The medievalist Adolphe d'Avril registered a number of specific objections. The problem of verisimilitude disturbed him, for one thing. The five-day duel stretched reader credulity too far, especially since, after a time, the weapons were tree trunks. Avril was devout, and he considered it inappropriate for the poet to mention a sorcerer and two pagan deities, Bacchus and Apollo. Avril also complained that, instead of ending, "Le Mariage de Roland" simply breaks off. He saw no reason why the poet should have substituted a secular ending for the divine apparition that brings the episode to a close in *Girart de Vienne*. What happens in the epic "est purement et simplement admirable, non seulement au point de vue religieux, mais comme ressort dramatique," he asserted. Finally, he regarded the poem's last few lines as vulgar: "Et maintenant buvons, car l'affaire était chaude." That Roland should suggest, once the duel is over and his engagement decided, that he and Olivier should celebrate by drinking together is shocking. Roland and Olivier look like two stolid *crocheteurs* who, having cudgeled one another soundly, are making peace as they down a few pints. "Et le lecteur va rester sous l'impression d'une petite scène de cabaret." Avril agreed with Prosper Tarbé, who, editing the epic, saw the duel as an ominous foreshadowing of future events. Alluding to an unseen "tombe toujours entr'ouverte," Tarbé commented that in the original epic "au milieu de ce cliquetis d'armes, de ces cris de guerre... , le poète fait sans cesse poindre à l'horizon la journée fatale de Roncevaux. C'est sans doute une conception dramatique que de placer une image de la mort au milieu de ce qui respire la vie la plus active, la plus ardente, la plus avide de l'avenir.... On doit aimer tous les jeunes coeurs brûlant des affections les plus saintes et sur lesquels une mort inévitable et prochaine étend déjà sa main froide et sans pitié."[34] Tarbé was also undoubtedly concerned over the dilemma involving Aude. Into her life death intrudes, keeping her and Roland from union. Tarbé implied that their story contains the plot of a gripping drama. Hugo of all people should have sensed this. Three years before Achille Jubinal's article, however, the failure of *Les Burgraves* drove Hugo from the theater, and he had no desire at this point to exploit the situation's dramatic potential.

"Aymerillot" follows "Le Mariage de Roland" in the *Légende des siècles* but did not appear with it in the *Revue des Deux Mondes*. Departing from Jubinal once once, Hugo reinterpreted the main character, making him a more ingratiating figure than he is in *Aymeri de Narbonne* and in Jubinal's summary. The poem tells how, returning from Spain, Charlemagne sees the town of Narbonne. He calls upon his proven barons to capture it for him, but each gives a courteous excuse and declines. Finally Aymerillot, an obscure lad of twenty, volunteers and succeeds. Henceforth he is known as Aymeri de Narbonne.[35]

The beginning of the poem commands our attention, since here the battle of Roncevaux and Roland's death are evoked. In writing this segment of his poem, as in "La Guerre d'Espagne," the author appears to have relied upon tradition rather than printed sources. As Charlemagne rides along, gloomy and downcast, he thinks about the recent disaster. "Le bon roi Charle est plein de douleurs et d'ennui," declares the poet. "Charlemagne, empereur à la barbe fleurie, / Revient d'Espagne; il a le coeur triste, il s'écrie: / 'Roncevaux! Roncevaux! ô traître Ganelon!' / Car son neveu Roland est mort dans ce vallon / Avec les douze pairs et toute son armée." Later, "Il pleure; l'empereur pleure de la souffrance / D'avoir perdu ses preux, ses douze pairs de France, / Ses meilleurs chevaliers qui n'étaient jamais las, / Et son neveu Roland." Aside from his personal loss, he has an added reason for dejection. He foresees that the disaster will be commemorated in songs and epics. He knows "Qu'on fera des chansons dans toutes ces montagnes / Sur ses guerriers tombés devant des paysans." Thus the humiliation will be perpetuated. Believing that there had been local, probably spontaneous *chansons*, Hugo echoes an idea that J.P. Picquet had advanced in 1789 and that Gaston Paris would shortly elevate to the status of theory. Apparently the poet also believed that Roland's attackers were not Moslem or Gascon soldiers but mountaineer civilians. Later Jean Richepin would suggest a similar view. Hugo implies too that Roland, Olivier, and the other victims were either left on the battlefield or buried where they fell. The emperor mulls over what he has left on the other side of the mountains. "Et les os des héros blanchissent dans les plaines," he sadly reminds himself, but he also praises his "compagnons couchés dans la tombe profonde." Nothing is said about interment in France. Such details constitute additional evidence that the poet was not familiar with the *Chanson de Roland* when he wrote the poem. In "La Guerre d'Espagne," written much earlier, Roland's body was left behind, but it had been buried. Hugo is consistent in thinking that the corpse remained at Roncevaux.

In the midst of his sorrow and brooding Charlemagne sees Narbonne and is distracted. When each of his nobles is unwilling to assault the town, he recalls painfully that among his slain heroes there were two who would not have hung back. "O comtes palatins tombés dans ces vallées, / O géants qu'on voyait debout dans les mêlées, / Devant qui Satan même aurait crié merci, / Olivier et Roland, que n'êtes-vous ici! / Si vous étiez vivants, vous prendriez Narbonne, / Paladins!" At last a bold but unproven lad in his entourage takes the town for him. Despite the boy's manly achievement, Paul Verlaine referred to him as an *éphèbe*. Verlaine applied the same term to a boy in another of Hugo's Roland poems, Nuño, king of Galicia, who was fifteen and had "la peau plus blanche qu'une femme."[36] Verlaine seems not to have noticed that Olivier and Roland are described as "deux enfants," "roses comme des filles."

Probably "Le Petit Roi de Galice" was written around 1846, a little earlier than "Le Mariage de Roland" and "Aymerillot."[37] It was published in the *Légende des siècles* in 1859. While it has overtones of Ariosto, its plot is wholly imaginary. Here Roland is shown as a knight errant before the battle of Roncevaux. He is in Spain, just back from Brittany, Sicily, Egypt, and Arabia, where he has won great renown. The poem tells about ten villainous princes, all brothers, who have kidnapped their adolescent nephew, a little king. Camped at a spot near Compostela, they are trying to decide how to get rid of him and then divide his kingdom among themselves. Nuño is tied on a mule while "cette collection de monstres se concerte." Heatedly, they discuss "Trois avis: le cloîtrer au prochain monastère, / L'aller vendre à Juzaph, prince des sarrasins, / Le jeter simplement dans un des puits voisins."

Suddenly, Roland rides up to the group. How this paladin of France happens to be in Spain is not explained. Prince Lucien Bonaparte had said that Roland was "le soutien . . . de l'orphelin," and now it will be demonstrated. When Roland suspects that the men are up to mischief and makes inquiries, they respond with threats at first. Then, learning his identity, they flatter and attempt to bribe him. "Tant d'illustres combats / Font luire votre gloire, ô grand soldat sincère, / Que nous vous aimons mieux compagnon qu'adversaire," the cleverest of the brothers tells him, offering him two towns if he promises not to interfere. Astounded, Roland gives the young monarch his horse and bids him rush into town. Nuño hurries back to his capital, where he is welcomed enthusiastically.

Meanwhile, Roland kills the wicked uncles, along with their soldiers, except for the shrewd one, who gets away. The action is narrated in minute, vivid detail. Although he wins, the hero does not emerge from the carnage unscathed. He is wounded but undaunted.

In "Le Petit Roi de Galice" Hugo seems more concerned with Durandal than with its owner. The sword's rapid, daring thrusts are described with great care: "Durandal flamboyant semble un sinistre esprit; / Elle va, vient, remonte et tombe, se relève, / S'ébat, et fait la fête effrayante du glaive." Tearing into the evil conspirators, it wreaks terrible destruction.

> Durandal, à tuer ces coquins s'ébréchant,
> Avait jonché de morts la terre, et fait ce champ
> Plus vermeil qu'un nuage où le soleil se couche;
> Elle s'était rompue en ce labeur farouche;
> Ce qui n'empêchait pas Roland de s'avancer;
> Les bandits, le croyant prêt à recommencer,
> Tremblants comme des boeufs qu'on ramène à l'étable
> A chaque mouvement de son bras redoutable,
> Reculaient, lui montrant de loin leur coutelas;
> Et, pas à pas, Roland, sanglant, terrible, las,
> Les chassait devant lui parmi les fondrières;
> Et, n'ayant plus d'épée, il leur jetait des pierres.

At the end of the poem Roland has killed most of his enemies and put the others to flight. Still, he has no sword. It has broken or crumbled, but he is undisturbed. His lack of concern remains a mystery unless one reads a few lines that the poet decided not to use in the *Légende des siècles*. The discarded lines demonstrate that, to the poet, the sword possessed magic properties.

> Durandal était fée;
> Elle pouvait se rompre en un combat sanglant,
> Pour que tout fût égal entre un autre et Roland,
> Mais elle renaissait. Après l'avoir laissée
> Sur le champ de bataille en vingt morceaux brisée,
> Le lendemain matin Roland la retrouvait
> En s'éveillant, pendu au clou de son chevet;
> C'était sa Durandal splendide, aiguë et dure,
> Et l'on n'y voyait point de trace de soudure,
> Ayant été refaite à la forge du ciel.

Presumably, if his sword broke during an encounter, Roland momentarily resorted to tree trunks or whatever else might be handy until the sword was ready again. These lines of Hugo's were not published until 1970.[38] We now realize why ostensible problems with his sword never perturbed Roland. Problems with his horse are another matter. One was killed beneath him during the fight with Olivier. In "Le Petit Roi de Galice" he lost another by lending it to Nuño, who never returned it. How he went on his way after ridding the world of the wicked uncles is never elucidated. The poet also neglects to tell us what mount his hero was riding, having lost several others, when he had his fatal encounter with the Saracens.

Hugo's Roland, like the traditional one, is a mixture of good and bad traits. Modest he certainly is not. He knows his worth and does not hesitate to boast about it to Nuño's malevolent uncles. Nevertheless, on the whole one must agree with the poet's description of him as a "bon chevalier." His motives consistently are the best, and in making use of the superhuman prowess with which he has been endowed, he generally promotes laudable ideals. On his various travels, he does remarkable deeds, all in the interests of a noble cause. Writing in the *Revue des Deux Mondes* on 15 October 1859, Emile Montégut expressed admiration. Hugo, the critic believed, had set out to reconcile history and legend. In depicting Roland as he had done, the poet had reconstructed the cruel realities of a barbaric era and at the same time had done justice to the chivalric ideal to which that era had clung. Hugo himself indulged in characteristic overstatement in the preface to the *Légende des siècles*. He declared that, while permitting himself an occasional "fiction," he had remained faithful to "la couleur des temps et à l'esprit des civilisations diverses." "Le Mariage de Roland" and "Aymerillot" "jaillissent directement des livres de geste de la chevalerie. C'est de l'histoire écoutée aux portes de la légende."[39] Poetically Hugo implied that he had read the epics instead of reading about them.

In "La Guerre d'Espagne" Hugo championed the altar as well as the throne, but this is not true of the later Roland poems. No monks or priests appear, or at least no good ones. Roland is devout and so is Nuño, but to practice their faith they do not need men of the cloth as intermediaries. Rescued, a grateful King Nuño gives thanks to God, but he does it directly, not through a priest. Increasingly anticlerical, the poet had taken care to place a priest in the camp of the thieving and murderous uncles, however. "Un prêtre est avec eux qui lit son bréviaire." By keeping company with such rogues and by doing nothing to help their pathetic prisoner, this priest has repudiated the principles to which he is committed. Another priest, Archbishop Turpin, is conspicuously absent from these poems. Also missing is the angel, another intermediary between God and man, who in *Girart de Vienne* ended Olivier and Roland's violent dispute.

"Le Mariage de Roland," "Aymerillot," and "Le Petit Roi de Galice" have roots in articles the writer chanced to read. Even so, the protagonist owes at least as much to his creator's imagination. In all these poems Roland's impulsiveness, his elevated sense of his own worth, and his unswerving dedication to the best human and religious values make the hero look very much like the protagonist in the *Chanson de Roland*, which the poet almost certainly had not read when he wrote the poems. Both Rolands brandish weapons that have extraordinary powers. Hugo, not one to give his hero a sword blessed by a priest, provides him with a magic one. The *Chanson de Roland*'s hero wields a sword that may have supernatural properties, but these attributes seem to derive from the relics in its pummel. Curiously, long after he wrote "Le Mariage de Roland," "Aymerillot," and "Le Petit Roi de Galice," Hugo finally read the *Chanson de Roland*. Around 1865 he scribbled some lines of verse on the back of a letter: "Durandal, lame auguste, avait dans son pommeau / Du sang de saint Basile, une dent de saint Pierre."[40] The lines come straight from the epic, in which readers are told that "En l'orient punt asez i ad reliques: / La dent seint Perre e del sanc seint Basilie."[41] Hugo never used the lines, and they never found their way into later editions of the *Légende des siècles*. Perhaps the author could not bring himself to introduce material that ran counter to his own views in matters of religion.

Renan told Flaubert that Hugo did not like history, and he may have been right.[42] In any event, history could have told the poet only so much about the actual Roland. In conceptualizing his protagonist, Hugo did what he did best: he relied upon his extraordinary imagination.

Alfred Assollant (1827-86) was a journalist who also dabbled in history and wrote adventure novels. One of these, *La Mort de Roland*, subtitled *Fantaisie épique*, appeared in 1860. The tone is not too serious. The novel is filled with stories and adventures, and in one of them Roland narrates his life story. His childhood is the customary one, but Assollant has sprinkled it with numerous embellishments, including a few original details. Roland's mother was Berthe, Charlemagne's sister, "blonde comme un épi et belle comme une rose." Hunting in a forest one day, she was thrown from her horse. Comte Milon saved her. Soon he declared his love and asked the emperor for her hand. Charlemagne laughed at him, whereupon he and the princess eloped and married. In a distant land, "un hermite les maria comme il put. Je fus le seul fruit de cette heureuse union," Roland declares. Ten years later Milon was treacherously killed, and Berthe, with her little son, embarked "sur un vaisseau qui portait des marchands de Venise et de Marseille. Les vents poussèrent le vaisseau sur les côtes de France où il échoua, et ma mère, dépouillée de tout, mais pleine de courage et d'espérance, partit avec moi pour implorer le pardon de Charlemagne et lui présenter son fils. . . . Le seul bien que nous eussions conservé était Durandal, l'épée de mon père, que j'ai encore aujourd'hui."[43] Charlemagne had been about to leave on one of his forays against the Saxons. Hunting in the Ardennes Forest, he fell asleep near a fountain. Roland kills a lion and saves his life. The boy tells the emperor that he is his nephew. Berthe arrives a moment later, and all are reconciled. Roland is reared at court but never learns to read. He is restored to his father's fiefs and in due course is made a knight. At Charlemagne's side, he wars for a decade against the infidels. Roger is mentioned, permitting Assollant to remind readers that he knows *Orlando innamorato* and *Orlando furioso*. Roland admits that he was once enamored of Angelica but now happily is cured.

In *La Mort de Roland* readers see an irritable Charlemagne who is no longer young. "Sa barbe blanchissait à vue d'oeil, et il commençait, tout comme un autre, à aimer le coin du feu et les longs repas."[44] One evening after a copious meal, he calls upon Alcuin to entertain him and the twelve peers, and the learned monk prepares to give a reading of his *De arte rhetorica dialogus*. At this the illiterate Roland yawns noisily. Between uncle and nephew an envenomed argument results, leading to Roland's being banished and his fiefs confiscated. Roland is not disturbed. "Je vais en Espagne," he announces, "et là je me taillerai un royaume dans la peau des Sarrasins." Brandishing Durandal, he leaves the banquet hall, mounts his horse, "et sans s'inquiéter de la nuit noire, des brigands et des enchanteurs, il s'en alla lentement à travers la forêt." His horse, incidentally, is named Bride-d'Or, not Veillantif.

Naimes de Bavière tells the emperor that in the coming war with King Marsile of Saragossa, Roland will be needed and asks his master to recall him. Charlemagne claims that it is too late but remains pensive, as though he would like to retract his heated words. Ganelon, comte de Mayence, on the other hand, thinks the emperor should have hanged his nephew. Renaud de Montauban, a character the author remembered from *Orlando furioso,* suggests that the count do it himself. Trembling, Ganelon excuses himself. "Je suis homme de robe et justiciard: je ne suis pas porte-sabre," he points out. The others laugh. Ganelon is humiliated, and Roland was the indirect cause.[45]

Having crossed into Spain, Roland rescues a Moorish princess, Corisande, from a band of marauders. She had been on her way to France to implore Charlemagne's help against Ferragus, the son of King Marsile. Ferragus has killed Corisande's uncle, King Stordilan of Grenada, and kidnapped her cousin Doralice. Assollant found Ferragus, Stordilan, and Doralice's names in Ariosto, but their adventures he concocted himself. Roland is taken with the beautiful princess, and the two of them visit Marsile's court, where they are well received and entertained. Troubles eventually break out, and Roland kills one of the "chevaliers les plus renommés de la cour de Marsile, le fier Balugant, émir de Tolède."[46] Far from being angry, Marsile presses Roland to enter his service. Planning to take on his host's son, the proud knight refuses and takes his leave.

With Corisande, he pushes on to Grenada to deliver Doralice. There the entrenched Ferragus awaits him. In the streets Roland has a proclamation read outlawing the Moorish prince. Bluffing, he announces that Charlemagne has arrived beneath the city walls with a mighty army. A combat ensues during which the count kills the wicked kidnapper and usurper, thus making Doralice queen of Grenada. The two women now vie for Roland's love. For a time Doralice seems about to win, but Corisande gets her man.

Corisande and Roland have other adventures. At one point, while Roland is exterminating pagan enemies, his friend Olivier arrives, accompanied by Bernardo del Carpio, Turpin, and twenty thousand men. Charlemagne is said to be on his way with the main army. Turpin is described as "un des plus saints prélats et des meilleurs chevaliers de son temps. Ses cheveux blancs, sa barbe blanche, sa taille haute et majestueuse, ses yeux brillants, sa ferme contenance inspiraient le respect et la crainte."[47] From the outset, Bernardo del Carpio and Roland dislike one another, a dilemma del Carpio solves by joining the Saracens. Corisande, about to be married to Doralice's brother, an evil heathen prince, is rescued by her real lover. With Corisande, Olivier and Turpin, Roland sets out to meet his uncle's advancing army.

Between Roland and the emperor all is soon forgiven. Together they head for Saragossa, where they will attack Marsile. Among Charlemagne's lords is Ganelon, "ce traître, animé d'une haine implacable," who hates and fears Roland. Through subservience and flattery, he has ingratiated himself with the emperor and is thus a redoutable enemy. Soon an emissary from King Marsile arrives to propose peace. Charlemagne tells the emissary that, when he leaves the next day, an ambassador will leave with him bearing his answer. Taunting his adversary, Roland proposes Ganelon for the post. "S'il vous faut un homme pacifique," he tells his uncle, "prenez . . . ce pâle justiciard qui tremble les jours de bataille. Par lui, vous êtes bien sûr d'avoir une paix éternelle."[48] Afraid and enraged, Ganelon recoils but is appointed. During the negotiations that follow, he intimates to Marsile that Roland is the only obstacle to peace. When Marsile promises him three counties, the two men conspire to eradicate their common foe. It is decided that, as the French withdraw from the Iberian Peninsula, Roland must command their rear guard. "Je me charge du reste," Marsile declares. Loaded with presents, Ganelon returns to the French camp and tells his master that Marsile has agreed to his harsh terms. Corisande's baptism takes place the following day at Valencia. Corisande and Roland are to be married two weeks later in Bordeaux.

"Les deux amants ignoraient qu'ils ne devaient plus se revoir en ce monde," but they are nonetheless worried. Warned by terrible dreams, Corisande is loath to ride on ahead with the emperor and leave her fiancé behind. Roland too experiences somber presentiments, but he dutifully covers the main army's withdrawal. Most of the peers ride on ahead with their emperor, but Olivier and Turpin remain with Roland and his twenty thousand men near Roncevaux. As the bulk of the army disappears into the distance, Ganelon calls out to Roland, laughing and wishing him good luck. Roland answers that he sees no reason to be alarmed but asks Ganelon to tell the emperor that in case of trouble he will sound his horn for the emperor to turn back.[49] Roland then has a bad dream. Alone in Roncevaux Valley, he sees an earthquake piling up stones around him. From the mountaintops several enemies are pointing down at him and laughing. All the while, Satan tends the storm that accompanies the scene. The dream over, Roland and his men push on toward the sinister valley.

The French reach the valley hungry, wet, and disconsolate. They soon discover that they are trapped in a kind of amphitheater, Saracen soldiers having sealed off the entrance, with the Moors looking down at them from the mountains. Olivier advises blowing the horn, declaring that he is less afraid of the Moors than of the woods and mountains, the pagans' natural allies. Roland does not heed the warning. Pine trees, sawed in advance, begin to rain down into the enclosure, killing large numbers of men. Roland, with Olivier and Turpin at his heels, starts to scale the mountains to reach the attackers. An avalanche of stones comes hurtling down. After twelve hours of slaughter, Olivier again counsels his friend to blow his horn, but Roland believes it too late. Threatened by Turpin, he at last does so. Six leagues away, Charlemagne hears the call. Ganelon, who has not delivered his victim's message, assures him that Roland is bear hunting. Roland, Olivier, and Turpin all have serious wounds. Roland could escape, but he will not leave his companions. Turpin gives absolution to all those still alive. As the combat resumes, Roland, at Olivier's insistence, blows his horn once more. Olivier and Turpin expire. Although exhausted, Roland kills Bernardo del Carpio, who is fighting in the enemy ranks. For Assollant this was a patriotic touch. Spanish *romanceros* claim that del Carpio killed Roland.[50]

Confronting death, Roland has a clear conscience. He is certain to go to heaven but he wonders who will protect his fiancée. Then he tries to break his sword, "mais Durandal fendit la montagne, fit une brèche énorme et ne se brisa pas." Roland hurls it over the mountains. Assollant gives his own account of its fate: "La bonne épée tomba dans les eaux profondes d'un lac qui se cache à trois lieues de Roncevaux et qu'aucun voyageur n'a pu découvrir. C'est là qu'elle dort depuis bien des siècles, et elle y dormira jusqu'à ce qu'un héros pareil à Roland vienne l'y chercher."[51] Unless he was relying upon oral tradition, Assollant almost certainly invented this detail. There is no reason to believe that he knew such versions of the *Chanson de Roland* as the Manuscrit de Châteauroux and the Manuscrit de Lyon, in which the dying man throws his sword into a murky, stinking spring. Assollant's hero tosses his weapon over the mountains at random, whereas in these manuscripts Roland intentionally plunges the sword deep into the water.

Assollant's Roland weakly blows his horn one last time, breaking it with the effort. Then, stretching out on a rock, he looks at the sun, calls out to Corisande, and dies. Meanwhile, Charlemagne is convinced by a poet from Roland's entourage of Roland's peril. Ganelon is quartered on the spot, and the emperor rushes back to Roncevaux. When he gets there, it is all over. Tenderly, Corisande kisses her lover's remains and dies. Charlemagne punishes the evildoers and returns to France. Quickly consoled, Doralice marries someone else.

As is true in most versions of the Roland story, Assollant's hero is a superman. In addition to his other feats of derring-do, he throws his sword not just into a lake but into a lake three leagues distant. Obviously the sword did not wind up in a church or museum, as some writers would have it. *La Mort de*

Roland is not the first modern work to show the paladin in love with a Saracen princess. In *Das Thal von Ronceval*, Immermann had done it in 1819. Yet Assollant produced one of the nineteenth century's most imaginative treatments of the Roland legend. Charlemagne is shown not as a benevolent patriarch but rather as an irascible old man, not always wise, who likes his creature comforts. Readers learn that his wife, almost never mentioned elsewhere, is still living and that he has several daughters and, in addition to Roland, several nephews.[52] Alcuin, seldom introduced in Roland literature, did not settle at the Frankish court until after Roland's death. Nevertheless, he shows up here and indirectly provides a reason for Roland's going to Spain. An irritated Roland was already in Spain when Charlemagne arrived. While not unheard-of in such narratives, angry words between emperor and nephew followed in time by mutual forgiveness are another of Assollant's departures from tradition. It is curious, too, that the illiterate Roland should have a poet in his entourage.

When Princess Corisande met Roland she was on her way to ask Charlemagne to intervene in Iberian politics, and this is not far removed from Dupleix's and Sismondi's assertions that the Frankish king invaded Spain at the request of heathen princes with grievances against the ruling clique in their country. At Marsile's court there is a pagan monarch named Balugant, not Baligant. That he is emir of Toledo rather than of Babylon is a novel touch also. In addition to portraying the chief villain as a coward, Assollant breaks with literary tradition by making Ganelon a member of the *noblesse de robe* instead of the *noblesse d'épée*. When Roland derides his peaceable calling, Assollant creates his own version of how Ganelon came to hate Roland, who had unknowingly caused him to be humiliated. Finally, Roland's complicated love adventures, with the hero wavering for a time between the heathen princesses Doralice and Corisande, is a notable innovation. Back home no belle Aude awaits her fiancé's return.

No one would deny that *La Mort de Roland* is a highly original piece of writing, though few, if any, critics would claim that it is great literature. Some of Assollant's contemporaries, however, held him in rather high esteem. Emile Zola applauded his lively imagination. Referring to one of his other novels, Zola called him a "conteur primesautier" and complimented him on "la vivacité française dont il a fait preuve dans le roman."[53]

Like the Romantics, the Parnassians took an interest in the Roland legend. In the movement's early days, Xavier de Ricard, liberal political activist, patriot, and poet, was important in formulating the tenets of Parnassian doctrine and in winning an audience for the writers who became its apostles. Ricard's "La Mort de Rollant," written when the poet was quite young, is dedicated to Gérard Walch, who later edited it. The poem is divided into paragraphs rather than stanzas, and *rime plate* is used throughout. The lines are alexandrines, with caesuras occurring randomly. Ricard was ahead of his time in not capitalizing each new line of verse. Except to add a medieval touch, there seems to be no real reason why he chose to call Charlemagne "Karl" or Roland "Rollant." Ganelon is "Gannelon." Carle and Rollant could have been found in the *Chanson de Roland*, to be sure, but this does not explain Gannelon. The style, though engaging, is occasionally eccentric. Despite its oddities, the poem is a good one, and the narrative, presented with skill and imagination, arouses and holds the reader's attention. "On y trouve . . . une image de l'idée médiévale que pouvait avoir un parnassien," declared Robert Sabatier.[54]

For his narrative the poet constructed a frame, creating a story within a story. The enveloping action involves Hugh Capet, who has just become king of France. During a lull in one of his wars, the monarch wanders into a forest. To avoid a storm, he takes shelter in a cave that serves as the home of an ancient hermit. As a boy the hermit participated in the Franks' Spanish invasion and had been with Charlemagne on the homeward journey. Returning with the emperor to Roncevaux Valley, he had looked at the horrible spectacle and decided that, with Roland dead, the age of heroes was at an end. Only fifteen at the time, he threw away his arms, left the army, and became a *trouvère*. Charlemagne, Roland, and the Franks had given him the material for his epics. "Sentant que le siècle allait diminuer, / je jetai là l'armure et me fis besacier, / et, pendant soixante ans, sans repos, à grand'erre, / j'ai, dans mainte chanson, chanté, par mainte terre, / Karl, le grand Empereur, avec son grand neveu, / et les gestes des Franks qui sont les faits de Dieu." Having done this, he has withdrawn to his cave to die. At his visitor's request, however, he tells the story of the battle of Roncevaux. Like the hermit, the reader does not actually see the fighting. Instead, he is with Charlemagne, who, hearing his nephew's horn, guesses what is happening. Thus the battle is perceived through the emperor's reactions to the successive horn blasts. Like the emperor, the reader arrives on the scene only after the massacre has taken place.

Suffusing the narrative section of the poem is an atmosphere of doom. It begins with Charlemagne returning from the wars in Spain, where he has subdued the Moors. Roland has been the expedition's hero. With the Franks withdrawing, their erstwhile adversaries could make trouble. At dawn one morning, Charlemagne and his knights hold a council to discuss the matter. Ganelon addresses Charlemagne, saying, "Rollant, mon beau-fils, est un homme / des plus fameux parmi tous ceux que l'on renomme: / si nous voulons rentrer, sans être talonnés / par ces nègres païens, vrais diables incarnés, / à qui pouvons-nous mieux fier l'arrière-garde / qu'à Rollant?" As in the *Chanson de Roland*, here Roland knows that his stepfather dislikes him. He is not pleased at being named to command the rear guard but accepts the post when it is conferred. Charlemagne, haunted by sinister premonitions, rides away with his main army. "Avec toute sa baronie, / la barbe éparse sur sa cuirasse brunie, / Karl, angoisseux et triste, a quitté Roncevaux: / et la rumeur des pieds, des armes, des chevaux, / s'étend autour de nous à plus de quinze lieues!"

Vigny's "Le Cor" had shown the Franks in a happy mood as they headed for home. Here, on the contrary, the ride is dismal, as the soldiers wend their way through wooded mountain passes that are majestic but somber. Showing a Parnassian tendency, Ricard calls attention to the colors that dominate the scene. The men glitter with their "heaumes d'or vermeils," "écus lustrés," and "claires épées." Their polished armor is alive with "éclairs vibrants," and their banners are "pans fleuris rouges, et blancs, et bleus." The pine trees, the mountains, and the deep ravines also provide color, and, visible from the narrow passes, there are the "vallons profonds de ténèbres comblés." The austere landscape does nothing to relieve the emperor's gloom. "Il se sent en grand deuil pour Rollant." He weeps and, bowing his head, calls upon God to spare his young nephew. Were he older he would have acquired some wisdom, but he would also have lost some of the enthusiasm that makes him indispensable. Rash though he is, he is a solid bulwark "contre mes ennemis et ceux de votre Loi," Charlemagne tells the Lord.

After a time the pall momentarily lifts. With France almost in sight, the men begin to think about the honors, the castles, and the ladies that will be waiting for them. The procession has reached Gascony when suddenly the happy mood is dispelled. All at once, "derrière, du fond des défilés étroits, / grossie au formidable écho de mille combes, / tourbillonnante comme un hurlement de trombes," a terrible noise is heard. The main army comes to a halt, stunned. "Et chacun se regarde avec des pleurs aux yeux," as though sensing catastrophe. Again the sound is heard. This time, more insistent, it "se prolonge et s'irrite, affolée, / comme le bramement d'une fauve acculée." Recognizing the sound, Charlemagne orders his men to head back. "Nul cor, sinon le sien, n'aurait si longue haleine! / A l'aide, mes barons, car Rollant est en peine, / et des preux tels que lui n'appellent qu'en mourant!" At this point the horn is heard again, but now the sound no longer calls for help but signals despair. "C'est un râle à présent qui sanglote, âpre et long."

One more time the horn is sounded, this time "par hoquets brisés et haletants." Again the emperor begs God to save Roland. Of all the soldiers in the main army, only Ganelon is not weeping. Charlemagne and his men rush back to Roncevaux Valley. The ride is a "morne chevauchée, effroyable et farouche." It is sundown, and the fading light distorts the rugged natural scenery, making it forbidding. Preceding the others into the valley, the emperor calls out. There is no answer. Instead one sees "Des morts partout, des morts par tas et par jonchées!" Blood is everywhere, on the rocks and even on the flowers. There is no doubt that Roland and his comrades have been wiped out. The narrator, remembering that he had been present as an apprentice soldier, describes the scene. The victims have been crushed by rocks and trees sent hurtling down the mountains at them.

> Du plus haut de ses pics la montagne a croulé:
> elle gît tout entière emmi le val comblé:
> par vastes éboulis de forêts, ses pinèdes
> hérissent ce chaos rocheux de longs fûts raides
> écimés par leur chute en énormes épieux,
> et, pressés sous ces blocs massifs, vingt mille preux
> rendent, en longs filets qui courent par les herbes,
> l'âpre sang qui gonflait leurs poitrines superbes.

Again the poet underscores the vivid colors, calling attention to the blood shining in the brilliant sunset.

The emperor searches for his nephew. He remembers the young knight's having told him that, were he ever killed in battle, his face would be turned toward the pagans. Charlemagne climbs to the top of a hill, and there, lying in the grass near three stones, is the dead Roland. Beneath him are his sword and horn. He is pale, his eyes are clouded, and his head is turned toward Spain. Charlemagne faints. Roland's death has ended the happy period of his life and has also taken away his throne's main prop. Worse still, knighthood has reached its peak and now can only decline. At this point the hermit breaks off, declaring that he is out of breath. Probably he is overcome with emotion.

Obviously Ricard has read the *Chanson de Roland*, taking from it many of his plot elements. The council of war, Ganelon's proposing Roland for the rear guard command, Roland's angry acceptance, the twenty thousand men assigned to the contingent, Charlemagne's hunch that Roland will be killed, the circumstances in which the hero's body is discovered—these and other details have their source in the epic. The hermit's function, moreover, duplicates that of Turoldus.

On the other hand, what "La Mort de Rollant" did not borrow from the *Chanson de Roland* is equally intriguing. Ganelon suggests his stepson for a perilous task, but there is no reason to conclude that he has committed treason. In the poem he is not accused, tried, or executed. He appears to hate the infidels as much as everyone else. There is no Olivier or Archbishop Turpin in the poem. Perhaps Ricard was anticlerical or deist. No angels conduct the hero's soul to heaven, suggesting that Roland may not be headed in that direction at all. Ricard ended his poem on a purely human note, just as he omitted the miracle that allowed the emperor to pursue the villains and chastise them. There is no pursuit, and the evildoers do not get punished. Anticlericalism could explain some of this, but it hardly explains why Olivier, normally so vital to the narrative, has been left out.

Ricard's chief departure from the *Chanson de Roland* version involves the identity of Roland's attackers. In Ricard's poem, Charlemagne's expedition had been against the Moors, but they are not the ones who fall upon the rear guard and annihilate it. The hermit still wants the outlaws, or their descendants, punished. The king he is addressing came to the throne two centuries after the battle of Roncevaux, but the hermit now exhorts that king to avenge the disaster. He names the culprits. They are not the Moors, and they are not even a military people. Instead they are mountain shepherds who hated the Franks. The hermit tells his royal visitor that being Charlemagne's successor carries with it an obligation.

> Sache à quel dur labeur Dieu t'a prédestiné:
> il faut venger les Franks sur la race honnie
> des hommes d'Aquitaine et de Septimanie:
> ils détestent les Franks: ils ont vaincu les Franks.
> Nos chevaliers, les plus fameux et les plus grands,
> ont recontré chez eux d'étranges aventures;
> et tout sonnant de fer et tout tintant d'armures,
> ces preux entre les preux furent déconvenus
> par ces Romains furtifs, rasés et presque nus.
> Ils mouraient—assaillis d'une attaque soudaine
> de vils pâtres déchaux vêtus de brune laine,
> lestes coureurs, toujours présents, absents toujours,
> et qui, traquant nos preux comme ils traquent leurs ours
> à coups de javelots, de flèches et de pierres,
> tournent en fuite nos batailles les fières.

The hermit adds that unbelievers, whatever their persuasion, are bad, "mais cette race est pire." After all, these people are Christians.

"La mort de Rollant" is a curious poem, raising several questions. Olivier and Turpin are not so much as mentioned. Nor is it ever clear why the author put his *récit* into the mouth of a hermit who was more than two hundred years old when he related his narrative to a chance visitor seeking shelter from a storm. The poem's most unusual feature, however, is undoubtedly that the author, knowing the *Chanson de Roland* quite well, nonetheless provided villains other than those the epic designates. Ricard selected from the epic what he wanted, then felt perfectly free to combine this with an entirely different version of Roland's death. In "La Mort de Rollant," Ricard followed literary tradition up to a point and then departed from it completely, making Roland the victim of treacherous mountain shepherds. While Ricard emphasizes Charlemagne's grief, incidentally, no arrangements for burying the casualties are mentioned.

Another poet who considered the hero of Roncevaux an attractive literary figure was Théodore de Banville, in turn a Romantic, a Parnassian, and an independent. He was familiar with the *Chanson de Roland* and called attention to its "magnifiques inventions."[55] The 10 January 1870 issue of the liberal, republican newspaper *Le National* published Banville's poem "Pas de feuilleton." Banville explained in his poem, addressed to the publisher, Rousset, why he was not submitting his usual article on the week's events in the theatrical world. He had been idling and dreaming, he confessed. As a patriot, he had been pondering the Roland legend. "Pendant de longues journées, / J'entends Roland sonner du cor / Dans les gorges des Pyrénées / Que le sang baigne," he admitted, referring perhaps to Vigny's "Le Cor." Five years later the poem was reprinted in the author's *Rimes dorées*.

An earlier narrative poem entitled "Roland" (1863) is more detailed. It appeared in the periodical *Le Boulevard* on 12 April. Several archaic words such as *gésir* and *mécréants* remind readers that the setting is medieval. The poem does little more than present a tableau showing "le bon Roland" during his last moments. As the poem begins, Charlemagne hears his nephew's horn and turns back, but too late. The horn had been sounded to tell him that the situation was hopeless. While the emperor and his troops are rushing back, the melee goes on. One by one the gallant peers are slain. Olivier is killed also.

> Au pied des rocs de marbre, ils ne sont plus que trois:
> L'archevêque Turpin, qui, la mort sur la joue,
> Navre encor les païems. qu'on l'en blâme ou l'en loue,
> Et le brave Gautier de Luz, et puis Roland.
> Olivier est tombé, qui, déjà chancelant,
> Et l'oeil au Paradis qui devant lui flamboie,
> Hauteclaire à la main, criait encor: Montjoie!

Gautier de Luz must be the *Chanson de Roland*'s Gautier de l'Hum. In nineteenth-century French literature, Banville alone has him share Roland's last stand. His moments, like those of Turpin and Roland, are numbered, but he makes each blow count. Soon only Roland is left standing, and he is wounded. "Et Roland frappe, ayant une blessure au flanc, / Durandal avait tant travaillé que le sang / Ruisselait sur sa lame, et l'enveloppait toute / D'un humide fourreau vermeil, et goutte à goutte / Pleuvait en même temps de tous les points du fer."

Roland is so covered with blood that he is attracting vultures. His drenched sword looks as though it were thrashing about in a wet, red scabbard. Roland cannot stop to wipe it. All at once St. Michael hurries down "les clairs escaliers bleus du Paradis," wipes the sword on his tunic, and then returns to heaven. Roland resumes his task with even more gusto: "Sa grande épée, heureuse et rajeunie, ouvrait / Les fronts casqués; à chaque estocade nouvelle, / On en voyait jaillir le sang et la cervelle." A moment later Durandal is again dripping with blood, but the angel does not intervene. Instead, abruptly and dramatically, the poem comes to a close with its hero dying. Readers know that Charlemagne arrives too late and beholds a grim sight, described in the opening lines. "Couchés à jamais pour l'éternel repos, / Les païens gisent morts par milliers, par troupeaux, / Sur le sable, à côté des Français intrépides," who are just as dead as their assailants. The poem's visual effects are remarkable. Other original touches include the addition of Gautier de Luz to the cast of characters, and an angel's dropping in to wipe Roland's sword.

"Roland" appeared in Banville's *Les Exilés* (1867). Another poem in the collection is "La Belle Aude," which shows the aftermath of the contest between Moors and Franks. Although dated three years earlier than "Roland," the poem was first published in *Le Boulevard* on 8 June 1862. Unlike "Roland," it is in stanza form. Like the later poem, however, it contains occasional archaisms, such as *gente demoiselle*. Like the *Chanson de Roland*, it is written in decasyllabic verse. In the 1 June 1852 *Revue des Deux Mondes* Ludovic Vitet had summarized the *Chanson de Roland*. A few lines in "La Belle Aude" come from Vitet's article.[56]

"La Belle Aude" takes up the Roland legend at the point when Charlemagne, having returned to Aix, is trying Ganelon. Although the traitor's wickedness is about to be punished, another problem remains. Aude must be told what has happened. Hardly has the emperor returned when she asks the inevitable question. "Sire, dit-elle au roi pâle et tremblant / . . . . / Où donc est-il votre neveu Roland, / Qui m'a juré de me prendre pour femme?" The emperor is at a loss to answer. "A ce discours le puissant Empereur, / Le vieux lion couronné, le grand chêne, / Baisse la tête et frémit de terreur." Then he has to admit that her fiancé, "Cet artisan d'exploits, mon capitaine, / Le bon Roland, est mort à Roncevaux." To console her, he offers her his son Louis instead. Incredulous, she does not take him seriously. Surely he does not believe "Que, Roland mort, Aude reste vivante!" As in the *Chanson de Roland*, Aude falls dead at his feet. Later she is laid to rest in a convent, and the emperor mourns for another loved one. "Et Charles pleure encor cette pucelle / Qui fut sans tache ainsi qu'un diamant, / Et brave coeur et gente demoiselle."

In 1867 and 1868 Albert Glatigny worked as an actor in several cities in or near the Pyrenees Mountains: Bayonne, Bagnères, Pau, Eaux Bonnes. He loved the mountains and wrote to Théodore de Banville that they thrilled him much more than the Alps did. He would return to Bayonne in September 1872 in the hope of curing his tuberculosis. Returning to Paris in March, he died on 16 April 1873. Like Millevoye, he was not quite thirty-four.

Such literary giants as Sainte-Beuve, Flaubert, and Mallarmé liked, admired, and praised Glatigny. When *Les Flèches d'or*, the poet's best collection, appeared, Mallarmé penned a glowing review that the modest author, though touched, would not let him publish.[57] Writing in *Le Constitutionnel* on 12 June 1865, Sainte-Beuve complimented the work, stressing the poet's originality and calling him, approvingly, "un osé et un téméraire."[58] Favorable comment by the dean of French critics led to neither fame nor fortune. Bad luck continued to hound the hapless poet, who has undeservedly remained a rather marginal figure in French poetry.

Glatigny's "La Mort de Roland" was the finest French Roland poem since Vigny's "Le Cor," Peyrat's "Roland," and Fournel's "Romance de Roncevaux." Glatigny was familiar with Hugo's treatment of the legend. In 1870, at Beaumesnil for his precarious health, he wrote François Coppée that the site made him think of "Le Petit Roi de Galice" and its little king who took Roland's horse.[59] Probably he knew the *Chanson de Roland* also. "La Mort de Roland" appeared in *Les Flèches d'or*, published on 21 May 1864. It consists of twelve six-line stanzas and, like the *Chanson de Roland*, is in decasyllabic verse. By using an occasional archaic word such as *preux* or *félonie*, the poet contrived to give his work a medieval aura.

When "La Mort de Roland" begins, the battle of Roncevaux has just ended, and the Saracens have fled back into Spain. Archbishop Turpin and Olivier are dead, and the poet wonders who in the future will buckle on Olivier's famous sword Hauteclaire. Roland, mortally wounded, lies amid the debris and the casualties, overcome at seeing his brave companions lying still and cold. "Devant ses yeux, comme une vapeur rouge, / Monte le sang qui grise Roncevaux. / Autour de lui s'entassent les armures, / Pleines de cris d'angoisse et de murmures, / De râles sourds d'hommes et de chevaux." In dwelling upon the ghastly spectacle, Glatigny is one of the few authors to insist upon realistic moans and screams of the wounded soldiers and horses, even evoking their eventual death rattle. As night falls the terrible scene is all the more appalling. "Puis tout se tait, et la lune sanglante / Au sombre ciel apparaît, triste et lente; / La Mort livide emplit le val fumant, / Et dans la brume où son grand spectre nage, / Rendus joyeux par l'odeur du carnage, / Les noirs corbeaux volent confusément."

Peyrat had mentioned the vultures also. The sight is grim and sickening. Roland is even more distressed when it occurs to him that, should the Moors return, his sword will fall into the hands of a pagan warrior. To prevent this, he tries to break it by dealing desperate blows against a mountain close at hand. Durandal resists, and only the mountain is scarred. Roland is disheartened. "Son âme en pleure. Alors, aveugle, blême, / Pour la sauver de cet affront suprême, / Contre un rocher il heurte Durandal. / Le mont frémit sur sa solide assiette, / Le roc se fend et sous les coups s'émiette: / L'arme flamboie et ne sent aucun mal." Unable to destroy his sword, Roland reminds it that

"Le forgeron t'a faite belle et dure." He seeks consolation in recalling the exploits it has helped him carry out. Then he blows his horn and, with calm resignation, prepares to die. "Puis le héroes recommande son âme / A Dieu le Père ainsi qu'à Notre-Dame, / Croise, en priant, ses deux bras engourdis / Sur sa poitrine, et regarde l'Espagne, / Ayant tenu jusqu'au bout la campagne, / Et saint Michel l'emporte au paradis!"

Glatigny ended his poem on this note. As in Ricard's poem, here Roland dies gazing at the mountains into which his killers disappeared as they galloped back into Spain. No Charlemagne, however, is on the horizon to pursue and chastise the miscreants, punish a traitor in his own ranks, then claim and bury the hero's earthly remains. Roland is the sole character in the somber drama. An authentic medieval knight, he has done his duty to God and king and dies faithful to both. The poem says nothing about his guilt in having brought on the massacre by proudly refusing to call for help. He laments his comrades, for "Tous étaient fiers et de hardi courage," but he does not reproach himself for contributing to their deaths. In the poem, in fact, he is not shown as having done anything reprehensible.

In Massenet's opera *Esclarmonde* (1889), a Roland falls in love with an Oriental empress endowed with supernatural powers. While there are many similarities between him and the familiar Roland, there are important differences. Massenet's hero is a Comte de Blois, and the king he serves is named Cléomer, not Charlemagne. Instead of Turpin, there is a bishop of Blois. A quarter of a century earlier, however, the authentic Roland had appeared on the operatic stage. Auguste Mermet's *Roland à Roncevaux*, the composer's best opera, was first performed at the Académie Impériale de Musique on 3 October 1864.[60] Its four acts and a ballet had taken sixteen years to get to the stage. In addition to the music, the composer wrote the words, and he proved to be a talented librettist.

In Mermet's opera, Ganelon, named the guardian of Alde (not Aude) by her dying father, is compelling his young ward to marry him. As the distressed heiress tells a friend, "Du comte Ganelon je suis la prisonnière, / Au lit de mort mon père / Sur moi lui donna tout pouvoir. / Seul il commande en mon manoir; / La résistance est inutile." Roland remonstrates with Ganelon for using force to bring the marriage about, and the two men become enemies, their hostility increasing as Roland and Alde fall in love. Ganelon vows revenge. When the Franks invade Spain, he tells the Saracen emir of Saragossa, "Il est un vallon triste et sombre, / Entouré de rocs escarpés / Dans lesquels des soldats campés / A l'ennemi cachent leur nombre. / C'est le vallon de Roncevaux." There Roland, their common foe, can be ambushed and slain. Fighting with the Saracens at Roncevaux, Ganelon is killed by his rival, who then dies, exhausted, in Alde's arms as Charlemagne arrives.

One of Roland's important musical moments occurs when the hero sings "Superbes Pyrénées," which a chorus repeats.

> Superbes Pyrénées
> Qui dressez dans le ciel
> Vos cimes couronnées
> D'un hiver éternel,
> Pour nous livrer passage
> Ouvrez vos larges flancs;
> Faites taire l'orage,
> Voici venir les Francs.

In act 1 a shepherd and chorus sing a "Chanson de Roland" that recalls the Revolutionary and Napoleonic Roland songs. It is heard again at the end of act 4 when Frankish knights carry the dead Roland from the battlefield and the curtain falls.

> Dans les combats, soldats de France,
> Des preux chantez le plus vaillant:
> Tout fuit quand il brandit sa lance;
> Chantex, soldats, chantez Roland.
>
> J'entends au loin, dans les campagnes,
> Perçant les bois et les montagnes,
> Des ennemis glaçant le coeur,
> Son cor d'ivoire au son vainqueur.
>
> Dans les combats, soldats de France,
> Des preux chantez le plus vaillant:
> Tout fuit quand il brandit sa lance;
> Chantez, soldats, chantez Roland.
>
> Là-bas, dans la plaine sanglante,
> Brille une épée étincelante,
> Rouge comme un soleil couchant:
> C'est Durandal au dur tranchant.

Like many other writers, Mermet wondered about the fate of Roland's sword. For the librettist, it was left on the battlefield, red with pagan blood.

Curiously, in Mermet's opera Roland dies less because Ganelon and the emir conspire against him than because he has broken a vow never to fall in love. As he declares to Turpin in act 3, an angel had appeared to him once in a dream. He sings the aria "Le Rêve de Roland."

> J'étails bien jeune encor, lorsque je vis en rêve
> Un ange radieux, le bras armé d'un glaive.

> Il marchait devant moi, me montrant le chemin. . . .
> Sans peur je le suivais. . . . Quand j'aperçois soudain
> Une église en ruine, un sombre cimetière. . . .
>   L'ange s'arrête; à sa voix l'éclair luit. . . .
>
> Il me montre une tombe, en soulève la pierre,
> Y jette son épée . . . et tout s'évanouit!
> Je l'avais déjà vu, ce sombre cimetière:
> Dès le matin j'y cours, et, sous la pierre,
> Je découvre au milieu d'ossements, de débris,
> Un glaive sur lequel je vois ces mots écrits:
>   "Je suis Durandal,
>   Du plus dur métal.
>   Sans craindre personne,
>   Qui me portera
>   La victoire aura,
>   Son coeur s'il ne donne."
> Et moi, voulant remercier
> L'ange radieux de mon rêve,
> Vers le ciel je tendis le glaive
> Et lui promit d'avoir un coeur d'acier.

Digging it up in a cemetery is the nineteenth century's most unusual way of having Roland acquire his famous sword. Later another librettist would simply let him inherit it from his father, as Assollant's hero had done. At any rate, Roland acknowledges to Turpin that he has not kept his promise to the angel. Turpin exhorts him to stick to his vow. Nevertheless, Roland succumbs to love, despite the archbishop's appealing to Alde in his presence.

> De cet amour, montre-lui la démence
> Et relis sur ce fer la fatale sentence:
>   "Je suis Durandal,
>   Du plus dur métal.
>   Sans craindre personne,
>   Qui me portera
>   La victoire aura
>   Son coeur s'il ne donne."

Love wins out, the paladin pays the price with his death.

The important role of love is Mermet's most startling deviation from the standard legend. Generally, stage productions require a love story. Moreover, operas have sopranos, and sopranos must have arias and pretexts for singing them. Operatic heroines also need to witness their lovers' deaths or at least be on hand to lament the lovers' fates. Mermet bent the plot accordingly and had Alde follow Charlemagne's army to Spain. This is certainly one of his more striking innovations. Her rushing onto the battlefield undoubtedly appealed to his sense of the dramatic, but operatic convention virtually dictated it. Mermet almost certainly did not know that thirteenth-century "romanticized" versions of the *Chanson de Roland* show her arriving at Charlemagne's camp at Blaye and dropping dead on learning what has befallen her fiancé at Roncevaux.[61] This is about what happens, for example, in the Manuscrit de Venise 4, in which she spends some time alone with the remains of her brother and fiancé. The manuscript was not published until 1877, thirteen years after the opera.

Given the standard operatic need for a love interest, having Alde's dying father name Ganelon to look after his daughter was a logical touch. It motivates Roland's interest in the girl and her problems and later triggers the animosity that springs up between her champion and her guardian. Ganelon's wanting to marry her is pure invention, of course. According to legend, he is already married to Roland's mother. His death in the enemy ranks at the battle of Roncevaux is another new twist. Still another occurs in act 2, in which the emir, not by Ganelon but by Roland himself, sends Charlemagne gifts and a placating message. Having Roland carried from the battlefield by his grieving comrades is a touch that Mermet could have picked up from Arlincourt.

Directed by Emile Perrin, *Roland à Roncevaux* was a sensation. Reviewing it on 11 October 1864, the *Journal des Débats* forgave the composer the liberties he had taken with the plot, calling them a "fantaisie toute personnelle." On 15 October the *Revue des Deux Mondes* was elegiac.[62] So was *Figaro* the next day, praising the marvelous costumes and decors as well as the splendid cast. Roland's role was sung by Louis Gueymard, a leading tenor of the day. Pauline, his wife, had been entrusted with the role of Alde. Jules Belval, a bass, was Turpin, and Jean Charles Cazaux, another durable bass, appeared as Ganelon. The shepherd, with what one critic called his "douce mélancolie," was Victor Warot, later a distinguished teacher. The lavish sets were the work of artists Charles A. Cambon and Joseph Thierry. Advance publicity had stirred up considerable interest, and it paid off. In the audience when the curtain rose, with a visiting prince in tow, sat Napoleon III.

Traditionally Paris theaters presented revues at the end of each year poking fun at the season's most popular plays and operas. In view of its tremendous success, *Roland à Roncevaux*'s was inevitably parodied. Presented at the Bouffes Parisiens on 27 December 1864, the *Revue pour rien* was the work of Paul Sirodin, Ernest Blum, and Louis François Clairville.[63] Clairville had produced many of these diversions and would produce many more. The music was written by Florimond Ronger, better known as Hervé, who would soon be famous as an operetta composer.

The *Revue pour rien* has a loose plot intended merely to link musical skits, the last of which is the two-act *Roland à Rongeveau*. In the *Revue pour rien* characters who are supposed to be tradesmen, theater patrons, and a provincial who has come to Paris to see the town dart about and stumble into the skits, taking roles and conversing with each other and the audience. The provincial is Grosmulot, who is as doltish as his name suggests. Early on, he tells a storekeeper that he has arrived from Mézidon in Calvados. He has seen a poster announcing *Roland à Rongeveau* at the Bouffes Parisiens. Having played Roland in an amateur theatrical back home, he is anxious to find out how the hero looks on a big city stage. Getting cheated several times, he finally obtains a "free" ticket that costs him much more than he would have paid at the box office and takes his seat in the theater. The evening is drawing to a close, and the final skit, *Roland à Rongeveau*, is about to begin. The actor scheduled to appear as the hero is believed to be ill, and Grosmulot, handing over thirty francs more, walks on and takes his place. Two prop men step onto the stage and set up the decor, which consists of a sign that reads: "CECI REPRÉSENTE LES SUPERBES PYRÉNÉES."

Full of puns and pointed allusions, the parody is comical. In it, as in the opera, the heroine is being forced to marry Ganelon, who is called Galon, meaning "chevron" or "braid trimming." The heroine appraises her unwelcome suitor, telling the audience at the outset that she is aware of how much *galon* is worth by the yard. Her name is not Alde but Alte-la.[64]

Roland à Rongeveau opens with an expository scene in which the heroine explains to a confidante that, much against her will, she is having to marry Chevalier Galon. When the confidante tries to interrupt, presumably to console or advise, she is silenced with the reminder that her dramatic function is merely to listen. Shrinking from the match that awaits her, Alte-la states her position in her first song: "Je repousse cet hymen, / J'aimerais mieux, je te le jure / S'il fallait lui donner ma main, / La lui donner sur la figure."

Meanwhile, the improvised Roland wanders into the heroine's apartment, his arrival giving her an idea. She tells him that he suits her purposes. He must elope with her immediately. "Car si vous me faites attendre, / J'épouse dès ce soir le chevalier Galon." Roland observes, not at all relevantly, "Quand on prend du galon, on n'en saurait trop prendre." Uninterested in this comment, the heroine insists upon an elopement, anywhere. Alas, it is too late. Galon's squeaking boots are heard approaching, and in a moment their wearer appears. With him has come someone to draw up a marriage contract. "O ma charmante demoiselle," announces Galon, "Pour signer un contrat si beau / J'amène Turlupin, notaire à Rongeveau." Turning to Galon, Roland calls upon him to desist, and the two rivals draw their swords. Turlupin intervenes, assuring them that more important events lie ahead for them in Spain. "Arrêtez, preux de Charlemagne! / Lorsque vous allex de l'Espagne / Combattre le noir tyran / Sans vous rougir de votre propre sang, / Tous deux revenez blancs d'Espagne. / Blancs d'Espagne!" Roland then sings a comic paraphrase of Mermet's "Superbes Pyrénées."

> Superbes Pyrénées
> Où, pour guérir leurs maux,
> Les belles fortunées
> S'en vont prendre les eaux,
> Pays des chiens modèles,
> Pays des montagnards,
> Pays des infidèles,
> Tu m'attends et je pars.

After the chorus repeats this, the two prop men appear once more, putting up a new sign telling spectators that "LE THÉÂTRE REPRÉSENTE LE PALAIS DE L'ÉMIR, À SARAGOSSE," and the second act begins.

Exactly why Roland, Alte-la, Turlupin, and the chorus should now be in the emir's palace, especially since the emir himself never appears, is not explained. Galon has disappeared and presumably has gone off to join the enemy between acts. Roland appears carrying a sword and reading something on it—a promise, etched into the blade, by which the sword swears to make him victorious. Roland likewise must swear to love the sword to the exclusion of everything else. At this the heroine enters and declares her eternal love. Roland admits that her charms are alluring but that all his love must go to the sword. "Si je vous aime, adieu, bonsoir, / Mon bancal n'a plus de pouvoir." When it looks as if he might yield to human love after all, Turlupin arrives to admonish him. "Roland, renonce à l'amour qui t'enflamme. / La gloire vaut mieux qu'une femme. / La gloire mène à l'immortalité, / La femme à l'imbécilité."

Roland thinks he would still rather have the lady, but at this critical moment the choice ceases to be his. The chorus announces that hosts of bellicose pagans have materialized and seem bent on mischief. "Trahison, trahison, les combats recommencent. / Pour nous attaquer de nouveau, / Cent mille Sarrasins s'avancent / Dans les plaines de Rongeveau." Twice the chorus enjoins Roland to blow his horn, which he does. Apparently all will now end happily, and a final song, the "Marseillaise de Roland," is heard.

> Portez à notre auteur
> Votre cri vainqueur.
> En ce jour de fête,
> Crions à tue-tête.
> Le public vaillant
> Va suivre Roland.
> Chacun beuglera,
> Vociférera,
> Et l'on sortira
> Sourd de l'opéra.

This is repeated while "on danse une farandole à l'imitation du ballet de *Roland à Roncevaux*," a reference to an interlude in Mermet's opera.

At the conclusion of the dance the curtain falls, ending a clever but by no means memorable spoof of Mermet's important work. One assumes that, far from being killed, Roland will marry Alte-la and live happily ever after. Galon, unless he has been killed, will be punished for his wickedness, and Turlupin will continue drawing up marriage contracts. Mermet's opera came out of it all unscathed. Discussing it in the *Revue des Deux Mondes*, Henry Blaze de Bury was enthusiastic. "Musique, drame, mise en scène, tout vous émeut," he wrote. He even liked the ballet.[65] The opera continued to hold the boards and during its first three years had numerous performances.

5
Despair, Hope, and Triumph

In July 1870 France let herself be lured into war with Prussia. Less than a year later, she lay beaten and prostrate, stripped of Alsace and part of Lorraine. Whatever reasons they gave for the humiliating defeat, totally unexpected, people agreed that the lost territory had to regained. Morally and militarily speaking, Frenchmen had to set their house in order, then retake what was theirs. As intense nationalism mounted, writers called upon their countrymen to emulate one of the nation's most eminent heroes, Roland. Thereafter, Roland's weaknesses were minimized or forgotten in literature, and only his valor and commitment to the highest ideals were set forth. Even when his immediate enemies were Saracens, the public was never allowed to lose sight of the fact that evil Germans, lurking about somewhere, were ready to pounce. Eventually, France would strike back.

After the disastrous Franco-Prussian War, the French poet Joseph Autran saw Roland as a national rallying point. His *Légende des paladins*, which deals with the medieval hero, was probably written during a three-week period in June 1871.[1] Against Hugo's advice, the devastating Treaty of Frankfurt, dictated by Bismarck, had been signed on 10 May. When Autran wrote, German troops were occupying French territory, as they had been when Cuvelier de Trie and Chandezon staged their *Roland furieux* in 1817. Dating his work 1874, the author published it in 1875. By this time the Germans were gone, but the French were humiliated. The book was dedicated to France, "mère des paladins errants." Frenchmen were told in the dedication, "A ce récit, peuple des Francs, / Si ton coeur bat, tu peux revivre," and the epilogue called upon contemporaries to unite and emulate their ancestors. Having become once more "la race des vainqueurs," Frenchmen could then disarm and "pardonner au monde."

In addition to a dedication, a prologue, and an epilogue, the *Légende des paladins* is made up of twenty-two individual poems. For source material the poet drew upon the *Psudo-Turpin Chronicle* at least as much as he did upon the *Chanson de Roland*, and he chalked up a minor debt to *Orlando innamorato* and

Orlando furioso.[2] He did not hesitate to use pure invention as well. Like occasional predecessors and several contemporaries, he now and then used an Old French word such as *occire* or *glouton* to add medieval flavor. Evident in each line are the poet's deep religious convictions.

Autran is one of the rare authors treating the Roland legend to describe his characters' appearance, Christians and Moors alike. Ganelon the traitor, for instance, is pale and has green eyes and a reddish beard. Charlemagne is pious, learned, wise, immense, Herculean, all but invincible. He has "la barbe fleurie," which almost all writers give him, plus "l'oeil brillant, le nez droit, les traits calmes." He shares his soldiers' hardships. Going to war against the Moors, "Il transformait soudain toutes ses habitudes. / Des plus tranquilles moeurs il passait aux plus rudes. / C'est ainsi qu'on le vit, sous le ciel espagnol, / Se nourrir de pain noir et dormir sur le sol, / Et lui-même, une nuit de veille solennelle, / Tout seul, autour du camp, rester en sentinelle!" Turpin is "le vieux moine soldat" "qui, soldat patriarche, / Accompagnait toujours la vieille armée en marche, / Et qui distribuait aux preux les sacrements." Olivier, "le plus pur de tous," is young and handsome, "dans la fleur de son mâle printemps." This man is sensitive but firm. His body is discovered when the emperor returns to the scene of the massacre. "C'est le jeune Olivier que trouve Charlemagne. / La mort, dans son éclat riant et printanier, / A moissoné le fils du vaillant Régnier. / Il est là, comme un lis tout meurtri par l'orage, / Celui pour qui Roland eut, dès son premier âge, / Cette belle amitié dont le ciel fut témoin."

Thus Autran, unlike Hugo, does not date the two men's closeness from the combat in which neither was able to subdue the other. Autran, departing from both the *Chanson de Roland* and the *Chronicle*, endows his characters with traits he imagines. In this case he emphasizes Olivier's youth and comeliness. Olivier is not shown as a prudent foil to Roland's rash boldness, the opposition stressed in the *Chanson de Roland*. As Charlemagne's nephew, Roland is "le premier baron." Blond and blue-eyed, he is also the handsomest man in the army. "Lion par le courage, agneau par la douceur," he is devout, charitable, courteous, valiant, and an accomplished warrior. A pious man, he burns candles and endows monasteries and convents. If in his campaigns he appropriates his enemies' goods, he keeps nothing for himself. "C'est toujours à l'autel qu'il portait son butin." On only one occasion had he failed to do this.[3] Aude wears a circlet of rubies he had made after smashing a king's crown and removing the gems. He became engaged to the damsel on returning from a campaign in Asia. After the Spanish expedition, which he intends to be his last, the two are to be married.

Inspired by the *Pseudo-Turpin Chronicle*, the *Légende des paladin*'s initial poem is entitled "Le Chemin de Saint-Jacques."[4] Charlemagne is at Aix, where he has a dream. He sees a line of stars stretching to Galicia. Then St. James appears and promises help if the emperor will seize the province and erect a suitable tomb for him there. Charlemagne sets out.

Another episode in the *Légende des paladins* is "L'Allée de frênes," partly based on the *Pseudo-Turpin Chronicle*. On the eve of a battle with the Moors, Charlemagne has a second dream. St. James appears to him, this time to announce that in the next day's clash the first encounter will be disastrous to his advance guard, but the ultimate victory will be his. The angel's prediction turns out to be correct, and the slain knights are buried in two rows. As a memorial, each man's spear, made of ash wood, is stuck in the ground over his grave. The survivors retire for the night. Next morning a miracle awaits them.

> Chaque lance était verte et portait quelques fleurs.
> Aux tombes des martyrs en terre sarrasine
> Chacune avait poussé sa féconde racine;
> Et ces arbres sont ceux qui, si grands et si beaux,
> Sont encore aujourd'hui debout sur les tombeaux,
> Et qui, sous le soleil dont l'Espagne est brûlée,
> Vous mènent à Burgos par une sombre allée!

Threads from the *Chronicle* went into the fabric of this poem, but the poet's inventive mind was at work also. According to his source, on the eve of a battle with the Saracens the Christians planted their spears in the ground in front of their tents. In the morning those who would die in battle found their spears in bloom. When the spears were cut down so they could be used, they left roots from which trees, still to be seen, sprang up. The *Chronicle* does not mention a double row of trees, however, nor is anything said about Burgos.[5]

Still another episode, "Le Baptême du géant," takes place beneath the walls of Pamplona. Like the preceding episodes, this one owes much to the *Pseudo-Turpin Chronicle*, which nevertheless localizes the action outside the town of Nájera. In Autran's poem a giant, Ferragus, comes out to taunt the French emperor's soldiers, daring one of them to come out and measure arms with him. Several do so and meet with no success. Then Roland steps forward. He and Ferragus duel for three days, each unable to overcome the other. Tired, they decide to call a truce until the following day. When the time comes to resume the battle, Ferragus instead calls upon his opponent to explain certain Christian articles of faith. He listens with interest but does not seem convinced. He then proposes that the duel resume, with the victor's God to be declared the true one. Roland agrees, and, harsher than ever, the combat is renewed. Finally Roland strikes his opponent in his one vulnerable spot, his navel. As the colossus dies, he has an ultimate revelation and asks for baptism. Roland dashes off to a nearby stream, returns with water, baptizes the unlikely convert, and sends him off to paradise in a hastily acquired state of grace. In the *Chronicle*,

Ferragus dies wounded in the navel but screaming to Mohammed for aid. As for the catechism lesson, what in the *Chronicle* had been a debate becomes in the modern poem a desire to hear various doctrinal issues elucidated.[6]

Autran took even more liberties when he recounted the fate of Bramimonde, Marsile's widow. In the *Chanson de Roland* Bramidonie, as Autran calls her and as the Oxford Manuscript sometimes does, accompanies the French victors to Aix and becomes a Christian, taking a new name. Such is not the case in the *Légende des paladins*. In "Bramidonie," one autumn afternoon at sunset when the war between the French and the Moors is at its worst, Archbishop Turpin is walking near some snow-covered mountains muttering his prayers. All at once a beautiful woman appears. When the archbishop asks who she is, "Je suis Bramidonie, / Lui dit-elle, je suis l'épouse du vieux roi / Marsile, et c'est ton Dieu qui m'amène vers toi." Falling to her knees, she asks to be baptized. Turpin receives her into the Church, then sends her back to her husband. "Quel que soit le sceau de ta nouvelle foi / Retourne à ton époux et retourne à ton roi. / Il est écrit là-haut, dans une loi jalouse: / "Rien ne désunira le mari de l'épouse." / Va donc; et, si tu peux, douce et tendre pour lui, / Communique à son coeur la clarté qui t'a lui." Returning to her husband's palace, the queen tells Marsile what she has done. Furious, he hurls her from a tower into the river below. Autran spares us none of the details:

> On put voir cette pâle victime,
> La tête échevelée et les mains en avant,
> Tourbilloner dans l'air comme une paille au vent,
> Et venir se briser sur les roches profondes
> Du torrent, qui la prit aussitôt dans ses ondes
> Et longtemps la roula dans son cours orageux,
> Comme un lis que le vent lui jette dans ses jeux.

Not at all distressed at learning what has happened, Turpin comments that this woman has at least saved her soul, whereas the devil will get her husband's.

In the *Légende des paladins*, Ganelon's reason for betraying Roland is not irritation with his stepson. Taking a hint from the *Chronicle,* Autran gave Ganelon purely venal motives. In battle Roland hears from a Moslem adversary what took place. Prince Zurfalou, Marsile's son, calls on him to surrender, giving him a good reason.

> A quoi bon résister? Ganelon t'a vendu!
> C'est lui qui nous apprit, par un furtif message,
> Et le nombre des tiens et l'heure du passage;
> C'est lui qui t'a livré. . . .
> ....

> Ah! vous parlez d'honneur et de chevalerie!
> ....
> Vous vous dites les Francs, les barons, les chrétiens,
> Et voilà cependant ce qu'a fait un des tiens!

Autran's résumé of the battle of Roncevaux is a moving account. Homeward bound, Charlemagne hears Roland's horn and turns back. Riding swiftly toward the ambush site, he is an imposing figure, with the wind blowing in his beard. He arrives too late, naturally. Breathing his last, Roland tells the emperor that Ganelon sold the rear guard, and Charlemagne swears that the traitor will receive the punishment he deserves.

Roland was the last to die. One by one the French barons had perished, including Olivier and Turpin. "Roncevaux, Roncevaux, / Tu seras dans l'histoire un lieu sombre et funeste! / De mes vieux compagnons, c'en est fait, nul ne reste!" Roland exclaims. His dying prayer, rather wordy in the *Chronicle*, is short in Autran. "Je sens bien," he declares, "'Que mon âme retourne à son juge suprême. / Recevez-la, Seigneur, dans votre paradis!' / Ainsi parle Roland, sous ces rochers maudits." Roland's address to Durandal, which he is anxious to break in order to keep it from falling into Saracen hands, is more elaborate. "A mon épée, ô chère et vaillante compagne, / Que n'avons-nous pas fait pour le roi Charlemagne? /.... / Par toi, noble instrument de tournois et de guerre, / J'ai soumis à mon roi presque toute la terre." He hits a rock with the sword, but it will not break. How could it be otherwise, the poet asks, when it contains not only a tooth of St. Peter's and a bone of St. Denis's but also a tress of the Virgin Mary's hair? It is not until Roland commends his soul to God that the sword, of its own accord, shatters. "Dans sa droite, enfin, sa Durandal éclate; / Et lui-même, affaissé sur la ronce écarlate, / Il retombe, et la mort, à pas silencieux, / Approche, éteint son souffle et referme ses yeux." In the *Chronicle* Roland does not denounce Ganelon nor does he succeed in breaking his sword.

The final poem of the *Légende des paladins* is "La Fiancée." Back in Aix, Aude, blonde and radiant, dressed in rich apparel, watches as the emperor and his soldiers parade into town. Not seeing Roland among these veterans, she asks where he is but receives no answer. Guessing the truth, she senses that it will kill her. The emperor's offering her his own son is to no avail, and she dies. The poet describes her burial and an ornate tomb raised in her and Roland's honor.

> On l'enterra, le soir, au fond d'une chapelle.
> Les cloches dans les airs, pleurant Aude la belle,
> Accompagnaient en choeur son âme dans l'azur.
> On lui fit un tombeau du marbre le plus pur,

> Merveille où le ciseau du statuaire habile
> Donna la vie et l'âme à la pierre immobile.
> On y voyait Roland et ses hardis travaux,
> Ses victoires partout, sa chute à Roncevaux.
> Dans l'autre bas-relief, c'était la bien-aimée
> Au passage du roi tombant toute pâmée.
> C'est là qu'on déposa le virginal cercueil;
> Et pendant six cents ans les pèlerins en deuil
> Virent, sur ce tombeau tout brodé de pilastres,
> Trois rangs de lampes d'or briller comme des astres!

For this conclusion Autran relied upon his imagination, since the *Chronicle* does not mention Aude and the *Chanson de Roland* merely says that she was buried with pomp beside an altar in a church and that she was mourned. Nothing is said about an elaborate tomb.[7] Autran chose to dwell on the love between Aude and Roland, a love totally absent from the *Chronicle* and about which little is said in the *Chanson de Roland*. Autran's denouement provides a more romantic, more spectacular ending than either.

Autran's most obvious borrowings are from the *Pseudo-Turpin Chronicle*. From the *Chanson de Roland* he took the idea for Aude's death and embroidered upon it. Because of the *Chanson de Roland*, he likewise made Archbishop Turpin die at the hero's side rather than head back toward France with the main army. Other incidents that the *Chanson de Roland* contributed are Olivier's accidentally hitting Roland on the head with his sword during the rear guard's last stand, Roland's stretching his dead comrades out at Turpin's feet to receive the archbishop's final blessing, and Ganelon's being turned over to Charlemagne's cook for safekeeping until the French get back to Aix.

In his famous *voyant* letter, Rimbaud called Autran an imbecile. He was wrong. The *Légende des paladins*, though not great, is certainly a good verse narrative. Armand de Pontmartin, a contemporary critic, thought it "saisissante dans sa simplicité héroïque" and praised its "heureux contrastes" "tour à tour gracieux et terribles." Of the various poems, he called special attention to "L'Allée de frênes," "La Messe," "Le Baptême du géant," "La Sieste," "Bramidonie," and "La Fiancée." The *Légende des paladins*'s virile call to action, he thought, should arouse an "émulation féconde."[8] No doubt the work helped raise French readers' morale during the somber years that settled over France after her shocking defeat.

Another writer at the end of the nineteenth century treated an episode in the *Pseudo-Turpin Chronicle* that had attracted Autran's notice. Unlike Autran, he hinted that France may have incurred God's wrath by not living up to her noblest moral ideals. Leconte de Lisle was one of those contemporaries who admired this stern Christian moralist, Edmond Haraucourt. While he was far from sharing the younger poet's religious convictions, probably the bitterness that underscores so much of his own verse made him recognize a kindred spirit in the future author of *Les Ages*.

Writing in 1898, Haraucourt took an incident from the *Chronicle,* changing it slightly and making it occur after Roland's death. In this provocative sequel the poet set out to show the hiatus between Christian doctrine and Christian practice and above all to condemn forced conversion. Haraucourt's poem is entitled "Marsile." Prince Lucien Bonaparte had considered the heathen monarch an attractive character and so did Haraucourt.

Charlemagne has returned too late to Roncevaux and has pursued the Moors, capturing their leader. "Le roi sarrazinois Marsile est prisonnier." Baligant is not mentioned. Marsile must either be baptized or be put to death, the French emperor tells him. Meanwhile the emperor conducts his prisoner to a banquet hall, seats him on his right, and proceeds to devour his food like a glutton. The prisoner does not eat or drink but watches the Frenchmen, first with curiosity, then amazement, and then horror. "Le musulman, rigide et grave, ne boit pas, / Ne mange pas: il pense, il écoute, il regarde, / Stupéfait des hanaps, de la rumeur bavarde, / Des blocs de viande rouge et des buveurs goulus." At last he questions the emperor: "Quels sont ces hommes chevelus / Qui mâchent sans dégoût les cadavres de bêtes?" He is told that these are "mes faiseurs de conquêtes, les Preux." The men in ornate costumes, rubicund and chubby, are the bishops and "les prêtres du Dieu vrai qui donne la victoire." The timid ones with downcast eyes are the mendicant friars, the preachers. Then Marsile indicates "Ceux-là, demi-nus, qui dans les plats d'argile / Recueillent les morceaux qu'on jette au lévrier, / Qui vous tendent les mains comme pour vous prier, / Et qui sortent des coins en rampant sur les dalles / Pour ramasser des os rongés, sous vos sandales," and is told, laconically, that these wretched creatures are the poor. The prisoner is aghast. "Vous traitez le pauvre comme un chien," he exclaims and calls upon his captor to put him to death. "Tuez-moi. J'aime mieux être mort que chrétien." If the complacent, sanctimonious Levites he sees around him, the coarse, insensitive gluttons, represent Christianity, then Marsile wants no part of it. The *Chanson de Roland* depicts Marsile as a fanatic who would rather die than renounce Mohammedanism. Haraucourt suspected that he had a nobler reason for dying. He was appalled by the barbarous manners and inhumane coldness of the Christians.[9] Nothing is said about his wife, who, in the *Chanson de Roland,* is taken back to France and converted.

Perhaps Haraucourt's immediate inspiration was "Les Convives du roi," a poem in Autran's *Légende des paladins.* If so, then Haraucourt made several changes. In Autran's poem Charlemagne is not dealing with Marsile but with Aigoland, another Mohammedan ruler, who is not a prisoner. Nor is the war over. Rather, a truce has been declared and the two leaders have chanced to encounter one another and are taking a stroll together. As they talk, a poor man accosts them, his hand outstretched. Aigoland turns him away with harsh words, whereupon the French emperor reproves the Saracen, pointing out that "Ces pâles mendiants qui n'ont ni feu ni lieu / Sont tous auprès de nous les envoyés de Dieu." Unbeknown to Charlemagne, his companion is impressed.

The next day Charlemagne is presiding over a splendid feast when Aigoland, the truce still in effect, comes to visit him. Charlemagne points out the warriors, the princes of the blood, the counts, barons, and knights who have won his battles, as well as the churchmen, the bishops, deacons, canons, abbots, and monks who are concerned with the men's souls. And who, the Mohammedan asks, are the others?

> Des hommes en haillons, groupe triste et hagard,
> Qui, pieds nus, habillés de quelque robe sale,
> Pêle-mêle, attendaient, dans un coin de la salle.
> —Ces derniers conviés, dont tu vois la maigreur,
> Ce sont les mendiants, répondit l'empereur,
> Ce sont les vagabonds qui, d'une âme inquiète,
> Viennent attendre là qu'on leur jette une miette.
> —Empereur, dit l'émir, j'étais venu vers toi,
> L'esprit ouvert d'avance aux clartés de ta foi.
> Désertant Mahomet, je voulais ce soir même
> Recevoir de ta main la faveur du baptême;
> Mais, puisque c'est ainsi que l'on traite en ce lieu
> Ceux qui sont, m'as-tu dit, les envoyés de Dieu,
> Je sors, n'estimant pas que votre loi chrétienne
> Satisfasse le coeur beaucoup plus que la mienne.[10]

In Autran's poem there are no coarse soldiers, no gluttons. No Mohammedan prince has to choose between death and conversion, but, disenchanted, he does decide not to embrace the invaders' faith. Haraucourt's poem is an indictment. Autran's work had ended on a didactic but much pleasanter note. Haraucourt makes the abashed Charlemagne learn to practice what he has preached. "Charles baissa la tête, et dit: 'Il a raison.' / Et, depuis ce jour-là, dans sa grande maison, / Pauvres et mendiants, tous ceux que l'on pourchasse, / Furent toujours assis à la première place!" Autran's source and, ultimately, Haraucourt's was the *Pseudo-Turpin Chronicle*. Autran had added his own touches and omitted details when he wished. The *Chronicle* insists that the emperor was in despair when he realized that his own bad example made the Moor recoil from accepting Christianity.

Haraucourt would have another opportunity to refer to the Roland legend during World War I. A poem dating from that period is called "A la mémoire des écrivains Français morts pour la patrie." Praising these writers, the author pointed out that were it not for such heroes, French civilization, as represented in the nation's literature, would have vanished. The *Chanson de Roland* might never have existed had there not been traditional links between France's soldiery and her writers.[11]

Henri de Bornier's *La Fille de Roland,* which had its Comédie Française premiere on 15 February 1875, reflected French despair and aspirations following the Franco-Prussian War. Barbier and Hugo were among those who acclaimed the play. Pointing out that the dramatist had not paid as much attention to the *Chanson de Roland* as he might have done, Théodore de Banville was only a trifle less enthusiastic.[12]

Conceived in 1864 and finished in 1865, an initial version called *Le Chemin de St-Jacques* had been rejected by Comédie Française. France vanquished? An emperor humiliated? Such things could never happen and should not be shown. Bornier reworked his play, calling it *Gérald.* Offered to the Comédie Française in 1870, it was accepted in principle but put aside due to the outbreak of hostilities with Prussia. After the war, things had changed. Now an emperor had been humiliated and France had been overrun. Revised once more, the play was submitted as *Le Comte Amaury.* This time it went into rehearsal. In charge was Emile Perrin, who had directed Mermet's *Roland à Roncevaux.* Perrin did not like the title, however, and it was changed to *La Fille de Roland.*[13] Starting on 15 February 1875, large audiences began to see and feverishly applaud this version.

Bornier's dramatic technique owed much to the theater of François Ponsard. To Ponsard's son the author supposedly remarked that the idea for the play came from four stanzas of Ponsard's "Galésinde au couvent." The stanzas deal with Charlemagne's call to his vassals, Roland's departure, and the battle of Roncevaux.[14] Bornier's Roland, like Ponsard's, seems to have been from the Rhine River area. In both works, moreover, a man abandoned as dead is discovered and nursed back to life by a kindly monk or hermit. Basically, however, Bornier's plot is his own, and Ponsard's sixteen lines could have given the dramatist little more than his starting point.

In Victor Hugo's work, Roland and Aude had married. Bornier's Roland not only got married but also had a daughter. When we see her, she is a grown woman. *La Fille de Roland* takes place in 813 and 814 and involves a simple if implausible scenario. After the ambush at Roncevaux, Ganelon was tried and sentenced to death. Left for dead, he did not die. Radbert, a kindly monk, discovered him and nursed him back to health, then retired with him to the distant Château de Montblois, near the Rhine River. Here Ganelon took a new name, Amaury. While he has tried to put the past behind him, his conscience tortures him. At Montblois he has reared a valiant son, Gérald. Having the same mother as Roland, Gérald is almost identical to his dead half-brother to whom he has no idea he is related.[15] Ganelon's pain intensifies as he sees Roland's features in Gérald. Speaking of his son, he points out that "Il rappelait Roland par son visage même, / Au point que mon esprit quelquefois ne savait / Si mon fils était mort ou si Roland vivait!" Gérald is eager to try his luck and win distinction as a knight. He has taken Roland as his model, little suspecting that his hero is a half-brother who died before he was born. He is equally ignorant that his father was the chief cause of his hero's death.

When the curtain rises, Ganelon has just returned from a visit to Roncevaux. "J'avais soif de revoir le théâtre du crime," he tells someone. Hardly has he returned when visitors begin to arrive at his castle. The first is Berthe, Charlemagne's grandniece. En route to the emperor's palace at Aix, she was attacked by a band of marauding Saxons. Gérald saved her, taking Ragenhardt, the Saxon leader, prisoner. Next to arrive is Duke Naimes, who, with a detachment of soldiers, has come to escort Berthe the rest of the way. At a banquet in Berthe's honor, Ganelon asks his son, who has had lessons from a minstrel, to entertain their guest with "quelque nouveau poème," "quelque chanson de geste." A modest lad, Gérald declines, but Radbert urges him to sing what could be called Bornier's "Chanson de Roland," "cette chanson dont un moine est l'auteur." Thus prodded, Gérald agrees.

> La France, dans ce siècle, eut deux grandes épées,
> Deux glaives, l'un royal et l'autre féodal,
> Dont les lames d'un flot divin furent trempées;
> L'une a pour nom Joyeuse, et l'autre Durandal.
>
> Roland eut Durandal, Charlemagne a Joyeuse,
> Soeurs jumelles de gloire, héroïnes d'acier,
> En qui vivait du fer l'âme mystérieuse,
> Que pour son oeuvre Dieu voulut s'associer.
>
> > Toutes les deux dans les mêlées
> > Entraient jetant leur rude éclair,
> > Et les bannières étoilées
> > Les suivaient en flottant dans l'air!
> > ....
> > Durandal a conquis l'Espagne;
> > Joyeuse a dompté le Lombard;
> > Chacune à sa noble compagne
> > Pouvait dire: Voici ma part!
> > Toutes les deux ont par le monde
> > Suivi, chassé le crime immonde,
> > Vaincu les païens en tout lieu;
> > Après mille et mille batailles,

Aucune d'elles n'a d'entailles
Pas plus que le glaive de Dieu!

Hélas! La même fin ne leur est pas donnée:
Joyeuse est fière et libre après tant de combats,
Et quand Roland périt dans la sombre journée,
Duandal des païens fut captive là-bas!

Elle est captive encore, et la France la pleure,
Mais le sort différent laisse l'honneur égal,
Et la France, attendant quelque chance meilleure,
Aime du même amour Joyeuse et Durandal!

Captured at the battle of Roncevaux, Roland's sword is still in Spain. Sancho Panza, we recall, thought it was in the Armería Real in Madrid. Quinet thought so too.

Gérald has already told his father that he would like to go to court and serve the emperor. Soon, however, he confesses that he has fallen in love with Princess Berthe. Ganelon is appalled and tries to dissuade his son. If his son were to marry the emperor's grandniece, sooner or later his own past would surely be revealed. He persuades the young man to renounce the idea. Soon complications develop when Berthe admits that she has fallen in love with her rescuer and the duke extends him an invitation to come to court. Having made his father a promise, Gérald declines. Instead, he goes off to fight the Saracens in Africa.

A year later, old and humbled, Charlemagne sits on his throne in Aix wondering why God seems to have abandoned him. A task calling for a proven hero has arisen, and none of his courtiers is equal to it. For a month a Saracen emir, Noéthold, has been coming to the palace each day to taunt him and his nobles, shouting that he had seized, "étant enfant, / Le jour de Roncevaux, sous le corps de Roland, / Durandal, son épée, et je viens vous la rendre. / Mais je ne la rendrai qu'à qui pourra la prendre!" In the *Chanson de Roland,* as Bornier knew, Roland had placed his sword beneath him before dying. According to Bornier, Noéthold found and removed it, justifying Roland's concern that it might fall into pagan hands. All of Charlemagne's young barons are eager to take up the Moor's challenge, but, realizing that not one of them measures up to the emir, the emperor has withheld his permission. When Noéthold finally blusters that "De ton neveu Roland je remporte l'épée, / Durandal," and invites him to look at it one last time, the emperor, old as he is, decides to duel with the intruder himself. Suddenly Gérald appears and claims the honor. Elated, Charlemagne lends him his sword Joyeuse for the contest. Berthe adds her own encouragement. From the comments of Berthe and Charlemagne, watching from a window, one learns what is happening. Gérald is the victor, of course, and returns with Roland's sword, which will be placed in Roland's tomb. Charlemagne rewards the young knight by announcing, "Gérald, voici le prix que ta valeur réclame: / La fille de Roland demain sera ta femme." Roland's daughter is being awarded to the champion who has reclaimed Roland's sword. All would seem to be on the point of ending happily.

Ganelon, using his new name, has arrived at the palace to witness his son's triumph and also, because his estate is a crown dependency, to take his oath as the emperor's vassal. Charlemagne recognizes him almost at once, flies into a rage, threatens, reconsiders, and then forgives the penitent traitor. It is decided, however, that the erstwhile culprit must go on a pilgrimage to the Holy Land. Gérald still does not know his father's terrible secret. Only when Gérald's Saxon prisoner threatens to reveal the truth does Ganelon makes a clean breast of things. Stunned, Gérald feels that it will take more than an imperial pardon to erase the past. An "expiation éclatante et suprême" is still needed to redeem his own and his father's honor. In refusing to marry Berthe, he explains his decision to the astonished but compassionate court:

> Je suis le fils du crime, et non du repentir!
> Afin qu'aux yeux de tous la leçon soit plus haute,
> Je veux que le malheur soit plus grand que la faute!
> Et le père sera d'autant mieux pardonné
> Que le fils innocent se sera condamné!
> ....
> Mon père s'exilait; nous partirons ensemble;
> Il sied que le destin jusqu'au bout nous rassemble.

Berthe pleads with him, but Gérald has too lofty a concept of duty and honor.[16] He will not permit Roland's daughter to wed the son of Roland's murderer. Reluctantly, the emperor acquiesces but gives Durandal to Gérald. Gérald leaves, hoping to find death in battle somewhere. As he withdraws, Charlemagne orders his courtiers to do him honor: "Barons, princes, inclinez-vous / Devant celui qui part: il est plus grand que nous!" And so the play turns into a tragedy.

The play was a tremendous success, due to the climate of the times, the superb directing, and the splendid casting. Sarah Bernhardt was Berthe, Mounet-Sully was a thrilling Gérald, Henri Dupont-Vernon was Ganelon, Henri Mauband was Charlemagne, and J.A.F. de Laroche was the Saxon prisoner. Commenting on the production fourteen years later, Bornier declared that the Divine Sarah was "ravissante, chaste, noblement passionnée, princesse et femme à la fois—ou plutôt elle ressemblait à une statue d'ivoire sur un autel dans une cathédrale gothique."[17] *La Fille de Roland* was Bornier's masterpiece. It did much to help France recover its flagging spirits. Its noble sentiments and able verse still deserve respect. A hostile Jean Moréas compared Bornier to Campistron, Racine's mediocre rival, but Flaubert judged him more equitably. "Bornier est un poète," he wrote.[18] Nevertheless, the play's extraordinary verbal beauty cannot hide a number of flaws, including several weighty *invraisemblances*.

One of these has to do with Roland's having had a half-brother. The *Pseudo-Turpin Chronicle*, to be sure, had assigned him a brother, Baudouin, but Bornier invented a different one. Since Gérald did not know at the beginning of the play that he had a half-brother, we can presume that he was born after Roland's death, although on one occasion the dramatist hints otherwise. That Gérald could have grown up unaware of his father's despicable act of treason seems preposterous. Had it never occurred to this lad, so deeply interested in chivalry, to wonder why his father never rode away to take part in Charlemagne's wars? A reformed Ganelon does not come as a complete surprise, since Prince Lucien Bonaparte has already shown us one. Ganelon's escaping death, though, is a different matter. Did Bornier know that in the *Chanson de Roland*'s later, rhyming versions, dating from the twelfth and thirteenth centuries, the villain does indeed get away?[19] Probably not. But there are other problems as well. How has Bornier's Ganelon contrived to live for years at the Château de Montblois without paying homage to Charlemagne for his fief? Also, since he and his son have spent the previous year in different parts of the world, how did Ganelon know at what exact moment he should appear at Aix to witness his son's triumph? For that matter, why, instead of going back home, did Gérald turn up in Aix after leaving Africa? After all, he had promised to return home directly. And what has become of Ganelon's wife, Charlemagne's sister and the mother of Roland and Gérald? Has the emperor made no attempt to locate and care for his unhappy sister? What has her life been like in exile, or has she died heartbroken? In passing, one is amazed at how long her childbearing years lasted. At about the time Gérald was born, she had already lost an adult son in the wars. But the play is filled with other troublesome matters as well. For instance, what happens to Gérald's Saxon prisoner during the year his captor spends in Africa? Why should he have left the Château de Montblois and ended up at the emperor's palace?

The most unlikely circumstance in *La Fille de Roland*, though, is one that seems to bother none of the characters—the matter of incest. Victor Hugo, we recall, had Roland and Aude marry. Berthe is their child. As Roland's half-brother, Gérald is Berthe's uncle. A dispensation, at least, would have been required if the two were ever to be married. Never once is the lovers' blood relationship mentioned in the play, nor is it given as a reason for their ultimate separation. In fact, Bornier even considered allowing them to marry, thus giving the play a happy ending.[20] We wonder too about Berthe's childhood. Aude died on hearing that Roland had been killed. Did Charlemagne rear her baby daughter? The play does not enlighten us.

Despite these caveats, *La Fille de Roland* is a moving play, with dramatic action, lofty sentiments, and some good poetry. It is the author's only treatment of the Roland legend.[21] A patriotic piece, the play contains lines about evil Germans such as the ones who attacked Berthe, which were certain to stir French audiences in 1875. Moreover, Gérald's retrieving Roland's sword from a wicked enemy who had seized it must have reminded those same audiences that the time might come when they could do the same thing with Alsace and Lorraine.

René Fabert's historical drama *Charlemagne*, also in verse and dating from 1875, was first performed at the Troisième Théâtre Français on 23 January 1878. The action takes place at about the same time as *La Fille de Roland*. Charlemagne is locked in a death struggle with the Saxons. The dead Roland is mentioned several times. Fearful that the Moors will resume their raids, the emperor is having them watched on his western frontier. "Renaud, puis Aimery, du haut des Pyrénées, / Surveilleront le Maure aux perfides menées; / Songeant à Roncevaux, toujours se rappelant / Que c'est là que périt mon bon neveu Roland," he points out. Later his son Louis, during a tender moment with a Saxon priestess, hears a horn in the distance. When he hears it a second time he senses disaster, becomes worried, and, in lines reminiscent of "Le Cor," exclaims: "Dieu, c'est le cor qui sonne, / Et si plaintivement que tout mon corps frissonne. / C'est comme à Roncevaux." As in "Le Cor," in Fabert's play Turpin has survived the Roncevaux massacre.

Fabert's drama is creditable. Still, *La Fille de Roland* was the first to reach the theater, and it seized audiences' imagination and kept it. It had come at a crucial time in French history, and Frenchmen would remember it at other desperate moments. The Comédie Française revived it on 25 December 1914 before an elated audience. A few months earlier, the battle of the Marne had saved Paris from another German occupation. Much later, as darkness was about to descend over the country in 1940, a new edition came out.

Henri Rabaud, who would later conduct the Paris Opéra and the Boston Symphony Orchestra and who would succeed Gabriel Fauré as head of the Paris Conservatoire, was a noted composer. At the turn of the century Bornier's drama was still vividly remembered, and Rabaud decided to turn it into an opera.[23] The libretto, which often follows the play word for word, was the work of Paul Ferrier, a minor dramatist and prolific librettist. Bornier had called his play a *drame*. Rabaud described the opera as a *tragédie musicale*.

The opera's plot seldom deviates from that of the play. Rabaud eliminated Roland's squire, a minor character in the play. Rabaud also stretched his audience's credulity a little less than Bornier had done by making the action take place twenty rather than thirty-five years after the battle of Roncevaux. In the opera characters have fresher memories of the disaster. And, of course, when she cannot marry Gérald, Berthe is still young enough to land another husband, assuming she does not take the veil.

In the opera, as in the play, Ganelon is a kind master, loved and honored in his household, but he is tormented. Pouring out his feelings to Radbert, he recalls the purpose of a recent trip.

> Sous le remords qui m'étouffait,
> J'ai fait de Roncevaux l'affreux pèlerinage!
> J'ai revu le vallon témoin de mon forfait!
> Hélas! depuis vingt ans je pleure!
> Combien lente s'écoule l'heure
> Pour qui succombe au repentir!
> Et ces vingt ans de pénitence,
> Vingt ans qui du coupable auront fait un martyr,
> N'ont pas effacé la sentence!
> (Act 1, scene ii)

He prays that God will forgive him for his crime. In the opera, but not in the play, there is a chorus of execration once when his real name is mentioned. "Il a trahi les fils de France, / Il a trahi comme Judas! / Il a vendu son alliance / Aux meurtriers de nos soldats! / Maudit soit Ganelon! Maudit soit Ganelon!" (act 2, scene 4).

Soon Berthe appears and, learning of the hazards of proceeding to Aix, she decides to remain at Ganelon's castle until an escort arrives to conduct her to her uncle's palace. Berthe resembles her father. As the emperor exclaims at one point, "O Roland! qu'elle est bien ta fille! / Dans son regard c'est ton regard qui brille! / Sois donc bénie, enfant, à qui je dois / Le vivant souvenir des gloires d'autrefois (act 3, scene 2)." The chorus comments that Gérald, shares traits with his hero and model. "Même bravoure et même orgueil," it is decided. The coincidence that he, like Berthe, looks very much like Roland seems to occur to no one. As in the play, in the opera Ganelon tries to quash his son's interest in Berthe. With great reluctance, he finally consents to letting the attachment continue.

Gérald's "Chanson de Roland" duplicates the one in the play, with the omission of the song's two lengthy middle stanzas. When Noéthold taunts Charlemagne and his barons, the emperor resigns himself to allowing "ce more insolent" to go home, taking Roland's sword with him. Only at the last moment does he decide to accept the boastful intruder's challenge himself. At this critical point Gérald appears and kills the interloper, rescuing the sword. Now Durandal can be placed in Roland's tomb. In the distance the chorus sings a Te Deum, not mentioned in the play.

As the opera ends, Gérald and Ganelon leave together, going into what they consider an exile. Nothing has been said, however, about Ganelon's making a pilgrimage. Much earlier, on the other hand, Ganelon had described his trip to Roncevaux Valley as a "pèlerinage." As father and son withdraw, the stage directions do not call for the son's deserted sweetheart to point heavenward, as she does in the play.

One never loses track of the opera's patriotic motive. Despite the fact that much of the action takes place in Aix, there is never a doubt that Charlemagne's barons are Frenchmen. The emperor complains about France's present lamentable state and expresses his deeply felt wish that she will recover her honored position among the nations (act 3, scenes 2, 4). He hopes that her prestige will, "aux époques prochaines, / Croissant comme croissent les chênes / Aux autres peuples qui naîtront / Offrir, par le glaive et le verbe, / De ses rameaux l'abri superbe / Et l'ombre douce de son front!" Evil invaders must be driven out. "Haut les coeurs, chevaliers de France! / Faites avec moi le serment, / Sur ce sol qui frémit sous un joug infâmant, / De lutter pour sa délivrance! (act 3, scene 4)." The allusion to Alsace and Lorraine could hardly have been clearer.

While not innovative, Rabaud's music is expressive and now and then imaginative. Depending upon plot circumstances, it is brisk, suspenseful, majestic, or tender. The premiere, at the Opéra Comique on 16 March 1904, was considered a highly important event. The composer chose his cast prudently. All the major roles were entrusted to the theater's principal singers, and thus almost no one in it was not a star. The *Echo de Paris* and *Figaro* heaped lavish praise on the artists.[24] Berthe's role went to Marguerite Carré, a remarkable prima donna. Léon Beyle, the Opéra Comique's leading tenor, was Gérald. The Belgian Hector Dufranne, a baritone who had been Golaud in the first performance of Debussy's *Pelléas et Mélisande* two years before, was Ganelon, and Félix Vieuille, a bass who had also helped launch *Pelléas et Mélisande*, was given the role of Charlemagne. Charles Bianchini's impressive costumes contributed visual splendor, as did Lucien Jusseaume's sumptuous decors. Both men's talents had been put to use in the *Pelléas et Mélisande* production.[25] Still, although it was revived several times in the early 1920s, Rabaud's opera has not remained in the repertoire.

Baron Adolphe d'Avril (1822-1904) was a diplomat and an erudite medievalist. In 1865 he produced a rather literal *Chanson de Roland* translation, complete with an extensive introduction, that went through a number of editions. Like Dumas, he was interested in Roland's childhood. His *Les Enfances Roland* appeared in 1892 in the Nouvelle Bibliothèque Bleue collection.[26] The work was for children and adolescents, but it had something for older readers as well. Children would not have understood a passage from the Old French *Chanson d'Antioche*, but the lines were translated, making them accessible to all readers. Frequently the writer took a didactic stance, due no doubt to the main audience he hoped to attract.

Although Avril made no claim to originality, he did demonstrate in *Les*

Enfances Roland that he was an accomplished medievalist. While drawing upon other works, he relied essentially in this prose narrative upon the *Reali di Francia* and the Old French *Aspremont* and *Girart de Vienne*. The medieval specialist brought to his narrative an expert's knowledge of the period. Occasionally he added his own comments or elucidations. Regarding Olivier and Roland's duel, for instance, he explained that the actions of the two champions were based on the chivalric code governed by the strictest protocol.[27] He was particularly anxious to combat the notion that people in the Middle Ages were barbarians. He inserted material intended to prove that lords and ladies, at least, were polite and cultivated at the time. A thick medieval aura results from the use of such archaic words as *lors, avesprée, chu, coi, ouïr, quérir,* and *occir,* as well as obsolete locutions, phrases, and even spellings. "Ce jour d'huy" is encountered, and sometimes *le, la,* and *les* are omitted. Like medieval epic poets, the author used repetition.

As an artist, Avril was less than perfect. Occasionally an insignificant digression slows the momentum. Sometimes the author discarded useful plot material from his source. During a lull in their duel, Olivier tells Roland that he would like to see his sister Aude become his adversary's wife. Inside the Château de Vienne, Aude cannot hear the conversation. Yet a little later she calls Roland her fiancé.[28] Generally, however, Avril needs no excuses. He tells a good story and tells it well.

Avril makes Roland the son of Charlemagne's sister, whom he calls Gillie, although the *Reali du Francia* calls her Berta.[29] Gillie, without her brother's consent, has married Milon. Learning about this secret union, Charlemagne explodes in anger, and the couple flees. Dumas père had the lovers go to Spain, but Avril settles them in Ravenna. There, poor and proscribed, they rear their son Roland, who goes to school and turns out to be a natural leader and an excellent student. We recall that Assollant let him grow up illiterate. While on an expedition to rescue the pope, Charlemagne discovers the lad and, thanks to an accident, his parents as well. Charlemagne's rancor has not cooled, but Roland intercedes and his parents receive the emperor's forgiveness.

We next see Roland when he is about fifteen. Charlemagne has returned home. King Aigoland, a pagan, sends an ambassador, who appears on Ascension Day and calls upon the emperor to become his master's vassal. Charlemagne prepares to go to war. Before he leaves, his impetuous nephew and four companions are sent, under Turpin's supervision, to a fortress in Laon. Overcoming the gatekeeper, they escape, seize horses, and join Charlemagne. At Aspromonte, in Calabria, a battle with the pagans ensues. In the battle Roland saves his uncle's life and kills Aigoland's son Yaumont. Roland claims Yaumont's dappled horse Veillantif as well as his sharp sword Durandal. The French win, and in Rome the pope blesses Durandal as Charlemagne knights its new owner.

Avril's third and last episode is the longest. With his uncle, who plans to name him his eventual successor, Roland has returned to France. Sometime later, having defied his emperor, Girart de Vienne has retired to his castle with his brothers Hernaut and Renier as well as Hernaut's son Aymeri de Narbonne and Renier's daughter and son, Aude and Olivier. Avril did not approve when Hugo, who had little taste for research, made Olivier Girart's son rather than Renier's. Actually, Avril was not above altering facts himself. In his basic source, Girart has insulted no one when he withdraws to his castle. Rather, Charlemagne's empress has played a low trick on him. But anxious to maintain his contention that wellborn medieval men and women were highly cultivated, Avril eliminated details that would suggest the empress's bad manners.

Charlemagne has pursued his recalcitrant vassal and laid siege to the Château de Vienne, setting up camp beneath its steep battlements. Roland meets Aude on the castle ramparts, and the two are attracted to each other. When the siege has gone on for six months, Olivier proposes a *combat singulier* on an island in the Rhone River to decide the issue between emperor and vassal. Olivier is his uncle's champion, and Roland is the emperor's. Torn between love for her brother and love for Roland, Aude prays, hoping for a miraculous outcome that will exonerate her uncle, please the emperor, and humiliate neither her brother nor her lover. The warriors are well matched. "Ils luttent bien assortis," Avril comments. "Jamais deux chevaliers ne furent si vaillants, ni si hardis, ni combattant si fièrement."[30] The awesome warriors fight on and on. Each has his horse killed. How Veillantif will eventually be resurrected to serve his master at Roncevaux is not explained. When Olivier's sword breaks, Roland allows his opponent to send to the castle for a new one as well as for some wine. Olivier selects Hauteclaire. Then, having served his opponent wine, he renews the battle.

Such a contest could have ended only with the death of one of the contenders had there not been divine intervention. Aude's entreaties are answered. A cloud descends between the two adversaries and an angel orders them to stop their duel. Their valor will be needed against the pagans. Here as elsewhere in the narrative, there are allusions to the somber events that will come to pass at Roncevaux. Olivier and Roland, who admire each other, vow eternal friendship. In Hugo's version Olivier brought matters to a sudden conclusion by proposing that his antagonist marry Aude. Here Roland takes the initiative and asks Olivier for his sister's hand. The request is granted, and the emperor ratifies the engagement. Roland gives Aude a ring, and she presents him with a white banner. "Ainsi la paix fut faite." Charlemagne and Girart are reconciled. Then emissaries arrive with news that the infidels are crossing into France. Charlemagne summons his barons and heads for Spain. "Vous connaissez bien la chanson de geste," the author concludes. Through

Ganelon the French were betrayed and Roland, with twenty thousand other Frenchmen, perished.[31]

Avril treated the Roland legend on another occasion, this time writing for adults. In 1875 he wrote a verse drama called *Le Mystère de Roland*. Believing that dialogue problems would make it impossible to produce, he reluctantly recast it as prose drama. Epics, the author believed, have a natural dramatic configuration, and he followed the *Chanson de Roland* as much as he could, imitating its inversions, repetitions, and recapitulations. A commentator, who acts as a chorus, is called a *maître du jeu*, for medieval flavor. The play is divided into six tableaux. Entitled *Le Mystère de Roncevaux*, it appeared in 1893.[32] There is no record that it has ever been performed.

Realizing that the battle scene could not be staged, Avril resolved to present it as a *récit*. The author recalled that St. Giles, destined to become a hermit later on, was supposed to have been present at Roncevaux. Avril quoted lines from another epic, the *Chanson de Hugues Capet:*

> Cent ans avoit et plus,
> Trez le tamps Charlemaigne estoit au bos repus
> Et fu en Raincheval ou Rolans fu perdus;
> Et la fist il le veu, quant il fu combatus,
> Que si Deux li volloit faire telle vertus
> Qu'il peuist escapper dez paiiens malostrus,
> Il devenroit tantost hermitez ou renclus.

Probably Avril did not know the Provençal *Cansó d'Antiocha*, with its digression on the battle of Roncevaux in which Giles, though killed, is mentioned.[33] Perhaps he was relying upon Stricker's *Karl*, dating from the first half of the thirteenth century, in which Giles brings Charlemagne the the bad news. Avril let Giles survive and recite the massacre.

Thus the quatrième tableau, called "Sur la route de France," contains a narrative. Badly wounded, "le preux Gille" wanders away from the carnage and staggers out to meet Charlemagne, who, having heard Roland's horn for the third time, is turning back to come to his nephew's aid. Giles tells the emperor that Ganelon has betrayed the French, and Ganelon is turned over to the head cook to await trial. Giles's long account follows the sequence of events in the *Chanson de Roland*. A few passages will demonstrate Avril's treatment of material in the epic that did not lend itself to dramatization. In addition to recounting events, Giles comments, as the epic does. "Aux quatre premiers chocs, le combat alla bien pour les chrétiens," he states. "Le cinquième leur fut funeste et terrible. Tous sont tués, les chevaliers français, hormis soixante, que Dieu a épargnés. Avant qu'ils meurent, ils se vendront bien cher." Roland and Olivier quarrel. Hearing them, Archbishop Turpin calls on them to desist. To blow the horn now will serve no purpose, he tells them, but he advises Roland to do it anyway. "Que l'empereur vienne, il nous pourra venger et les infidèles ne s'en retourneront pas joyeux. Nos Français mettront pied à terre: ils nous trouveront et morts et taillés en pièces: ils nous porteront en bières sur des bêtes de somme. Ils nous pleureront par douleur et par pitié: ils nous enfouiront dans les parvis des monastères: loups, porcs et chiens ne nous mangeront pas." Commending this reasoning, Roland puts the horn to his lips and blows. "Le comte Roland, avec peine et effort et grande douleur, sonne son cor. Le sang clair lui jaillit par la bouche. Les tempes de son cerveau en sont déchirées." This concludes the *récit*.

In the cinquième tableau, entitled "A Roncevaux," Roland addresses his slain comrades, assuming the blame for what has taken place. Olivier dies, and Roland, reconciled to him, weeps. The Saracens flee. Archbishop Turpin dies. Aware that his own death is imminent, Roland tries to break his sword, but to no avail. He talks to it, recalling the deeds it has helped him accomplish and mentioning the relics it contains.[34] "Quand je ne puis plus me servir de vous, je ne puis plus vous conserver. . . . Durandal, que tu es belle et sainte!" he exclaims pathetically. Then he confesses his sins, murmurs a short prayer, and dies. St. Gabriel and St. Michael descend and carry his soul to heaven. Charlemagne arrives to find his nephew dead.

The final tableau takes place at Aix. Roland's sword has been placed on the altar at St. Seurin's in Bordeaux. Roland, Olivier, and Turpin have been buried in white marble tombs at St. Romain's. Ganelon has been convicted and punished. Aude, learning that her fiancé has been killed, dies and is buried in a convent. The *maître du jeu* sums up with several stanzas of verse.

> Belle Alde est morte! En l'église on l'inhume.
> Charle a vengé la mort du preux Roland.
> Suivant la loi de Dieu et la coutume
>   Du royaume des Franks.
>
> Dieu ne veut pas que le felon se vante,
> Et de son crime qu'il recueille le prix;
> Mais Dieu reçoit une vierge innocente
>   Dans son saint paradis.
>
> Adieu, Roland; les douze pairs, adieu,
> Morts pour Jésus et la France en Espagne!
> Le roi de France est le sergent de Dieu;
>   Gloire à Charle-le-Magne. . . .

St. Gabriel tells the emperor in a dream that the Christian cause needs him in other places. The emperor is reluctant but admits that he must do as commanded. He and his suite wax enthusiastic finally, knowing that "le Christ . . . aime les Français."

Mermet had shown operagoers an adult Roland. With the century drawing to a close they saw an adolescent one. *L'Enfance de Roland,* described by the composer as a *légende lyrique,* deals with two boyhood episodes in the paladin's life. Both music and libretto were the work of the Belgian composer Emile Mathieu (1844-1932). Although published in 1893, the four-act opera was initially performed at the Théâtre de la Monnaie in Brussels on 16 January 1895.[35]

Mathieu appears to have known German. His libretto, he wrote, had been inspired by Uhland's "Klein Roland" (1808) and "Roland Schildträger" (1811).[36] Deeply interested in the Roland legend, Uhland also wrote a "Roland und Alda" (1811), for which he had transcribed much of *Girart de Vienne* in the Bibliothèque Nationale in 1810. In "Klein Roland" Uhland had told the story of how Bertha, Charlemagne's sister, had eloped with Milon d'Anglant, married, and settled in a small Italian town near Siena. The destitute couple lived in a cave, and in time they had a son. Hoping to improve his family's status, Milon leaves to seek his fortune elsewhere. While he is away, Charlemagne, returning from Rome, stops in the town where Bertha lives. Neither he nor his sister is aware of the other's presence. Not only is Bertha distressed about being on bad terms with her brother and concerned about her absent husband, but she is also hungry and thirsty. Little Roland, knowing that the king is in town, takes it upon himself to provide for his mother. Not far away, Charlemagne is seated at a table, surrounded by his court, enjoying a banquet. He looks up and sees a boy enter the room, boldly remove a dish from the table, and leave with it. A little later the boy returns and takes the king's own goblet. When Charlemagne questions him, he answers that he is taking the food and wine to his mother, a great lady. He adds that he is her only servant. When he leaves, Charlemagne instructs three noblemen and three ladies to go with him and bring the lady back. Timidly, Bertha returns with the courtiers. Roland's manner and speech win the king over completely and effect a happy reunion between brother and sister. Bertha assures the king that her son will grow up to serve him well. At the end of the poem, Milon has not returned.

"Roland Schildträger" shows the diminutive hero in a different situation. Charlemagne expresses a desire to own a precious stone now in the possession of a giant living in the Ardennes Forest. Six nobles set out, hoping to wrest it from its current owner. By now Milon has returned and is a prominent courtier. Like the others, he hopes to get the jewel. One by one each of the noblemen returns with one of the giant's weapons or a part of his body. The giant had already been killed when each located him. Roland, serving as Milon's shieldbearer, had killed him while his father was taking a nap but has not mentioned the fact. When Milon discovers the corpse, he returns, disappointed, to court. Because his son has slipped the jewel into his father's shield as an ornament, Milon is about to be credited with having seized it, but the truth is quickly learned. Roland is already showing his merits.

Dumas père treated these episodes in his *Chronique de Charlemagne* in 1842, and Adolphe d'Avril had treated one of them in *Les Enfances Roland* fifty years later. Either Mathieu did not know his French predecessors' work or else preferred the German poems. In any event, he did not hesitate to tamper with his source material, changing and adding so much that the original anecdotes are barely recognizable. He even added characters that, while not in Uhland's poems, are nevertheless indispensable to his plot.

Heading *L'Enfance de Roland*'s cast of characters is Charlemagne, depicted as a patriarch. In the opera his name is Karl, probably due to metrical considerations. Dame Berte and Roland appear, of course, and the three named courtiers are Duke Naimes of Bavaria, Count Richard, and Count Garin. No name is assigned to the giant. Among the invented characters is Princess Imma, Charlemagne's niece. She appears nowhere else in Roland literature. There are also various Saxon prisoners, who are free on parole. One of these, Sigmar, proves as necessary to the plot as Roland himself. Roland is supposed to be fourteen, and his role calls for a soprano voice.

The setting for act 1 is a terrace in front of Charlemagne's palace at Ingelheim, beside the Rhine River. It is an April morning. As the curtain rises, the king, with his niece and courtiers, comes out to meet some Moslem ambassadors bearing gifts and an unexpected suggestion. An interpreter addresses the king: "Prince auguste, pasteur des peuples d'Occident, / Le Sultan de l'Islam, le maître de l'Asie, / S'offre pour ton sincère et fidèle allié, / Ainsi sera le monde enfin pacifié." The proposal of an alliance comes as a surprise, but a chorus of knights and commoners welcomes it with enthusiasm. Charlemagne and Imma are dazzled by the gifts—rich silks, a casket encrusted with precious stones, scimitars in velvet scabbards, an ivory horn, and a scepter with a ruby tip. Looking at the scepter, the king muses about a giant who lives in the Ardennes Forest and has a marvelous red jewel that is valuable and magic.

> Combien doit resplendir dans la forêt profonde
> L'escarboucle magique au brassard du géant.
> ....
> Je vois son infernal sourire
> Insulter ma faiblesse et railler mon délire.
> Muet, fasciné, je l'entends me dire,
> "Va, ton pouvoir n'est que néant."
> Tant qu'elle resplendit dans la forêt profonde,

> L'escarboucle magique, au brassard du géant,
> Grand roi qui fais trembler le monde,
> Va, ton pouvoir n'est que néant.

Charlemagne craves the stone. He sinks into a chair, and the chorus warns the audience that he is slipping into his strange illness. His seizures do not last, but they recur and threaten his reason. Imma thinks she has the solution. Tearfully, she addresses the Frankish knights and asks them to try to get the stone. Duke Naimes, Count Richard, Count Garin, and other paladins reply that trying to get the carbuncle is quixotic, that each of them has attempted it. Imma is determined.

> Et bien! je fais serment sur le saint Evangile
> De ne donner ma main qu'au valeureux guerrier
> Qui saura conquérir l'escarboucle subtile,
> Quand il ne serait qu'un pauvre chevalier.
> Fût-il simple homme d'armes, à son blanc bouclier
> Un tel exploit mettra de telles armes
> Qu'il sera désormais des premiers le premier.

A chorus compliments her on her noble sentiment, but it will prove to have been rash.

Noticing that the king is reviving, Imma calls for silence. Charlemagne thanks his niece for her concern and assures her that one of her caresses is enough to chase away the evil spirits. Soon fully in control once more, he invites the ambassadors into the palace, announcing a hunt. As the others leave, Sigmar hangs back. To himself and the audience he confesses that he loves Imma and thus is almost willing to accept the Franks' domination of his country. He implores Freya, the Norse goddess of love, to help him master "tous ces coupables transports," and Odin is invoked to keep him true to his people and their deities. Just then Imma returns to ask why he does not participate in the festivities. He answers that his people's lot and his own captive status hardly dispose him to merriment. After flirting a little, Imma turns to the wonders of nature and spring. "Partout la vie éclate," she exclaims. Sigmar agrees but continues to pine for his homeland and people, a "race altière, / Dans sa pauvreté libre et fière." Although she thinks she knows that he loves her, the princess coquettishly wonders aloud whether there is a sweetheart back home. Sigmar assures her that there is not.

Then Roland appears for the first time. Stopped and questioned by Imma, he excuses his temerity in approaching the palace by saying that he has heard of the kindness of those who live there and would like to offer them his services. As for his background, "Mon père était un pauvre chevalier. / Il mourut, sans ressources abandonnant ma mère. / Comme Dieu vient en aide à qui ne désespère, / Elle sut m'élever, / Aussi me suis-je mis en tête / De lui gagner fortune et rang." Sigmar admires his charm and pluck, and Imma wants to help him. Roland knows that the princess is said to be a good person and that she has vowed to marry no man except the one who presents the giant's magic carbuncle to the king. A clever observer, he guesses that she wants the Saxon prisoner to be that man. When he says as much, Imma blushes, confirming his suspicions. He tells the princess and her suitor that his mother lives on the edge of the Ardennes Forest, the home of the giant. Having grown up there, he knows the area well and can lead Sigmar to the giant's lair. Leading someone there, actually, is the service he had come to offer. Imma and Sigmar, leaping at this chance to win the king's approval, declare their love.

In the next scene the king emerges from the palace to say that the hunt is about to begin. Suddenly messengers arrive with the news that the Saxons, under their leader Wittikind, are on the march. The king, who loves peace, will now have to make war. He orders the hostages put in chains. A distressed Imma pleads on their behalf, but the king is inflexible and orders the peers to meet that evening to decide the prisoners' fate. Roland witnesses the scene and assures the princess that he will save her lover. The courtiers and ambassadors leave for the hunt.

Act 2 takes place in the Ardennes Forest a little later. The curtain rises on Dame Berte seated at the entrance to her cave. Several things are troubling her. She is still estranged from her brother, presumed hostile. She has lost her husband, Milon d'Anglant, who has died in a drowning accident. At present she is awaiting the return of her son, who has been gone for some time. Her "orgueil, amour, espoir," Roland is all she has left. Suddenly a horn announces the approach of a hunt, and Roland cries out to her that he is back. Faithful to the promise he made to Imma, he has helped Sigmar escape. He introduces him. Berte discloses that the giant is protected by magic. Nevertheless, for one hour one night a year he is defenseless. That moment comes on Holy Thursday and commemorates Judas's greeting Jesus with a treacherous kiss. Conveniently, this is Holy Thursday. The giant's dim lair is at the intersection of three ravines in the forest. The brilliant jewel will be shining, indicating where one should strike. As the blow is struck, Jesus' name must be invoked. Sigmar, having other religious commitments, would rather not do this, but Berte assures him that it is essential. Even though Roland will only be a squire, his mother tells him that he is too young to go along. "J'ai coeur et force d'homme," he insists, reminding her of David and Goliath. Berte relents and gives him his father's sword. This, one assumes, is Durandal. Roland is elated and feels invincible. Martial music is heard as he and Sigmar stride away and Berte prays for their safety.

The giant is aware that Sigmar and Roland are on their way. He will have the warrior thrown over a cliff, he decides, but will merely rebuke the boy for his audacity. Forest spirits watch over the endangered colossus. In the darkness Sigmar and Roland get separated. Roland, realizing that he may have to face the enemy alone, calls upon God and the angels to protect him. Soon, at a point where three ravines come together, he is standing at the foot of a mountain. At its peak is the giant's abode. Suddenly a brass instrument sounds, and the giant comes into view, his presence revealed by the reddish glow of a jewel in his brassard. He calls on his diminutive opponent to abandon his foolish project and enter his service, in return for his life. Roland answers that, while he does not want to kill his adversary, he must have the precious stone. The giant calls him an "insolent avorton" and prepares for trouble. All at once Sigmar appears and strikes, invoking Odin as he does so. He breaks his sword. Raising his own weapon with both hands and calling out to Jesus, Roland deals a mighty blow. The giant falls dead. Stage directions tell us that "Roland lui arrache l'escarboucle et la brandit d'un geste de triomphe."

Aix-la-Chapelle is the setting for act 3. Some time has elapsed. The first scene shows Imma waking up, clutching at a dream about her absent lover. A lady in waiting reminds her that Naimes, Richard, and Garin have been gone for three days. Each has been searching for the giant and the carbuncle. Imma realizes that she was too hasty in promising to marry whoever came back with the gem. If Sigmar is not the winner, she declares, she will enter a convent, there to await eternal union with him. It does not occur to her to wonder what heaven would be like with a heathen consort, assuming he got there.

The next scene is in the palace's Salle d'Or. The Saxons have been subdued and pacified. Now the principal rebel leaders are seated at the king's table with the Frankish knights, celebrating the end of hostilities. Berte and Roland enter. The lad promises his hesitant mother that he will have her reinstated in her royal rank, using the carbuncle. Meanwhile, the king has everyone's goblet filled and refilled. Roland refuses the goblet offered him and walks resolutely to the royal table, where he seizes the king's. He also takes food. Here Mathieu injects a bit of dialogue that closely follows a passage in "Klein Roland." Charlemagne calls on the lad to desist. Roland looks him in the face, and his stern features relax. Then Roland tells him that his mother must have food and drink befitting a person of royal birth. At this the king orders three lords and three ladies to go fetch this queen. Roland points out that there is no need to do so: "Point n'est besoin d'un tel cortège, / Dame Berte, venez! Le Roi, que Dieu protège, / Près de lui vous mande à l'instant." Berte, wearing pilgrim's garb, kneels before the king. Charlemagne bids her rise and has a royal mantle thrown over her shoulders. Roland greets him as his uncle. The tableau concludes happily as Berte predicts that Roland will serve her brother well, conquering many provinces for him. "Son nom remplira les annales du saint Empire Romain," she prophesies.

Then an officer of the palace announces that Naimes, Richard, and Garin have returned, their squires loaded with booty. Charlemagne, knowing that the loot should include the giant's weapons and the miraculous jewel, is delighted. The nobles and their squires enter with weapons belonging to the giant. At this point Roland disappears and Imma enters with her ladies. The three paladins tell the king that they have brought him many trophies but no precious stone. On reaching the giant's lair, they found that someone had already killed the monster and made off with the carbuncle. Roland, with Sigmar in tow, reappears and stands in the doorway. When he holds out the jewel, a grateful Charlemagne invites him to choose his reward. His recompense will be a selfless one.

> Sire, votre clémence en accueillant ma mère
> Combla mon plus ardent désir.
> Mais il est un autre salaire
> Par serment promis au vainqueur:
> A la princesse Imma,
> Devant tous, je réclame le droit
> De disposer de sa main, de son coeur.

Roland tells the king that the husband Imma would like, "fameux parmi ceux de sa race," struck the giant first but broke his sword in the process. Roland then names this warrior, assuring the king that, far from being an "ôtage déloyal" violating his parole, he had only fled the palace at Roland's urging. Roland is quick to add that his new friend has been converted. Sigmar, who has had time to meditate about Odin's not having helped him when he needed it, confirms this. Asked to express her wishes, Imma states that the new convert is indeed the husband of her choice, and Roland places her hand in Sigmar's.

Although Charlemagne is not yet an emperor, the chorus forecasts that the king will achieve imperial status. In the opera's closing moments Roland is the center of attention. The chorus emphasizes Berte's prediction. "L'enfant, pareil à son prince," "avide d'exploits glorieux," will conquer many a land. His name will live in the annals of the Holy Roman Empire. Presumably Mathieu did not know that the Frankish chroniclers would say almost nothing about Roland, since to discuss him would have entailed acknowledging the disaster in which he lost his life and a whole army was wiped out. Instead, the opera ends on a happy note. Nothing foreshadows the catastrophe that lies ahead.

L'Enfance de Roland has not survived in the repertoire, although it has a certain melodic charm. The music, often brisk and spirited, sometimes quite moving, is generally better than the libretto. Mathieu's plot stands out markedly. Not much remains of the tale from the old *Reali di Francia* that had drawn Uhland's and Dumas's attention. Basically, Mathieu combined "Klein Roland" and "Roland Schildträger," but he took an important liberty in suppressing Milon d'Anglant, essentially giving his role to the imaginary Sigmar. Like Mermet before him, Mathieu realized that his plot needed a love theme to insure interest. An adolescent boy would hardly provide it. Mathieu could have kept Milon and let his reunion with Berte constitute the romantic element. Instead, the composer chose to invent a new intrigue, making a noble prisoner of war fall in love with a princess created for the purpose. The princess's mother, never seen, is supposed to have been Berte's sister. Hence Mathieu constructed a secondary plot that resembles the original story about Berte and Milon.

Some of Mathieu's plot changes were less drastic. Whereas Uhland had envisaged his hero as a young boy, Mathieu made him a teenager. Mathieu's protagonist does not go around carrying someone else's weapons for him. Mathieu's Roland is more observant than other depictions of him at an early age. Avril, however, did credit him with being a bright student.

All the action of *L'Enfance de Roland* occurs along the Rhine River or in the Ardennes Forest. One wonders why Berte arrives at her brother's court dressed in pilgrim's clothing, since she has not come far. Uhland had situated "Klein Roland" in Italy and had had the reunion take place there as well. There are other minor differences between Mathieu's libretto and the German poems that inspired it. In "Roland Schildträger" the giant's coveted jewel is embedded in a shield, not in an armband, and six paladins instead of three go looking for it. Mathieu gave the paladins two reasons instead of one for seeking it—the king wants it, and the princess's hand will reward the man who returns with it. In Uhland's poem, the search takes four days; in the opera it requires only three.

The elaborate subplot about the location of the giant's lair, the spirits protecting it, and the giant's one vulnerable hour is pure invention. Mathieu's giant is less horrendous, incidentally, than the one in "Roland Schildträger." Though described as a miscreant, he does not seem particularly evil. He is only too willing, for example, to spare the life of a youthful antagonist. Still, he has no intention of giving up his precious stone without a fight.

In constructing his plot, Mathieu introduced other changes. Archbishop Turpin does not appear in the opera, as he does in "Roland Schildträger." Charlemagne's seizure is another addition to the basic plot. Regarding the stone itself, Uhland gave the king no particular reason for wanting it other than a desire to possess a rare gem. Dumas provided a religious motive. Mathieu's Charlemagne wants the stone for its supernatural properties and also because, powerful though he is, it is something that he has been unable to acquire. Imma wants him to have it because possessing it will dispel his seizures.

With historical matters Mathieu did not cope as well as he might have. A peace-loving Charlemagne does not coincide with our usual idea of one who brought most of western Europe to heel. Mathieu's reluctant conqueror, on learning that the Saxons are in revolt, asks wearily, "Faudra-t-il toujours verser des flots de sang?" One suspects that, under his leadership, Roland will have a hard time becoming a distinguished soldier. Still, Charlemagne does not protest when someone predicts that his nephew will add many new territories to his realm, presumably with the sword. His achieving peace with the Saxons, who were in constant rebellion throughout his reign, is as implausible as his diplomatic arrangement with the Mohammedan ambassadors. His dividing the known world between himself and a sultan is something that never happened. Nevertheless, such fanciful episodes did make it possible for Mathieu to conclude his opera happily.

A few weeks after the first performance of *L'Enfance de Roland,* the opera was staged at the Opéra Royal in Ghent. For the premiere Henri Seguin sang the role of Charlemagne. Gabrielle Lejeune was Princess Imma, Camille Cosset was Sigmar, and Emma Cossira was Dame Berte. The Russian soprano Mme Bellina appeared as Roland. Destined to have the most dazzling career of all the cast members was the bass singing the giant's role. This was Marcel Journet, a Frenchman who had been at the Théâtre de la Monnaie less than a year. Later he would captivate audiences at the Opéra, the Opéra Comique, Covent Garden, the Metropolitan, and especially La Scala.

Not all French writers of the nineteenth century revered Charlemagne and Roland. Louise Michel, schoolteacher, poet, and revolutionary, had little good to say about kings and emperors. The Commune's Vierge Rouge, she was deported to New Caledonia after the movement was crushed. Pardoned but unrepentant, she returned to Paris a decade later, castigating the Third Republic as vehemently as she had ever inveighed against the Second Empire. She thought the Middle Ages had been as cruel as the modern era. Then an emperor had turned a deaf ear to his nephew's desperate call for help. The poet believed that the people should revolt and bring about the happier times that Maxime Du Camp may have had in mind. She expressed the idea in the first stanza of "Les Temps héroïques." "Ce n'est plus le vieux Charlemagne, / Qui sourd à l'appel de Roland / S'en revient triste de l'Espagne; / Ce sont des peuples en campagne, / Et la mort sonne l'Oliphant."[37]

Like Michelet, this poet took a stern view of Charlemagne, accusing him of having deliberately ignored Roland's appeal. As an epigraph she quoted in modern French, "La terre a des tressaillements," a rough translation of the *Chanson de Roland, laisse* 110, l. 1427, "E terremoete ço i ad veirement." In France, while Roland is battling the Saracens, a terrible earthquake occurs. To Louise Michel, the people's eventual rising up will be an immense upheaval comparable to the seismic one in the epic. Clearly the poet knew the *Chanson de Roland.* She published her poem in the *Revue de France* in November 1897. By this time the *Revue* was rather moderate. Gone were the fiery days when it published the Commune's decrees.

Michel's "Le Vautour" was originally called "Champ de bataille." The author presents it as a *légende italienne*, but it reads like a description of Roland's death at Roncevaux. On a plain surrounded by mountainous peaks, the sole survivor of a momentous battle prepares to die as his victorious opponents ride into the distance. "Il entend dans la nuit la fanfare lointaine, / Que jette en s'éloignant à la funeste plaine / L'ennemi triomphant." As he dies, the hero thinks of his fallen companions. "Et le blessé songeant à la gloire flétrie / Pleure ses compagnons, perdus pour la patrie, / Tous jeunes et vaillants." Like Peyrat's ambushed knights, they have died for freedom rather than for a king or a creed. "Mais toujours on entend dans la sinistre plaine / Passer remplissant l'air de puissantes haleines / L'appel de liberté."[38]

Despite her violent ideas, Louise Michel had respectable well-wishers, including Victor Hugo, whom she idolized and whom she had met in 1851, as he was going into exile himself. She addressed several poems to him and remained in contact through the years.[39] Hugo wrote "Viro major," later published in *Toute la lyre,* on her behalf as she was being deported. He claimed to respect her "majesté farouche," and while conceding that mercy was not one of her obvious qualities, he suggested that she might be a seer, noting "le divin chaos des choses étoilées / Aperçu tout au fond d'un grand coeur inclément."

Another poet at this time was not awed by Charlemagne or Roland. Jean Richepin's "Sonnet moyen-âge" dates from 1877. Perhaps the poet was alluding to Roland when he wrote: "Aux accords d'un rebec la belle musicienne / Chante son chevalier, le fier preux au poil blond / Qui combat sans merci le Sarrasin félon. / Elle garde sa foi comme il garde la sienne."[40] Whatever the case, Richepin would soon write a poem specifically about Roland. "Le Roncevalais" appeared in 1884 in *Les Blasphèmes.*

> Vieil Empereur à la barbe fleurie,
> A Roncevaux se tient l'hôtellerie
> Où vont dormir tous tes preux chevaliers
> Qui plus jamais ne seront réveillés.
> ....
>
> Frappe d'estoc, Roland, frappe de taille!
> Tu livres là ta dernière bataille.
> Et ceux qui vont te mettre à leurs genoux,
> Ce ne sont pas les Sarrasins, c'est nous,
> Roncevalais fiers et vivants sans règles.
> Fils des glaciers, frères aînés des aigles.
> Sonne, Roland, sonne ton olifant!
> Voici que le montagne se défend.
> La bonne mère avec nous t'assassine.

> Pour te broyer son coeur se déracine.
> Nous t'en jetons les lambeaux arrachés.
> Il pleut des pins. Il grêle des rochers.
> Sonne, Roland! La montagne t'écrase . . .
> El l'Empereur aura la barbe rase.[41]

Probably the "hôtellerie" is not the Roncevaux hospice where pilgrims used to stop over but rather the battlefield itself, where Charlemagne's ambushed peers will sleep forever. Of course, the reference could be to the chapel cellar where a few writers believed some of the victims were buried. Richepin's "blasphemy" lies in the irreverent handling of a national hero. The poem's graphic presentation of Roland's death provides one of its chief interests. It seems as if the mountain were carrying out an execution, punishing the hero for having hacked at its crest and created the Brèche de Roland. The mountain's agents are the local people. "Et ceux qui vont te mettre à leurs genoux, / Ce ne sont pas les Sarrasins, c'est nous, / Roncevalais fins et vivants sans règles," an allusion to the genuine natives or to the independent, vengeful Basques, Gascons, or Aquitainians who, instead of the Moors, may have initiated the attack that led to Roland's death. Michelet had described the natives as inhospitable, adding that the rocks themselves seemed ready to crush whoever ventured into their dismal recesses.

Verlaine found *Les Blasphèmes* distasteful, calling them "cochonneries" in which "la grosse trivialité du fond ne le cède qu'au banal de la forme."[42] Probably Verlaine's strictures did not bother the poet. In any event, Richepin outlived his rebellious, bohemian period and eventually become a sedate traditionalist and patriot. World War I provided an opportunity for him to demonstrate his patriotism and look at Roland in a new way.

"Sous l'Arc de Triomphe" appeared originally in *Lectures pour tous* on 1 December 1918. The war over, France's heroes were returning, "le plus humble étant un Roland." A similar idea was expressed in "Pour nos poilus." On 15 April 1917 a ceremony had been held in the Sorbonne's Grand Amphithéâtre to celebrate the entrance of the United States into the war. For the occasion Richepin had composed and recited "Le Baiser des drapeaux," which, like the other poems, came out in *Poèmes durant la guerre* (1919).[43] Here the poet asserted that France's dead heroes were cheering on their modern counterparts from the other world. One of the dead heroes was "Roland sonnant du cor."

Out of World War I came Richepin's *Allons, enfants de la patrie,* a collection of thirty-three poems about heroic individuals and deeds in French military history. The poet's patriotism was at its zenith. Intended to glorify the French soldier, the volume was intended as a children's book, but not exclusively. "Pour les enfants, d'abord," wrote the author, but "aussi pour les grandes personnes qui ont le suprême bonheur de rester enfants le plus tard possible," retaining their love for heroes and legends. "Roland," the second poem in the collection, is, like the others, short and moving, though not great.

> Souffle, Roland, souffle dans ton cor!
> Souffle sans fin! Souffle encor, encor!
>   Souffle à rendre l'âme!
> Ton âpre appel, depuis tant de jours,
> Nous entendons toujours et toujours
>   Tout ce qu'il nous clame.
>
> "A l'aide! A l'aide! On entre ehez nous!
> L'étranger veut nous mettre à genoux!
>   Redressons nos tailles!"
> Tel est l'appel de ton cor, Roland,
> Dont l'âme ainsi va toujours soufflant
>   Toutes nos batailles.
>
> La Marne en fut le dernier écho,
> Quand claironna son cocorico
>   Chassant l'aigle immonde;
> Si bien, ô preux à l'olifant clair,
> Qu'on vient encor, avec ton vieil air,
>   De sauver le Monde.[44]

The three stanzas demonstrate the extent to which Richepin had evolved since his earlier, desecrating poem.

Readers familiar with *Le Jongleur de Notre-Dame* (1906) and the *Vie de Jeanne d'Arc* (1908) realize that Anatole France had more than a passing interest in the Middle Ages. He knew the *Chanson de Roland*, referring to it several times in his own work.[45] He wrote a prose narrative, "Le Gab d'Olivier," in which the epic's heroes abound, though not to their best advantage. First published on 22 February 1893 in *L'Echo de Paris*, the narrative later turned up in the *Contes de Jacques Tournebroche* (1908), a collection of short stories. For a medieval touch, the author used the Old French word *gab*, meaning "boast" or "wager." Ultimately the tale derives from the Old French *Pèlerinage de Charlemagne*, the plot altered in only a few details.

The narrative begins with Charlemagne and his twelve peers, who have already made a pilgrimage to Jerusalem, deciding to visit King Hugo in Constantinople. On their arrival there is a lavish reception, after which the emperor and his lieutenants retire to their sumptuous, if communal, sleeping quarters. The irreverent Anatole France was less than awed by knights and their pastimes. The French visitors, a bit drunk, are unable to sleep at first. "Ne pourvant goûter le sommeil, ils se mirent à gaber, selon la coûtume des chevaliers de France." Starting with the emperor, each boasts that he will play a prank on their host. Some of the pranks are brutal, but all require superhuman strength. Roland's turn comes at last, and the bet is that he will saunter outside the city walls and blow his horn so hard that the gates will fall off their hinges. King Hugo overhears the inordinate bragging and angrily informs his guests to be prepared to carry out their vaunts the next day or be beheaded. Considerably sobered, the worried visitors at last get to sleep. In the morning they proceed to their host's palace, where they kneel and call upon the Virgin Mary to give each man the strength to make good his boast. When the men disperse hoping to perform their tasks, "Roland gagne les remparts. . . . Au bout de très peu de temps une rumeur terrible comme celle qui annoncera aux hommes la fin du monde gronda jusque sans la salle du palais . . . et secoua le roi Hugon dans son trône d'or. C'était un bruit de murailles écroulées et de flots mugissants, que dominait le son déchirant d'un cor." Roland accomplished his feat, as did all his cohorts.[46]

When Anatole France wrote the story, his attitude was not hostile but merely tongue in cheek. He had simply not taken a national hero too seriously. Fifteen years later, when "Le Gab d'Olivier" took its place in the *Contes de Jacques Tournebroche*, the country had been through the Dreyfus Affair, and Anatole France had joined the liberal ranks. If the story had been rewritten at this time, perhaps the author would have presented the military hero more ironically or even somewhat grimly.

Joseph Fabre (1842-1916) was a teacher, Christian philosopher, and republican statesman. Interested in the Middle Ages, he wrote extensively on the career and trial of Joan of Arc. When he published his *Chanson de Roland* translation in 1901, France was divided into two hostile, bitter camps over the Dreyfus Affair. Unlike many other intellectuals, Fabre revered the military establishment, and he dedicated his book to the army: "A l'armée nationale est dédiée cette traduction de l'épopée du patriotisme." The epic was a "poésis simple et passionnée," the translator thought. Serving as a preamble to the translation is "Roland et la belle Aude," Fabre's poetic prose narrative about events preceding the Franks' foray onto the Iberian Peninsula. Divided into eighteen chapters, the novelette relies heavily upon *Girart de Vienne* but borrows details from other epics as well. The author makes no attempt to repress his imagination.

When the action begins, difficulties between Charlemagne and one of his vassals have reached the crisis stage. "Gérard de Vienne, puissant seigneur, avait bravé Charlemagne," and the emperor has laid siege to his splendid castle. "La forteresse semblait imprenable. Epais étaient ses murs et hauts ses tours."[47] Roland and Olivier, Charlemagne's and Gérard's nephews respectively, are named their uncles' champions. Before the duel, however, Aude, with other ladies, comes out onto the battlements. Roland sees her and is struck by her beauty. She tells him that she is Aude, Gérard's niece and

Olivier's sister, adding that she will never wed save with her uncle and brother's consent. When Roland identifies himself, Aude is distressed that this man and her brother are about to engage in combat. She turns and goes inside. Clearly a mutual interest has sprung up, and the circumstance does not escape the emperor. A few days later, Olivier summons Roland to the appointed duelling place, an island in the Rhone River. There, astride their horses, the two rush at one another with gusto. Sure that he will triumph, Roland boasts that the Château de Vienne will be razed and Gérard executed. Olivier calls attention to his opponent's "vantardise," a characteristic trait of Roland's.

Brandishing Durandal, Roland soon cuts Olivier's horse in two, but Olivier deals his opponent's mount a similar blow. Fabre does not explain how Roland managed to revive his horse and later ride him at the battle of Roncevaux. In no time both knights are on foot and locked in close combat. Stalwart, they are described as "plus fiers que lions and léopards." On each side, anxious well-wishers look on and pray for their champion. Aude, her emotions a jumble, hopes that the outcome will somehow be glorious for both men. She vows, however, that if Roland kills her brother, she will never marry him. As the battle continues, each champion admires and even compliments his adversary's valor and skill. When Roland breaks Olivier's sword, he allows his opponent to send for another, and the two rest and chat while they wait. Gérard sends his nephew a sword that turns out to be Hauteclaire.

A digression relates how Roland at age fifteen came into possession of his horse Veillantif and his sword Durandal. Challenged by a messenger from King Aigoland, Charlemagne had gone to Aspromonte, in Calabria, to fight the powerful Saracen. Considering Roland too young to go, his uncle had left him in the fortress of Laon, but Roland overpowered the gatekeeper, escaped, and arrived on the battlefield in time to rescue his uncle. "Le vieux Charlemagne, qui avait bien même coeur que jadis, mais non même force," had been toppled from his horse by Aigoland's son Yaumont, who was riding Veillantif and brandishing Durandal. Roland beheaded Yaumont, keeping horse and sword for himself. Delighted with his nephew's feat, the emperor knighted him on the spot. Avril had used the same story in *Les Enfances Roland*.

The duel between Roland and Olivier resumes. At one point Roland pretends to tire and expresses a desire to rest. Olivier, always courteous, agrees and offers to fan his opponent while he takes a nap. Unlike Hugo's Roland, Fabre's claims that he had not been serious. "Je combattrais aisément quatre jours de suite," he brags. The two men continue fighting. As the contest wears on, both become irritated. "Ils devenaient violents, exaspérés, farouches," but neither would surrender.

Meanwhile, Aude has been watching the towers. Believing that one of the adversaries will have to die and not wishing to survive either, she prays. God answers her appeal and intervenes. As night is falling, a cloud comes down from heaven. An angel appears in it and assures the warriors that honor has been satisfied. God, with an important mission in store for them, forbids their continuing. "Désormais, c'est côte à côte, en Espagne, aux dépens de la gent païenne, que vous devez signaler votre valeur," they are told. Overcome, the two champions put down their swords. Each decides that the other is the man he most esteems. Roland announces that he would like to marry Aude. Olivier is ecstatic, and the two new friends embrace. Presumably Charlemagne's quarrel with Gérard de Vienne is settled.

In May Charlemagne, surrounded by his knights, is holding court in Gérard's castle. A modest Aude, richly clad, is led in, and her presence illuminates the entire castle. Charlemagne formally asks Gérard for his niece's hand so that Roland and Aude can be married. Gérard agrees, declaring that his niece "ne pouvait avoir mari de plus haute valeur." With the assembled barons and Archbishop Turpin as witnesses, the emperor proclaims the solemn commitment, and a day is set for the wedding. While the Franks are celebrating, messengers rush in to announce that Moorish enemies are preparing to invade France. "On doit tout quitter pour courir sus aux païens." Roland presents his fiancée with a ring, and she gives him a white banner. This undoubtedly is the white pennant that, attached to a lance, Roland will later carry into battle. But Roland will not return to his beloved. "Roland ne reviendra plus: il mourra à Roncevaux."

Fabre ends his tale at this dramatic moment, choosing not to mention, as his principal source did, the emperor's preparations for the coming contest with the heathens. Fabre concentrates on the duel between Roland and Olivier and the sudden but deep love between Aude and Roland. One could wish that the author had made the love element less sudden and consequently more plausible. Still, Aude emerges as a believable character, and her role is vital. As a direct result of her prayer, divine intervention puts an end to a duel that would have marred her happiness, no matter who won. Although she would subsequently lose both brother and fiancé, both would die at the same time, in battle against a common foe.

Several features distinguish Fabre's tale from Victor Hugo's presentation. For one thing, Aude interested Fabre more than she did his predecessor. Fabre centered the action around her, in marked contrast with "Le Mariage de Roland," in which she is not a developed character at all. Unlike Hugo, Fabre also takes care to make Olivier the recalcitrant vassal's nephew, not his son, and thus avoids a mistake the other writer had made. In Fabre's version the duel appears to last only one day, although Roland tells his opponent that he could go on for several more. In "Le Mariage de Roland," the two champions hack at each other for four or five days. Furthermore, there is no divine intervention in Hugo's poem, in which the two heroes, worn and harried, end matters with a solution of their own. In Fabre's work, Roland mentions wanting to marry Aude only after an angel has made peace between him and her brother. In "Le Mariage de Roland" Olivier proposes that Aude and Roland get married, whereas Fabre makes the idea originate with Roland. Finally Hugo actually marries the two lovers. Sticking closer to the source epic, which Fabre knew and Hugo did not, Fabre is content to show the engaged pair planning to marry but having to postpone things until Roland has dealt with the Moors. The marriage, of course, will never occur.

Maurice Bouchor (1855-1929) was a friend of Jean Richepin and in his youth was as precocious and wild as his companion. Like Hugo, Banville, and Richepin, he had published a collection of poems during his teens. In time his work took on moral, patriotic qualities, like Richepin's. Some of Bouchor's early poems, the *Poèmes historiques et légendaires,* demonstrated the poet's penchant for legends and the Middle Ages. Bouchor was also much interested in education for the masses. When a competition was announced in 1893, he entered his *Chants populaires pour les écoles,* winning the prize. The book was soon published, and the second, didactic phase of the author's career began. During this period Bouchor translated the *Chanson de Roland* in verse, using decasyllabic *huitains* and an *a b a b b a b a* or *a b a b b c b c* rhyme scheme. Bouchor published it in the *Revue hebdomadaire* in 1898.[48] The following year it appeared in book form "à l'usage des écoles."

Not surprisingly, Bouchor had already written an original Roland poem. This "Chanson de Roland" appeared in the *Chants populaires pour les écoles* in 1895. Bouchor belonged heart and soul to the Third Republic. Writing in the thick of the Dreyfus Affair, when the army was under heavy attack, he may have been proclaiming with his poem that he was not one of the army's hostile critics. The poem presents its author's view of the Roland legend.

> Le noble Charles, roi des Francs,
> Avait passé monts et torrents.
> Restait l'arrière garde
> Ayant pour chef Roland le preux.
> Voilà qu'il se hasarde
> Au fond d'un val bien ténébreux.
>
> Hélas! le traître Ganelon
> A fait garder ce noir vallon:
> Car une armée immense
> Soudain descend des pics voisins.
> La lutte à mort commence,
> Aux cris stridents des Sarrasins.
>
> L'épée au poing, fier et sanglant,
> Il crie aussi, le bon Roland.

> Il court dans la bataille,
> Jonchant de morts le sombre val.
> Il frappe, il brise, il taille;
> Partout rayonne Durandal.
>
> Blessé trois fois, sire Olivier
> Dit à Roland: "Beau chevalier,
> Là-bas est Charlemagne.
> Sonnez vers lui, sonnez du cor,
> Sonnez par la montagne!"
> Le bon Roland dit: "Pas encor."
>
> Enfin, percé de part en part,
> Roland sonna: c'était trop tard.
> Autour de lui, dans l'ombre,
> Râlaient les gens et les chevaux,
> Vaincu, mais par le nombre,
> Roland mourut à Roncevaux.

Predominating in this poem is the eight-syllable line that had become the norm. Clearly Bouchor does not interpret or add to his material to any great extent. When Roland blows his horn, no urgent reason is given for his belatedly deciding to do so. The poem comes to a close before Charlemagne returns to gather his dead and punish the Saracens. The poem's unusual feature is the assertion that Ganelon has had the valley guarded. Taking the initiative, Ganelon presumably not only conspired with the Saracens but also took a hand in setting up the attack. Thus Bouchor may be implying that Ganelon played an active role in the attack and may even have helped plan strategy. A teacher's manual accompanying the *Chants populaires* would seem to bear this out.

Bouchor considered his poem instructive in republican virtue. In the teacher's manual, a collaborator bolstered this position, calling the *Chanson de Roland* an "oeuvre rude et naïve," "profondément émouvante dans sa simplicité." The collaborator reproves Roland for his foolish pride but admires his courage. "En grande partie coupable du désastre, il a fait, du moins, des efforts surhumains pour sauver ses compagnons. Sa mort héroïque n'est-elle pas l'expiation de ses fautes? Ainsi en a jugé le peuple de France, qui, généreux pour ce noble vaincu, ne se rappellera que sa haute vaillance, son coeur fraternel et son infortune. Le souvenir du bon et brave Roland vivra toujours dans le coeur des Français." Bouchor published his poem with a musical setting, a melody "populaire dans le pays basque," provided by Julien Tiersot.[49]

A little more than two decades later Bouchor returned to his hero in the *Programmes de réunions civiques et familiales*, devoting one of his popular culture talks to the *Chanson de Roland*. His remarks spring from personal reactions to the epic and owe little to the author's predecessors. Evoking the Middle Ages and its poetry, Bouchor told his unlikely audience that the *Chanson de Roland* was "le plus ancien et le plus célèbre de ces poèmes." The Roncevaux disaster made a deep impression upon the popular imagination, he said, and the event gave rise to a legend that in turn inspired various poems. Finally, a particularly gifted *trouvère* put together what is now known as the *Chanson de Roland*. Yet "on peut dire qu'elle a été un peu l'oeuvre de tout le monde en France: c'est l'émotion de la foule qui créa la légende, qui en imposa le sujet au poète et qui lui en inspira l'accent."[50] Thus Bouchor detected multiple voices in the epic's gradual composition but believed that the ultimate product was the work of a single, unknown individual.

Bouchor told his listeners that the poem came into being on the eve of the Crusades, and naturally the villains were Moslems. Having changed his mind since writing his poem, Bouchor asserted that Roland's attackers were actually Basques, "hordes guerrières et pillardes." That Ganelon had had a hand in the business he now considered dubious. Unfortunately the epic is not devoid of unpleasant episodes, but this at least demonstrates the poet's frankness. Justice was often brutal and cruel. "Dans la *Chanson de Roland*, c'est d'après le résultat d'un duel à mort que l'on décide qui est l'innocent, qui est le coupable." There were also in the poem "les terribles excès du fanatisme. Contraindre les infidèles à opter entre le baptême ou la mort, cela semble . . . chose tout à fait légitime ou, plutôt, méritoire" in the epic. Bouchor pointed out that the Saracens were by no means heathen idol worshipers.[51] Unlike Prince Lucien Bonaparte and Napoléon Peyrat, he did not go on to praise them, however.

Bouchor stressed the *Chanson de Roland*'s characterization, interpreting as he did so. The characters are rendered in realistic detail, although they are not what they might have been had the epic been written earlier. Writing centuries after the historic disaster, the *Chanson de Roland* poet made no effort to "représenter ses personnages comme ils étaient du temps de Charlemagne. L'idée ne lui est probablement pas venue qu'ils eussent été différents de ses contemporains. Il les a représentés exactement comme des hommes du onzième siècle, c'est-à-dire comme ceux qu'il voyait autour de lui. Les moeurs féodales comme les armures qu'il nous décrit, tout est de son propre temps."[52] This kind of thing had worried Stendhal.

In his poem Bouchor had called Charlemagne the king of the Franks. Here, however, the characters are not Franks but Frenchmen. As the author phrased it, "les héros de la *Chanson de Roland* sont déjà français 'de la tête aux pieds.' Impressionables, expansifs, enthousiastes, la riposte vive, les puissants barons ont même plus d'un trait commun avec les braves gens de nos faubourgs et de nos villages." Much earlier Michelet had come close to the same view, but he would not have endorsed the rest. Charlemagne, to Bouchor, was an ideal monarch. "Avec sa cordiale brusquerie," he is "le roi le plus dévoué au bien de tous, le chef le plus vigilant, l'homme le plus tendrement attaché à ses compagnons d'armes." As for Turpin, he stands out in bold relief. "On peut le trouver trop batailleur pour un homme d'église; mais . . . ses armes sont toujours loyales. Il est plein de vie et plein de coeur, ce bouillant prélat." Olivier, "toujours maître de lui, sans que sa bravoure en soit moins éclatante," is another engaging figure. "Quant à ce Roland si chevaleresque et si fier, si tendre pour les siens, comment ne pas l'aimer malgré les fautes où l'entraîne sa folle passion de la gloire?" He is "le plus français de tous, par ses défauts . . . comme par ses qualités; et il n'est pas surprenant que notre peuple, fier de ses vertus et indulgent à ses faiblesses, l'ait tant aimé, chanté, glorifié." Bouchor was touched by the skill with which Olivier and Roland's relationship was handled. "Notre vieux poète a exprimé le sentiment de l'amitié avec beaucoup de force et même de délicatesse. Il atteint le sublime de l'émotion lorsqu'il chante, après la querelle de Roland et d'Olivier sur le champ de bataille, leurs instants suprêmes, ennoblis par la tendresse et le dévouement, et leur admirable mort."[53]

Even though Bouchor had translated the *Chanson de Roland* and cited it constantly in his lecture-essay, he nevertheless mentioned the persistent legend, not found in the epic but encountered frequently in the nineteenth century, about Roland and his companions being crushed by boulders hurled down from the mountains overlooking the battle site. "Les Français, inférieurs en nombre, serrés dans le vallon étroit, écrasés par les quartiers de roc que, d'en haut, l'ennemi lançait sur eux, périrent jusqu'au dernier."[54] Nothing is said about this in Bouchor's "Chanson de Roland."

Bouchor's presentation concludes with the remark that the epic, while primitive and even a little barbaric, is very French, brimming over with life, emotion, and grandeur. Its concluding lines, after scenes depicting the era's harsh realities, are restful. Bramimonde's voluntary conversion gives the poem a serene denouement. Gentle persuasion rather than violence has convinced the pagan queen. "Seule de son peuple, Bramimonde n'a pas été baptisée de force. Sa qualité de reine lui a valu, sans doute, ces égards; mais sa condition de femme y a été aussi pour quelque chose. C'est donc en faveur d'une femme que s'adoucit, pour la première fois, le fanatisme guerrier du moyen âge—au moins suivant notre poème—en attendant que la vieille intolérance ait enfin désarmé en faveur de l'humanité tout entière."[55]

France's defeat in the war with Prussia stunned the French citizenry, creating a deep sense of humiliation that permeated all classes. From humiliation to an active desire for revenge was but a short step. Before long intellectual and political leaders, Hugo included, were telling their compatriots that the lost territories had to be wrested from the victors' grasp. In the minds of some, this presupposed revitalizing the nation, returning to old, respected values and traditions that had been neglected or even lost, and making France not only militarily able but spiritually worthy to resume her place in the international community. To many the means to achieve such an end lay in massive religious renewal. Others called for a moral regeneration involving secular considerations as well. Whatever their drives, all these spokesmen were intensely patriotic, and, in practical terms, their goals were identical. The scandals that shook the Third Republic in its infancy, disappointing and even appalling to the proponents of *redressement,* made the task more formidable, but they also intensified people's aspirations. Retaking the forfeited provinces thus became a highly emotional crusade, at once religious and political.

As the nineteenth century drew to a close and as World War I approached and then materialized, explosive patriotism was definitely in the air. Audiences listening to Rabaud's opera might well have asked themselves if the time had come for an intrepid hero to appear, reclaiming the land that a wicked enemy had occupied. Once again writers turned to Roland.

Charles Péguy, who would be one of the war's first French victims, gave an expressive voice to the patriotic outburst. On the eve of the war, he was thinking of Roland and other national heroes and heroines. In the posthumously published *Ballade du coeur qui a tant battu,* Berthe au Grand Pied and "le preux Charlemagne" are among the medieval personalities evoked. Perhaps the poet had the "Soldat de Charlemagne / Et de Roland" in mind when, alluding to "le château sarrasin," he mentioned the "bataillons fauchés ras" as gallant French soldiers died on the battlefield.[56]

Previously Péguy's magnificent lyrical trilogy *Jeanne d'Arc* (1897) had shown its heroine in the first play, *À Domremy,* at prayer (part 1, act 3). Humbly she asks God to lead France back to the pure religious fervor it had known in Roland's day.

> Que notre France après soit la maison divine
> Et la maison vivante ainsi qu'au temps passé,
> La maison devant qui tout malfaisant s'incline,
> La maison qui prévaut sur Satan terrassé;
>
> La maison souveraine ainsi qu'au temps passé,
> Quand le comte Roland mourait face à l'Espagne
> Et face aux Sarrasins qu'il avait éblouis,
> Quand le comte Roland mourait pour Charlemagne;
>
> La maison souveraine ainsi qu'au temps passé
> De monsieur Charlemagne ou de monsieur saint Louis,
> Tous les deux à présent assis à votre droite.[57]

Péguy saw Jeanne as striving to bring back Christian France's apogee, the era of Charlemagne and Roland. Her God, like Roland's, is militant. He will come to the aid of his elite and even live among them. Like Roland, Jeanne aroused animosities but nevertheless came to be considered one of France's great national standardbearers, brave and emblematic. In serving their temporal masters, both were also serving the Lord. Both had a mission and accomplished it, although they perished doing so. Péguy remembered the detail from the *Chanson de Roland* about Roland's dying facing his antagonists.

Later, in the *Mystère de la charité de Jeanne d'Arc* (1910), Madame Gervaise tells Jeanne, who cannot understand why Jesus' followers deserted their master at a critical moment, that biblical prophecies had to be fulfilled. Jeanne is incredulous. French men and women of the pious Middle Ages would never have done such a thing, she contends. "Jamais des chevaliers français, jamais des paysans français. . . , jamais Charlemagne et Roland."[58] Like his heroine, Péguy was dedicated to a principle of honor. Edmond Rostand would hold that, like Roland and Joan of Arc, Péguy himself was a hero.

Several other poets of the period knew the Roland legend and admired its hero but had little to say about either. Francis Jammes, for example, considered the *Chanson de Roland* one of the world's greatest books but, despite his being from the Pyrenees Mountains, let it go at that. Some of Jean Cocteau's war poems, though the poet chose not to exploit his hero's name, are dedicated to Roland Garros, the aviator. "Roland Garros" contrasts the French with the Germans by setting the "cor de Roland" in opposition to the "cor de Tristan," but the idea is not developed.[59]

Succeeding Léon Dierx, Paul Fort became Prince des Poètes in 1912. Fort's war poems are not his best. He had a love for medieval literature, including epics, those "vierges accents de nos chants primitifs." He regarded Charlemagne not only as a great king and emperor but also as a unique one. In his prose poem "Charlemagne ou le rêveur et l'innocent," his hero's achievements, but not his losses, are enumerated. Charlemagne is credited with having subdued the Aquitainians, for example, but nothing is said about the Roncevaux massacre. Among "tous les vainqueurs de nos grandes batailles" he named Charlemagne and Roland. When Rheims was being heavily bombarded early in World War I, Fort called upon the city's children to be brave, telling them that they might have to die. Given their imminent peril, perhaps the poet would have done well to remind his young readers that even heroes are sometimes struck down, that Roland, far from routing his enemies in his last great battle, was defeated and killed. To Fort and his contemporaries, Roland and his companions were brave, whatever their fate. Even before the war, Emile Verhaeren had extolled French soldiers' valor, even though that valor was sometimes as foolhardy as Roland's had been. One poem shows the French, rash and resplendent in their plumes and armor, hurling themselves into a melee, "Téméraires, comme autrefois à Roncevaux." More than four thousand of them were slaughtered.[60]

We have seen that Jean Richepin, so contemptuous of Roland and his legend in *Les Blasphèmes,* reversed himself and became an articulate patriot with the advent of the war. His "Roland," included in *Allons, enfants de la patrie* (1920), atoned for his earlier poem and held the paladin up for his readers to admire and, if old enough, to emulate.

Maurice Barrès, a close friend of Frédéric Mistral, was from Lorraine, and part of his native province was occupied. An intransigent nationalist, Barrès knew the *Chanson de Roland* in Old French. Sponsored by the British Academy, he delivered an address in London on 12 July 1916, in the middle of the war. When the French go to war, he told his audience, they do so with a sense of divine mission. "Les premiers, ils ont inventé l'idée de guerre sainte." Quoting a line from the *Chanson de Roland,* he declared that a voice from their consciences or from above assures them that, should they be killed, they will have their reward in heaven: "Se vos morez, esterez saint martir." It was a line with which Archbishop Turpin had exhorted the beleaguered soldiers of the rear guard.[61]

Poet, dramatist, patriot, and conservative political activist, Paul Déroulède incarnated most of Barrès's militant views. Serving in the war with Prussia, he had been captured and had escaped. Alsace and Lorraine he saw as more than a crushing disaster. Their loss had humbled France and cost her other nations' respect. Urging national renewal and repossession of the lost provinces, he founded the Ligue des Patriotes and its newspaper *Le Drapeau* to publicize his ideas. Barrès's admiration for him was unbounded. For a time Barrès even edited the newspaper. Déroulède did not live to see his dreams realized. When he died in 1914 on the eve of World War I, Barrès wrote in his diary that the fallen leader had been a knight in the noblest French tradition. "La patrie a perdu son chevalier," he wrote, adding that Déroulède had gone to join other French heroes, including Roland.[62] Barrès lived to see the two provinces reincorporated into France.

Another French writer remembered the *Chanson de Roland* as the crisis approached. The dramatist and poet Edmond Rostand, a Provençal, quoted Frédéric Mistral and also liked Hugo's "Le Petit Roi de Galice." Moreover, he nourished a sentimental attachment to the Pyrenees Mountains. As a boy he used to vacation in the area, and in time he would settle there. Leaving Cambo, his villa in the Basses Pyrénées, he enjoyed taking his carriage and driving in the evening between the Nive River and the Col de Ronceveau. He and Rosemonde Gérard, his wife, explored the area. Both had a detailed knowledge of the Roland legend. "Comment oublier le fidèle ravin / Qui d'un pas de Roland voulut garder l'empreinte," Mme Rostand would ask in the poem "Le Pays basque."[63] She alludes to the tradition that a shallow concave impression in a rock at the battle site was made by Roland or his horse treading on it. Faget de Baure preferred to think that the horse left the print.

As was usual in nineteenth-century France, Rostand's career began with a book of verse, *Les Musardises*. In 1890, the year he married, he published it, later expanding it. "Le Contrebandier," the last poem in the expanded version, narrates an encounter in the mountains with an old smuggler, one of whose oaths is "par le cor de Roland." This uncommon individual preaches idealism and admires heroism. Wandering about in the mountains, he has seen the ghosts of Roland and his slain companions. Pointing to the horizon, "Là, j'ai des Douze Pairs vu les douze ombres tristes," he tells the poet-narrator. Peyrat and Hugo had talked about Roland's ghost, too.

With the advent of World War I, Roland's presence became increasingly real to the poet. Most of Rostand's war poems appeared in the posthumous *Vol de la Marseillaise*, in which the writer poured out harmonious vitriol on the ancient enemy, Germany. Roland had already been called great and Roncevaux had been mentioned as a battle site in earlier poems: "Fable des insectes," "Un Soir à Hernani," *Cantique de l'aile*. Men from the Pyrenees Mountains were among the patriotic soldiers the author noticed as, under the aegis of Joan of Arc and Roland, the French marched off to war.

In these poems some of the heroes and victims were Francophones, though not French. Belgium sustained determined attacks during the war, and most of the country was occupied. Holding out to the end, however, its popular young ruler, known to his contemporaries as the Chevalier Roi, showed remarkable courage and quickly became a popular hero. Rostand was one of those who paid him tribute.[64] In "Horreur et beauté," Albert I is compared not with Charlemagne but with Roland, whom the poet seems to have viewed as more a man of action. At the same time Cardinal Mercier, Albert's primate and helper, is likened to Archbishop Turpin. "Mais Roncevaux n'a rien de plus beau, sous son Pin, / Rien de plus pur, sous son Laurier, la Fable Greque, / Que ce jeune Monarque et son vieil Archevêque: / C'est Achille et Nestor, c'est Roland et Turpin." In the *Chanson de Roland* the dying hero lies beneath a pine tree: "Li quens Rollant se jut desuz un pin." Hence Rostand alludes to Roncevaux "sous son Pin."

Rostand was naturally concerned with the French more than the Belgians in their struggle with the German Empire. France, declared the poet in "Le Chant des astres," is the land "Où Roland a son cor et Jeanne son pennon." Rostand believed that all who took up arms in the nation's defense and paid for it with their lives were acting, like Roland and Joan of Arc, in accordance with a personal relationship with St. Michael, France's patron saint. In addition to the one with St. Michael, Roland had such a relationship with St. Gabriel. "Ceux qui sont morts pour la Patrie ont vu l'Archange. / Qu'il soit le Chevalier de soleil et de fer / A qui le gantelet de Roland fut offert, / Ou du pommier lorrain le Visiteur étrange." All these dead heroes, declared the poet in his concluding lines, have encountered one of the militant saints and have agreed to serve the national cause, whatever the cost. "Tous—quand, se soulevant sur un bras douloureux, / Comme Roland son gant ils lui tendaient leur vie— / L'ont vu, de fer et d'or, et qui venait sur eux!" Although Rostand mentions only one saint in these lines, he has in mind Roland's dying gesture, chronicled in the *Chanson de Roland*. Here, as he draws his last breath, Roland extends his right gauntlet to heaven in token payment for his sins. The *Chanson de Roland* is somewhat ambivalent about which saint was the first to arrive on the scene to receive the proffered glove, thus warranting Rostand's failure to be specific. Rostand lived to see the French victorious. On 22 December 1918, six weeks after the armistice ended the war, he died. At the Académie Française many years before, he had succeeded Henri de Bornier.

With Rostand, Roland's legend and practical role had come full circle. In 1792 Roland had been invoked as the French stormed into battle against their enemies, largely German. Now in 1914 and the years that followed, his name was being used in a similar cause and against the same foe. Both times he was serving his country, but there were some differences. The ebullient Roland of the 1790s, preoccupied with winning battles, set his comrades an irresistible example and whipped up their courage, spurring them on to help him in his task. He was little concerned with the monarch and deity he had championed in the Middle Ages. French governments changed swiftly as the eighteenth century ended and the nineteenth began. As the new century wore on, French writers saw even more changes as regimes came and went. Likewise, religion experienced ups and downs in public esteem. Still, Roland retained his appeal whatever coteries were in power, whatever ideologies dazzled people's imagination. He held his own under kings, emperors, and republics, anticlericals as well as the orthodox brandishing his name.

Writers during World War I invoked his name, but contrary to what had been done in 1792 and 1793, no effort was made this time to separate him from God and king. Péguy had shown him dying "pour Charlemagne," not France. As the war ran its course, Rostand could draw a parallel, without seeming ridiculous, between a brave modern king and a hero whom the socialist poet had praised. No blame attached itself to his reputation if the writer mentioned an archbishop in the same poem and if he showed Roland seeking to atone for his sins by holding out his gauntlet to God and having saints come down to earth to receive it. This would never have happened in 1792 and 1793.

To be sure, like his predecessor, the new Roland was both an impetus and an example to a generation at war. But he had regained his religious character and was no longer ashamed to be seen in the presence of kings. The development was natural, since Barrès, Rostand, and their contemporaries saw World War I as a crusade. When the French Revolution broke out, Roland's task had been to assail enemies, and with skill and luck he could hope to survive. Deities and rulers had little to do with his world. His twentieth-century promoters knew that in a crusade in which the weapons might include chemicals, tanks, and planes, even the most valiant heroes ought to be prepared to die. But, equally important, in a crusade one is fighting for God, and if a dedicated hero happens to find a good king on his side, there is no reason to think that the pious cause is diminished. Thus by World War I the resurrected paladin had come to look very much like the hero of the *Chanson de Roland*.

6
A Hero for All Seasons

Shortly before the French Revolution, Roland began attracting writers' attention. During the turbulent years that followed, his value as a tool of propaganda was exploited. He became a boisterous patriot and an imperial dragoon, shouting slogans as he manhandled his country's enemies. Radically different from the pious knight of the *Chanson de Roland*, he is barely recognizable in this incarnation. As the final allied coalition drove deeper and deeper into France in 1814 and 1815, Aimé Martin and Creuzé de Lesser hoped he could save the day. It was not to be, and soon France was occupied. Unrealistically, Cuvelier de Trie and Chandezon tried to resuscitate him and have him drive the invaders out. Marchangy and Arlincourt let him die but deplored his loss to the nation, disabled without his mighty sword.

Then came Romanticism and, with it, continued evolution in Roland's portrayal. The new Roland was sensitive, too superior for fate not to find a way to strike him down in the midst of his noble deeds. Fact and legend lent themselves to such an interpretation, of course. Vigny saw Roland as a doomed idealist. Michelet came to view him in this light as well, showing him abandoned by the very entities, human and divine, to whose advancement he had devoted his life. For Maxime Du Camp he would be something of a social reformer. Later, traces of the romanticized hero as victim would persist in the poems of Glatigny and Banville. But Romanticism had another kind of hero as well—the highminded, swashbuckling extrovert, all action, succeeding in whatever he did. This is how Dumas and Hugo envisaged their protagonist. To make him fit the pattern, they took care to show him only in winning situations and thus did not have to explain how so accomplished a knight could, in the end, be overcome.

With the July Revolution, Pétrus Borel, then a hotheaded young liberal, invoked Roland's name as he urged all revolutionaries to claim their due. "En avant, compagnons! plus terribles, plus braves / Que Bayard et Roland," he declaimed, with a view to inciting them.[1] During the July Monarchy, when Frenchmen were fighting Mohammedans in North Africa, poems about

Roland continued to be written. In the 1840s Auguste Barbier composed his "Roland" and Charles Fournel his "Romance de Roncevaux."

Under the Second Empire, Napoleon III's victories inspired confidence. Perhaps this helps explain why Roland continued to attract authors and readers during the period. Roland had been killed, it is true, but he had set a glowing example and instilled pride. Then the Franco-Prussian War brought defeat and humiliation and, in many people's minds, a craving for revenge. As the disasters multiplied, some looked for a scapegoat. Hugo found one in Marshal Achille Bazaine, who had surrendered to the Prussians at Metz on 27 October 1870. "Si cet homme eût voulu, la France triomphait," shrieked this son of a French general who twice had let the Prussians march into Thionville, a town close to Metz. Vituperating but giving no details, the poet unjustly compared his victim with Ganelon, trying him as summarily as Charlemagne is supposed to have tried the Count of Mainz.[2] Wounded spiritually and materially, France thought of Roland again. Joseph Autran's *Légende des paladins* and Henri de Bornier's *La Fille de Roland* date from this period. Roland had long since been killed, but his spirit lived on and one day would help Frenchmen smite their enemies. To Autran's and Bornier's contemporaries, this meant driving out the Germans who had seized and occupied all of one French province and part of another.

With the Third Republic came disappointments and scandals, and some lost faith in heroes, or at least took them down from their pedestals. Rimbaud scoffed at *oriflammes* and derided servicemen in railroad stations who postured and seemed to be vaunting their prowess as they waited for their trains. For such "Rolands" he had no use.[3] Likewise, soldiers hoping to dazzle girls at parties with their flashy uniforms irritated Laforgue, and he warned a young lady about "les Roland, les dentelles / Du bal qui vous attend ce soir!"[4] Anatole France's short story "Le Gab d'Olivier" is an irreverent look at Roland, Olivier, and their companions. Anything but awestruck, Jean Richepin seemed to feel that in Roncevaux Valley Roland had gotten what he deserved. Before long, however, events gave the military, in some quarters at any rate, a new luster. After all, soldiers would undoubtedly be needed if the lost provinces were to be retrieved. In the late 1880s General Georges Boulanger appeared to be leading the nation toward military dictatorship, and he attracted an enormous following. On the heels of this phenomenon came the Dreyfus Affair. Some Frenchmen came to dislike their soldiery while others, conversely, espoused an exaggerated brand of hero worship. This period gave rise to such works as Maurice Bouchor's "Chanson de Roland." One wonders how many literate Frenchmen at this time would have endorsed Gide and Valéry's decision that the epic it was based upon was "dumb."

Then came World War I. For almost everybody, patriotism was the order of the day. As war had grown more and more inevitable and when at last it was declared, Péguy, Barrès, Verhaeren, and Rostand all invoked Roland while execrating an enemy for whom he was also a national hero. Richepin now had a change of heart. Though a little altered, Roland was now as much an icon as he had been in 1792. After the war, Jules Vodoz published a book called *Roland, un symbole*. The title summed up the paladin's status with the era's readers.

Some writers over the years had viewed Roland with things in mind other than patriotism. To some he had an appeal because of their own historical, archeological, or religious bents. For Faget de Baure, born and bred in the Pyrenees Mountains, he had a sort of hometown aura about him that easily blended with the essayist's delight in folklore. To Adolphe d'Avril, not only a scholarly medievalist but a devout believer as well, the knight was an outstanding exemplar of Christian commitment. Some, like Ramond de Carbonnières, Picquet, and Taine, were tourists or mountain climbers who, as they gazed at Roncevaux Valley and the steep crags overlooking it, were reminded of the paladin who had been slain there centuries before.

One of the truly striking features of nineteenth-century French Roland literature is its incredible diversity of plot and characterization. Some of this is due to the source material authors employed. Even though Louis de Musset called Charlemagne a saint, he is by no means consistently presented as a benign, even-tempered, sagacious monarch. He is usually characterized as a stern but wise and kind "empereur à la barbe fleurie," but this is not always the case.[5] Prince Lucien Bonaparte, perhaps thinking of his own brother, depicted him with more than his share of human weaknesses, which include a nasty temper and taking a new wife without having properly disposed of her predecessor. Several authors hinted at incest with his sister.[6] Assollant thought him irascible. More often than not, he was shown jumping to hasty conclusions about Ganelon's treason. Only Arlincourt, incidentally, showed him as the young man he was at the time he decided to invade Spain.

Writers have not agreed as to his whereabouts when he made the decision. Aix-la-Chapelle is the usual place, but Chasseneuil, Paderborn, Ingelheim, and Paris have also been mentioned. A few authors, especially those concerned with historical accuracy, have impugned the invasion's motives, concluding that religion played but a small part in it. Alexandre de Laborde went so far as to contend that Charlemagne never invaded Spain. Prince Lucien agreed. Creuzé de Lesser had him send Roland, then change his mind and arrive to take personal command. Napoléon Peyrat had no doubt that he had ventured onto the Iberian Peninsula and came up with literature's most original reason for the junket: Charlemagne was pursuing Moorish swains guilty of abducting Frankish maidens. Peyrat can also be interpreted as having placed him at the battle of Roncevaux, fighting beside his nephew. Michelet and Barbey d'Aurevilly said he was callous for not turning back instantly when Roland blew his horn. Other writers have blamed Ganelon and Turpin for dissuading him. Collin de Plancy asserted that he did not hear the blasts and that he never returned at all. In Népomucène Lemercier's *Charlemagne,* the emperor learned what happened and had the guilty punished, but only much later.

Roland's mother is generally agreed to have been Princess Berthe, Charlemagne's sister. In a love match, she married Milon, whose surname and title vary somewhat. Authors refer to him as Milon d'Angers, Milon d'Angletz, Milon d'Ayglant, Milon d'Anglant, Milon d'Anglante, and Milon d'Anglaure. What about his son's title and rank? To Banville and most others who mention the topic, Roland was a count. Dumas, however, made him a duke, and Musset called him a prince. To some he was simply a peer, his exact rank unspecified. Most present him as devout. Musset and Collin de Plancy called him "blessed," and Gustave Le Vavasseur considered him a saint. His piety disappears, however, at the time of the French Revolution and Napoleon.

Several authors have focused on Roland's childhood. Dumas said he was reared in Spain, but other places have been listed also. Hugo imagined him as a little boy, blond and frolicsome, given to martial sports. Dumas and several others showed him devoted to his mother and, well before he was big enough, killing a giant. Avril wrote an entire book about his youthful adventures. Authors drawing upon the *Pseudo-Turpin Chronicle* usually said that he had brothers. Now and then a brother named Baudouin crops up, and on one occasion one named Thierry is mentioned.[7] Henri de Bornier would invent a half-brother, a Gérald born after the paladin's death.

Some writers ventured to guess what Roland looked like. Gustave Kahn talked about his good looks. Hugo was sure that he was blond and had delicate features. Autran awarded him blue eyes. Barjaud decided that his hair was black and that he was deeply tanned. Assollant fixed his age at twenty-eight when he was killed, but J.P. Picquet and Baron Isidore Taylor reported an inscription that would have made him forty-two.

Authors borrowing from the *Pseudo-Turpin Chronicle* generally did not include a love element. With its solemn religious didacticism, the *Chronicle* had no room for profane love. Although Autran is an exception, authors who used it did not as a rule show a fair Aude waiting for Roland back at Aix. In versions in which she is mentioned or actually appears, her role is variable. In Banville she is purely and simply her lover's betrothed. In Hugo she marries him before he leaves for Spain. Coincidentally, the hero and his beloved are indeed husband and wife in the Provençal *Rollan a Saragossa,* but Hugo certainly would not have known this. In Mermet's opera *Roland à Roncevaux,* Aude rushes onto the battlefield. Peyrat imagines her ghostly form haunting it long after her fiancé's death. Assollant, Dumas, Ponsard, and Kahn omitted her altogether, replacing her with someone else. Prince Lucien Bonaparte had the dying Roland think of Ariosto's Angelica and ask to be remembered to her. Chandezon and Cuvelier de Trie betrothed him to Marphise. Arlincourt referred to his protagonist as a faithful lover but did not identify the sweetheart. Delécluze let him die without a thought for her, but Assollant's hero was very much concerned about the fate of the woman he was leaving behind.

Two nineteenth-century French authors had Roland canter off to Spain alone or with companions, not as part of Charlemagne's invasion force. Prince Lucien and Assollant showed uncle and nephew at odds with one another, so that the nephew, annoyed in one case and very angry in the other, departs for the Iberian Peninsula on business of his own. While these two authors gave other reasons for the ill feeling, from the beginning of the fourteenth century an Upper Italian tradition described Charlemagne and Roland quarreling as a result of Roland's taking the city of Nobles without his uncle's consent.

At the battle of Roncevaux, normally several or all of the peers are with Roland. Dumas said the odds against the Franks were a hundred to one. Probably Prince Lucien is the writer who put his hero at the greatest numerical disadvantage: In *Charlemagne* Roland has only a hundred men with him. Fournel gave him ten thousand, Creuzé de Lesser twelve thousand. The usual count, based on the *Chanson de Roland*, is twenty thousand. Pitted against the rear guard, according to Fournel and Creuzé de Lesser, were one hundred and two hundred thousand enemy troops respectively. Taine said there were three hundred thousand. The *Chanson de Roland* put the figure at four hundred thousand, counting reserves. Ganelon, to Maurice Bouchor, was much more actively involved in the massacre than is ordinarily the case. For his part in it, he is usually tried and punished, either near the disaster site or back in Aix, depending upon whether authors were following the *Pseudo-Turpin Chronicle* or the *Chanson de Roland*. Creuzé de Lesser had him and his relatives herded into an enclosure on or near the battlefield and slaughtered, with no trial anywhere. Prince Lucien Bonaparte imagined him dying in Paris, tormented by his conscience. In Bornier and Rabaud, he is left for dead but revives and repents. Mermet had him die fighting in the enemy ranks.

How long did Roland's duels and battles last? On their island in the Rhone River, Roland and Olivier struggle for two to five days, depending on the writer. As for the battle of Roncevaux, which Peyrat set in the winter and which Kahn suggested may have been fought at night, there is no time consensus either. Collin de Plancy allotted it one day. Peyrat, constantly revising his poem, was unable to make up his mind, in one version letting it go on for a hundred days. Ordinarily there are no survivors. Collin de Plancy was emphatic about it, but not everyone agreed. Avril and Assollant allowed one eyewitness to get away. Ricard let a boy view the aftermath from the edge of the battlefield and spend the next two hundred years talking about it. In Dumas, Ponsard, and Kahn, the hero himself lived through it all, only to die later of a broken heart.

As a rule, whether Archbishop Turpin was with Charlemagne or Roland at the time of the battle depends upon whether a given author was following the *Pseudo-Turpin Chronicle*. Vigny's Turpin, for example, based in part on the *Chronicle*, is riding with the emperor when the ambush occurs. Fournel and many others placed him at the disaster site. Sometimes, as in Michelet, he is scarcely mentioned. He is absent from all but one of Hugo's Roland poems. It comes as a surprise that Olivier, in Arlincourt's version, is not at Roncevaux at his friend's side. Bouchor does not mention him as being there either. Prince Lucien has him die after Roland. Cuvelier de Trie and Peyrat, remembering Ariosto, omit him, substituting Renaud de Montauban.

When, desperate at last, Roland finally agrees to summon help, he blows his horn so hard that blood vessels burst. In the *Chronicle* he shatters the nerves and veins of his neck. In the *Chanson de Roland* his temples burst. Generally writers relying upon each of these followed their model's lead. In Edgar Quinet, curiously enough, the blood vessels in the hero's chest rupture. Oddly, Michelet the historian agreed with the spurious *Chronicle*, stating that veins in his neck exploded. Picquet, reflecting the *Chronicle*, claimed that the horn itself burst.

What became of the horn in the various accounts? And what happened to Durandal, Roland's sword? At a monastery on the presumed battle site, Baron Isidore Taylor was shown weapons that according to the monks had belonged to the rear guard commander.[8] Writers permitted themselves latitude about the fate of the horn. Usually it was thought to have been made of ivory. In the *Pseudo-Turpin Chronicle* it bursts. Vigny's Roland dies clutching it. Fournel allows the pagans to suspect that it possessed magic powers. Peyrat came close to believing that himself, calling the horn a "trompe merveilleuse." According to Peyrat, Roland had it with him but may not have used it during his ordeal. Maxime Du Camp has him hurl it into the sky before dying. After his death, it plunges back to earth, plowing into the ground at the exact spot from which it was thrown. There it will lie buried until the unknown, appointed day when it will announce humanity's deliverance.

Variation involving Roland's sword is even greater. Authors who expressed an opinion did not agree about how Roland acquired it in the first place. According to the *Chanson de Roland*, Charlemagne gave it to him. For one or two writers such as Assollant, he inherited it from his father. Remembering the epic *Aspremont*, Avril had him capture it at the battle of Aspromonte, taking it from King Aigoland's son Yaumont. In Mermet's *Roland à Roncevaux*, an angel showed it to him in a dream. On waking up, he went to a cemetery and found it under a tombstone, where it was supposed to be.

Normally, fearful lest the sword fall into pagan hands after his death, Roland, knowing that his time is running out, is depicted as trying to destroy it. It neither shatters nor breaks in the *Chanson de Roland*. In the *Chronicle* its owner strikes a rock with it three times. The rock splits but the weapon suffers no damage. Authors liked using this episode, since it enhanced their hero's prowess and allowed them to give a superhuman explanation for the Pyrenees Mountains' famed Brèche de Roland, which the paladin supposedly opened up with his sword. While Dumas, Amable Tastu, and one or two others allowed him to break it, most writers have emphasized the weapon's hardness. Some even attributed occult properties to it. Hugo let it crumble in battle, only to mend miraculously overnight to be ready for the next day's heroic deeds. After the dying Roland has said his prayers, Autran has the sword shatter of its own accord. Creuzé de Lesser lets it break and remain broken. Here, for his final devotions, the expiring knight makes a cross with the two pieces. A variant of this is that the weapon, unbroken but divided naturally at the hilt by its protective guard, looks enough like a cross to be used as one. Gaillard said that Roland broke the blade and threw the pieces away. Assollant's novel shows him tossing it over the mountains, letting it fall into the deep waters of a lake three leagues away, where it will stay until a hero as remarkable as its owner comes along to claim it. Fournel's Roland, though exhausted, manages to drag himself to a crevice and drop it in, making sure no pagan will ever find it. In Du Camp's poem he seeks neither to hide nor destroy it. In Mermet's opera, it gets left on the battlefield. Only in Bornier's *La Fille de Roland* and in the opera based on it does a pagan manage to get possession of it. Much of the play involves Charlemagne's attempting to retrieve it. To some writers, including Prince Lucien, it was buried with its owner in Roncevaux Valley. Others held that it was deposited in a church in France. Quinet claimed to have seen it in the Armería Real in Spain.

From the point at which Charlemagne hears his nephew's horn and decides that trouble is afoot, there is considerable variation in plot. Traditionally the emperor returns to the ambush site, takes stock of what has happened, pursues the perpetrators, usually heathens, and punishes them. But in Vigny's "Le Cor" he merely contemplates the disaster. Sadly, he plans his knights' burial in Fournel's "Romance de Roncevaux." Prince Lucien Bonaparte and Napoléon Peyrat had everyone interred in Roncevaux Valley. Arlincourt, Amable Tastu, and Chateaubriand felt that Roland's grave was in Roncevaux Valley, and Michelet implied the same thing. Bornier, mentioning a tomb in Aquitaine, offered no details. Hugo believed that the body remained behind also, but he was not sure that it was buried. Faget de Baure asserted that the twelve peers, including Roland, were all buried in Roncevaux Valley. Gaillard reported a tradition in which Charlemagne erected a chapel on the massacre site and buried thirty of the most important victims in the cellar. Mistral claimed that Roland's tomb was at Bédaille, near the Spanish border. No matter where the dead were laid to rest, ghosts have always haunted the battlefield, according to Millevoye, Peyrat, Hugo, Ponsard, Mermet, and Rostand.

Following the *Pseudo-Turpin Chronicle*'s lead, a number of writers declared that some of the bodies were taken back to France and buried in different places. Of course, since he supposedly wrote it, Archbishop Turpin does not get killed in the *Chronicle*, and authors using this source did not have to account for the prelate's tomb. According to the *Chronicle*, Olivier was interred at Belin. Roland was laid to rest in Blaye at the church of St. Romain, his sword at his head, his horn at his feet. Most of the others were buried in Arles or Bordeaux. In the *Chanson de Roland* Turpin and the other peers were buried at St. Romain's, although Roland's horn was left at St. Seurin's in Bordeaux. Writing in 1620, Scipion Dupleix stated that Roland had been interred at St. Romain's and that, according to tradition, his sword had been placed at his head and his horn at his feet. Later, he added, the sword was taken to Rocamadour, while the horn was deposited in St. Seurin's. Mérimée, Inspecteur Général des Monuments Historiques, was in an excellent position to know where such things ought to be, and he thought the sword was still at Rocamadour. Frédéric Mistral was convinced of it. Mérimée's friend Alexis de Valon was not so sure and held that it had been removed from Rocamadour at the time of the French Revolution and replaced by another one not at all resembling it. Prince Lucien had the sword, along with its owner, interred at Roncevaux. For Peyrat, Roland, his sword, and his horn were all buried where the paladin was struck down. Cervantes, we recall, believed that the sword was in the Madrid museum where Quinet claimed to have seen it.

Alexandre de Laborde, author of an enormously popular book on Spain, denied that the Franks had invaded the peninsula or that there had ever been a battle of Roncevaux.[9] Few authors agreed. But just who attacked and killed Roland is a topic on which writers have not seen eye to eye. In Dumas, Ponsard, and Kahn's accounts, he manages to survive the disaster, though wounded. Having recovered, he goes on to grapple with deeper, more personal problems. Traditionally, Roland was done in by the Saracens, or at least this has been the most popular literary view. Nevertheless, basing their position on the historians or falling back on persistent oral tradition, some have sought the culprits elsewhere. The Basques, the Gascons, the Aquitainians, the Navarrese, and the Asturians, alone or in combinations, have all come in for their share of blame. Richepin asserted that the inhabitants of the tiny hamlet of Roncevaux did it themselves. Hugo's Charlemagne credited local peasants with the deed. Ricard blamed mountain shepherds.

One of the most intriguing variants in the Roland legend concerns what precisely struck the hero down. Literary tradition presents him, after his interminable struggle with the Saracens, dying wounded and exhausted after his enemies have fled. The *Chronicle* adds the curious detail that as death approaches he is unusually thirsty. Many times, however, an extraordinary reason is given for his death. Sometimes alone, sometimes not, he is shown as having been crushed beneath a rain of stones and trees that the pagans or other

enemies, high above him in the surrounding mountains, have set in motion. A visual representation of this event greeted visitors to the 1819 Salon when they paused in front of Achille Michallon's *Mort de Roland*. This is how Vigny finished off his protagonist. In "Le Cor" one sees the hero after the massacre, when all his comrades except his closest friend have been killed. When Charlemagne finds him, the knight is lying, almost dead, crushed beneath a dark rock. He has succumbed to rocks and trees, not battle weariness. Depending upon the author, sometimes there is one boulder, sometimes there are many. Generally the trees are pines, but occasionally they are firs. For Prince Lucien they are pines and oaks. Although the best known, Vigny was not the first French writer to kill the hero in such a manner, nor was he to be the last. Prior to "Le Cor" Prince Lucien, Creuzé de Lesser, Arlincourt, Marchangy, and Amable Tastu had done the same thing. Much later, Assollant and Richepin would do it as well. Richepin imagined a gripping scene as from the mountain peaks the rocks and trees began to topple into the valley below. It was as if the mountain were an active participant in killing the beleaguered victim, according to the poet.

Determining the source of this denouement is problematic. Certainly this is not how the proud knight meets his end in the *Chanson de Roland* or the *Pseudo-Turpin Chronicle*. Scipion Dupleix mentioned it, however. In all likelihood, oral tradition is the basic explanation. Dupleix, accounting for the fate of Roland's horn and sword, referred to tradition, we remember. J.F. Boudon de St-Amans, Picquet, Faget de Baure, Collin de Plancy, Taine, and Rostand all called attention to the oral tradition that still existed in the mountains as late as the 1950s. Mistral reminded correspondents a decade or so later that there was such a tradition in Provence as well, and Joseph Fabre noted one in the Paris Basin.[10]

Hugo's Charlemagne worried about how posterity would view the events. The earliest annals, written under his watchful eye, did not even mention the disaster, much less the villains and their wicked deed. Fifteen years after his death the event was at last recorded but without details. Perhaps the version so often encountered in nineteenth-century literature is, after all, the correct one. It could well be that, set upon by hidden adversaries, the Franks, Roland among them, were annihilated by boulders and trees rolled or hurled down from the mountains by a timorous but determined enemy, entrenched and well concealed in the peaks' stony recesses and protected by both distance and altitude. If this is indeed what occurred, the event must have left a durable impression upon the untutored mountaineers, who remembered and passed it on orally.

Several French authors in the nineteenth century appear to have been familiar with Gabriel Henri Gaillard's *Histoire de Charlemagne* (1782). Part of the story of the trees and rocks had found its way into this popular work. Gaillard,

narrating what took place, declared that "Les Français, ne pouvant . . . atteindre un ennemi presque invisible, effrayés par la vue des précipices et par le bruit des torrens, étoient écrasés par de grosses roches qu'on rouloit sur eux du haut des montagnes ou percés par des flèches lancées d'un lieu sûr."[11] Vigny's Roland, along with Olivier, is discovered lying in a stream, smashed by a huge rock. Still, Gaillard does not allude to the trees that, according to various authors, were also sent tumbling down the mountains. Like Gaillard, Michelet talked about stones but said nothing about trees. Did Gaillard fail to recall everything that he or his sources had heard about the matter? Did he intentionally omit a detail that he considered incidental or unlikely? In the absence of conclusive written evidence, the best way to account for the story of the trees and stones is probably to ascribe it to orally transmitted folklore. In any event, it is clear that the Roland legend, once it started becoming literature, included some divergent plot elements. Writers who wished to portray Roland as being first and foremost a religious martyr no doubt thought it more appropriate for him to die in a holy cause, struck down in a dastardly ambush by heathen soldiers who, hating the faith he represented but unable to vanquish its champion in open battle, finally resorted to cowardly tactics. Dying on the battlefield defending the true faith against pagan hordes is a more fitting end for a devout paladin than getting flattened beneath cascading rocks and trees unleashed by concealed opponents who, technically at least, might have been of the same religious persuasion as their victim. The story about a Christian knight succumbing, in spite of his virtues and prowess, to superior pagan numbers may have prevailed because, in the eyes of its early purveyors, this is the way it should have been. That a persistent alternate account has survived, containing still other variants that are perhaps just as close to the truth, is puzzling.

Although many nineteenth-century writers treated and interpreted Roland, there were those who regrettably did not. While Adolphe d'Avril had a great deal to say about the doomed knight, his brother-in-law Gobineau merely mentioned him in *Le Roman de Manfredine* and passed on. In a poem to Lamartine, Delavigne praised Roland's upright character but did not elaborate. Unfortunately Stendhal never wrote about him, nor did George Sand. Stéphane Ajasson de Grandsagne, who had probably been Sand's lover, published Napoléon Peyrat's "Roland," one of the nineteenth century's best and most gripping poems dealing with the legend. As for Sand herself, while she visited the Pyrenees Mountains in 1825 and was thrilled with their barren grandeur, in neither her letters nor her *Histoire de ma vie* does she allude to the terrible disaster that took place there in 778. While *Une Vieille Histoire* (1833), *Lélia* (1833, 1839), *Le Nuage rose* (1872), and *Lavinia* (1873) are set in the mountains, neither the Roncevaux catastrophe nor its chief victim is mentioned. As a boy, Dr. Laurent Bielsa, the narrator of *Ma Soeur Jeanne* (1874), spends time climbing around Le Marboré and the Brèche de Roland, but this is as close as the author gets to the historical events associated with the location. But in *Le Géant Yéous* (1873), which has the same setting, one learns that among the books Miquel and his sisters read is the *Chanson de Roland*. When Flaubert spent a month in the area in the summer of 1872, Sand urged her friend to see the Cirque de Gavarnie, but he had already done so.[12]

While he visited the Pyrenees Mountains several times, Flaubert mentioned neither Roland nor the battle of Roncevaux. For receiving his *baccalauréat* in 1840, he was rewarded with a trip that included a visit to the region. Setting out in late summer, he was thrilled as the mountains came into view and in no time set about exploring them. His travel notes, not published until the twentieth century, describe what he saw. The scene was grandiose. Le Chaos, with its "splendeurs tragiques," he mentioned as "un lieu plein de rochers entassés les uns sur les autres, comme un champ de bataille d'un combat de montagnes où ces cadavres immenses seraient restés." To Peyrat, the piles of stone looked as if they could have been a monument to Charlemagne's nephew. Flaubert was overwhelmed by Le Marboré. "Les masses grises des montagnes du Marboré, bordées de neige, se détachaient dans le bleu du ciel et au-dessus d'elles roulaient quelques petits nuages blancs dont le soleil illuminait les contours. On reste ravi," he declared. The Cirque de Gavarnie and la Brèche de Roland were even more breathtaking. "Tout s'oublie vite quand on arrive dans le Cirque de Gavarnie. C'est une enceinte de deux lieues de diamètre, enfermée dans un cercle de montagnes dont tous les sommets sont couverts de neige et du fond de laquelle tombe une cascade. A gauche, la Brèche de Roland et la carrière de marbre, et le sol sur lequel on s'avance, et qui de loin semblait uni, monte par une pente si raide qu'il faut s'aider des mains et des genoux pour arriver au pied de la cascade." According to Peyrat, this is where Roland and Renaud de Montauban took their nightly baths. Flaubert considered it the most spectacular thing he had seen during his trip, and he returned to his lodgings in a dreamlike state.[13] If his dreams included Roland and the battle of Roncevaux, the fact is not recorded.

Béranger, who also did not write about Roland or the battle of Roncevaux, was the protégé of Prince Lucien Bonaparte, who did. In turn, he was the patron of Rouget de Lisle and Peyrat. Heredia has a sonnet in which, without comment and without mentioning Roland, the author alludes to Aude's "blonds cheveux" and "fier profil," all part of her "beauté terrible."[14] Roland did not inspire Baudelaire, Verlaine, or Mallarmé, though he kindled the interest of their friends Fournel, Glatigny, and Banville. Little interested in orthodox religious heroes, especially historical ones, Zola was not attracted to Roland. Daudet and Maupassant, concerned with the modern world, were not of a mind to exploit medieval legends, but Anatole France was, and he wrote a tale about Charlemagne, Roland, and the peers.

Speculating about Roland works that were contemplated or planned and, in some cases, even written but never published provokes curiosity, however frustrating it may be. "Le Cor," as we have seen, is not our only proof that Vigny recognized the Roland legend's literary possibilities. Some memoir fragments tell us that in 1851 he planned to write something he would call "Le Miroir de Roland." Apparently he never wrote it. During her *pensionnaire* years in Paris, Fournel's friend Louise Ackermann wrote a poem or poems about the paladin, but whatever she wrote has never surfaced. Neither have the lines Stuart Merrill translated from the *Chanson de Roland,* which were recited on 7 December 1891 at the Théâtre d'Art. Serving as an appropriate backdrop was a Symbolist painting by Paul Serusier and Henri G. Ibels, specially done for the occasion. In it gold warriors, conceived in a manner reminiscent of the primitives, stood out against a green background. Though admired, Merrill's *vers sonores* do not seem to have been published.[15]

A marionette play dealing with the legend was seen by a Dutch visitor to Paris at Rodolphe Salis's famed art cabaret in 1891. A friend of Richepin, Marcel Schwob, and other French men of letters, the Dutch visitor was W.G.C. Byvanck. Interested in the French Middle Ages, he wrote on François Villon. With Schwob and Alphonse Allais he went to the Chat Noir one night. The Chat Noir's shadow plays were becoming famous, but what he saw that evening was a puppet show with live actors and an actress reciting the dialogue. Byvanck described the event.

> Le rideau du théâtre se lève . . . et c'est une vraie scène qui se montre à nos yeux avec des petites coulisses qui représentent un palais.
>
> Tout à l'heure le décor changera et nous serons dans un défilé sombre des Pyrénées. C'est la tragédie de Roland et de sa mort à Roncevaux. Un monsieur et une dame, debout auprès du piano, prêtent leur voix au paladin et à sa chère Aude, les petits fantoches de la scène, qui se déclarent leur amour mutuel dans le langage ardent qui caractérisait les passions du moyen âge.
>
> Pour rendre la jouissance de l'oeil plus intense, ces voix se taisent, quand l'armée de Charlemagne passe, superbe, parmi les montagnes couvertes de neige.
>
> Ici, un effet grandiose a été atteint par des moyens infimes: donnez-moi un peu de carton peint et quelques fils de fer, dit l'artiste, et je bouleverserai votre âme de fond en comble par l'image de rochers, d'abîmes et de troupes de guerriers, marchant à la mort sous le regard de leur empereur.[16]

From Byvanck's account, it is clear that the production was excellent, with splendid scenery and remarkable puppets. There may have been musical accompaniment, since a piano is mentioned as having been close to the marionette box. The dialogue, which sadly does not seem to have been preserved, was ardent, the total effect moving. We note that the love theme involving Roland and Aude loomed large in the production.

Especially given the simplicity of the basic narrative, clearly the nineteenth-century French picture of Roland shows unexpected diversity. The puppet play Byvanck witnessed occurred immediately before the period during which Bouchor, Fabre, Barrès, Péguy, and others began making their patriotic utterances using Roland as a focus. Having been invoked to encourage France as she went to war with Austria in 1792, Roland came full circle in 1914, when once more Austria, seconded by Germany, found herself at war with France. Roland had continued to be remembered and resurrected in moments of national triumph or crisis as the decades succeeded one another and as World War I approached, bringing the era to a noisy, jolting halt.

Notes

Toponymy

1. Hippolyte Taine, *Voyage aux Pyrénées* (Paris: Hachette, 1887), 218; A. Philibert Abadie, *Itinéraire des Hautes-Pyrénées* (Paris: Didier, 1833), 139.
2. Gerard J. Brault, ed., *The Song of Roland* (University Park: Pennsylvania State U P, 1978), 1:62.

1. Vague Recollections and New Beginnings

1. Miguel de Cervantes, *Don Quixote*, pt. 2, chaps. 8, 9. Both ballads are from the *Cancionero de Amberes*.
2. This Roland has been studied by Sijbrand Keyser, *Contribution à l'étude de la fortune littéraire de l'Arioste en France* (Leiden: M. Dubbeldeman, 1933), and Alexandre Cioranescu, *L'Arioste en France des origines à la fin du XVIIIe siècle* (Paris: Les Editions des Presses Modernes, 1939). Despite Cioranescu's modest title, his book lists a number of works based on Ariosto appearing in France during the nineteenth century.
3. Among the few writers invoking the foreign Roland well into the ninteenth century was Prosper de Barante, who mentions him in a discourse read to the Académie Française on 5 Jan. 1843: "Au chantre de Roland le pape Léon Dix / Accordait en riant sa part de Paradis."
4. *Satire* X. Boileau feared that a wife returning from the opera might be tempted to be as unfaithful as mad Roland's beloved Angelica. Tremble, he warns every husband, lest "Elle n'aille à l'instant, pleine de ces doux sons, / Avec quelque Médor pratiquer ces leçons."
5. Gluck, known to be writing one himself at the same time, decided not to compete, leaving his own *Roland* unfinished. Spire Pitou, *The Paris Opera* (Westport, Conn.: Greenwood, 1983), 1:304-5.
6. Louis de Musset, "De l'épée considérée comme signe de religion et en particulier de l'épée de Roland," *Mémoires de l'Académie celtique* 3 (1809): 359-69.
7. Raoul Mortier, ed., *Le Manuscrit de Châteauroux* (Paris: La Geste Francor, 1943), vol. 4 of *Les Textes de la "Chanson de Roland."*
8. Louis de Musset, "Légende du bienheureux Roland, prince français," *Mémoires et dissertations sur les antiquités nationales et étrangères publiés par la Société Royale des Antiquaires de France* (Paris: Fournier, 1817), 1:151.
9. Ibid., 151-60.
10. Ibid., 170.

11. Musset based this upon the historian Jean Dutillet's assertion that Louis VII created a special category of peers in 1179 and that, under Philippe Auguste, these peers, who had ceremonial functions and attended the king when he administered justice, came into prominence. "Ce n'est que depuis le temps où ces douze pairs ont paru avec éclat que les romanciers et les poètes en ont parlé, et, par cette raison, nous pensons que *li romant de Roncevals* est postérieur au règne de Philippe Auguste" (Ibid., 171). Thus, a poet of Philippe Auguste's period was committing an anachronism or at least using a modern word to describe something that did not exist in Roland's time.

12. Ibid., 167-68.

13. Roland has indeed been revered as a saint: for example, the cathedral chapter at Magdeburg, Germany, placed him on its calendar of sainte in 1459. How much Musset knew about local Roland cults is impossible to determine. See Robert Folz, *Le Souvenir et la légende de Charlemagne dans l'empire germanique médiéval* (Paris: Les Belles Lettres, 1950), 512.

14. Bédier touched upon Musset's article some decades ago. See Joseph Bédier, "De l'édition princeps de la *Chanson de Roland* aux éditions les plus récentes," *Romania* 63 (1937): 441-42.

15. François René de Chateaubriand, *OEuvres complètes* (Paris: Garnier Frères, 1859-61), 11:481-82.

16. A description of these events can be found in Ludovic Vitet, "La *Chanson de Roland*," *Revue des Deux Mondes*, 14 (1852): 820-23, and Paul Thibault, "Le Manuscrit de Châteauroux," in *Les Textes de la "Chanson de Roland,"* ed. Mortier, 4:ix-xiv. Vitet later published his article in book form.

17. Vitet, "La *Chanson de Roland*," 819.

18. Henri Monin, *Dissertation sur le "Roman de Roncevaux"* (Paris: Imprimerie Royale, 1832), 65-72; Francisque Michel, *Examen critique* [of Monin's *Dissertation*] (Paris: Silvestre, 1832), 16pp; Monin, "Addenda," in *Dissertation*, 5.

19. Antoine Le Roux de Lincy, *Le Livre des légendes* (Paris: Silvestre, 1836), 61-67. Silvestre published both the *Livre des légendes* and the *Chanson de Roland*.

20. Vitet, "La *Chanson de Roland*," 822.

21. See Edgar Quinet, *Des Epopées françaises inédites du douzième siècle*, in *OEuvres complètes* (Paris: Hachette, n.d.), 9:480, 495, 502; Edgar Quinet, "L'Epopée française," *Revue des Deux Mondes* 9 (1837): 32.

22. Prosper Mérimée, *Correspondance générale* (Paris: Le Divan; Toulouse: Edouard Privat, 1941-64), 6:196-97, 203-4, 210; 7:7-8.

23. Twentieth-century editions of the *Pseudo-Turpin Chronicle* include the one edited by Ronald N. Walpole, published by the University of California Press in 1976, and the one edited by Claude Buridant, published by Droz in the same year. In 1937 H.M. Smyser edited a Latin text, published under the auspices of the Medieval Academy of America.

24. Scipion Dupleix, *Histoire générale de France, avec l'estat de l'église et de l'empire* (Paris: Claude Sonnius, 1639), 1:314-23, esp. 320-21.

25. Gabriel Henri Gaillard, *Histoire de Charlemagne* (Paris: Moutard, 1782), 3:339-40.

26. Gaillard gives the French title of the work as *Chronique des prouesses et faits d'armes de Charlemagne* and lists Paris editions in 1505, 1527, and 1583. Galliard notes that the *Chronicle* was supposed to have been translated from the Latin by Charles VIII's

librarian, Robert Gaguin. Some of Gaillard's information may be erroneous, however. The Bibliothèque Nationale catalog gives no 1505 or 1583 editions. A 1583 *Chronique de Turpin*, published in Lyon, is actually an edition of *La Conquête de Trébizonde*, a chivalric romance. In 1843, Baron Isidore Taylor quoted from the rich prose of the 1527 edition, published by Regnauld Chauldière. Gaillard did not know who wrote the *Pseudo-Turpin Chronicle* but believed that the author was a monk whose name may have been Robert and who may have been attached to the Abbaye de St-Denis. Gaillard rejects the notion that he might have been Spanish. Gaillard, *Histoire de Charlemagne*, 3:343, 378, 397.

27. Ibid., 343-45, 373-75, 377-78.
28. Ibid., 347-48.
29. Ibid., 411-19, 353-55, 359, 407-19.
30. Ibid., 2:94, 97-102, 86-120, 129, 180-81, 448, 121, 127-28, 133, 168, 178-80, 228, 409, 413, 179, 172-76, 235, 237-41.
31. Ibid., 2:189-91, 192-94, 202.
32. Ibid., 2:195, 94, 117, 203, 195-96.
33. Ibid., 2:196-99.
34. Ibid., 2:199-202, 204.
35. Ibid., 2:235, 207.
36. Pierre de Gorsse, "L'Invention des Pyrénées: Ramond de Carbonnières," *Villégiatures romantiques* (Paris: Editions du Pavois, 1944), 13-42.
37. Charles Augustin Sainte-Beuve, "Ramond de Carbonnières," *Causeries du lundi* (Paris: Garnier Frères, n.d.), 10:476; Cuthbert Girdlestone, *Louis François Ramond* (Paris: Lettres Modernes, 1968).
38. Jean Fourcassié, *Le Romantisme et les Pyrénées* (Paris: Gallimard, 1940), 26-27, 334.
39. Louis Ramond de Carbonnières, *Voyage dans les Pyrénées*, ed. André Monglond (Lyon: Henri Lardanchet, 1927), 63, 69. This is an edition of Ramond de Carbonnières's *Observations*.
40. Ibid., 83-84.
41. Jean-Florimond Boudon de St-Amans, *Fragmens d'un voyage sentimental et pittoresque dans les Pyrénées* (Metz: Devilly, 1789), 49.
42. Louis Ramond de Carbonnières, *Carnets pyrénéens* (Lourdes: Editions de l'Echauguette, 1931), 9, 19, 121, 123.
43. J.P. Picquet, *Voyage dans les Pyrénées françaises* (Paris: Le Jay Fils, 1789), 28-29, 170. Slightly expanded, several editions of the book were published in the 1820s and 1830s.
44. Ibid., 285-86. Gaillard seems to have thought Charlemagne was literate but left open the possibility that he may not have been. The emperor is said to have written a book called *Livres carolins* but he could have had someone else write it, the historian notes. Similarly, Pope Adrian praised him in a poem, and when the Pope died Charlemagne composed a Latin epitaph for him that, again, could have been someone else's work. "On voit encore cette épitaphe gravée sur une table de marbre auprès de la porte de l'église du Vatican." Gaillard, *Histoire de Charlemagne*, 2:57, 392. In the following century Collin de Plancy believed that Charlemagne, "voulant tout savoir," read and studied. Jacques Albin Simon Collin de Plancy, *La Reine Berthe aux grand pied* (Paris: Putois Cretté, 1859), 240. In his *Les Pyrénées*, Baron Isidore Taylor scoffs at the idea that Charlemagne could have composed the epitaph Picquet mentions. If the emperor had a

tomb built for his nephew at Roncevaux or Blaye, it is absurd to think he could have written an epitaph. "Le prétendu vieil historien est un de ces écrivains . . . qui, par dérision ou avec une audace inouïe, comptant sur l'ignorance et la crédulité publique, composent des documents historiques. Nous donnerons cependant cette épitaphe parce que nous croyons que dans un essai sur un fait si intéressant de l'histoire de France, nous ne devons rien omettre et notre foible érudition rien oublier." Taylor then gives the following version of the Latin epitaph, somewhat different from the one reported by Picquet: "Tu patriam repetis; nos triste sub orbe relinquis: / Te tenet aula nitens; nos lacrymosa dies. / Tu qui lustra gerens octo binos super annos, / Ereptus terris, justus ad astra redis." Isidore Taylor, *Les Pyrénées* (Paris: Gide, 1843), 550-51. The epitaph in question would have made Roland forty-two at the time of his death.

45. Picquet, *Voyage*, 286-87.

46. Etienne de Jouy, *L'Ermite en province*, in *OEuvres complètes* (Paris: Jules Didot, 1823), 8:242.

47. Stendhal's curious remark is found in an essay printed as an appendix to Pierre Martino's edition of *Racine et Shakespeare*. See "Qu'est-ce que le romantisme," *Racine et Shakespeare*, ed. Pierre Martino (Paris: Champion, 1925), 2:33.

48. See R. Fountès, "Faget de Baure," in Jean Charles Roman d'Amat et al., eds., *Dictionnaire de biographie française*, 13 (Paris: Letouzey et Ané, 1975): 459. Consult also Henri Martineau, *Petit Dictionnaire stendhalien* (Paris: Le Divan, 1948), 164-65.

49. François-René de Chateaubriand, "De quelques ouvrages historiques et littéraires," *OEuvres complètes* (Paris: Garnier Frères, 1859-61), 6:553-54.

50. Jacques Joseph Faget de Baure, *Essais historiques sur le Béarn* (Paris: Denugon, 1818), 24-25.

51. Emile Vignancourt, ed., *Poésies béarnaises* (Pau: Imprimerie et Lithographie Emile Vignancourt, 1852), vi-vii.

52. See Henri Jacoubet, *Le Comte de Tressan et les origines du genre troubadour* (Paris: Presses Universitaires de France, 1923); Roger Poirier, *La Bibliothèque universelle des romans* (Geneva: Droz, 1976); and Angus Martin, *La Bibliothèque universelle des romans* (Oxford: Voltaire Foundation, 1985). Martin's book constitutes vol. 231 of *Studies on Voltaire and the Eighteenth Century*.

53. Antoine René de Voyer d'Argenson de Paulmy, "Fin de l'histoire de Roland," *Bibliothèque universelle des romans* 12 (1777): 211.

2. Patriot Warrior

1. Julien Tiersot, *Rouget de Lisle: son oeuvre, sa vie* (Paris: Charles Delagrave, 1892), 98-318. Texts of "Roland à Roncevaux" are hard to find. See Constant Pierre, *Musique des fêtes et cérémonies de la Révolution Française* (Paris: Imprimerie Nationale, 1899), 461-62.

2. The play was first performed at the Théâtre Historique on 3 August 1847. Text and music of the song are found in Guillermo M. Tomás, *La France héroïque dans sa musique militaire, guerrière, et patriotique* (Havana: El Siglo XX, 1918), 45-46. In the play, the first stanza, with the refrain, is sung at the beginning of act 5. The second and last stanza, again with the refrain, concludes the play. See Alexandre Dumas, *Théâtre complet* (Paris: Calmann Lévy, 1886-99), 11:139, 165-66. A year before, Dumas had ended his novel by quoting from Rouget de Lisle's original refrain but without inserting his own "Chant des Girondins."

3. Marie Jeanne Durry, *Les Autographes de Mariemont*, pt. 2 (Paris: Nizet, 1959), 1:312, 326; Julien Tiersot, *Histoire de la "Marseillaise"* (Paris: Delagrave, 1915), 107-8.

4. E. Guieysse-Frère, *Sedaine, ses protecteurs et ses amis* (Paris: Flammarion, 1907), 328-30.

5. André Grétry, *Mémoires ou essais sur la musique* (Paris: Imprimerie de la République, 1797), 2:50; Pierre Bossuet, *Histoire des théâtres nationaux* (Paris: Editions et Publications Contemporaines, n.d.), 83.

6. Michel Sedaine, *Guillaume Tell: drame en trois actes en prose et en vers* (Paris: Maradan, 1793), 36-37.

7. Alexandre Duval, *OEuvres complètes* (Paris: J.N. Barba, 1822-23), 5:5, gives 16 December 1803 as the date of the first performance. C. Beaumont Wicks, *The Parisian Stage*, vol. 1, *1800-1815* (University of Alabama P, 1950), 31, lists 4 February 1804.

8. Duval, "Notice sur *Guillaume le conquérant*," *OEuvres complètes* 5:22; autograph letter of Lucien Bonaparte to Antoine Arnault in *Catalogue Thierry Bodin* 28, no. 40 (1986).

9. See Friedrich Blume, *Die Musik in Geschichte und Gegenwart* (Kassel: Bärenreiter Verlag, 1949-86), 2:1403; 8:1902. Méhul's music was published in Paris by the Magasin de Musique, 1804. Choron's setting, likewise printed in Paris, was published by Auguste Leduc, n.d.

10. Duval, "Notice," 25. According to the *Mercure du XIXe siècle*'s issue of 9 April 1825, Duval's plays could not be staged because of government censorship.

11. J.B. Weckerlin, *Chansons populaires du pays de France* (Paris: Hengel et Cie, 1903), 1:151; Philothée O'Neddy, "Méhul et Boïeldieu," *OEuvres complètes*, ed. Ernest Havet (Geneva: Slatkine Reprints, 1968), 2:210; Théophile Dumersan, ed., *Chants et chansons populaires de la France* (Paris: Garnier Frères, 1848), vol. 1, not paginated.

12. Claude Auguste Nicolas Dorion, *La Bataille d'Hastings ou l'Angleterre conquise* (Paris: Firmin Didot, 1822), 2:71-72.

13. "E! Durandal, cum ies e clere et blanche! / Cuntre soleil si luis et si reflambes! / .... / Jo l'en conquis Escoce, Gwale, Islande / E Angleterre que il teneit sa cambre." Le Vavasseur quoted *laisse* 172, 11. 2316-17, 2331-32.

14. Gustave Le Vavasseur, "La Chanson de Roland," *Poésies complètes* (Paris: Alphonse Lemerre, 1888-96), 3:215-17.

15. *Chansonnier des grâces* (Paris: Mme Louis, 1805), 10:61.

16. Pierre Ladoué, *La Vie et l'oeuvre de Millevoye* (Paris: Perrin, 1912), 250.

17. Charles Hubert Millevoye, *Charlemagne à Pavie*, chant 4, in *OEuvres complètes* (Paris: Ladvocat, 1822), 3:53-54.

18. Charles Hubert Millevoye, *Emma et Eginhard*, in *OEuvres complètes*, 3:237.

19. Ladoué, *Millevoye*, 250-51.

20. Théophile Dumersan and Noël Ségur, *Chansons nationales et populaires* (Paris: Garnier Frères, 1866), 2:481.

21. "Roland" was first published in an album containing two other romances by Dalvimare and La Mothe-Langon. Published in Paris, rue St-Marc, but no date given.

22. See Claire Labrosse's index to Henri Gougelot, *La Romance française sous la Révolution et l'Empire* (Melun: Legrand et Fils, 1938), 115, and J.M. Quérard, *Les Supercheries littéraires dévoilées* (Paris: Paul Daffis, 1869-79), 2:636-37.

23. Stylistic features assign the song to the First Empire period. See Henri Gougelot, *Catalogue des romances françaises parues sous la Révolution et l'Empire: Les Recueils de romances* (Melun: Legrand et Fils, 1937), 65, 69.

24. J.B. Barjaud, *Homère . . . , suivi de fragments d'un poème intitulé "Charlemagne"* (Paris: Blanchard, Patris, and Lebour, 1811), 76-77.

25. Aimé Martin, *Epître sur les sujets que le règne de Buonaparte offre à la poésie*, 1814.

26. Martin's course is discussed in the *Mercure de France* 58, January, February, and March 1814. Quote in March issue, p. 591.

27. Henri Jacoubet, *Le Comte de Tressan et les origines du genre troubadour* (Paris: Presses Universitaires de France, 1923), 397-98. None of Martin's remarks about Roland are quoted in the *Mercure de France*.

28. Bonaventure de Roquefort, *De l'état de la poésie françoise dans les douzième et treizième siècles* (Paris: Fournier, 1815), 138, 135-36.

29. Auguste François Creuzé de Lesser, *La Chevalerie ou les histoires du moyen âge* (Paris: F. Ponce-Lebas et Cie, 1839), 283-94. See also 439, 512, 532-39.

30. Népomucène Lemercier, *Charlemagne*, in *Suite du répertoire du Théâtre Français* (Paris: Dabo, 1822), 10:111.

31. Ferdinand Dugué, *Gaïffer*, in *Théâtre complet* (Paris: Calmann Lévy, 1891-94), 1:319.

32. His brother, King Louis of Holland, agreed. See Louis Bonaparte, *Mémoire sur la versification et essais divers* (Florence: Guillaume Piatti, 1819), 7. King Louis's book was dedicated to the Académie Française, despite Prince Lucien's exclusion.

33. Lucien Bonaparte, *Charlemagne ou l'église délivrée* (London: Longman, Hurst, Rees, Orme, and Brown, 1814), 1:367.

34. Ibid., xiii.

35. Ibid., x-xi. According to the poet's introduction, Waifar and Lupus are cousins and are, respectively, dukes of Aquitaine and Gascony. For reasons of his own, Prince Lucien prefers calling Lupus "Théodebert." He also changes the name of Carloman's widow.

36. Ibid., 362.

37. As Prince Lucien did not know the *Chanson de Roland*, Roland's dying thoughts here are not for Aude but rather for Angelica, the heroine of *Orlando furioso*.

38. Most of the segments of *Charlemagne* devoted to Roland are found in cantos 2, 4, 6, and 13.

39. The chapel is discussed in Ramón Menéndez Pidal, *La "Chanson de Roland" et la tradition épique des Francs* (Paris: Picard, 1960), 223-26. Menéndez Pidal's plate 4 shows it around 1880. In 1934 and 1951 excavations on the site uncovered human remains.

40. Some historians would have it that Roland was set upon not by Moors or Gascons but by Basques. With this theory in mind, it is interesting to note that Louis Lucien Bonaparte, Prince Lucien's erudite son, would one day write a Basque grammar and several other works on the Basque language and its dialects. It is probably another coincidence that Prince Lucien had a grandson named Roland. This Prince Roland in time became a scientist and writer who set up two laboratories, or stations, for studying glaciers. One of the observatories was in the Pyrenees Mountains.

41. Louis Antoine François de Marchangy, *La Gaule poétique ou l'histoire de France considérée dans ses rapports avec la poésie, l'éloquence, et les beaux-arts*, 8 vols. (Paris: C.F. Patris and Chaumont Jeune, 1813-17).

42. Louis Antoine François de Marchangy, *La Gaule poétique*, 3d ed. (Paris: C.F. Patris, 1819), 3:11.

43. Stendhal, "Lettre V," *Racine et Shakespeare*, vol. 2, in *OEuvres complètes*, ed. Georges Eudes (Paris: Pierre Larrive, 1951-54), 16:64; Prosper Mérimée, *Correspondance générale*, 16:2; Victor Hugo, *Les Misérables* (Paris: Gallimard, 1951), 123; Gustave

Flaubert, *Par les champs et par les grèves*, in *Voyages*, ed. René Dumesnil (Paris: Société les Belles Lettres, 1948), 1:172; George Sand, *Correspondance*, ed. Georges Lubin (Paris: Garnier Frères, 1964-89), 1:254-55, and vol. 6:678.

44. Later he would write *Tristan le voyageur*, about fourteenth-century France, in which he showed the period more in depth than he had in *La Gaule poétique*.

45. Marchangy calls Aigoland "Agramant," borrowing the name from *Orlando furioso*.

46. Marchangy, *La Gaule poétique*, 3d ed., 3:71-72, 73.

47. Ibid., 74.

48. Ibid., 75-78.

49. Ibid., 78.

50. Reference works generally give the year of Arlincourt's birth as 1789, but pointing out that the author lied about his age, the *Dictionnaire de biographie française* insists that it was 1788. See J.M. Roman d'Amat et al., *Dictionnaire de biographie française* 3:646-48.

51. Germaine de Staël, *De l'Allemagne*, ed. Pauline de Pange (Paris: Hachette, 1958-60), 5:134. Arlincourt omits the word "romantique." See Charles Victor d'Arlincourt, *Charlemagne ou la Caroléide* (Paris: Lenormant, 1818), 1:xvii. Arlincourt's "Hymne funèbre de Roland" is on 212-15.

52. Arlincourt, *Charlemagne*, 1:xi.

53. Ibid., 7.

54. Ibid., 236.

55. Alphonse de Lamartine, *Correspondance Lamartine-Virieu* (Paris: Presses Universitaires de France, 1987), 2:232; Charles Augustin Sainte-Beuve, "Le Vicomte d'Arlincourt," *OEuvres* (Paris: Gallimard, 1966), 1:81.

56. Amable Tastu, *La Chevalerie française* (Paris: Ambroise Tardieu, 1821), 97-100, 111-25.

57. Ramón Menéndez Pidal, *La "Chanson de Roland" et la tradition épique des Francs* (Paris: Picard, 1960), 223-26.

58. Robert Sabatier, *La Poésie du dix-neuvième siècle* (Paris: Albin Michel, 1977), 1:402; Charles Augustin Sainte-Beuve, "Madame Tastu," *Portraits contemporains* (Paris: Didier, n.d.), 1:383.

59. Victor Hugo, *Les Misérables* (Paris: Gallimard, 1951), 122-24.

60. Jean Guillaume Antoine (or Auguste) Cuvelier de Trie and Léopold Chandezon, *Roland furieux, pantomime chevaleresque et féerie* (Paris: Fages, 1817), 3.

61. Ibid., 6-7.

62. Ibid., 19-23.

63. Ibid., 37-38.

64. Balzac's awareness of the French Roland legend is indicated by his allusion to "les sons lointains du cor de Roland." The paladin's desperate call for help is mentioned in *Physiologie du mariage* (1829). Generally, though, Balzac thought of Roland as Ariosto's lunatic, maddened by love and representing the "révolutions désordonnées, furieuses, impuissantes qui détruisent tout sans rien produire," rather than as a national hero whom one should admire and emulate. Roland, he believed, demonstrates that, in love as in everything else, there is no explaining taste. Why should Ariosto show his readers "Angélique préférant Médor . . . à Roland dont la jument était morte et qui ne savait que se mettre en fureur," he wondered. Balzac, *La Vieille Fille*, in *Comédie humaine* (Paris: Gallimard, 1976-81), 4:935-36.

65. J.C.L. Simonde de Sismondi, *Histoire des Français* (Paris: Treuttel et Würtz, 1821-44), 2:259

66. Ibid., 263.

67. A few years earlier Sismondi had dealt with the *romanceros* in *De la littérature du midi de l'Europe* (Paris: Treuttel et Würtz, 1813), 2:224, in which he alluded to Bernardo del Carpio's "victoire sur Roland à Roncevaux." In the *Histoire des Français*, he is supposed to have "étouffé Roland dans ses bras." Ibid., 265.

68. Sismondi, *Histoire*, 2:264-65.

69. Ibid., 263-64.

70. J.C.L. Simonde de Sismondi, *De la littérature du midi de l'Europe* (Paris: Treuttel et Würtz, 1813), 1:284-85.

71. Ibid., 284, 285, 287.

72. Ibid., 286-88.

73. Ibid., 280, 290-91. *Les Chroniques de St-Denis* are now generally called *Les Grandes Chroniques de France*.

74. Ibid., 288-89.

75. Sismondi was a Swiss Protestant.

3. The Romantics' Roland

1. François René de Chateaubriand, *Mémoires d'outre-tombe* (Paris: Flammarion, 1950), 3:178.

2. François René de Chateaubriand, *Essai sur les révolutions*. Idem, *Génie du christianisme*, ed. Maurice Regard (Paris: Gallimard, 1978), 955. See Ramón Menéndez Pidal, *La "Chanson de Roland" et la tradition épique des Francs* (Paris: Picard, 1960), 222-25.

3. François René de Chateaubriand, *OEuvres complètes* (Paris: Garnier Frères, 1859-61), 10:96-98, 99, 23.

4. Ibid., 9:433, 440.

5. Consult Jules Viard, ed., *Les Grandes Chroniques de France* (Paris: Champion, 1923), 3:204-87. Sismondi believed that the Roland episode in *Les Grandes Chroniques* derived essentially from the *Pseudo-Turpin Chronicle*. Chateaubriand gives the source of his hunch about where the *Chanson de Roland* might be found as the *Mémoires de l'Académie des Inscriptions* 1 (1815): 317. He also lists Charles Du Fresne Du Cange's *Cantilena Rollandi* and Dom Antoine Rivet de la Grange's *Histoire littéraire de la France* (Paris: Imprimerie Nationale, 1733-63), 7:73 (*avertissement*).

6. Chateaubriand, *Mémoires*, 3:552.

7. Charles Augustin Sainte-Beuve, *Chateaubriand et son groupe littéraire sous l'Empire*, ed. Maurice Allem (Paris: Garnier Frères, 1948), 1:128, 2:344.

8. Charles Augustin Sainte-Beuve, *OEuvres* (Paris: Gallimard, 1966), 1:446.

9. Françoise Dehousse, "Le 'Cours d'Ancienne Littérature' professé à Liège par Sainte-Beuve," *Sainte-Beuve et la critique littéraire contemporaine* (Paris: Les Belles Lettres, 1972), 45; André Billy, *Sainte-Beuve: sa vie et son temps* (Paris: Flammarion, 1952), 2:126.

10. Alfred de Vigny, *Correspondance* (Paris: Presses Universitaires de France, 1989-), 1:181.

11. Pierre de Gorsse, *Villégiatures romantiques* (Paris: Editions du Pavois, 1944), 90. See also Alfred de Vigny, *Journal d'un poète*, in *OEuvres complètes* (Paris: Gallimard, 1960), 2:590, and Vigny's *OEuvres complètes* (Paris: Gallimard, 1986), 1:871-72, 1532-33. A fairly recent study of "Le Cor" is H. Vaucheret, "Les Pyrénées, cadre médiéval dans 'Le

Cor'," in *Vigny, les Pyrénées, et l'Angleterre* (Pau: Marrimpouey Jeune, 1978), 63-78. Notes for Vigny's projected tragedy about the historical Roland have been published in Madeleine Ambrière et al., *Alfred de Vigny et les siens: documents inédits* (Paris: Presses Universitaires de France, 1989), 207.

12. Alfred de Vigny, *Mémoires inédits, fragments, et projets*, ed. Jean Sangnier (Paris: Gallimard, 1958), 407-8. See also Vigny, *OEuvres complètes*, 1:355.

13. It has been claimed that Vigny used this work since he retained an error from it. Early in the poem he apostrophizes the area around Roncevaux: "O montagnes d'azur! ô pays adoré! / Rocs de la Frazona, cirque du Marboré, / Cascades qui tombez des neiges entraînées, / Sources, gaves, ruisseaux, torrents des Pyrénées." In Dusaulx's work "Frazona" is supposedly a misprint designating a mountain peak near Le Marboré. See Jean Fourcassié, "Recherches sur le premier paragraphe du 'Cor'," *Revue universitaire* 47 (1938), 426-28. But "Frazona" is what French residents and tourists in Vigny's day ordinarily called the crag. See Harry Redman, Jr., "Vigny, 'Le Cor' et 'Frazona'," *Revue d'histoire littéraire de la France* 88 (1988): 241-42.

14. A text of this song, along with Silcher's music, is in Max Walter and Anna Woods Ballard, eds., *French Songs* (New York: Charles Scribner's Sons, 1916), 41. Silcher published the song as "Wis lieblich schallt durch Busch und Wald," with German words by Christoph von Schmidt. For their help in identifying this song I thank Liselotte Andersson of the Maxwell Music Library, Tulane University, and Professor Hermann Josef Dahmen of the Silcher Archiv in Schnait, Germany. It is not generally known that Schmidt's lyric is based on a French song.

15. Jules Vodoz, *Roland: un symbole* (Paris: Champion, 1920), 68-69.

16. Jules Barbey d'Aurevilly, *Un Prêtre marié*, in *OEuvres complètes* (Paris: Gallimard, 1964-66), 1:939. It appeared as a serial in 1864, in book form in 1865.

17. Jules Barbey d'Aurevilly, *Premier mémorandum*, in *OEuvres complètes*, 1:747.

18. Heinrich Heine, *Atta Troll* IV. Letter to Guillaume Trebutien, in Jules Barbey d'Aurevilly, *Correspondance générale*, (Paris: Les Belles Lettres, 1980-89), 5:43. In his letters Barbey uses the expression "cor de Roland" several times.

19. Jules Barbey d'Aurevilly, *OEuvres complètes* 2:93.

20. Napoléon Peyrat, "Le Capitaine Dusson ou le siège du mas d'Azil," *L'Arise* (Paris: Librairie de Charles Mayrueis et Cie, 1863), 265.

21. Henri Lardanchet, *Les Enfants perdus du romantisme* (Paris: Perrin, 1905), 257-69; Félicité de Lamennais, *Correspondance générale* (Paris: Armand Colin, 1971-82), 7:248; Charles Augustin Sainte-Beuve, *Correspondance générale* (Paris: Stock, Privat, and Didier, 1935-83), 13:476, 343; Charles Asselineau, "Napol le Pyrénéen," *Les Poètes français* (Paris: Hachette, n.d.), 4:659-60; Anatole France, "Anthologie," *La Vie littéraire*, in *OEuvres complètes illustrées* (Paris: Calmann Lévy, 1925-35), 6:569. Originally France's review article of Alphonse Lemerre's *Anthologie des poètes français du XIXe siècle* appeared in two installments in *Le Temps* on 26 August and 23 September 1888. In the conclusion of the second installment the reviewer discussed Peyrat and "Roland."

22. Jacques Joseph Faget de Baure, *Essais historiques sur le Béarn* (Paris: Denugon, 1818), 25.

23. Ibid.

24. Jean Richepin, "Le Baiser des drapeaux," *Poèmes durant la guerre* (Paris: Flammarion, 1919), 85.

25. Asselineau, "Napol le Pyrénéen," 300; Charles Baudelaire, *Mon coeur mis à nu*, in *OEuvres complètes* (Paris: Gallimard, 1983), 707, 1512.

26. France, *OEuvres complètes illustrées*, 6:568-69.

27. Fernand Gregh, *Portrait de la poésie française au XIXe siècle* (Paris: Delagrave, 1936), 154-58.

28. Edgar Quinet, *Rapport . . . sur les épopées françaises du douzième siècle* (Paris: F. G. Levrault, 1831), 27, 28. The report would be incorporated into the author's works. See *Des épopées françaises inédites du douzième siècle*, in *OEuvres complètes* (Paris: Hachette, n.d.), vol. 9. The minister was collecting such reports, and Ludovic Vitet, who would later write on the *Chanson de Roland*, provided him with another one at the same time.

29. "M. Génin, qui depuis a donné une si remarquable édition de l'un de ces chants épiques, me niait publiquement qu'il y eût des poèmes carlovingiens en vers de douze syllabes," Quinet recalled in an *avertissement* written in 1857. Quinet did not retract his contention, but the two men became friends. See also Edgar Quinet, "L'Epopée française," *Revue des Deux Mondes* 9 (1837): 32.

30. Quinet, "L'Epopée française," 37. In 1839 the article appeared in *Allemagne et Italie*. Virtually unchanged, it constitutes chaps. 9, 10, 11, 12, 13, and 14 of the *Histoire de la poésie*. Still near its original form, it appeared, along with *Des Épopées françaises inédites du douzième siècle* and *Mes vacances en Espagne*, in vol. 9 of Quinet's *OEuvres complètes*.

31. Quinet, "L'Epopée française," 26, 33.

32. Gaston Paris, *Histoire poétique de Charlemagne* (Paris: Franck, 1865), 463.

33. Quinet, "L'Epopée française," 33-34, 28.

34. Ibid., 36-37.

35. "Histoire de Guérin de Montglane," *Bibliothèque universelle des romans* 10 (1777): 82-84. Reprinted in Louis de Tressan, *Corps d'extraits de romans de chevalerie* (Paris: Pissot, 1782), vol. 2.

36. *Roman de Fierabras* (Berlin: Reimer, 1829). Some of these details are in Frederick G. Yeandle, ed., *Girart de Vienne* (New York: Columbia U P, 1930), 1-2.

37. Quinet, "L'Epopée française," 44.

38. Ibid., 35.

39. Victor Hugo, *L'Ane* (Paris: Flammarion, 1966), 105.

40. "Extrait de la Chronique des prouesses et faits d'armes de Charlemagne," *Bibliothèque universelle des romans* 7 (1777): 154.

41. Edgar Quinet, *Mes vacances en Espagne* (Paris: Les Imprimeurs Unis, 1846), 12, 28. This is the sword Sancho Panza mentions in *Don Quixote*.

42. Ibid., 396.

43. Edgar Quinet, *Merlin l'enchanteur* (Paris: Calmann Lévy, 1860), 1:93, 97, 366; 2:105, 274, 339.

44. Lucien Refort, ed., *Tableau de la France*, by Jules Michelet (Paris: Les Belles Lettres, 1949), xv.

45. Jules Michelet, *OEuvres complètes*, ed. Paul Viallaneix (Paris: Flammarion, 1971–), 4:349.

46. Ibid., 278-79, 350.

47. Ibid., 278-79.

48. Ibid.

49. Jules Michelet, *OEuvres complètes*, 3:50; Michelet, *OEuvres*, 4:418.

50. Jules Michelet, *OEuvres complètes*, 7:56, 58. Robert Casanova edited this volume.

51. Ibid., 57. Michelet believed that the epic existed, in nascent form, well before

1100. "C'est vers le dixième siècle . . . que, sans nul doute, commencèrent les chants de Roland. Ces chants, déjà antiques sous Guillaume le Conquérant, en 1066, ne sont pas, comme on le croit, l'oeuvre du pesant âge féodal, qui n'a fait que les délayer. De telles choses ne datent pas d'un âge de servitude, mais d'un âge vivant, libre encore. . . . La noble *Chanson de Roland* est antérieure, on le sent partout, à cette mauvaise époque" (56-57).

52. Jules Michelet, *Histoire de France* (Paris: Albert Lacroix, 1876-77), 3:209, 205.

53. Ibid., 206, 205. "Charlemagne . . . a laissé périr Roland." John R. Williams has some interesting comments on Michelet's view of the *Chanson de Roland*, particularly during the author's last phase, in "Jules Michelet and Medieval French Literature," *Res Publica Litterarum* 2 (1979): 347-58.

54. Jules Michelet, *La Montagne* (Paris: Librairie Internationale, 1868), 85.

55. Jacques Albin Simon Collin de Plancy, *Dictionnaire infernal* (Paris: Librairie Universelle de P. Mongie Aîné, 1825-26), 2:122.

56. Jacques Albin Simon Collin de Plancy, *La Reine Berthe au grand pied* (Paris: Putois-Cretté, 1859), 235.

57. Ibid.

58. Ibid., 236.

59. Jacques Albin Simon Collin de Plancy, *Dictionnaire critique des reliques et images miraculeuses* (Paris: Guien et Cie, 1821-22), 3:43-45.

60. Alexis de Valon, "La Corrèze et Rocamadour: rêveries à travers champs," *Revue des Deux Mondes* 9 (1851): 460. For some of his material Valon relied upon Dupleix's *Histoire de France*. The *Chanson de Roland* quotation comprises ll. 2316-17. Valon was using Génin's édition, published in 1850.

61. Prosper Mérimée, *Correspondance générale* 2:189.

62. Ibid., 7:8.

63. Ibid., 8:444.

64. Ibid., 6:197.

65. Eugène Rosary, *Les Pèlerinages de France* (Rouen: Mégard et Cie, 1865), 97.

66. Jean Boutière, ed., *Correspondance de Frédéric Mistral avec Paul Meyer et Gaston Paris* (Paris: Didier, 1978), 105, 108.

67. Ibid., 200-201.

68. Frédéric Mistral, "Lou Duran-Dai," *Revue du Sud-Est* (1906): 20-21.

69. In an editorial in the 1875 *Almanach provençal* Mistral wrote of the "enthousiasmes de la poésie sainte." For a presentation of Mistral's religious attitudes, see E. Flavien Girard, *Du sentiment religieux chez Mistral* (Montpellier: Déhan, 1960). The poet insists upon the use of Provençal in two poems, notably, of *Les Óulivado*, "La Respelido" ("La Renaissance") and "A linmaculado councepcioun" ("A l'immaculée conception").

70. Alexandre Dumas père, *Chronique de Charlemagne*, in *Aventures de Lyderic* (Brussels: Méline et Cie, 1842), 241-47, 255-65.

71. Ibid., 241-47.

72. Ibid., 255-65

73. Alexandre Dumas père, *Une Aventure d'amour* (Paris: Plon, 1985), 144. In two poems, "Klein Roland" and "Roland Schildträger," Uhland recounted basically the same anecdotes. Probably he used the same sources as Dumas.

74. Alexandre Dumas père, *Excursions sur les bords du Rhin* (Paris: Calmann Lévy, 1887), 2:7-12. Dumas revisited the Rhine area in 1844, 1852, and 1857.

75. Harry Redman, Jr., *German Romantic Poetry's Treatment of the Roland Legend* (Stuttgart: Akademischer Verlag Stuttgart, 1988), 77ff. In the early nineteenth century the variant appeared several times in British literature: Thomas Campbell's poem "The Brave Roland" (1820), Letitia Landon's "Roland's Tower," and, in prose, Edward Bulwer-Lytton's *The Pilgrims of the Rhine* (1834) treated the legend.

76. Victor Hugo, *Le Rhin* (Paris: Nelson, n.d.), 1:199.

77. Xavier Marmier, *Voyage pittoresque en Allemagne* (Paris: Morizot, 1858), p. 82.

78. Redman, *German Romantic Poetry's Treatment*, 79-82; Jacques Vier, *La Comtesse d'Agoult et son temps* (Paris: Armand Colin, 1959), 2:68-69.

79. Jacques Vier, *La Comtesse d'Agoult et François Ponsard d'après une correspondance inédite* (Paris: Armand Colin, 1960), 1:55.

80. François Ponsard, "Lettres à la duchesse Decazes," *Revue de Paris* 4 (1901): 404-5.

81. Poem collated from François Ponsard, *OEuvres complètes* (Paris: Calmann Lévy, 1876), 3:334-36, and Vier, *La Comtesse d'Agoult et François Ponsard*, 1:55-56.

82. Ponsard, "Lettres à la duchesse Decazes," 405.

83. Gustave Kahn, "L'Image Roland," *Revue blanche* 13 (1897): 307-8; J.C. Ireson, *L'OEuvre poétique de Gustave Kahn* (Paris: Nizet, 1962), 342.

84. See Stéphane Mallarmé, *Correspondance*, ed. Henri Mondor and Lloyd James Austin (Paris: Gallimard, 1959-85), 10:50 n. 3.

4. Magnificent Braggart and Doomed Lover

1. *Chants et chansons populaires de la France* (Paris: H.L. Delloye, 1843-44), 2:n.p. Rimbaud's petulant remark is in his famous letter to Paul Demeny of 15 May 1871.

2. Auguste Barbier, *Rimes héroïques* (Paris: P. Masgana, 1843), 21-22, 152.

3. Etienne Jean Delécluze, *Roland ou la chevalerie* (Paris: Jules Labitte, 1845), 1:xv.

4. Ibid., 1:23, 36, 2:iii; 1:35, xii.

5. Ibid., 1:347, 38-39.

6. Ibid., 1:36, 37; 2:vii-viii.

7. Charles Magnin, "Roland ou la chevalerie," *Revue des Deux Mondes* 14 (1846): 943, 953, 954.

8. See Tribout de Morembert's article on Fournel in Roman d'Amat et al., *Dictionnaire de biographie française*, 14:794. Mallarmé's correspondance for the 1860s is also helpful.

9. *Année littéraire* 5 (1863): 20-22. See Luc Badesco, *La Génération poétique de 1860* (Paris: Nizet, 1979), 1:1322. Vapereau did not include Fournel in his *Dictionnaire universel des contemporains* or in his dictionary of authors, but he did not include Mallarmé either.

10. The *Bibliographie de la France* lists the publication of Hugo's *Les Rayons et les ombres* on 16 May 1840. For Fournel's *Ombres et rayons*, published in Frankfurt, no specific publication date can be ascertained.

11. Gabriel Faure, *Mallarmé à Tournon* (Paris: Horizons de France, 1946), 30-32. This appeared earlier in article form in the *Revue des Deux Mondes* on 1 March 1937 (106-17).

12. For a text of the poem see Charles Fournel, "Romance de Roncevaux," *Poésies* (Paris: Renouard, 1848), 147-70.

13. Friedrich de La Motte Fouqué, *Romanzen vom Thale Ronceval* (Berlin: In der Realschulbuchanglung, 1805), 54pp.

14. Harry Redman, Jr., *German Romantic Poetry's Treatment of the Roland Legend* (Stuttgart: Akademischer Verlag Stuttgart, 1988), 2, 12-13.

15. Adolphe Thiers, *Les Pyrénées et le midi de la France pendant les mois de novembre et décembre 1822* (Brussels: Méline, Cans et Cie, 1840); A. Philibert Abadie, *Itinéraire topographique et historique des Hautes-Pyrénées* (Paris: Didier, 1833), 139, 142-43.

16. Isidore Taylor, *Les Pyrénées* (Paris: Gide, 1843), 542-43.

17. Ibid., 543, 572-73. Taylor also summarizes, quotes, and comments upon the *Pseudo-Turpin Chronicle*, the Spanish *romances*, and Pulci's *Il Morgante*.

18. Ibid., 561. The road around Roncevaux was rebuilt in 1813 so that Marshal Soult's artillery could get through, and today this road is still known as the Chemin des Canons or the Chemin de Napoléon. See Ramón Menéndez Pidal, *La "Chanson de Roland" et la tradition épique des Francs* (Paris: Picard, 1960), 225-26, and Louis Colas, "La Voie romaine de Bordeaux à Astorga dans sa traversée des Pyrénées," *Revue des études anciennes* 14 (1912): 180.

19. Jean Fourcassié, *Le Romantisme et les Pyrénées* (Paris: Gallimard, 1940), 284-85; Hippolyte Taine, *Voyage aux Pyrénées* (Paris: Hachette, 1860), 224-26.

20. Hippolyte Taine, *Histoire de la littérature anglaise* (Paris: Hachette, 1863), 1:91-93.

21. Hippolyte Taine, *Philosophie de l'art* (Paris: Hachette, 1924), 2:296-97.

22. Edmond and Jules de Goncourt, *Journal* (Monaco: Editions de l'Imprimerie Nationale, 1956-58), 12:62-63.

23. Quotations are from Maxime Du Camp, "Le Cor d'ivoire," *Les Convictions* (Paris: Librairie Nouvelle, 1858), 87-92.

24. Hugo's evolution can be seen in the prologue to *L'Année terrible*, in *OEuvres poétiques* (Paris: Gallimard, 1984), 3:286, 917. The poet alludes indignantly to the death of General Rafael del Riego, one of the Spanish Cortes's leading generals, who was hanged for his part in the rebellion (7 November 1823). François René de Chateaubriand, *Mémoires d'outre-tombe* (Paris: Flammarion, 1950), 3:212.

25. Victor Hugo, *Odes et ballades*, in *OEuvres poétiques*, 1:504, 355-56.

26. Victor Hugo, *France et Belgique, Alpes et Pyrénées* (Paris: Nelson, n.d.), 460, 553. A modern edition, with commentary, of that part of the work dealing with this region is *Les Pyrénées*, ed. Danièle Lamarque (Paris: Editions La Découverte, 1984). Victor Hugo, *Les Travailleurs de la mer* (Paris: Gallimard, 1984), 612.

27. Victor Hugo, *L'Art d'être grand-père*, in *OEuvres poétiques*, 3:639.

28. See Jacques Truchet's note and comment in the Pléiade edition. Victor Hugo, *La Légende des siècles* (Paris: Gallimard, 1955), 139.

29. Jubinal would join Mérimée in defending Comte Guillaume Libri, accused of stealing rare documents and books from French libraries and selling them in England. The Old French scholar Paulin Paris also came to Libri's defense.

30. The 1850 edition of *Girart de Vienne* was the work of Prosper Tarbé. In Germany there had been an incomplete edition as early as 1829, when, to his edition of the *Roman de Fierabras*, Immanuel Bekker added the 4060 lines of *Girart de Vienne* that Uhland had transcribed in the Bibliothèque Nationale nearly twenty years before. Hugo used neither of these. *Aymeri de Narbonne* was not published until Louis Demaison's 1887 edition. Hugo's borrowings from the Jubinal article are discussed in Paul Berret, *Le Moyen Age dans la "Légende des siècles"* (Paris: Henry Paul et Cie, 1911), 27-59, and Patricia A. Ward, *The Medievalism of Victor Hugo* (University Park: Pennsylvania State U P, 1975), 10, 90.

31. "L'épée est une illustre et fière Closamont / Que d'autres quelquefois appellent Haute-Claire." "Closamont" is a misreading by Jubinal. Hugo knew that people generally called the sword Hauteclaire; this corroborates his having had independent knowledge of the Roland legend.

32. In the epic, Roland tells Olivier that he would like to rest. When Olivier agrees, Roland claims that he was merely testing him. Roland declares that he could keep going for four more days. Perhaps these additional four days gave the poet the idea of prolonging the struggle.

33. Joseph A. Fabre, trans. *La Chanson de Roland . . . précédée de "Roland et la belle Aude"* (Paris: Belin Frères, 1902), 50.

34. Ibid., 98-99 (quoted).

35. Writing in the 1850s, Hugo could not have known that this exploit is part of the *Chanson de Roland*'s Manuscrit de Venise 4, since this version of the epic was not published until 1877. As in the case of "Le Mariage de Roland," Jubinal's article was the poet's main source.

36. Paul Verlaine, "A propos du dernier livre posthume de Victor Hugo," in *OEuvres posthumes* (Paris: Albert Messein, 1922-29), 1:296. "Les éphèbes, entre parenthèses, portent toujours bonheur à Victor Hugo, un féminin, en somme," Verlaine added.

37. Françoise Lambert, ed., *La Légende des siècles*, by Victor Hugo (Paris: Flammarion, 1970), 8.

38. Ibid., 169.

39. Emile Montégut, "La *Légende des siècles* de M. Victor Hugo," *Revue des Deux Mondes* 23 (1859): 992, 993. Montégut later reprinted the review in a collection of critical essays, *Mélanges critiques* (Paris: Hachette, 1887). Hugo, *Légende des siècles* 5.

40. Quoted in Lambert, ed., *Légende des siècles*, 10, 297.

41. *Chanson de Roland*, laisse 173, 11. 2345-46. Hugo undoubtedly read François Génin's translation.

42. Ernest Renan, *OEuvres complètes* (Paris: Calmann Lévy, 1947-61), 2:1136.

43. Alfred Assollant, *La Mort de Roland, fantaisie épique* (Paris: Hachette, 1860), 128, 127. Assollant calls Roland's mother Berthe aux Grands Pieds, although the sobriquet is more often reserved for Charlemagne's mother.

44. Ibid., 2.

45. Ibid., 4-5.

46. Ibid., 36.

47. Ibid., 226.

48. Ibid., 292.

49. Ibid., 298, 299-300.

50. Bernardo del Carpio is supposed to have choked Roland. Louis Viardot's novel *Lettres d'un Espagnol* (1826) contains a minor character, a mule driver, who sings "le refrain de quelque vieille romance sur la mort de Roland, étouffé à Roncevalles par Bernard del Carpio." Louis Viardot, *Lettres d'un Espagnol* (Paris: Monge, Gosselin, et Ponthieu, 1826), 2:8. The mule driver's song was probably this one, taken from the *Romancero de Bernardo del Carpio*:

> De la sangrienta batalla
> sale el valiente Bernardo,

> dexando a Roldán herido,
>   aquel paladín gallardo,
> de siete grandes heridas
>   todas dadas por su mano,
> y a Oliveros el famoso
>   de parte a parte pasado,
> sin otro muchos franceses
>   que en la lid a degollado,
> arrastrando las banderas
>   y el estandarte de Carlos,
> dándoles bien a entender
>   el esfuerço castellano
> de aquella sangre de godos,
>   de quien el mundo a temblado.

See Ramón Menéndez Pidal et al., eds., *Romancero tradicional de las lenguas hispánicas. Romanceros del rey Rodrigo y de Bernardo del Carpio* (Madrid: Editorial Gredos, 1957), 241-42. Note editors' comments, 144-45. Don Quixote and Sancho Panza heard a plowman singing a ballad about the French defeat at Roncevaux.

51. Assollant, *La Mort de Roland*, 316.

52. Ibid., 2, 290.

53. Emile Zola, *L'Atelier de Zola: textes de journaux 1865-1870*, ed. Martin Kanes (Geneva: Droz, 1963), 43. This book review appeared in *L'Evénement* on 10 June 1866.

54. Gérard Walch, ed., *Anthologie des poètes français comtemporains* (Paris: Librairie Delgrave, 1937), 1:210-15; Robert Sabatier, *La Poésie du dix-neuvième siècle* (Paris: Albin Michel, 1977), 2:76.

55. See Banville's review of Henri de Bornier's play, *La Fille de Roland*, in *Le National*, 22 February 1875.

56. Ludovic Vitet, "La *Chanson de Roland*," *Revue des Deux Mondes* 14 (1852): 817-64, esp. 850.

57. "Je vous remercie de votre article, mais il ne faut pas le publier. Vous parlez de moi d'une telle sorte." The poet was embarrassed. See Albert Glatigny, "Lettres à Stéphane Mallarmé," ed. Paul Morel, *Mercure de France*, nos. 1221-22 (1965): 477.

58. Charles Augustin Sainte-Beuve, "De la poésie en 1865," in *Nouveaux lundis* (Paris: Calmann Lévy, n.d.), 10:120.

59. See Jean Reymond, *Albert Glatigny: la vie, l'homme, le poète* (Paris: Droz, 1936), 166.

60. C. Beaumont Wicks, *The Parisian Stage* (University: U of Alabama P, 1950-79), 4:198.

61. Jules Horrent, *La "Chanson de Roland" dans les littératures française et espagnole au moyen âge* (Paris: Les Belles Lettres, 1951), 377; Ramón Menéndez Pidal, *La "Chanson de Roland" et la tradition épique des Francs* (Paris: Picard, 1960), 115, 117.

62. See Henry Blaze de Bury's review in *Revue des Deux Mondes* 53 (1864): 997-98.

63. Paul Souday, "La Parodie," *Les Livres du temps* (Paris: Emile Paul Frères, 1914-30), 2:454; *Revue pour rien* (Paris: Dentu, 1865), 66pp. The text of the revue was

haphazardly printed, with numerous typographical errors. The parodists' intent was to get their text into public hands as quickly as possible, perhaps another indication of the opera's continuing popularity.

64. The name may have been a learned pun. Apart from its obvious resemblance to that of the opera heroine, it recalls the literary traditionalists' derisive reaction when Chateaubriand's *Atala* appeared in 1801. To Boileau's scorn for two late tragedies by the declining Corneille, summed up in the couplet "J'ai vu l'*Agésilas*—Hélas! / Mais après l'*Attila*—Holà!" an antiromantic wit added the often-cited quip "Après *Atala*, halte là!"

65. Blaze de Bury, review, 1002-3.

5. Despair, Hope, and Triumph

1. Armand de Pontmartin, *Nouveaux samedis* (Paris: Michel Lévy Frères, 1867-81), 15:41. Pontmartin's *Samedis* were articles of literary criticism appearing in the *Gazette de France*. This one is dated May 1877. That the *Gazette* was a Bourbonist periodical and that Pontmartin was a friend of Autran lends interest to the poet's calling upon his countrymen, in the epilogue, to work together, "quel que soit le drapeau." Autran may have been one of many who in the early 1870s favored a Bourbon restoration in the person of the Comte de Chambord. The Bourbons' symbol was their dynasty's white flag, not the tricolor banner that other French regimes favored.

2. From Ariosto he borrowed the Moor Grandogne, a character in "La Rançon."

3. In "Le Butin" Roland seizes a flotilla bearing gifts being sent to Marsile by the emperor of Persia and decides to turn them over to Charlemagne. The women on board he intends to place in a convent, presumably in order to convert them.

4. See Ian Short, *The Anglo-Norman "Pseudo-Turpin Chronicle" of William de Briane* (Oxford: Blackwell, 1973), 32-33, and Ronald N. Walpole, ed., *The Old French Johannes Translation of the "Pseudo-Turpin Chronicle"* (Berkeley: U of California P, 1976), 131, 134.

5. Short, *Anglo-Norman "Pseudo-Turpin Chronicle,"* 38-39; Walpole, *Old French Johannes Translation*, 140.

6. Short, *Anglo-Norman "Pseudo-Turpin Chronicle,"* 50-54; Walpole, *Old French Johannes Translation*, 151-56.

7. No such tomb seems to exist today. Mabillon's *Annales ordinis. S. Benedicti* has an engraving of three caryatid statues of Charlemagne, Roland, and Aude in the Meaux Basilica, but this could not be the ornate tomb described in Autran's poem. By specifying that the tomb was admired for six hundred years, the poet may be referring to a monument that was later destroyed.

8. Armand de Pontmartin, *Nouveaux samedis*, 12:243-46. Pontmartin wrote many articles on Autran. This one is called "La Poésie nationale."

9. Edmond Haraucourt, "Marsile," *Les Ages: l'espoir du monde*, in *OEuvres* (Paris: Alphonse Lemerre, 1899), 111-12. The poem is one of the four the author placed in the section "Huitième siècle." Despite the publication date, the *achevé d'imprimer* is 27 December 1898.

10. Joseph Autran, "Les Convives du roi," *La Légende des paladins*, in *OEuvres complètes* (Paris: Calmann Lévy, 1874-81), 5:185-87. See Short, *Anglo-Norman "Pseudo-Turpin Chronicle,"* 46-47; Walpole, *Old French Johannes Translation*, 148-49.

11. Edmond Haraucourt, "A la mémoire des écrivains français morts pour la patrie," *Choix de poésies* (Paris: Charpentier, 1922), 237-38.

12. Banville's review appeared in *Le National* on 22 February 1875.

13. Nancy Stewart, *La Vie et l'oeuvre d'Henri de Bornier* (Paris: Droz, 1935), 67-68, 82, 89-90, 94-96. See also Jules Claretie, "La Vie à Paris," *Le Temps,* 21 June 1912, p. 3.

14. The four stanzas are quoted from Bornier's notes in Stewart, *La Vie et l'oeuvre d'Henri de Bornier,* 66-67.

15. One can only speculate about what prompted Bornier to name his young hero Gérald. The idea could have come from the Portuguese *romanceiro,* which has its *matière de France* and indeed its Charlemagne cycle. Gerinardo or Geraldo, a page serving the emperor, is a recurrent figure in the poems: "Gerinardo, Gerinardo, / Pagem d'el-rei tão amigo." Once it is hinted that, like Roland, he is related to his master: "Se sou genro querido / Tambem lhe quero explicar, / Sou filho d'el-rei de França / Neto do rei de Cascaes." Theophilo Braga, ed., *Romanceiro geral portuguez,* 2d ed. (Lisbon: Manuel Gomes, 1906), 229. See also "Estoria de Gerinardo" and "Dom Geraldo" (193-94).

16. Probably Bornier's protagonist owes something to Corneille, whom the writer admired. Bornier's "Ode à Corneille" was recited at the Comédie Française on 6 June 1871 by J.A.F. de Laroche. Further evidence of Bornier's interest in Corneille is found in the poem "Napoléon à Corneille" (1874).

17. Letter of Henri de Bornier, 21 January 1889, in Thierry Bodin Catalogue 26, no. 162 (1986). Contrary to Bornier's recollections, according to Francisque Sarcey, Laroche was named a *sociétaire* just before the premiere rather than at the time it took place. See Sarcey, *Comédiens et comédiennes: la Comédie Française* (Paris: Librairie des Bibliophiles, 1876), 1:25.

18. "L'ombre de Campistron exulte: / . . . . / Bornier de son art a le culte." See Michel Décaudin, *Jean Moréas, écrivain français* (Paris: Minard, 1969), 810, and Gustave Flaubert, *Lettres inédites de Gustave Flaubert à son éditeur Michel Lévy,* ed. Jacques Suffel (Paris: Calmann Lévy, 1965), 236.

19. See Ramón Menéndez Pidal, *La "Chanson de Roland" et la tradition épique des Francs* (Paris: Picard, 1960), 77, and Henry Chanteux, *Recherches sur la "Chanson de Roland"* (Caen: Académie de Caen, 1985), 59-64.

20. Stewart, *Bornier,* 87 n. 1.

21. From various versions of the play several poems or songs mentioning Roland were deleted, including the "Chanson de fer," the "Chanson de Berthe," and "Le Perron d'acier." Bornier included the poems in his *Poésies complètes.*

22. René Fabert [Augustin Fouquet], *Charlemagne,* in *Théâtre inédit du XIXe siècle* (Paris: Garnier Frères, n.d.), 2:253, 256, 295.

23. Henri Rabaud, *La Fille de Roland* (Paris: Choudens, 1904), 371pp. The French copyright is dated 1903, and a first edition appeared that year.

24. Henry Gauthier-Villars, "La Fille de Roland," *Echo de Paris,* 17 March 1904, p. 4; Gabriel Fauré, "La Fille de Roland," *Figaro,* 17 March 1904, p. 4. Rabaud would eventually succeed Gabriel Fauré as director of the Paris Conservatoire.

25. Denis Bablet, *Esthétique générale du décor de théâtre de 1870 à 1914* (Paris: Centre National de la Recherche Scientifique, 1965), xv.

26. Adolphe d'Avril, *Les Enfances Roland* (Paris: Petithenry, 1892), 101pp. For interesting comments on the epic, see Avril's introduction to his translation of the *Chanson de Roland* (Paris: Joseph Albanel, 1867), cxvi-cxvii.

27. Avril, *Enfances,* 54.

28. Ibid., 69.

29. Normally, Charlemagne's sister is called Berthe, but sometimes Gille. The prose *Roman de Berthe* calls one of Charlemagne's sisters Gille, as does the *Karlamagnus-Saga*. Génin's *Chanson de Roland* quotes a Lorraine fragment in which a sister is so named. The Fragments Michelant, vol. 2, *laisse* 12, l. 21, call Charlemagne's sister Gille, and so do the Manuscrit de Paris (*laisse* 260) and the Manuscrit de Lyon (*laisse* 121). The Fragments Michelant, vol. 2, *laisse* 12, ll. 22-23, also mention that Gille's first marriage was to Duke Milon and that her second was to the "coward" Ganelon.

30. Avril, *Enfances*, 60-61.

31. Ibid., 82, 89.

32. Adolphe d'Avril, *Le Mystère de Roncevaux* (Paris: Maison de la Bonne Presse, 1893), 18.

33. Paul Meyer published the *Cansó d'Antiocha* in *Archives de l'Orient latin* 2 (1883): 467-509. More recently it has been studied by Rita Lejeune, "Une Allusion méconnue à une *Chanson de Roland*," *Romania* 75 (1954): 145-64.

34. They are not the ones Autran lists. In *Le Mystère de Roncevaux* Roland states to Durandal, "Dans ta garde d'or, il y a tant de reliques: une dent de saint Pierre et du sang de saint Basile et des cheveux de monseigneur saint Denis; il y a du vêtement de sainte Marie." Avril, *Mystère de Roncevaux*, 106. Unlike Autran, Avril was adhering to the *Chanson de Roland*.

35. Emile Mathieu, *L'Enfance de Roland, légende lyrique* (Leipzig: Breitkopf et Härtel, 1893), 187pp. A German translation by Friedrich Fremery accompanied Mathieu's French text. For details about Mathieu, see Jules Toussaint de Sutter, "Notice sur Emile Mathieu," *Académie Royale de Belgique: Annuaire* (1959): 3-24.

36. For good modern texts of the poems see Hans Rüdiger Schwab, ed., *Werke*, by Ludwig Uhland (Frankfurt: Insel Verlag, 1983), 1:152-56, 185-91.

37. Louise Michel, *A travers la vie et la mort*, ed. Daniel Armogathe and Marion V. Piper (Paris: François Maspéro, 1982), 200.

38. Ibid., 106-7.

39. Raymond Escholier, *Un Amant de génie, Victor Hugo* (Paris: Arthème Fayard, 1979), 434.

40. Jean Richepin, *Les Caresses* (Paris: Charpentier, 1917), 22.

41. Jean Richepin, *Les Blasphèmes* (Paris: Charpentier, 1919), 229-30.

42. Paul Verlaine, *Les Hommes d'aujourd'hui*, in *OEuvres complètes*, (Paris: Albert Messein, 1922), 5:321.

43. Jean Richepin, *Poèmes durant la guerre* (Paris: Flammarion, 1919), 84, 90, 198.

44. Jean Richepin, *Allons, enfants de la patrie!* (Tours: Alfred Mame et Fils, 1920), 8, 14.

45. For example, "Je ne peux pas mieux dire, comme dit Charlemagne quand il donne son fils à la belle Aude." Quoted in Alvida Ahlstrom, *Le Moyen Age dans l'oeuvre d'Anatole France* (Paris: Les Belles Lettres, 1930), 97.

46. Anatole France, "Le Gab d'Olivier," *OEuvres complètes illustrées* (Paris: Calmann Lévy, 1925-35), 19:5-16.

47. Joseph A. Fabre, trans., *La Chanson de Roland . . . précédée de "Roland et la belle Aude"* (Paris: Belin Frères, 1902), 45. Fabre's work had several editions, the earliest in 1901.

48. *Revue hebdomadaire* 11 (1898): 316-51.

49. *Chants populaires pour les écoles: Livre du maître*, 2d ed. (Paris: Hachette, 1901), 60;

Chants populaires pour les écoles: Poésies de Maurice Bouchor, mélodies composées ou recueillies par Julien Tiersot, ser. 1 (Paris: Hachette, 1895), 17. Words and music can also be found in Max Walter and Anna Woods Ballard, eds., *French Songs* (New York: Charles Scribner's Sons, 1916), 53-54. In the Walter and Ballard edition, the third and fourth stanzas are in reverse order.

50. Maurice Bouchor, "La *Chanson de Roland,*" *programmes de réunions civiques et familiales* (Paris: Ministère de l'Instruction Publique, 1919), 4:7, 10.

51. Ibid., 9-10, 11-12, 37.

52. Ibid., 10.

53. Ibid., 12-13.

54. Ibid., 9.

55. Ibid., 37.

56. Charles Péguy, *Ballade du coeur qui a tant battu,* ed. Julie Sabiani (Paris: Klincksieck, 1973), 161-65.

57. Charles Péguy, *À Domremy: Jeanne d'Arc* (Paris: Gallimard, 1967), 32.

58. Charles Péguy, *Le Mystère de la charité de Jeanne d'Arc* (Paris: Gallimard, 1962), 174-75.

59. See Paul Hazard, *Don Quichotte de Cervantes, étude et analyse* (Paris: Mellottée, 1949), 360; Jean Cocteau, "Roland Garros," *Poésie* (Paris: Gallimard, 1925), 101.

60. Paul Fort, "Charlemagne, ou le rêveur et l'innocent," *Le Monde nouveau* 2 (1920): 783-86; republished in *Hélène en fleur et Charlemagne* (Paris: Mercure de France, 1921), 205-24. Paul Fort, "Enfants de Reims," *Heures de guerre,* in *Les Enchanteurs* (Paris: Mercure de France, 1919), 239; Emile Verhaeren, "Guillaume de Juliers," *Les Héros* (Brussels: Deman, 1908), 28. This was the battle of Courtrai, 11 July 1302, in which a Flemish archdeacon repelled a French invasion.

61. Maurice Barrès, *Les Traits éternels de la France* (New Haven: Yale U P, 1918), 42. This is a reprint, with notes, of the address as it appeared in the *Proceedings of the British Academy.* It also appeared in the *Revue des Deux Mondes* 34 (1916): 481-504. Barrès made a few spelling mistakes, corrected here, in quoting from the *Chanson de Roland.*

62. Maurice Barrès, *Mes cahiers* (Paris: Plon, 1929-49), 10:304-5.

63. Edmond Rostand, "Un Soir à Hernani," *La Cantique de l'aile,* in *OEuvres complètes illustrées* (Paris: Pierre Lafitte, n.d.), 2:117; Simone [Pauline Benda], *Sous de nouveaux soleils* (Paris: Gallimard, 1957), 162-63; Rosemonde Gérard, "Le Pays basque," *L'Arc-en-ciel, poèmes* (Paris: Charpentier, 1926), 197.

64. Edmond Rostand, *Vol de la Marseillaise* (Paris: Charpentier, 1919), 49. The collection was published posthumously, but some poems appeared before Rostand's death.

6. A Hero for All Seasons

1. Pétrus Borel, "Le Chant du réveil," *Rhapsodies,* in *OEuvres complètes* (Geneva: Slatkine Reprints, 1967), 2:183-85. Borel's 1831 poem entitled "Au médaillon d'Yseut," in which Roland is mentioned, appeared in the same collection (54). After the French Revolution sent her into exile, Mme de Genlis had published *Les Chevaliers du cygne ou la cour de Charlemagne* (1795), a novel that contains not one allusion to Roland. Philothée O'Neddy's *Histoire d'un anneau enchanté* (1842) mostly takes place at the same court. Here Roland and Olivier, though not characters in the tale, are referred to several times.

Olivier has "élégance"; Roland has "adresse." Much later, in "Les Visions d'un mort vivant," the author alluded to Roland as the "grand Roland." Philothée O'Neddy, *OEuvres complètes,* ed. Ernest Havet (Geneva: Slatkine Reprints, 1968), 1:34-105, esp. 46 and 84; 2:410.

    2. Victor Hugo, "Le Prisonnier," *La Légende des siècles* (Paris: Gallimard, 1984), 627. In writing a poem such as this, Hugo may have been striking a pose and making a bid for popularity. At the time of Bazaine's court-martial and imprisonment, his political ambition knew no bounds except the voting public's unwillingness to further it. Serious extenuating circumstances need to be weighed in assessing both Léopold Hugo's and Achille Bazaine's capitulations.

    3. Arthur Rimbaud, "Villes," *Illuminations,* in *OEuvres complètes* (Paris: Gallimard, 1983), 135. Rimbaud was hardly a patriot at this time. "Maintenant je suis maudit, j'ai horreur de la patrie," he wrote in *Une Saison en enfer.* "Mauvais sang," *OEuvres complètes,* 96.

    4. Jules Laforgue, "Dimanches," *Des Fleurs de bonne volonté,* in *Poésie complète* (Rome: Edizioni dell' Ateneo, 1966), 2:65.

    5. The "barbe fleurie" is a reminiscence of the *Chanson de Roland,* l. 2353.

    6. During the Middle Ages a legend persisted that Roland had indeed been Charlemagne's son, not his nephew. The belief found expression in the Old Norse *Karlamagnus-Saga,* in which the emperor confesses his sin to St. Giles, the Midi's principal saint.

    7. In addition to figuring in the *Chronicle,* Baudouin is found in the *Chanson de Roland* Manuscrit de Venise 4. It was not published until 1877 and had little, if any, effect upon nineteenth-century Roland literature.

    8. Isidore Taylor, *Les Pyrénées* (Paris: Gide, 1843), 542.

    9. Alexandre de Laborde, *Itinéraire descriptif de l'Espagne* (Paris: Nicolle and Lenormant, 1809), 2:88.

    10. Joseph A. Fabre, trans., *La Chanson de Roland . . . précédée de "Roland et la belle Aude"* (Paris: Belin Frères, 1902), 343.

    11. Gabriel Henri Gaillard, *Histoire de Charlemagne* (Paris: Moutard, 1782), 2:197.

    12. Gustave Flaubert and George Sand, *Correspondance,* ed. Alphonse Jacobs (Paris: Flammarion, 1981), 392.

    13. Gustave Flaubert, *Voyages,* ed. René Dumesnil (Paris: Les Belles Lettres, 1948), 1:28-30.

    14. José Maria de Heredia, "Email," *Les Trophées* (Paris: Alphonse Lemerre, n.d.), 106.

    15. Reported, for example, in the 14 December 1891 *Le Gaulois* and the January 1892 *Mercure de France.* See *Mercure de France* 4 (1892): 83-84; Denis Bablet, *Le Décor de théâtre de 1870 à 1914* (Paris: Centre National de Recherche Scientifique, 1965), 152; and Frantisêk Deák, "Symbolist Staging at the Théâtre d'Art," *The Drama Review* 20 (1976): 119.The date can be ascertained because on the same program was the initial performance of Maeterlinck's *Les Aveugles.*

    16. W.G.C. Byvanck, *Un Hollandais à Paris en 1891* (Paris: Perrin et Cie, 1892), 32-33. There were Roland puppet shows in Belgium and Italy also. See Gerard J. Brault, "The French Chansons de Geste," in *Heroic Epic and Saga,* ed. Felix J. Oinas (Bloomington: Indiana U P, 1978), 208.

Selected Bibliography

Aebischer, Paul. *Des Annales carolingiennes à Doon de Mayence*. Geneva: Droz, 1975.
———. *Préhistoire et protohistoire du "Roland" d'Oxford*. Bern: Editions Francke, 1972.
Brault, Gerard J., ed. *The Song of Roland: An Analytical Edition*. University Park: Pennsylvania State U P, 1978.
Buridant, Claude, ed. *La Chronique de Pseudo-Turpin*. Geneva: Droz, 1976.
Caluwé, Jacques de. *Le Moyen âge littéraire occitan dans l'oeuvre de Frédéric Mistral*. Paris: Nizet, 1974.
Cellier, Léon. *L'Epopée romantique*. Paris: Presses Universitaires de France, 1954.
Chanteux, Henry. *Recherches sur la "Chanson de Roland."* Caen: Académie de Caen, 1985.
Cioranescu, Alexandre. *L'Arioste en France des origines à la fin du XVIIIe siècle*. Paris: Editions des Presses Modernes, 1939. Reprint. Turin: Bottega d'Erasmo, 1963, 1970.
Cook, Robert F. *The Sense of the "Song of Roland."* Ithaca, N.Y.: Cornell U P, 1987.
Dakyns, Janine R. *The Middle Ages in French Literature, 1851-1900*. London: Oxford U P, 1973.
Folz, Robert. *Le Souvenir et la légende de Charlemagne dans l'empire germanique médiéval*. Paris: Les Belles Lettres, 1950.
Fourcassié, Jean. *Le Romantisme et les Pyrénées*. Paris: Gallimard, 1940.
Griffiths, Richard. *The Reactionary Revolution: The Catholic Revival in French Literature, 1870-1914*. New York: Frederick Ungar, 1965.
Horrent, Jules. *La "Chanson de Roland" dans les littératures française et espagnole au moyen âge*. Paris: Les Belles Lettres, 1951.
Jubinal, Achille. "Quelques romans chez nos aïeux." *Journal du dimanche*, 1 November 1846.
Lanson, René. *Le Goût du moyen âge en France au XVIIIe siècle*. Paris: Van Oest, 1926.
McKitterick, Rosamond. *The Frankish Kingdoms under the Carolingians*. London: Longman, 1983.
Menéndez Pidal, Ramón. *La "Chanson de Roland" et la tradition épique des Francs*. Paris: Picard, 1960.
Oinas, Felix J., ed. *Heroic Epic and Saga*. Bloomington: Indiana U P, 1978.
Segre, Cesare, ed. *La Chanson de Roland*. Translated by Madeleine Tyssens. 2 vols. Geneva: Droz, 1989.
Sholod, Barton. *Charlemagne in Spain: The Cultural Legacy of Roncesvalles*. Geneva: Droz, 1966.
Smyser, Hamilton M., ed. *The Pseudo-Turpin*. Cambridge, Mass.: Medieval Academy of America, 1937.
Vitet, Ludovic. "La *Chanson de Roland*." *Revue des Deux Mondes* 14 (1852): 817-65.

Wace. *Le Roman de Rou*. Edited by A.J. Holden. Paris: Picard, 1970.
Walpole, Ronald N., ed. *The Old French Johannes Translation of the "Pseudo-Turpin Chronicle."* Berkeley: U of California P, 1976.
Ward, Patricia A. *The Medievalism of Victor Hugo*. University Park: Pennsylvania State U P, 1975.
Wicks, C. Beaumont. *The Parisian Stage*. 5 vols. University: U of Alabama P, 1950-79.

Index

Abadie, A. Philibert, 129
Ackermann, Louise, 123-24, 217
Ackermann, Paul, 123-24
Adalgis (Lombard prince), 16, 50
Agout, Marie, comtesse d', 113-14
Agramant. *See* Ariosto, Ludovico; Boiardo, Matteo Maria
Aigoland (Mohammedan king), 5, 11, 57, 72, 168-69, 178, 194, 211
Aix-la-Chapelle, ix, 12, 109-11, 118, 153, 163, 165-66, 172, 174, 177, 181, 186, 208-10
Ajasson de Grandsagne, Stéphane, 84, 215
Alcuin, 48, 143, 147
Alfonso VI (king of Castile and Leon), 72-73
Allais, Alphonse, 217
Angelica. *See* Ariosto, Ludovico; Boiardo, Matteo Maria
Aquitaine, 13, 48, 52, 71, 101-2, 151, 191, 212-13
Aragon, 17, 109
Ardennes Forest, 109, 143, 182-83, 185-88
Argout, Apollinaire, comte d', 92, 228 n 28
Ariosto, Ludovico: *Orlando furioso*, x, 2, 21-22, 28, 40, 44, 46, 51-54, 57, 59, 63, 67-70, 72, 78-79, 85, 95, 121, 129-30, 140, 143-44, 163, 209, 211, 219 nn 2, 3, 224 n 37, 225 n 64, 234 n 2
Arles, 12, 106-7, 213
Arlincourt, Charles Victor d', 59-62, 86, 89, 158, 208, 211-12, 214, 225 n 50
Armería Real, 1, 96, 172, 212-13
Aspremont, 178, 194, 211

Asselineau, Charles, 84, 90
Assollant, Alfred, x, 18, 143, 146-47, 157, 178, 208-12, 214, 232 n 43
Asturias, 70-71, 98, 213
Autran, Joseph, 10, 12, 162, 164, 166-68, 207, 209, 212, 234 n 1, 236 n 34
Autun, 71
Avril, Adolphe d', 108, 113, 138, 177, 194; *Les Enfances Roland*, 177-80, 183, 188, 209, 211; *Le Mystère de Roncevaux*, 180-82, 208, 210, 215, 236 n 34
Aymeri de Narbonne, 136, 139, 179, 231 n 30

Baligant, 5, 147, 168
Balzac, Honoré de, 69, 225 n 64
Banville, Théodore de, 10, 151-53, 170, 206, 209, 216, 233 n 55, 235 n 12
Barante, Prosper de, 219 n 3
Barberino, Andrea da, x, 2, 4, 28, 110, 178, 187
Barbey d'Aurevilly, Jules, 9, 83, 100, 208
Barbey d'Aurevilly, Léon, 82-83
Barbier, Auguste, 10, 119-20, 124, 170, 207
Barcelona, 17, 102
Barguette, 130
Barjaud, J.B., 43, 209
Barrès, Maurice, 202, 204, 208, 218, 237 n 61
Basques, 13, 91, 98, 100, 191, 213, 224 n 40
Bastide, J.F. de. *See Bibliothèque universelle des romans*
Baudelaire, Charles, 90, 119
Baudouin (Roland's brother), 5, 12, 64, 174, 209, 216, 238 n 7

Bazaine, Achille, 207, 237 n 2
Beauvarlet-Charpentier, Jacques Marie, 40
Bédaille, 106, 212
Bédier, Joseph, 220
Belin, 12, 14, 213
Bellina, Mme, 189
Belval, Jules, 158
Benevento, duke and prince of, 16, 54, 56
Béranger, Pierre Jean de, 31, 49, 84, 216
Bernardin de St-Pierre, Henri, 19, 43
Berni, Francesco, 24, 44
Berthe (Charlemagne's sister), 5, 16, 18, 108-9, 143, 178, 182-88, 209, 232 n 43, 236 n 29
Berthe (Roland's daughter in Bornier's *La Fille de Roland*), 171-77
Beyle, Léon, 177
Bianchini, Charles, 177
Bibliothèque universelle des romans, 3, 7, 24-29, 34, 36, 39-40, 42, 44-45, 56-57, 76, 79, 94-95, 110
Bigorre, 21, 23, 136
Bismarck, Otto von, 162
Blaye, 158. *See* St. Romain, Abbaye de
Blaze de Bury, Henry, 161
Blum, Ernest, 158, 233 n 63
Boiardo, Matteo Maria: *Orlando innamorato*, 2, 24, 44, 51-54, 57, 59, 63, 96, 129, 143, 162
Boileau, Nicolas, 2, 51, 219 n 4, 234 n 64
Bonaparte, Joseph (king of Spain), 87
Bonaparte, Napoleon. *See* Napoleon I
Bonaparte, Prince Lucien, 16, 34, 49-51, 54-56, 59, 61-62, 71, 103, 135, 140, 168, 174, 198, 208-14, 216, 224 n 40
Bordeaux, 12, 14, 145, 181, 213
Borel, Pétrus (Pierre Borel d'Hauterive), 206, 237 n 1
Bornier, Henri de, 170-71, 173-75, 204, 207, 209-10, 212, 235 nn 15, 16, 17
Bouchor, Maurice, xii, 196-99, 207, 210-11, 218, 236 n 49
Boudon de St-Amans, Jean-Florimond, 20, 214
Bouffes Parisiens, 158-59
Bourdillon, Antoine Jean Louis, 8
Bourgeat, L.A.M., 44

Brèche de Roland, xi, 19-20, 23, 47, 58, 75-76, 83, 85, 97, 101, 104, 106, 115, 129, 135-36, 146, 191, 212, 216
Brittany, 13, 99, 102, 119-20, 140
Byvanck, W.G.C., 217-18

Cambon, Charles A., 158
Campistron, Jean Galbert de, 174, 235 n 18
Cancionero de Amberes, 219 n 1
Canino. *See* Bonaparte, Prince Lucien
Cansó d'Antiocha, 106, 180, 236 n 33
Capet, Hugh, 148, 180
Carcassonne, 71
Carpio, Bernardo del, 48, 144-46, 226 n 67, 232 n 50
Carré, Marguerite, 177
Catalonia, 17
Cazaux, Jean Charles, 158
Cervantes, Miguel de: *Don Quixote*, 1, 172, 213, 228 n 41, 232 n 50
Chandezon, Léopold, 66, 69, 95, 163, 206, 209
Chanson d'Antioche, 177
Chanson de Hugues Capet, 180
Chaos, Le, xi, 46, 216
Charles X (king of France), 31
Chasseneuil, ix, 70-71
Chateaubriand, François René de, 3, 7-8, 19, 23-24, 51, 56, 66, 70, 75-78, 135, 212, 234 n 64
Châteroux, Manuscrit de, 6, 8, 146
Choron, Alexandre, 36
Clairville, Louis François, 158, 233 n 63
Coblenz, 111
Cocteau, 201
Cole, Sir G.L., 130
Collin de Plancy, Jacques Albin Simon, 101-4, 106, 120, 208-10, 214, 221 n 44
Cologne, 118
Comédie Française, 48, 170, 175
Compostela, 5, 11, 140
Coppée, François, 154
Cordova, 11
Corisande, 144-47
Cosset, Camille, 189
Crépet, Eugène, 84
Creuzé de Lesser, Auguste François, xi,

Index

44-48, 55, 59, 61, 91, 206, 208, 210, 212, 214
Cuvelier de Trie, Jean Guillaume Antoine (or Auguste), 66, 69, 95, 163, 206, 210-11

Dalvimare, Martin Pierre, 41-42
Daniel, Gabriel, 18, 64
Dante Alighieri, 2, 7; *Divina commedia*, 1; *Inferno*, 2; *Paradiso*, 2
Daudet, Alphonse, 216
Debussy, Claude, 177
Décade, Le, 3
Decazes, Egédie, duchesse, 114, 116
Delavigne, Casimir, 215
Delécluze, Etienne, 9, 120-22, 210
Didier, king of the Lombards, 16, 50
Dierx, Léon, 201
Doralice, 144-46
Dorion, Claude Auguste Nicolas, 36-38
Drouet, Juliette, 135
Du Camp, Maxime, 132-34, 189, 206, 211-12
Dufranne, Hector, 177
Dugué, Ferdinand, 49
Dumas, Alexandre père, 16, 30-31, 108-13, 115-16, 118, 135, 177-78, 183, 187-88, 206, 209-10, 212-13, 222 n 2, 229 nn 73, 74
Dumersan, Théophile, 41
Dupleix, Scipion, 12-14, 17, 19, 48, 55, 98, 105, 108, 147, 213-14, 229 n 60
Dupont-Vernon, Henri, 173
Duroc, G.C., 54
Durozoir, Charles, 56
Dusaulx, Jean, 79, 227 n 13
Dutillet, Jean, 220 n 11
Duval, Alexandre, 3-4, 35-36, 38, 41-42, 119

Echo de Paris, L', 177, 192
Einhard, 16, 18, 40, 51, 58, 70, 79, 97-98, 108
El-Mouménim (Mohammedan king in Peyrat's "Roland"), 88
Emma (Charlemagne's daughter), 16, 40, 79, 108
Eudo (duke of Aquitaine), 13

Fabert, René, 175
Fabre, Joseph, 138, 193-96, 214, 218
Faget de Baure, Jacques Joseph, 22-23, 85-86, 99, 203, 208, 212, 214
Faure, Gabriel Auguste, 123
Fauré, Gabriel Urbain, 175
Ferdinand VII (king of Spain), 78, 87, 135
Ferragus (giant), 5, 11, 22, 46, 57, 72-73, 129, 144, 164-65
Ferrier, Ida, 111
Ferrier, Paul, 175
Figaro, 158, 177
Flaubert, Gustave, 56, 132, 143, 153, 174, 216
Flégier, Ange, 81
Fort, Paul, 201
Fourcassié, Jean, 131
Fournel, Charles, ix, 82, 122-28, 154, 207, 210-12, 216-17
France, Anatole, 84, 192-93, 216, 227 n 21
Freiligrath, Ferdinand, 113
Friuli, dukes of, 16, 54, 56
Froila (Spanish Christian king), 13

Gabriel, St., 134, 181, 203
Gaillard, Gabriel Henri, 15-19, 56, 64, 72-73, 79, 94, 103, 110, 130, 212, 214-15, 220 n 26, 221 n 44
Galésinde, 114-16, 170
Galicia, 5, 10, 136, 140-42, 163
Garibaldi, Giuseppi, 134
Garnier, Germain, comte, 8
Gascony, 13, 17, 49, 52, 55, 70-71, 98, 100, 103-4, 120, 139, 149, 191, 213, 224 n 40
Gavarnie, xi, 19, 87, 91, 97; Cirque ce, xi, 46, 78, 86, 89, 97, 129, 135, 216
Gèdre, xi, 19-20, 85, 91
Geibel, Emanuel, 81
Génin, François, 9-10, 92, 104-5, 131, 228 n 29, 229 n 60
Geoffroy, Roland's brother, 5
Gérald (Roland's half-brother in Bornier's *La Fille de Roland*), 170-76, 209
Gide, André, 207
Giles, St., 128, 180-81, 238 n 6

Girart de Vienne, 78, 93-94, 136-38, 178-79, 182, 193, 231 n 30
Glatigny, Albert, ix, 10, 153-55, 206, 216, 233 n 57
Gluck, Christoph W., 219 n 5
Gobineau, Arthur de, 215
Grandes Chroniques de France, Les (*Les Chroniques de St-Denis*), 73, 77, 226 nn 73, 5
Gregh, Fernand, 90
Grétry, André, 31-32
Gueymard, Louis, 158
Gueymard, Pauline, 158
Guizot, François, 9
Guyot des Herbiers, Claude Antoine, 6, 8

Haraucourt, Edouard, 168-70
Harold (king of England), 37
Heine, Heinrich, 83
Heredia, José Maria de, 216
Herstal, 101
Hervé. *See* Ronger, Florimond
Hilberte, 117-18
Hildegonde, 111-12
Homer, 75, 94-95, 105, 122, 131-32
Hugo, Victor, 4, 10, 56, 66, 77-78, 84, 87, 90, 107, 113, 123, 135-36, 139, 141-43, 162-63, 170, 179, 190, 199, 206-7, 212, 231 n 24, 237 n 2; "Aymerillot," 136, 139-40, 142, 213-14; "J'aime un groupe d'enfants," 135, 209; "La Grand'mère," 134-35, 211; "La Guerre d'Espagne," 135, 139, 142, 212; "Le Mariage de Roland," 136-39, 142, 170, 174, 195-96, 209, 232 n 32; "Le Petit Roi de Galice," 136, 140-42, 154, 202; *Le Rhin*, 113

Ibals, Henri G., 217
Ibnal or Ibinalarabi (king of Saragossa), 14, 18
Immermann, Karl, 18, 147
Ingelheim, 111, 183

James, St., 5, 10-11, 72, 102, 163-64
Jammes, Francis, 201
Josephine, Empress, 41, 51, 63

Journal des Débats, 3, 121, 158
Journet, Marcel, 189
Jouy, Etienne de, 22
Jubinal, Achille, 136-37, 139, 231 n 29, 232 nn 31, 35
Jusseaume, Lucien, 177

Kahn, Gustave, 116-18, 210, 213
Karlamagnus-Saga, 236 n 29, 238 n 6

Laborde, Alexandre de, 208, 213
Laforgue, Jules, 81-82, 207
Lamartine, Alphonse de, 19, 61, 63, 66, 84, 215
Lamennais, Félicité de, 2, 84
La Motte Fouqué, Friedrich de, 127-28
La Motte-Langon, Etienne Léon de, 41-42, 223 nn 21, 22, 23
Laroche, J.A.F. de, 173, 235 nn 16, 17
La Rue, Gervais de, 7
Leconte de Lisle, Charles Marie, 119, 167-68
Lejeune, Gabrielle, 189
Lemercier, Népomucène, 48, 209
Leoprandus (dean of the Cathedral of Aix-la-Chapelle), 10
Le Roux de Lincy, Antoine, 9-10, 36, 119-20
LeVavasseur, Gustave, 38, 209, 223 n 13
Liszt, Franz, 113
Louis (Charlemagne's son), 48, 166, 175
Louis IX (king of France), 99, 105
Louis XV (king of France), 99
Louis XVI (king of France), 8, 29, 32, 41, 60
Louis XVIII (king of France), 22, 135
Louis Philippe (king of the French), 60
Lully, Jean Baptiste, 2
Lupus II (duke of Aquitaine), 17-18, 52-53, 64, 70, 86-87, 91, 98, 129-30, 224 n 35
Lyon, Manuscrit de, 146, 236 n 29

Magnin, Charles, 122
Malézieu, Nicolas de, 131
Mallarmé, Stéphane, 123, 153-54, 216
Marboré, Le, xi, 20, 46, 84-85, 129, 216
Marchangy, Louis Antoine François de,

Index   245

16, 55-63, 79, 86, 89, 93, 100, 214, 225 n 44
Marie Antoinette (queen of France), 31-32
Marie Louise, Empress, 41-51
Marmier, Xavier, 113
Marmontel, Jean François, 3
Marseille, 143
Marsile, 5, 46-48, 54, 70, 124-29, 131, 144-45, 147, 155, 165, 168
Martin, Aimé, 43-44, 206, 224 nn 26, 27
Massenet, Jules, 155
Mathieu, Emile, 182-83, 186-89, 236 n 35
Mauband, Henri, 173
Maupassant, Guy de, 216
Méhul, Etienne, 36
Menéndez Pidal, Ramón, 64, 224 n 39
Mercure de France, 44
Mérimée, Prosper, ix, 5, 9, 56, 104-6, 121, 213, 231 n 29
Mermet, Auguste, xii, 28, 31, 87, 155-59, 161, 182, 188, 209-12
Merrill, Stuart, 217
Meyer, Paul, 106-8
Michael, St., 152, 155, 181, 203-4
Michallon, Achille, 53, 80, 214
Michel, Francisque, ix, 9-10, 46, 77, 96, 104-5, 121
Michel, Louise, 189-90
Michelet, Jules, ix-x, 6, 10, 19, 28, 77, 83, 91, 97-101, 105, 132-33, 136, 189, 198, 208, 211-12, 215, 228 n 51
Millevoye, Charles Hubert, 38-41, 50, 63, 69, 153, 212
Milon, comte d'Angers, 5, 11, 16, 18, 51, 78, 108-10, 143, 178, 182-85, 188, 209, 236 n 29
Mistral, Frédéric, 5, 105-8, 202, 212-14, 229 n 69
Molinet, Jean, 3
Monin, Henri, 6, 8-9, 95, 98, 121
Montégut, Emile, 142
Montpensier, Antoine Marie Philippe Louis d'Orléans, duc de, 129
Moréas, Jean, 174
Mortier, Raoul, 6
Mounet-Sully (Jean Sully Mounet), 173

Moussa (Mohammedan prince in Peyrat's "Roland"), 89
Musset, Alfred de, 4, 6
Musset, Louis de, 4-8, 72, 103, 208-9, 220 nn 11, 13, 14

Naimes (duke of Bavaria), 16, 144, 171, 183-84, 186
Napoleon I, 19, 22, 29, 31, 34, 36-38, 41-44, 48-49, 51, 54-56, 60, 66, 75, 87-88, 105, 130, 209, 235 n 16
Napoleon III, 158
Narbonne, 71, 89, 136, 139-40
Navarre, 13, 23, 57, 70-71, 98, 213
Nîmes, 71
Nobles (city), 210
Noailles, Natalie de, 75
Nodier, Charles, 3, 19, 24
Noéthold (Mohammedan king), 172, 176
Nonnenwerth, 111-13, 115-16

Odéon, 118
O'Neddy, Philothée (Théophile Dondey), 36, 237 n 1
Opéra, 155
Opéra Comique, 177

Paderborn, 101
Pamplona, 5, 11, 13, 17, 57, 70, 102, 164
Paris, 8, 12, 58, 80, 91
Paris, Gaston, 21, 93, 106-7, 139
Paris, Manuscrit de, 8, 236 n 29
Paris, Paulin, 78, 231 n 29
Paulmy, Antoine René de Voyer d'Argenson, marquis de. See *Bibliothèque universelle des romans*
Péguy, Charles, 200-201, 204, 208, 218
Pèlerinage de Charlemagne, Le, 192
Perrin, Emile, 158, 170
Peyrade, La, xi, 20, 91
Peyrat, Napoléon, xi-xii, 20, 83-91, 96, 104-7, 135, 154, 190, 198, 208-13, 215-16; "Bertran de Born," 91; "La Peyrada," 20, 91
Philippe Auguste (king of France), 7, 220 n 11
Piccini, Niccolò, 3

Picquet, J.P., 20-21, 23, 139, 208-9, 211, 214, 221 n 44
Pinabel, 12
Pius VII, Pope, 49
Pixérécourt, René Charles Guilbert de, 66
Poitiers, battle of (732), 71; battle of (1356), 3, 9, 24, 77
Ponsard, François, 113-16, 118, 170, 209-10, 212-13
Pontmartin, Armand de, 167, 234 n 1
Pulci, Luigi, 24, 44, 231 n 17

Quinault, Philippe, 2
Quinet, Edgar, ix, 8-10, 91-97, 132, 136-37, 172, 211-13, 228 nn 28, 29

Rabaud, Henri, 175, 177, 210, 212
Racine, Jean, 174
Ramond de Carbonnières, Louis, 19-21, 56, 208
Reali di Francia. See Barberino, Andrea da
Refort, Lucien, 97
Renan, Ernest, 143
Revue blanche, 116
Revue de France, 189-90
Revue de Paris, 132
Revue des Deux Mondes, 78, 92, 95, 104-5, 122, 136, 139, 142, 153, 158, 161
Revue hebdomadaire, 196
Rhine River, 1, 111, 113-16, 118, 170
Ricard, Xavier de, 147-51, 155, 210, 213
Richepin, Jean, 87, 139, 190-92, 196, 202, 207-8, 213-14, 217
Rimbaud, Arthur, 90, 119, 167, 207, 238 n 3
Rocamadour, 14, 85, 103-8, 213
Roderick (king of the Visigoths), 85, 88
Rolandseck, 111, 113, 115-16
Rolandswerth, 111
Rollan à Saragossa, 106, 209
"Romance del conde Guarinos," 1
"Romance del moro Calaínos," 1
Ronger, Florimond, 158, 233 n 63
Ronsavals, 106
Roquefort, Bonaventure de, 44
Rosary, Eugène, 106

Rostand, Edmond, 202-4, 208, 212, 214
Rouget de Lisle, Claude Joseph, 19, 29-33, 36, 38, 216, 222 n 1, 2
Roussillon, 17, 70, 106

Sabatier, Robert, 148
St. Romain, Abbaye de, 6, 12, 14, 21, 181, 213, 221 n 44
Sainte-Beuve, Charles Augustin, 19, 63, 66, 77-78, 84, 120, 153-54
Salis, Rodolphe, 217
Sand, George (Aurore Dudevant), 56, 215-16
Saragossa, 5, 12-13, 18, 57, 70, 98-99, 102, 145, 155
Schwob, Marcel, 217
Sedaine, Michel, 31-33, 36, 38
Seguin, Henri, 189
Ségur, Noël, 41
Septimania, 151
Serusier, Paul, 217
Silcher, Friedrich, 79, 227 n 14
Sirodin, Paul, 158, 233 n 63
Sismondi, Jean Charles Léonard Simonde de, x, 12, 70-71, 99, 147, 226 n 67
Somport, xii
Soult, Nicolas Jean de Dieu, French marshal, 130, 231 n 18
Staël, Germaine de, 4, 56, 60, 70
Stendhal (pseud. of Henry Beyle), 22-23, 41, 56, 87, 120, 215
Stricker, Der, 128, 180

Taillefer (minstrel), 3, 34, 37-38, 76-77, 99
Taine, Hippolyte, ix, xi, 97, 131-32, 136, 208, 210, 214
Talleyrand, Charles Maurice de Talleyrand-Périgord, prince de, 54
Tarbé, Prosper, 138, 231 n 30
Tassilo, duke of Bavaria, 16
Tastu, Amable, 63-64, 66, 212, 214
Taylor, Isidore, baron, xii, 129-31, 209, 211, 220 n 26, 221 n 44, 231 n 17
Théodoric, 12
Thierry (Roland's brother), 5, 209
Thierry, Augustin, 76

Thierry, Joseph, 158
Thiers, Adolphe, 129
Thiodoric, 64
Tiersot, Julien, 197, 222 n 1, 236 n 49
Timbal, Prosper, 84-85, 88
Toledo, 72
Toulouse, 85, 88, 98-99
Tours, 7
Tressan, Louis de La Vergne, comte de. *See Bibliothèque universelle des romans*
Troisième Théâtre Français, 175
Tunis, 109

Uhland, Ludwig, 94, 182-83, 186-88, 229 n 73, 231 n 30

Valencia, 145
Valéry, Paul, 207
Valon, Alexis de, 5, 104-6, 108, 213, 229 n 60
Vapereau, Gustave, 123
Varney, Alphonse, 30
Venise 4, Manuscrit de, 158, 232 n 35, 238 n 7
Verhaeren, Emile, 201, 208, 237 n 60
Verlaine, Paul, 140, 191, 216, 232 n 36
Vernet, Horace, 63

Vieuille, Félix, 177
Vignancourt, Emile, 23
Vigny, Alfred de, xii, 78-83, 124, 149, 152, 154, 206, 211-15, 217, 226 n 11, 227 n 13
Villemain, Abel, 72
Viollet-le-Duc, Eugène Emmanuel, 121
Virgil, 105
Vitet, Ludovic, 9-10, 105, 153, 220 n 16, 228 n 28
Vodoz, Jules, 80, 208
Voltaire, François Marie Arouet de, 14-15, 131

Wace, 3, 37, 76-77
Waifar (duke of Gascony), 17-18, 49, 51-53, 86, 91, 98, 103, 224 n 35
Walpole, Horace, 60
Walsh, Gérard, 147
Warot, Victor, 158
Wellington, Arthur Wellesley, duke of, 59
William I, the Conqueror (king of England), 3, 33-34, 36-38
Wittikind (Saxon chieftain), 16, 70, 185

Zola, Emile, 147, 216